Leopardi's Nymphs
Grace, Melancholy, and the Uncanny

LEGENDA

LEGENDA, founded in 1995 by the European Humanities Research Centre of the University of Oxford, is now a joint imprint of the Modern Humanities Research Association and Maney Publishing. Titles range from medieval texts to contemporary cinema and form a widely comparative view of the modern humanities, including works on Arabic, Catalan, English, French, German, Greek, Italian, Portuguese, Russian, Spanish, and Yiddish literature. An Editorial Board of distinguished academic specialists works in collaboration with leading scholarly bodies such as the Society for French Studies, the British Comparative Literature Association and the Association of Hispanists of Great Britain & Ireland.

MHRA

The Modern Humanities Research Association (MHRA) encourages and promotes advanced study and research in the field of the modern humanities, especially modern European languages and literature, including English, and also cinema. It also aims to break down the barriers between scholars working in different disciplines and to maintain the unity of humanistic scholarship in the face of increasing specialization. The Association fulfils this purpose primarily through the publication of journals, bibliographies, monographs and other aids to research.

Maney Publishing is one of the few remaining independent British academic publishers. Founded in 1900 the company has offices both in the UK, in Leeds and London, and in North America, in Philadelphia. Since 1945 Maney Publishing has worked closely with learned societies, their editors, authors, and members, in publishing academic books and journals to the highest traditional standards of materials and production.

ITALIAN PERSPECTIVES

Editorial Committee
Professor Simon Gilson, University of Warwick (General Editor)
Dr Francesca Billiani, University of Manchester
Dr Manuele Gragnolati, Somerville College, Oxford
Dr Catherine Keen, University College London
Professor Martin McLaughlin, Magdalen College, Oxford

Founding Editors
Professor Zygmunt Barański and Professor Anna Laura Lepschy

In the light of growing academic interest in Italy and the reorganization of many university courses in Italian along interdisciplinary lines, this book series, founded by Maney Publishing under the imprint of the Northern Universities Press and now continuing under the Legenda imprint, aims to bring together different scholarly perspectives on Italy and its culture. *Italian Perspectives* publishes books and collections of essays on any period of Italian literature, language, history, culture, politics, art, and media, as well as studies which take an interdisciplinary approach and are methodologically innovative.

Managing Editor: Dr Graham Nelson, 41 Wellington Square, Oxford OX1 2JF, UK
www.legendabooks.com

Leopardi's Nymphs

Grace, Melancholy, and the Uncanny

❖

Fabio A. Camilletti

LEGENDA

Italian Perspectives 28
Modern Humanities Research Association and Maney Publishing
2013

Published by the
Modern Humanities Research Association and Maney Publishing
1 Carlton House Terrace
London SW1Y 5AF
United Kingdom

LEGENDA is an imprint of the
Modern Humanities Research Association and Maney Publishing

Maney Publishing is the trading name of W. S. Maney & Son Ltd,
whose registered office is at Suite 1C, Joseph's Well, Hanover Walk, Leeds LS3 1AB

ISBN 978-1-907975-91-2

First published 2013

Printed in Great Britain

Cover: 875 Design

Copy-Editor: Charlotte Brown

CONTENTS

FOR MY GRANDMOTHER, ASSUNTA SPADARI

PREFACE

I quote Leopardi's *Canti* from Emilio Peruzzi's critical edition and the *Zibaldone* from that of Giuseppe Pacella, abbreviated as *Zib.* and followed by the page number in the manuscript and — when applicable — by the date. When required for philological reasons, I have checked the original manuscript in the CD-ROM edition by Fiorenza Ceragioli and Monica Ballerini. References to Leopardi's letters follow the edition of the *Epistolario* by Franco Brioschi and Patrizia Landi, abbreviated as E and followed by volume and page numbers; those to Leopardi's autobiographical writings follow Franco D'Intino's edition of the *Scritti e frammenti autobiografici*, abbreviated as SFA. Quotations from other texts are given from Lucio Felici and Emanuele Trevi's edition of Leopardi's *Tutte le poesie e tutte le prose*, abbreviated as TPP. For the English translation of texts, I have followed Jonathan Galassi for the *Canti*, Patrick Creagh for the *Operette Morali*, and the translation I completed with Gabrielle Sims of the *Discorso di un italiano poesia romantica*; for the letters, I have used Prue Shaw's translation, except for the few cases in which the letter in question was not part of her selection; translations from the *Zibaldone* use the English edition by Michael Caesar and Franco D'Intino. I have, however, allowed myself to slightly modify all these translations in order to preserve the literality of some passages, when it was required for the purposes of argumentation.

Quotations from the works of Sigmund Freud are given from James Strachey's *Standard Edition*, abbreviated as SE and followed by volume and page numbers, and verified, when required, in the German original of the *Gesammelte Werke*, abbreviated as GW. Those from Walter Benjamin's writings, other than the *Arcades Project*, follow the *Selected Writings* edited by Michael W. Jennings, Howard Eiland, and Gary Smith, abbreviated as SW and followed by volume and page numbers; when necessary, I have checked the original text in the German edition of the *Gesammelte Schriften* by Rolf Tiedemann and Hermann Schweppenhäuser, abbreviated as GS. Details of editions and translations of Aby Warburg's texts employed throughout can be found in the bibliography. Unless otherwise specified, all translations from primary and secondary sources are mine.

I wrote the embryo of this book in the summer of 2006, in an apartment in the Prague quartier of Vyšehrad — a few scattered notes on nymphs as the unacknowledged deities of modernity, with a view to some vague, future research project. They started to take a clearer and more defined shape one year later, at the Leopardi Centre in Birmingham, when Michael Caesar and Franco D'Intino encouraged me to pivot my analysis on Leopardi and the liminal writing of the *Zibaldone*. I can never thank them enough for this suggestion, as well as for their invaluable care, support, and supervision throughout these years. I would later refine my theoretical premises within the framework of a postdoctoral fellowship in Literature, Art History, and Psychoanalysis at the Berlin Institute for Cultural Inquiry. The wonderfully stimulating and interdisciplinary atmosphere of the ICI and of Berlin has intimately pervaded the writing of *Leopardi's Nymphs*, for which I am deeply thankful to Christoph Holzhey, the director, as well as to Luca Di Blasi and Claudia Peppel, and to the librarians, Corinna Haas, Magdalena Taube, and Constanze Reichstein for their sweet and professional help in my (frequently excessive) bibliographical needs. I materially wrote the book between the Marches and Warwick, where I could extensively discuss my work with my colleagues at the Department of Italian, Jennifer Burns, Ann Hallamore Caesar, Simon Gilson, Joanne Lee, David Lines, Loredana Polezzi, and Maude Vanhaelen. My most wholehearted thanks are for them, for this, but first and foremost for having made me feel home since my very first day at Warwick. I gave the manuscript its final shape in Pisa, in the autumn of 2012, while I was a visiting researcher at the Scuola Normale Superiore. The Scuola's library resources and the lively debate at seminars, to which I was well accustomed since my undergraduate years, proved to be an invaluable help for the last stages of my writing.

In the course of my research I received support from several institutions, which I would like to thank. In 2009–10 I was awarded a College of Arts & Law Scholarship from the University of Birmingham. In the same year I received a grant from the English-Italian cultural association 'Il Circolo', and an essay written in 2008, in which I outlined the main theories later developed here, was awarded the Rooke Prize: I would especially like to thank Clodagh Brook, from the University of Birmingham, who nominated me. The publication of this book was kindly supported by the Leopardi Centre at Birmingham and by the Department of Italian at Warwick. I would also like to thank Simon Gilson and the editorial board of the 'Italian Perspectives' series for having warmly welcomed the project of this book, and Graham Nelson for his kind help in all stages of the publication process. Some parts of this book have appeared in various journals and edited books in the course of years, although they have been extensively reshaped in the present form: '"On pleure les lèvres absentes": "Amor di lontano" tra Leopardi e Baudelaire', *Italian Studies*, 64, 1 (2009), 77–90; 'Il passo di Nerina: Memoria, storia e formule di pathos nelle *Ricordanze*', *Italianistica*, XXXIX, 2 (2010), 41–66; 'Oblique Gazes: The "Je ne sais quoi" and the Uncanny as Forms of Undecidability in post-Enlightenment Aesthetics', in *Tension/Spannung*, ed. by Christoph Holzhey (Vienna and Berlin: Turia + Kant, 2010), pp. 73–93; 'Voltaires Verwirrung', in *Phantasmata: Techniken des Unheimlichen*, ed. by Fabio Camilletti and others (Vienna and Berlin: Turia + Kant, 2011), pp. 185–202; 'Petrarchismo, "Phantasie" e costruzione della soggettività in Leopardi', *Rivista Internazionale di Studi Leopardiani*, 7 (2011), 25–40; '*Urszenen*: Dream-Logic and Myth in the First Page of Leopardi's *Zibaldone*', *Italian Studies*, 67, 1 (2012), 56–69. I thank all the series and journal editors of these publications for their kind permission to re-employ these materials. Finally, I would like to thank once again Jennifer Burns for her incommensurable help in reviewing the manuscript for publication, and Martina Piperno for her collaboration in preparing the index.

This book has benefited from the help of many people, with whom I could share ideas and who gave constant feedback and intellectual support in the course of its gestation: Alessandra Aloisi, Bruno Besana, Simone Brioni, Irina Chyzh, Maria-Silvia Cohut, Paola Cori, Enza De Francisci, Paolo De Ventura, Catharine Diehl, Martin Doll, Victor Fernandez Soriano, Sara Fortuna, Rupert Gaderer, Nicola Gardini, Manuele Gragnolati, Alessandro Grilli, Géraldine Hertz, Dominic Holdaway, Jan Niklas Howe, Pauline Julier, Camille Louis, Beau Madison Mount, Siouxzi L. Mernagh, Sotirios Paraschas, Anaïs Perrin, Ozren Pupovac, Paula Schwebel, Francesca Southerden, Emanuela Tandello, Filippo Trentin, and Katrin Wehling-Giorgi. My most special thanks are for Marco Scarponi and Roberto Barbini, for the nights at the *Pentolaio* in 2007, when I could understand, once and for all, what Leopardi meant.

Finally, I would like to thank my dearest ones: Alessandra Diazzi, for having made me turn from the past to the present; my mother and father, Maria Grazia Pancaldi and Giuseppe Camilletti; and my grandmother, Assunta Spadari, who loves Leopardi. This book is dedicated to her.

F. C., Filottrano, July 2013

L'Euridice che ho pianto era una stagione della vita. Io cercavo ben altro laggiù
che il suo amore. Cercavo un passato che Euridice non sa.

[The Eurydice I mourned was a season of life. I was looking down there
for something very different from her love. I was looking for a past which
Eurydice knows nothing of.]

CESARE PAVESE, 'L'inconsolabile', *Dialoghi con Leucò* (1947),
translation adapted from that of W. Arrowsmith and D. S. Carne-Ross

'You mean', I said rather tentatively, 'that we must eat again of the tree of
knowledge in order to relapse into the state of Innocence?'
'Certainly', he replied. 'That is the last chapter of the history of the world'.

HEINRICH VON KLEIST, *Puppet Theatre* (1810), translated by B. de Zoete

Perhaps the fracture that in our culture divides poetry and philosophy, art and
science, the word that 'sings' and the word that 'remembers', is nothing other
than one aspect of the very schizophrenia of Western culture that Warburg
recognized in the polarity of the ecstatic nymph and the melancholic river
god. We will be truly faithful to Warburg's teaching if we learn to see the
contemplative gaze of the god in the nymph's dancing gesture and if we
succeed in understanding that the word that sings also remembers and the one
that remembers also sings. The science that will then take hold of the liberating
knowledge of the human will truly deserve to be called by the Greek name
of *Mnemosyne*.

GIORGIO AGAMBEN, 'Aby Warburg and the Nameless Science' (1975),
translated by D. Heller-Roazen

INTRODUCTION

Mnemosyne

Anyone who describes his own city must travel into the past instead of into the distance. [...] the journey into the past, too, is a journey into the distance. [...] The city is still there, but that early period lies irrecoverably within it; this is a paradox that sharpens not only our pain but also our perception. [...] All the same, [...] the adult's glance does not yearn to merge with the child's glance. It is directed towards those moments when the future first announced itself to the child.

PETER SZONDI, 'Walter Benjamin's "City Portraits"'
translated by H. Mendelsohn

[Il mito della Gradiva] è nell'uomo il richiamo, proveniente dal profondo, di una primitiva immagine, retaggio di esperienze infantili, di una fanciulla amata e poi perduta [...] che spesso ci si illude di ritrovare, anche se di fatto (e qui [...], come lei vede, vi è una confluenza col mito di Orfeo) non la si ritrova più.

[The myth of Gradiva is, for man, the call, coming from the deep, of a primal image, the heritage of infantile experiences, of a girl once loved and then lost [...]. One often believes she has been regained, although, as a matter of fact (and here [...], as you can see, we witness a confluence with the myth of Orpheus), she is to be regained nevermore.]

CESARE L. MUSATTI, 'Consulenza psicologica per un film (Autointervista)'

Between Pisa and the Marches

On 5 September 1829 Leopardi writes from Recanati to Karl Bunsen, the Rome-based Prussian minister at that time:

Mio padre, il quale ama d'immaginarsi che nella casa paterna io stia meglio che altrove, le ha dato del mio stato un'idea ben diversa dal vero. Non solo i miei occhi, ma tutto il mio fisico, sono in istato peggiore che fosse mai. Non posso nè scrivere nè leggere nè dettare nè pensare. Questa lettera, finchè non l'avrò terminata, sarà la mia sola occupazione [...]. Condannato, per mancanza di mezzi, a quest'orribile e detestata dimora, e già morto ad ogni godimento e ad ogni speranza, non vivo che per patire, e non invoco che il riposo del sepolcro.[1]

[My father who loves to imagine that I am better off under the paternal roof than anywhere else, has given you an idea of my state very different from the reality. Not only my eyes but my whole physique are in a worse state than ever. I cannot write or read or dictate or think. Until I have completed it this letter will be my only occupation [...]. Condemned by want of means to this horrible and hated abode, and already dead to any enjoyment and any hope, I do not live except to suffer, and I ask for nothing but the repose of the grave.]

In talking about his father's house, Leopardi uses an expression that sounds interestingly close to another employed only a few days before, when writing to his publisher, Antonio Fortunato Stella, on 26 August: 'La mia salute è in un misero stato, e la mia vita è un purgatorio. In *quest'orrido e detestato soggiorno*, non ho più altra consolazione che ricordarmi degli amici passati' [my health is in a miserable state, and my life is a purgatory. In *this horrible and hated sojourn* I find no other consolation than remembering my past friends].[2] With the detachment of those who feel close to death, Leopardi speaks of himself as of an already ghostly creature, which is fighting against oblivion: 'Mi conservi Ella l'amor suo finché vivo, e mi raccomandi alla memoria de' suoi' [please keep your love for me as long as I live, and exhort your relatives to remember me].

These reciprocal reverberations are quite telling, for in these very same days — from 26 August to 12 September, as the manuscript testifies — Leopardi composes 'Le ricordanze' [The Recollections], a poem that precisely uses the space, both physical and emotional, of the 'paternal roof' as a battery of memory from which poetry may erupt. In the course of these weeks, it seems as if Leopardi's writing is progressively refined and crystallized by the totalizing dimension of poetry, which suppresses every other form of expression. Letters become scarce. After the one to Bunsen Leopardi responds briefly, on 23 September, to his friend Antonietta Tommasini, and two days later he even asks his sister to reply to Gian Pietro Vieusseux, justifying his silence by reasons of health.[3] In the same month, the reading lists that Leopardi had been updating in the course of many years, which had already become progressively laconic since the month of April, are interrupted, showing how reading — or, at least, the meticulous registration of books read — has become a somehow superfluous activity.[4] Finally, and most tellingly, on 5 September, Leopardi records in the *Zibaldone*, the intellectual journal kept since 1817, a quotation, without comment, from Cicero's *De officiis*. To some extent, the writing laboratory inaugurated twelve years before stops here: in 1829 Leopardi will make no further entries in the *Zibaldone*, and in the following years the journal witnesses only a few fragments, recorded between 1830 and 1832, that occupy no more than three pages. In the meantime, after 'Le ricordanze', Leopardi composes, one after the other, 'La quiete dopo la tempesta' [The Calm After the Storm] (17–20 September), 'Il sabato del villaggio' [Saturday in the Village] (29 September) and, on 22 October, the first draft of the 'Canto notturno di un pastore errante dell'Asia' [Night Song of a Wandering Shepherd in Asia], later completed in April 1830.

The return to poetry in early autumn 1829 is therefore framed within a return home that Leopardi perceives above all as a defeat — human, literary, and existential — and within a phase in which every other form of writing is extinguished. Several years before, in July 1821, Leopardi had drafted in the *Zibaldone* a plan of action aimed 'a scuotere la mia povera patria, e secolo' [to rouse my poor country and poor century].[5] He delineated there a quite naive self-representation as a complete intellectual, equally able to employ:

le armi dell'affetto e dell'entusiasmo e dell'eloquenza e dell'immaginazione nella lirica, e in quelle prose letterarie ch'io potrò scrivere; le armi della ragione, della logica, della filosofia, ne' Trattati filosofici ch'io dispongo; e le armi del ridicolo ne' dialoghi e novelle Lucianee ch'io vo preparando.

[the weapons of feeling and enthusiasm and eloquence and imagination in lyric poetry, and in whatever literary prose works I may write, the weapons of reason, logic, philosophy in the philosophical treatises that I am planning, and the weapons of ridicule in the Lucianesque dialogues and novellas I am preparing.]

This project corresponded to an ideal of synthesis between two opposite modes of intellectual action that Leopardi still hoped to reconcile. The first was inspired by his uncle, Carlo Antici, who since 1814 had directed the sixteen year-old philologist to a more active study of the classics with the purpose of acquiring an 'eloquence' that would lead to civil and moral action.[6] The other was Pietro Giordani's attempt, since 1818, to transform his pupil into the prototype of a new kind of intellectual, engaged in the renovation of the Italian literary tradition. Both expectations had been eluded, or, better, addressed elsewhere. The abandonment of poetry from the mid-1820s onwards had corresponded to a determined choice for prose, meticulously trained within the *Zibaldone*, in which the longing for literary and civil engagement was seen as a prelude to Leopardi's prospective entrance into the Bourbon Restoration's social *beau monde*. At the heart of this cultural project were the *Operette morali* [Moral Tales], as an aftermath of the dialogues inspired by Lucian already envisaged in 1821; its ideal corollaries were the projects of prose translation of Greek moral writers and the *Crestomazia de' prosatori* [Chrestomathy of Prose Writers], an anthology aiming to reassess the national literary canon.[7] All these works were part of a more global and common plan, in that they all proposed an intellectual renovation grounded in language and style, in the form of examples translated from Greek prose sources, of *morceaux choisis* from the national tradition proposed as stylistic models, and of a fresh demonstration of this mastery through the absolute originality of the *Operette*. All attempts culminated in a shipwreck. Whereas the project of *volgarizzamenti* was abandoned between 1827 and 1828 because of the indifference of publishers,[8] the *Crestomazia* was welcomed with a sort of embarrassed discretion by the contemporary literary scene,[9] and Leopardi's reaction to both responses shows a mixture of disappointment and disdain. On 25 February 1828, he writes to Antonio Papadopoli that:

Con questa razza di giudizio e di critica che si trova oggi in Italia, coglione chi si affatica a pensare e a scrivere. [...] Una raccolta delle mie traduzioni dal greco mi è stata anche fatta proporre da un libraio della Marca. Non so se avrò voglia di darmene pensiero.[10]

[Given the sort of judgement and criticism to be found today in Italy, anyone who puts a lot of effort into thinking and writing is a bloody fool. [...] A proposal has been made to me by a publisher from the Marches for a collection of my translations from the Greek. I don't know whether I'll want to bother with it.]

In a letter of 5 May 1828 to Pietro Giordani, Leopardi makes his disappointment more explicit: 'se negli studi potessi seguire ancora il mio genio, veduta la qualità dei giudizi di questo secolo, non mi darebbe più il cuore di logorarmi in far cose che mi contentassero' [if in my work I could still follow my own inclinations, seeing the quality of judgements of this age, I wouldn't have the heart to wear myself out doing things that satisfied me].[11] The *Operette* were to meet an even worse fate. On 13 February 1830, Vieusseux informs Leopardi that his book has not been awarded a prize announced by the Crusca Academy. Leopardi's reaction is desperate and decisive. 'Son risoluto', he replies on 21 March, 'di pormi in viaggio per cercar salute o morire, e a Recanati non ritornare mai più' [I am resolved to set out on a journey to seek health or to die, and never to return to Recanati again].[12] This is what he will actually do, leaving forever on 30 April.

Between these chronological and intellectual confines, however, Leopardi's poetry blossoms again, although in a radically different form from that of the 'liriche' projected in 1821. On the very same day, 25 February 1828, on which he writes to Papadopoli that 'Studiare e lavorare, sono cose che ho dimenticate, e dalle quali divengo alieno ogni giorno di più' [Studying and working are things I've forgotten, and they become more alien to me every day],[13] Leopardi sends to his sister, Paolina, a very famous letter:

> Io sogno sempre di voi altri, dormendo e vegliando: ho qui in Pisa una certa strada deliziosa, che io chiamo *Via delle Rimembranze*; là vo a passeggiare quando voglio sognare a occhi aperti. Vi assicuro che in materia d'immaginazioni, mi pare di esser tornato *al mio buon tempo antico*.[14]

> [I'm always dreaming about you all, asleep or awake: here in Pisa I have a delightful street, which I call *Street of Memories*: that is where I go to walk when I want to day-dream. I assure you that where imagination is concerned, I seem to be back *to my good, ancient times*.]

Similarly, three days before his letter to Giordani of 5 May, he writes again to Paolina that 'dopo due anni, ho fatto dei versi quest'aprile; ma versi veramente *all'antica*, e con quel mio cuore di una volta' [after two years I've written poems this April; but truly poems *in an ancient fashion*, and with the heart I once had].[15] For sure, Leopardi is referring here to 'A Silvia' [To Silvia], composed in the space of two days between 19 and 20 April.

Within the space of about one month, and speaking about the way in which a sort of anamnestic regression has brought him to return unexpectedly to poetry-writing, Leopardi employs twice, in his letters, the term 'antico', which for him is always (as we will see) the clue for a subterranean tension between history and memory. The return to the 'buon tempo antico' generating and inspiring poetry 'all'antica' describes, in a willingly ambiguous way, an existential rebirth that replaces such sedentary and rational activities as 'studying and working' with the fluctuating movements of strolling and daydreaming. Pisa propitiates this sort of *flânerie*, and in his letters, Leopardi — as he usually does — evokes the weather when alluding to an inner state.[16] In the enthusiasm of his first days in the city, on 27 December 1827, Leopardi writes to his father that in Pisa he can promenade, which in Recanati would be impossible: in Recanati it often rains or is windy, and on bright days there is no shade to give shelter; Pisa, on the contrary, has a mild climate, and seasons are organized in a delicate equilibrium that never turns into excess.[17] This praise sounds meaningful, especially since it comes from one who, in the 'Dialogo della Natura e di un Islandese' [Dialogue of Nature and an Icelander] of the *Operette*, had enumerated the manifold ways in which Nature is able to torment men at various latitudes: 'sono stato arso dal caldo fra i tropici, rappreso dal freddo verso i poli, afflitto nei climi temperati dall'incostanza dell'aria, infestato dalle commozioni degli elementi in ogni dove' [I have been seared with heat between the tropics, shrivelled with cold near the poles, afflicted in the temperate zones by the changefulness of the air, and troubled everywhere by the commotion of the elements].[18] Somehow, Pisa represents, therefore, the state of calm that the Icelander had been searching for in vain, and which in Recanati was only possible within the enclosed space of the library. 'Io le invidio', writes Leopardi to his father on 29 July 1828, 'il soggiorno della Libreria, nella quale mi ricordo bene di non aver mai conosciuta l'estate nè sentito molto l'inverno' [I envy you the time spent closed in the library, where I remember well never having even noticed the summer, nor having much suffered the winter].[19]

Pisa also differs from Recanati as far as its cityscape is concerned. Once in the city on 12 November 1827, Leopardi employs thrice, in three different letters, the same expressions: to Paolina, 'Pisa è un misto di città grande e di città piccola, di cittadino e di villereccio, un misto [...] romantico' [Pisa is a mixture of big city and small city, of urban and rustic, a romantic [...] mixture];[20] to Adelaide Maestri, 'trovo [...] un certo misto di città grande e di città piccola, di cittadino e di villereccio, un misto veramente romantico' [I find here [...] a certain mixture of big city and small city, of urban and rustic, a really romantic mixture];[21] and to Vieusseux, 'io trovo qui un misto di città grande e di città piccola, di cittadino e di rustico, tanto nelle cose, quanto nelle persone: un misto propriamente romantico' [I find here a mixture of big city and small city, of urban and rustic, in things as well as in people: a mixture that is really romantic].[22] His correspondents were plausibly unable to grasp its full implications, but Leopardi was probably anticipating here an acceptation of the adjective 'romantico' that he would make explicit, in the *Zibaldone*, one year later:

> Perchè il moderno, il nuovo, non è mai, o ben difficilm. romantico; e l'*antico*, il vecchio, al contrario? Perchè quasi tutti i piaceri dell'immaginaz. e del sentim. consistono in rimembranza. Che è come dire che stanno nel passato anzi che nel presente.[23]

> [Why is modernity, newness, never or unlikely to be romantic; and *antiquity*, oldness, the opposite? Because almost all pleasures of the imagination and feeling consist of remembering — which is the same as saying that they exist in the past rather than in the present.]

Pisa's 'romantic mixture' is therefore connected with the dimension of memory. The space perceived by Leopardi in November 1827 is a liminal one, torn between town and city, as well as between present and past.[24] Walking through the *Via delle Rimembranze* enacts a tension between closeness and distancing, through which recollections acquire a concreteness, albeit temporary, and can be crystallized within poetic speech.

The same tension between familiarity and otherness underlies 'Le ricordanze', transferred, however, from the domain of space to that of time. The subject returning to the 'paternal roof' is no longer the one who left it: in between, there stand Leopardi's existential and literary defeat, the death of his brother Luigi on 3 May 1829, and the forced detachment from the lively and international environment of Tuscany. A few months before writing this poem, in March 1829, Leopardi writes to General Pietro Colletta about his own literary projects: one of these is the 'Storia di un'anima', meant to be a novel in which 'poche avventure estrinseche e [...] delle più ordinarie' should relate 'le vicende interne di un animo nobile e tenero, dal tempo delle sue prime *ricordanze* fino alla morte', and a 'Colloquio dell'io antico e dell'io nuovo; cioè di quello che io fui, con quello che io sono; dell'uomo anteriore all'esperienza della vita e dell'uomo sperimentato' [The story of a soul, a Novel which would have little external action, and that very commonplace: but it would relate the inner experiences of a mind born noble and sensitive, from the time of its earliest *recollections* until death. [...] Conversation between the old me and the new me; that is between the man I was and the man I now am; between the man before he had experience of life, and the experienced man].[25] Both projects would find their ultimate concretization in 'Le ricordanze'. By re-activating the mythical theme of νόστος, 'Le ricordanze' shows Leopardi's return home as the confrontation of a grown-up subject with the illusions of his youth, bitterly declaring a loss of innocence.

Both 'A Silvia' and 'Le ricordanze' originate thus from failure, within a fluid and unstable moment in which the Recanati of Leopardi's youth is at the same time the 'hated' place of the letters to Bunsen and Stella, and the catalyst of memory that almost immediately turns into poetic speech. Both poems seem to have been written in a sort of trance, and for their author only. Between February and April 1828, while 'A Silvia' is plausibly emerging in his consciousness, Leopardi notes in the *Zibaldone* that poetry has no public or civil use, and that the only addressee of poetry is probably its own author, who, without bothering about the judgement of others, can re-read himself and confront his 'old' and 'new' selves:

> Uno de' maggiori frutti che io mi propongo e spero da' miei versi, è che essi riscaldino la mia vecchiezza col calore della mia gioventù; è di assaporarli in quella età, e provar qualche reliquia de' miei sentimenti passati, messa quivi entro, per conservarla e darle durata, quasi in deposito; è di commuover me stesso in rileggerli, come spesso mi accade, e meglio che in leggere poesie d'altri: [...] oltre la rimembranza, il riflettere sopra quello ch'io fui, e paragonarmi meco medesimo; e in fine il piacere che si prova in gustare e apprezzare i propri lavori, e contemplare da se compiacendosene, le bellezze e i pregi di un figliuolo proprio, non con altra soddisfazione, che di aver fatta una cosa bella al mondo; sia essa o non sia conosciuta per tale da altrui.[26]

> [One of the greatest fruits that I hope for and expect from my verses is that they will warm my old age with the heat of my youth. It is to savour them when I reach that age and to experience something that remains of my past feelings, placed there so it might be kept and last through time, as though in store. It is to move myself as I reread them, as often happens to me, and more so than when I read poems by other people. [...] Over and above the remembering, it is to

reflect on who I was, and to compare myself with myself. And finally, it is the pleasure of enjoying and appreciating one's own work, and of contemplating with contentment the beauties and the qualities of a child of one's own, with no other satisfaction than that of having made something beautiful in this world, whether or not it is recognized as such by others.]

Both poems are perceived as sudden and unexpected illuminations, and welcomed with a mixture of surprise and wonder. In writing to his sister about having 'written poems this April', Leopardi stresses the naive astonishment arising from a return to poetry that he himself almost believed to be impossible. The same sense of wonder is incorporated within the opening lines of 'Le ricordanze', 'Vaghe stelle dell'Orsa, io non credea | Di tornare ancor per uso a contemplarvi' [Shimmering stars of the Bear, I never thought that I'd be back again to see you shine].[27] In a moment of crisis and defeat, poetry seems to emerge outside the subject's control, establishing a fissure between a 'before' and an 'after'. On one side, there is Leopardi's youth, corresponding to an intentional self-construction as a philologist, poet, and philosopher: these are years made of reading, writing, experiments, and literary drafts, conceived within the *Zibaldone* as a laboratory, an interlocutor, and a palimpsest. On the other side, there is Leopardi's final escape from Recanati, the 1831 edition of the *Canti*, and the Neapolitan years, in which poetry remains almost the only medium of expression by reaching a radical and unprecedented balance between poetic lightness and philosophical density. The years 1828–29 can be considered as the moment of most productive tension between these two opposite poles; quite interestingly, when the subject recalls two prematurely dead feminine figures, bearing the names of Silvia and Nerina.

Nymphæ

These two *senhal* should alert us. It is difficult to think of their joint mention as a mere accident, especially if we consider that — as commentators generally highlight — the source seems to be the same. The two names appear together in Torquato Tasso's fable *Aminta* (1573), and are often coupled in the theatre and melodrama of the Academy of Arcadia (as in Domenico Lalli's 'pastoral fable', *Nerina*, performed in 1726).[28] Through this choice, Leopardi seems to evoke an uncontaminated 'spring' of the world, although readdressing the 'pastoral' levity of the original toward a pitiless reflection on the modern loss of innocence.[29] Still, it should not be forgotten that, in pastoral tradition, Silvia and Nerina are first and foremost the names of nymphs and as a classical philologist, Leopardi was unlikely to overlook this connection. In Leopardi's works, nymphs are scarcely present, but almost always connected with the demonic (or demoniac) sphere, as is best shown by the attention paid by Leopardi — between the *Zibaldone* and other writings — to the polysemy of the Latin term *nympha* and its evolutions in romance languages.

In December 1821, Leopardi notes in the *Zibaldone* how medieval writers seemed to consider *nympha* and *Lamia* as two substantially interchangeable terms, possibly suggesting a direct survival of ancient folkloric beliefs alongside the legacy of classical mythology that can be found in written sources:

Gli scrittori latt. adoperarono *Lamia* in senso di *strega*, o *fata* ec. e negli scrittori del trecento ella si trova, credo sempre, in senso di ninfa, tanto che i volgarizzatori di quel tempo, dove i testi latini dicono *nympha*, traducono regolarmente *Lammia*. Questa voce non la poterono dunque avere dagli scrittori latini, che l'adoprano in altro senso, ma dal volgare, il quale, come il volgo fu divenuto cristiano, e considerò le ninfe, e le altre deità del paganesimo come *demonj*, e mali spiriti, cominciò e costumossi a chiamar *Lammie* le ninfe de' Gentili. [...] Ovvero intendendo per *Lammie* le fate delle quali a que' tempi si discorreva, e la cui idea somiglia a quella delle streghe ec. e le fate essendo una specie di ninfe, e viceversa, prevalse questo costume di confonder le ninfe colle *Lammie*, tutte cose che dimostrano un uso volgare, e una perpetua conservazione della voce *Lamia* e dell'idea che significava, o di un'idea analoga alla medesima, nel volgare latino fino ai primordi dell'italiano [...]. E chi sa che gli stessi antichi latini (e greci) volgarmente non dicessero *Lamia* per ninfa? Considerando cioè la ninfa come un ente misterioso, e di misterioso potere, qual è appunto la *Lamia*.[30]

[The Latin writers used *Lamia* in the sense of *witch* or *fairy*, etc., and in the writers of the fourteenth century it is found — always, I think — in the sense of nymph, since the translators of that time, where the Latin texts say *nympha*, normally translate *Lammia*. They must therefore have gotten this word not from the Latin writers, who use it in another sense, but from the vernacular, and, as the populace became Christian, and considered nymphs and the other pagan deities to be *dæmons* and evil spirits, it began calling the pagan nymphs *Lammie*, and this became normal. [...] Or else it meant by *Lammie* the fairies who were much discussed in those days, and who resemble witches, etc., and since fairies are a kind of nymph and vice versa, this tendency to confuse nymphs with *lammie* prevailed. All these things demonstrate that the word *Lamia* was used colloquially, and that it and the idea that it signified, or an idea analogous to it, were permanently preserved in Vulgar Latin down to the beginnings of Italian [...]. And who knows that the ancient Latins (and Greeks) themselves did not colloquially say *Lamia* for nymph? Considering, that is, the nymph a mysterious entity, with mysterious powers, precisely like the *Lamia*.]

In this passage, the ungraspable nature of the nymph affords an understanding of an obscure and subterranean vein of ancient lore. The philologist's gaze takes the interchangeability of terms in medieval writers as a clue for detecting the way popular religion survives in oral culture, thus anticipating, in a proto-ethnographic way, the results of modern research on the survival of classical figures in popular beliefs about the 'little people'. These cultural patterns have been reconstructed by Laurence Harf-Lancner, who, however, credits Alfred Maury (1843) as the first to have identified in medieval fairies the descendants of ancient nymphs.[31] The undefined nature of the nymph becomes therefore an instrument for bypassing the classicist *fable*, approaching through a veritably mythological praxis a concealed core of ancient religion in which the sphere of the demoniac obliquely shines.[32]

Furthermore in the so-called 'Esercizi di memoria' [Memory Exercises], whose date is uncertain, Leopardi quotes Egidio Forcellini's Latin dictionary, remarking how nymphs seem systematically to have to do with the recomposition of opposite elements: 'Contrasto [...] (Ninfe, Forcellini), uniformare' [Contrast [...] (Nymphs, Forcellini), to make uniform].[33] This consideration reverberates in a 1823 passage of the *Zibaldone*, in which Leopardi, again referring to Forcellini, subsumes 'i fauni, le ninfe, i pani ed altre tali divinità, anzi semidivinità terrestri, acquatiche, aeree, insomma sublunari, reputate mortali' [the fauns, nymphs, pans, and other such divinities, or rather terrestrial, aquatic, airy, in short sublunary semidivinities reputed to be mortal] within the broader category of a 'genere partecipante dell'umano e del divino' [genus which participated in both the human and the divine], comparing these creatures to the figure of the hermaphrodite as the synthesis of an opposition.[34] The nymph is therefore, for Leopardi, an intermediary and liminal creature, and hence fully demonic in a Platonic sense,[35] which embodies a binary tension without solving it. In a *Hymn to Zeus* credited to Orpheus by the Neo-Platonist philosopher Porphyry in his treatise on simulacra (Περὶ ἀγαλμάτων), the absoluteness of the greatest of gods is precisely expressed by the coincidence of binary oppositions (first/last, beginning/end, male/female, heaven/earth), one of which is Zeus's aspect as ἄφθιτος [...] νύμφη [immortal maiden][36] — an expression, we may note, that comes perfectly close to the 'giovinetta immortal' [immortal maiden] evoked by Leopardi in the 'Canto notturno' with reference to the moon.[37]

In approaching the theme of nymphs, Leopardi seems therefore to grasp what Georges Dumézil terms 'the magnitude and the imprecision of nymphs' (l'ampleur et l'imprécision des *nymphaï*') in archaic Greek religion.[38] As Georges Didi-Huberman writes:

> Mortelle *et* immortelle, endormie *et* dansante, possédée *et* possédante, secrète *et* ouverte, chaste *et* provocante, violée *et* nymphomane, secourable *et* fatale, protectrice de héros *et* ravisseuse d'hommes, être de la douceur *et* être de la hantise, *Ninfa* assure bien la fonction structurale d'un *opérateur de conversion* entre des valeurs antithétiques qu'elle 'polarise' et 'dépolarise' alternativement, selon la singularité de chaque incarnation.[39]

> [Mortal *and* immortal, sleepy *and* dancing, possessed *and* possessing, concealed *and* revealed, chaste *and* provoking, raped *and* nymphomaniac, helpful *and* deadly, protector of heroes *and* kidnapper of men, sweet *and* haunting being , *Ninfa* assumes well the structural function of an *operator of conversion* between antithetical values that she alternately 'polarizes' and 'depolarizes', according to the singularity of each incarnation.]

This double and ambiguous nature of the nymph is confirmed by the semantic constellation of the Greek term νύμφη as synthesized by Liddell and Scott's dictionary: νύμφη denotes a 'goddess of lower rank', 'especially of springs' (so that νύμφη can also poetically mean 'water'), and is sometimes 'applied to souls seeking birth'; figuratively, νύμφη can also mean 'young wife, bride', 'marriageable maiden', 'daughter-in-law' or 'young girl'; finally νύμφη can also denote the 'doll, puppet', the chrysalis, the 'young bee or wasp, in the pupa stage', the 'opening rosebud' and, metaphorically, the clitoris.[40]

Already at a first glance, νύμφη seems to imply the idea of an undefined and indeterminate stage in a female being's development, tending between two opposite poles as a potentiality that has not been completely fulfilled: the chrysalis as a potential butterfly, the young girl who is no longer a child but not yet a woman, the nymph as a liminal creature between the human and the divine spheres, the soul that waits to be embodied. Such an ambiguous nature of the nymph has left persistent traces in Western cultural history. In his 1955 novel *Lolita*, Vladimir Nabokov recuperates the Elizabethan diminutive *nymphet* for designating those young girls 'who, to certain bewitched travellers, twice or many times older than they, reveal their true nature which is not human but nymphic (that is, demoniac)',[41] an unusual lexical choice that may have been inspired by the studies on nymphs in Renaissance literature and art promoted in the early 1950s by scholars connected to the Warburg Institute such as Erwin Panofsky and Otto Kurz.[42] Equally, in Leopardi, two nymphs' names are employed in order to address two ephemeral and fleeting existences, preserved by death in a chrysalis-like intermediary state. Silvia and Nerina are two young girls (in Greek κόραι, a term that is also employed, in the singular form Κόρη, to denote Persephone)[43] who have died prematurely (ἄωροι),[44] and who have been thus transfigured into liminal beings. From this angle, the notion of νύμφη intersects Leopardi's reflection on the ephemerality of human life and the vanishing of the illusions of youth; yet, it seems to me that the nymph manifests herself, in Leopardi's oeuvre, in a more intimate and deeper way, revealing herself in her most properly mythical aspect.

Certainly, if considered from a strictly literal angle, Leopardi's relationship with myth seems very unproblematic and would definitely preclude any reading along the lines suggested here. As we will see, Leopardi always employs the Greek notion of μῦθος in its literal meaning as 'untrue discourse'. This position does not change in the course of time: in the poem 'Alla primavera' (1822), ancient myths are defined as 'favole antiche' [To Spring, or on the Ancient Fables]; in the 1827 indexes of the *Zibaldone*, the entry 'Favole' is cross-referenced to 'Mitologie'. As a consequence, it is clear that Leopardi's *explicit* use of myth is always configured as a demystification;[45] still, this very position, inherited from Leopardi's rationalistic background, determines an oblique resurfacing of myth as a sort of 'toxic side-effect'.[46] From this angle, rather than of myth, Franco D'Intino speaks more properly of 'mythologem',[47] a term borrowed from the studies of Carl Gustav Jung and Carl Kerényi on the history of mythology:

> A particular kind of material determines the art of mythology, an immemorial and traditional body of material contained in tales about gods and god-like beings, heroic battles and journeys to the Underworld — 'mythologem' is the best Greek word for them — tales already well known but not unamenable to further reshaping. Mythology is the *movement* of this material: it is something solid and yet mobile, substantial and yet not static, capable of transformation.[48]

The point is therefore to detect an 'ancient' presence, which becomes manifest in small clues of the text: a subtle game that Leopardi doubtless encourages, by often concealing — in accordance with his anti-Neoclassical conceptualization of the survival of antiquity — Homeric or lyrical 'formulas of pathos' in those textual breaches that would suggest, at a first and superficial glance, a strictly mimetic representation of reality.[49] From this angle, Leopardi's secret use of myth interrogates the liminal zones between truth and imagination, actuality and illusion, that permeate his entire intellectual operation. How is it possible to make poetry in the age of disenchantment, and moreover while analyzing that very disenchantment by the means of the most rigorous philosophical thinking?

Thus, in the poems composed between Pisa and Recanati in 1828–29, νύμφη seems to be the 'unspeakable (hidden, crypted) word' whose 'rich, orderly polysemia [...] had to be lurking behind a regular [...] series of *cryptonyms*'.[50] The mythologem of the nymph, retraced in classical sources and in pastoral tradition, undergoes a process of cryptomnesia, namely the return of a forgotten memory which is not recognized as such by the subject and is therefore concealed in such clues of the text as onomastic choices or intertextual echoes.[51] The very first line of 'Le ricordanze' incorporates the secret word through a process of cryptomnesia, if, as Mario Fubini and Emilio Bigi have noted, the evocation 'Vaghe stelle dell'Orsa' conceals the intertextual remnant of the beginning of Tasso's poem, 'Vaghe Ninfe del Po, Ninfe sorelle'.[52]

My hypothesis is that the semantic constellation incorporated in the term νύμφη can be employed as a device for attempting a re-reading of Leopardi's poetry of 1828–29, and, at the same time, a reconfiguration of the 'poetic thinking' (*pensiero poetante*)[53] that unconsciously paves the way, in the preceding decades, to that unexpected outburst. Through the peculiar circumstances that characterize their genesis, 'A Silvia' and 'Le ricordanze' — to which we should add the 'Canto notturno' — powerfully polarize and reassess the entire development of Leopardi's intellectual trajectory. In this process, the resurfacing of the nymph's mythologem acts as a crucial element, both as a concealed and cryptic object of the poetic speech and as a power that secretly structures it at a formal level. Hence the choice of speaking of 'Leopardi's Nymphs', a term by which I do not uniquely mean Silvia and Nerina as nymph-like figures, but all the subterranean tensions (memory/ history, illusion/reality, myth/reason) deliberately left unresolved in Leopardi's speech, coexisting in the skilful elusiveness of the poetic signifier.

Ambiguity appears to characterize nymphs since their origins. As Jennifer Larson highlights, the study of archaic Greek religion reveals a strong affinity of the nymphs with the divinities known as Muses (Μοῦσαι), Graces (Χάριτες) and Hours (Ὥραι), 'The Muses, Charites, and Horai are groups closely allied to the nymphs, and they fulfil under other names many of the functions otherwise attributed to nymphs (e.g. [...] producing inspiration)'.[54] Often portrayed in groups of three,[55] nymphs, Muses, Graces, and Hours probably share a common origin, perhaps that of the three Mothers of Neolithic religion whose survival has been reconstructed by Carlo Ginzburg in Eurasian folklore.[56] The Mothers worshipped in the Sicilian temple of Engyon, were apparently connected to the nymphs, perpetuating the cult for a threefold feminine divinity connected to hunting and animals, and variously metamorphosed, in the Greek world, into images of nymphs, or those of Artemis and Hecate as personifications of the moon.

We can therefore legitimately think of the nymph as an impalpable creature, connected to the moon and to the three spheres of grace, poetry, and time. This threefold connection seems to be confirmed by the various guises the nymph has assumed even in recent times. As Didi-Huberman notes, nymphs are the veritable deities overlooking intellectual modernity between the nineteenth and twentieth centuries: among the examples he gives — Théophile Gautier's *Arria Marcella*, Nerval's *Aurélia*, Mallarmé's *Hérodiade*, Villiers de l'Isle-Adam's *L'Ève future*, Frank Wedekind's and Alban Berg's *Lulu*, Hofmannsthal's and Richard Strauss's *The Woman Without a Shadow*, André Breton's *Nadja* — Didi-Huberman includes the hysterical women beheld by Freud at the Salpêtrière hospital in Paris and a feminine figure from the Italian Renaissance, two apparitions that propitiate respectively the birth of a modern 'science of the soul' and of a modern 'science of images'.[57] The last reference is, of course, to the 'Nymph' described by the German art historian Aby Warburg, a feminine figure that crosses a Florentine fresco by Domenico Ghirlandaio and which becomes, throughout Warburg's oeuvre, the visible incarnation of a haunting 'survival of antiquity' (*Nachleben der Antike*),[58] as well as the veritable device for attempting a global reconfiguration of cultural history. The totalizing aspect of this image is made explicit by Warburg in a note of 1898:

> Die Ny[mpha] als Umfangsbestimmung endlich zusammen. Von Darwin über Filippino zu Botticelli durch Carlyle und Vischer zum Festwesen zu den Indianern und durch die Tornabuoni mit Ghirlandaio wieder zur Nymphe.[59]

> [The Nymph as the ultimate and over-encompassing dimensional determination. From Darwin going back to Filippino until Botticelli through Carlyle and Vischer up to the festive rituals of the Indians and through the Tornabuoni with Ghirlandaio back again to the Nymph.]

In Freud and Warburg, in other words, the feminine body in motion (the hysterical woman at the Salpêtrière, or the servant-maiden who crosses Ghirlandaio's painting) becomes the venue for an eruption of alterity subsuming and implicitly questioning the linearity of history — both in the spheres of ontogenesis and individual psychological development (for Freud) and of phylogenesis, thereby reconfiguring long-established modalities of interpreting cultural history and its paths (for Warburg).[60] In this sense, the legacy of Warburg's thought has allowed, in recent years, a global reconceptualization of the nymph as the ambiguous and ungraspable divinity overseeing intellectual modernity, thus challenging traditional forms of knowledge. Giorgio Agamben, who devoted several studies to Warburg over the years,[61] has recently spoken of the nymph as a hybrid being, resuming in her dancing gait a language of pathos articulated in terms of formulas: 'the nymph is an indiscernible blend of originariness and repetition, of form and matter', in the same way as Warburg's 'formulas of pathos' (*Pathosformeln*) 'are made of time: they are crystals of historical memory, crystals that are "phantasmatized" [...], and around which time writes its choreography'.[62] A few years before, in a lecture given at the Collège de France on 5 June 1992 and later published as an autonomous essay, Roberto Calasso began from Warburg's experience of mental disease in order to probe the roots of Greek myth, speaking of nympholepsy — the form of folly inspired by the nymphs — as a form of knowledge through demonic possession,[63] and of the nymphs as the very element of this possession.[64] Finally, the works devoted in recent years by Georges Didi-Huberman to Warburg and Walter Benjamin have stressed the intrinsically anachronistic nature of the nymph, which, as the incarnation of a haunting 'survival of antiquity', subverts the illusion of a linear structure of historical time, establishing at its place a history made of survivals, intermittencies, and discontinuities.[65]

In Warburg's, Freud's and Benjamin's oeuvres, the nymph recuperates therefore her ancient connection with grace, poetry, and time, thereby reconfiguring the relationship between image and movement, the role of possession as a modality of knowledge, and the survival of antiquity as an uncanny detail questioning every historicist dream of continuity. Quite interestingly, all three experiences happen to be located within the theoretical horizon of early twentieth-century Jewish-German cultural syncretism, that 'spiritual synthesis unique in its kind' — as Michael Löwy puts it — which, once annihilated by the National Socialist criminal apparatus, has later witnessed its theoretical and conceptual legacy being betrayed, or at least misunderstood, by a cultural milieu inclined to domesticate it within established academic categories.[66] The insertion of Leopardi within this constellation may sound problematic: in coming from such a different background as that of the aristocracy of the Papal States, born during the Napoleonic wars and intellectually raised in the years of the Bourbon Restoration, Leopardi would appear to be unrelated to the intellectual and political environment of the 'defeated generation'.[67] Yet Leopardi's intellectual legacy witnesses a lively afterlife in central European culture, thanks to his connections with such intellectual personalities as Karl Bunsen, Barthold Georg Niebuhr, and August von Platen, and to the posthumous attention paid to his works by Arthur Schopenhauer and Friedrich Nietzsche. Within the cultural environment of early twentieth-century Germany, Leopardi is therefore a well-recognized presence, especially for those — like Warburg — who had personal and intellectual connections with Italy. Also Benjamin, who reviewed a translation of Leopardi's *Pensieri* in 1928, had a direct knowledge of Leopardi's oeuvre, as testified by his quotations from the *Operette morali* in the *Arcades Project*.[68] Moreover, Leopardi's presence in the work of Warburg and Benjamin can also be seen as a latency, obliquely mediated by the second of Nietzsche's Untimely Meditations *Vom Nutzen und Nachteil der Historie für das Leben* [On the Use and Abuse of History for Life], of 1874, and by the writing *Über Wahrheit und Lüge im außermoralischen Sinn* [On Truth and Lies in a Nonmoral Sense], written in 1873 but posthumously published in 1903. As Didi-Huberman points out, Nietzsche's second *Untimely Meditation* has a crucial influence on Warburg's conceptualization of history,[69] and, as a manifesto of anti-historicism, equally underlies Benjamin's theses *On the Concept of History*. In his text, Nietzsche explicitly quotes Leopardi, but the whole *Meditation* — and especially its beginning — can be seen as an interweaving of motifs and themes, often clearly paraphrased, from Leopardi's poems such as 'Le ricordanze' and 'Canto notturno';[70] the same thing can be said about *On Truth and Lies*, inspired by the *Operette morali* in that it not only presents itself as a *conte philosophique*,[71] but is actually quintessentially shaped by Leopardi's thought at various levels. Either directly conveyed via editions and translations, or through Nietzsche's anti-historicist texts of the early 1870s, Leopardi's work may therefore be seen as a subterranean and latent influence, which somehow happens to shape Warburg's and Benjamin's reflections on time, memory, and the image.

It should also be said that Leopardi, like the 'defeated generation', has been intellectually defeated and betrayed, and often for similar reasons. The echo of his thought in his contemporaries, scarcely inclined to accept its radical newness, reverberates in a ramified intellectual legacy composed of more or less deliberate misunderstandings, which often tend to encapsulate it within fixed schemes and stereotypes.[72] Even in the twentieth century, Leopardi's thought remains unclassifiable, while the several attempts to insert his thought into pre-ordered ideological frameworks — progressive, nihilist, Marxist or existentialist ahead of his time — have often overlapped, and on many occasions replaced, analysis.[73] More than anything else, over Leopardi-related studies there seems to weigh what Antonio Prete, as early as 1980, named the historicist claim of Italian literary criticism:[74] precisely by being impoverished in terms of methods while analyzing a thinker whose radical newness actually consists in questioning historicist conceptualizations of time, historicism fails to grasp the intrinsically subversive strength of Leopardi's discourse for the very same reasons that have prevented it from fully receiving the legacy of early-twentieth-century Jewish-German thought. The newness of this thought consists in having questioned the assumptions of Idealism — linearity of historical time, predominance of will — through 'the eruption, within a magnetic field polarized by libertarian romanticism and Jewish messianism, of a new concept of history, including a new perception of temporality at variance with evolutionism and the philosophy of progress'.[75] From this angle, as Didi-Huberman writes, the general premises of classical aesthetics were verified by a rigorous philology, which was in its turn reoriented by a strongly philosophical and critical praxis.[76] This theoretical reflection entails a new attention to the infinitesimal detail, be it the mathematical infinitesimal, Benjamin's 'monad', philological detail, psychoanalytic symptom, or — finally — the anachronistic detail that, as a phobic significant, questions every illusion of continuity or order.[77] Once considered from this angle, Leopardi's operation, in being equally inclined to dismantle every illusion of teleological continuity, reveals subterranean affinities with the reflection of those who, 'because they were the defeated, because they were outsiders going against the tide of their era, and because they were romantics and incurable utopians', have witnessed their work 'becoming increasingly relevant and meaningful' for posterity.[78] In Didi-Huberman's terms, Leopardi's operation itself can be defined as a productively anachronistic reactivation of antiquity within the sphere of detail, nourished by a rigorous philology, which is in turn supported by the constant dialogue with a strong philosophical and aesthetical apparatus. In the same way as Warburg's *Bilderatlas Mnemosyne*, or Benjamin's *Arcades Project*, Leopardi's intellectual endeavour witnesses a substantial identity between work and laboratory, which finds its desperately modern nature in the deflagrated disjointedness of fragments.[79]

The nymph can be thus seen as the secret figure animating the hybrid nature and subterranean tensions of Leopardi's operation, acting — in compliance with her affinity with Muses, Graces and Hours — in the domains of grace, poetry and time. Hence the tripartite structure of this book, which takes its cue from the poems of 1828–29 in order to reconstruct Leopardi's 'poetic thinking' in relation to aesthetics and literary theory (Chapter 1), subjectivity, desire, and the poetic articulation of melancholy (Chapter II), memory, conceptualization of historical past, and the presence of myth (Chapter III), and the use of poetry as a way of circumventing the aporias of modern disenchantment (Conclusion). In the first case, the nymph-Χάρις can be seen as an allegory of the fleeting nature of grace, through which Leopardi grounds aesthetic enjoyment in undecidability; in the case of Leopardi's poetry as a melancholy discourse, the nymph-Μοῦσα embodies the knot between ungraspable *imago*, desire, and poetic speech; finally, the nymph-Ὥρα epitomizes the uncanny resurfacing of an out-of-time sphere of origin, acting as a survival of a both historical and memorial antiquity.

'Every age', wrote Warburg in a paper on the survival of ancient gods, 'can see [*schauen*] only those Olympian symbols which it can recognize and bear [*erkennen und vertragen*] through the development of its own inner visual organs [*inneren Sehorgane*]. We, for instance, were taught by Nietzsche a vision of Dionysus'.[80] He personally acknowledged that the time had come to see the nymphs, in the form of gracious, melancholy, and uncanny apparitions, haunting modernity as 'charming nightmare[s]':[81] and whose first manifestation can perhaps be retraced in an unexpected return to poetry, experienced between Pisa and the Marches, between 1828 and 1829.

Notes to the Introduction

1. E, II, 1686–87.
2. E, II, 1681, my emphasis.
3. E, II, 1697.
4. In September 1829 Leopardi only records the poem 'Amor fuggitivo' [Fugitive Love] by Torquato Tasso, one of the most influential authors in the composition of 'Le ricordanze'. Leopardi will restart his habit of drafting reading lists in the following year: see TPP, p. 1122.
5. *Zib.* 1394, 27 July 1821.
6. On this point see Franco D'Intino, *L'immagine della voce: Leopardi, Platone e il libro morale* (Venice: Marsilio, 2009), pp. 85–93.
7. On the *Crestomazia de' prosatori*, see Giulio Bollati's introduction to Giacomo Leopardi, *Crestomazia italiana. La prosa*, ed. by Giulio Bollati (Turin: Einaudi, 1968), pp. vii–xcviii. On Leopardi's editorial project for a collection of translated Greek moral writers, see Giacomo Leopardi, *Volgarizzamenti in prosa 1822–1827*, ed. by Franco D'Intino (Venice: Marsilio, 2012), pp. 91–105.
8. Leopardi, *Volgarizzamenti in prosa*, pp. 102–04.
9. Bollati's introduction to Leopardi, *Crestomazia italiana. La prosa*, pp. xviii–xxx.
10. E, II, 1460.
11. E, II, 1481–82.
12. E, II, 1719.
13. E, II, 1460.
14. E, II, 1459, my emphasis.
15. E, II, 1480, my emphasis.
16. See Franco D'Intino, 'I misteri di Silvia. Motivo persefoneo e mistica eleusina in Leopardi', *Filologia e critica*, XIX, 2 (1994), 211–71 (pp. 211–15).
17. E, II, 1437–38.
18. TPP, p. 534.
19. E, II, 1528.
20. E, II, 1400.
21. E, II, 1401.
22. E, II, 1402.

23. *Zib.* 4415, 22 October 1828, my emphasis.

24. On Leopardi and cities, see Emilio Bigi and others, *Le città di Giacomo Leopardi* (Florence: Olschki, 1991). On the specific case of Pisa, see: Luigi Blasucci, 'Leopardi e Pisa', in *Le città di Giacomo Leopardi*, pp. 105–31; Fiorenza Ceragioli (ed.), *Leopardi a Pisa: cangiato il mondo appar* (Milan: Electa, 1998), and Ceragioli, *Giacomo Leopardi e la stagione di Silvia* (Rome: Sossella, 2001); Attilio Brilli, *In viaggio con Leopardi* (Bologna: Il Mulino, 2000), pp. 77–83; Fiorenza Ceragioli and Marcello Andria, *Il percorso della poesia: Giacomo Leopardi a Pisa (1827–1828)* (Pisa: ETS, 2005).

25. E, II, 634, my emphasis. On the difference between 'the old me and the new me' and the philosophical consequences it entails in terms of conceptualizations of time and subjectivity, see Liana Cellerino, 'L'io antico e l'io nuovo', in *L'io del topo: Pensieri e letture dell'ultimo Leopardi*, by Liana Cellerino (Rome: La Nuova Italia Scientifica, 1997), pp. 87–103.

26. *Zib.* 4302, 15 February 1828.

27. Leopardi, 'Le ricordanze', ll. 1–2.

28. See the interesting reflections made by Floriana Di Ruzza on the names of Silvia and Nerina in connection to the *Aminta*, to the image of the moon-Artemis and to the deadly implications of Tasso's text: *Onomastica leopardiana: Studio sui nomi propri nei 'Canti', nelle 'Operette morali' e nei 'Paralipomeni'* (Rome: Nuova Cultura, 2010), pp. 57–66.

29. See Emerico Giachery, 'Convergenze su *Aspasia*', in *Motivo e parola* (Naples: Guida, 1990), pp. 23–42 (p. 31).

30. *Zib.* 2302, 29 December 1821.

31. Laurence Harf-Lancner, *Les Fées au moyen âge: Morgane et Mélusine: La Naissance des fées* (Geneva: Slatkine, 1984), p. 17.

32. On the difference between Ancien Régime *fable* and the construction of a veritable mythological form of scientific knowledge between the eighteenth and nineteenth centuries, see Jean Starobinski, 'Fable et mythologie aux XVIIe et XVIIIe siècles', in *Le Remède dans le mal: Critique et légitimation de l'artifice à l'âge des Lumières*, by Jean Starobinski (Paris: Gallimard, 1989), pp. 233–62.

33. TPP, p. 1107.

34. *Zib.* 3495–97, 22 September 1823.

35. On this aspect, see Elisabetta Brozzi, 'I demoni di Leopardi', in *La prospettiva antropologica nel pensiero e nella poesia di Giacomo Leopardi*, ed. by Chiara Gaiardoni (Florence: Olschki, 2010), pp. 443–59.

36. Porfirio, *Sui simulacri*, ed. by Mino Gabriele, transl. by Franco Maltomini (Milan: Adelphi, 2012), pp. 70–71, and the corresponding note at pp. 138–41 (III: 9).

37. Leopardi, 'Canto notturno', l. 99.

38. Georges Dumézil, *Fêtes romaines d'été et d'automne suivi de Dix questions romaines* (Paris: Gallimard, 1975), p. 41.

39. Georges Didi-Huberman, *L'Image survivante: Histoire de l'art et temps des fantômes selon Aby Warburg* (Paris: Minuit, 2002), p. 348.

40. Henry George Liddell and Robert Scott, *A Greek-English Lexicon* (Oxford: Clarendon Press, 1996), p. 1184.

41. Vladimir Nabokov, *The Annotated Lolita*, ed. by Alfred Appel Jr. (London: Penguin, 2000), p. 16.

42. Nabokov probably attended Panofsky's Norton Lectures in 1947–48, and may have come into contact with Kurz's essay 'Huius nympha loci', *Journal of the Warburg and Courtauld Institutes*, 16 (1953), 171–77. See Antonella Sbrilli, 'Le mani fiorentine di Lolita: Coincidenze warburghiane in Nabokov (e viceversa)', *Engramma* 43 (September 2005), <http://www.engramma.it/engramma_v4/rivista/saggio/43/043_sbrilli_nabokov.html> [accessed 28 May 2013].

43. See Giorgio Agamben and Monica Ferrando, *La ragazza indicibile. Mito e mistero di Kore* (Milan: Electa, 2010).

44. In Greek, the adjective ἄωρος means 'untimely', 'unripe', and as a noun denotes the ghost of those who have died prematurely: see Sarah Iles Johnston, *Restless Dead. Encounters between the Living and the Dead in Ancient Greece* (Berkeley, Los Angeles and London: University of California Press, 1999), pp. 164–65.

45. See Lucio Felici, *L'Olimpo abbandonato: Leopardi tra 'favole antiche' e 'disperati affetti'* (Venice:

Marsilio, 2005), p. 17. See also Patrizia Girolami, *L'antiteodicea: Dio, dei, religione nello 'Zibaldone' di Giacomo Leopardi* (Florence: Olschki, 1995).

46. Terry Castle, *The Female Thermometer: Eighteenth-Century Culture and the Invention of the Uncanny* (Oxford: Oxford University Press, 1995), p. 8.

47. D'Intino, 'I misteri di Silvia'.

48. Carl Gustav Jung and Carl Kerényi, *Science of Mythology: Essays on the Myth of the Divine Child and the Mysteries of Eleusis*, transl. by R.F.C. Hull (London and New York: Routledge, 2002), p. 3.

49. See Gilberto Lonardi, *L'oro di Omero. L''Iliade', Saffo: antichissimi di Leopardi* (Venice: Marsilio, 2005), p. 146.

50. Jacques Derrida, 'Fors: The Anglish Words of Nicolas Abraham and Maria Torok', transl. by Barbara Johnson, in *The Wolf Man's Magic Word: A Cryptonymy*, by Nicolas Abraham and Maria Torok, transl. by Nicholas Rand (Minneapolis: University of Minnesota Press, 1986), pp. xi-xlviii (p. xli).

51. The notion of cryptomnesia is employed by Freud in a small article of 1920, 'A Note on the Prehistory of the Technique of Analysis', SE, xviii, 263–65. It had been initially theorized by the psychiatrist Théodore Flournoy in analyzing the case of the medium Helen Smith, and had subsequently entered the psychoanalytical debate through Carl Gustav Jung's persistent interest in psychic phenomena. See Henri F. Ellenberger, *The Discovery of the Unconscious: The History and Evolution of Dynamic Psychiatry* (New York: Basic Books, 1981), p. 170.

52. In Giacomo Leopardi, *Canti*, ed. by Mario Fubini and Emilio Bigi (Turin: Loescher, 1964), p. 172 note.

53. I am clearly referring here to Antonio Prete, *Il pensiero poetante. Saggio su Leopardi* (Turin: Einaudi, 2006).

54. Jennifer Larson, *Greek Nymphs: Myth, Cult, Lore* (Oxford: Oxford University Press, 2001), p. 7.

55. Ibid., p. 259.

56. Carlo Ginzburg, *Ecstasies: Deciphering the Witches' Sabbath*, transl. by Raymond Rosenthal (New York: Pantheon Books, 1991), pp. 205–95.

57. Georges Didi-Huberman, *Ninfa Moderna: Essai sur le drapé tombé* (Paris: Gallimard, 2002), pp. 7–8.

58. On Warburg's nymph, see, among others, Sigrid Weigel, 'Aby Warburgs "Göttin im Exil". Das "Nymphenfragment" zwischen Brief und Taxonomie', *Vorträge aus dem Warburg-Haus*, 4 (2000), 65–104; Ulrich Raulff, 'Die Nimphe und der Dynamo. Warburg aus der Jugendstil', in *Wilde Energien. Vier Versuche zu Aby Warburg*, by Ulrich Raulff (Göttingen: Wallenstein, 2003), pp. 17–47; Silvia Contarini and Maurizio Ghelardi, '"Die verkörperte Bewegung": la ninfa', in *Aby Warburg: La dialettica dell'immagine*, ed. by Davide Stimilli (Milan: Il Saggiatore, 2004), pp. 32–45; Andrea Pinotti, 'Nimpha zwischen Eidos und Formel: phänomenologische Aspekte in Warburgs Ikonologie', in *Phänomelität des Kunstwerks*, ed. by Hans Rainer Sepp and Jürgen Trinks (Vienna: Turia + Kant, 2006), pp. 222–32; Claudia Cieri Via, *Introduzione a Aby Warburg* (Rome and Bari: Laterza, 2011), pp. 49–54.

59. Warburg Institute Archive, iii, 45.2.1.

60. 'Whereas Warburg spoke of the afterlife of antiquity, Freud referred to the return of the repressed. Both researchers explored images of motion for survivals of the past', Louis Rose, *The Survival of Images: Art Historians, Psychoanalysts, and the Ancients* (Detroit: Wayne State University Press, 2001). See also Georges Didi-Huberman, *L'Image survivante*, pp. 273–334, in which Rose's work is curiously not cited. On the psychoanalytic implications of Warburg's nymph see also Wolfram Pichler, Werner Rappl, and Gudrun Swoboda, 'Metamorphosen des Flussgottes und der Nymphe. Aby Waburgs Denk-Haltungen und die Psychoanalyse', in *Die Couch. Vom Denken im Liegen*, ed. by Lydia Marinelli (Munich: Prestel, 2006), pp. 161–86.

61. See, for example: 'Warburg and the Nameless Science' (1975), in *Potentialities: Collected Essays in Philosophy*, by Giorgio Agamben, ed. and transl. by Daniel Heller-Roazen (Stanford: Stanford University Press, 1999), pp. 89–103; 'Nymphs' (2007), transl. by Amanda Minervini, in *Releasing the Image: From Literature to New Media*, ed. by Jacques Khalip and Robert Mitchell (Stanford: Stanford University Press, 2011), pp. 65–80; *The Signature of All Things: On Method* (2008), transl. by Luca D'Isanto and Kevin Attell (New York: Zone Books, 2009).

62. Agamben, 'Nymphs', p. 71.

63. Roberto Calasso, 'La follia che viene dalle Ninfe', in *La follia che viene dalle Ninfe*, by Roberto Calasso (Milan: Adelphi, 2005), pp. 11–44 (p. 17).
64. Ibid., p. 31.
65. I refer here to Georges Didi-Huberman, *Devant le temps: Histoire de l'art et anachronisme des images* (Paris: Minuit, 2000), in which the author examines the notion of anachronism in Walter Benjamin's historical thought (pp. 85–155). Didi-Huberman's reflection on Warburg has been developed in two parallel works, both published in 2002, the previously mentioned *L'Image survivante* and *Ninfa moderna*.
66. On Benjamin and Warburg respectively see Didi-Huberman, *Devant le temps*, pp. 51–55, and *L'Image survivante*, pp. 27–34.
67. Quoted in Michael Löwy, *Fire Alarm: Reading Walter Benjamin's 'On the Concept of History'*, transl. by Chris Turner (London: Verso, 2005), p. 84.
68. Walter Benjamin, *The Arcades Project*, transl. by Howard Eiland and Kevin McLaughlin (Cambridge, MA, and London: Belknap Press of Harvard University Press, 1999), pp. 8, 18, 62, and 894.
69. Didi-Huberman, *L'Image survivante*, p. 160.
70. See Cesare Galimberti's notes to the beginning of the second *Untimely Meditation* in Friedrich Nietzsche, *Intorno a Leopardi*, ed. by Cesare Galimberti (Genoa: Il Melangolo, 1999), pp. 119–28.
71. This connection has been highlighted by Carlo Ginzburg, *History, Rhetoric, and Proof (The Menahem Stern Jerusalem Lectures)* (Hanover, NH: University Press of New England, 1999), p. 10.
72. Moving from René Girard's studies on the 'scapegoat', Cosetta Veronese speaks of Leopardi's nineteenth-century reception as of a case of 'scapegoating', and hence characterized by the two opposite and parallel movements of 'sacrifice and exclusion' and of 'sanctification and inclusion': *The Reception of Giacomo Leopardi in the Nineteenth Century: Italy's Greatest Poet After Dante?* (Lewiston, NY: Edwin Mellen, 2008), pp. 3–4 and, in more detail, pp. 36–42. The exaltation of Leopardi would therefore sound like the opposite and complementary aspect of the exclusion operated against the radical charge of his thought: the persistent jeremiad, inaugurated by Italo Calvino, on the alleged 'untranslatability' of Leopardi outside Italy and on the scarce consideration paid to his works by foreign readers and critics would be the most evident symptom of an unresolved conflict.
73. To reconstruct this prevalently Italian debate, whose recapitulation seems to have become a sort of *leitmotiv* for every introduction to a Leopardi-related book, falls definitely beyond my intentions.
74. Prete, *Il pensiero poetante*, p. 67.
75. Löwy, *Redemption and Utopia*, p. 3.
76. Didi-Huberman, *Devant le temps*, p. 54.
77. For these considerations I am indebted to Paula Schwebel's studies on the infinitesimal in Benjamin, Franz Rosenzweig and Hermann Cohen, which she presented on 11 November 2008 in the course of an internal workshop at the Berlin Institute for Cultural Inquiry with the title 'Dissolution and Intensity: Interpreting Benjamin's Monad'. On the paradigm of detail, see the still valuable study by Carlo Ginzburg, 'Morelli, Freud and Sherlock Holmes: Clues and Scientific Method', *History Workshop Journal*, 9, 1 (1980), 5–36.
78. Löwy, *Redemption and Utopia*, p. 2.
79. On Warburg's and Benjamin's fragmentary works see Matthew Rampley: 'Archives of Memory. Walter Benjamin's Arcades Project and Aby Warburg's Mnemosyne Atlas', in *The Optic of Walter Benjamin*, ed. by Alex Coles (London: Black Dog, 1999), pp. 94–117; and *The Remembrance of Things Past: On Aby Warburg and Walter Benjamin* (Wiesbaden: Harrassowitz, 2000).
80. From the manuscript *Die antike Götterwelt und die Frührenaissance im Süden und im Norden* [The World of Ancient Gods and the Early Renaissance in the South and the North], quoted in Ernst Gombrich, *Aby Warburg: An Intellectual Biography, with a Memoir of the History of the Library by F. Saxl* (Chicago: University of Chicago Press, 1986), pp. 190–91.
81. The expression is André Jolles's, from his fictive exchange of letters with Warburg on Ghirlandaio's nymph: quoted by Ernst Gombrich, *Aby Warburg*, p. 107.

CHAPTER 1

Grace

Il n'est rien de si précieux que ce temps de notre vie, cette matinée infini-
tésimale, cette fine pointe imperceptible dans le firmament de l'éternité, ce
minuscule printemps qui ne sera qu'une fois, et puis jamais plus. 'Le coq chante
et le jour brille. Lève-toi, mon aimé, c'est l'heure'. C'est l'heure: Hora! Tout
à l'heure, il sera trop tard, car cette heure-là ne dure qu'un instant. Le vent se
lève, c'est maintenant ou jamais. Ne perdez pas votre chance unique dans toute
l'éternité, ne manquez pas votre unique matinée de printemps.

[Nothing is as precious as this time of our life, this infinitesimal morning, this
imperceptible dot within the firmament of eternity, this minuscule spring that
will only ever be once, and then never more. 'The rooster is calling and the
day is shining. Wake up, my beloved, it's time'. It's time, the hour: Hora! Soon
it will be too late, because this hour only lasts one instant. The wind is rising,
it is now or never. Do not lose the only chance you have through all eternity,
do not miss your only morning of spring.]

VLADIMIR JANKÉLÉVITCH, *Le Je-ne-sais-quoi et le Presque-rien I*

Imaginary Breeze

Expressing what is vague and indefinable — for Leopardi, the only source of
aesthetic pleasure — can be, sometimes, like chasing butterflies; thus states a metaphor appearing in the *Zibaldone* as early as 1819:

Il sentimento che si prova alla vista di una campagna o di qualunque altra cosa
v'ispiri idee e pensieri vaghi e indefiniti quantunque dilettosissimo, è pur come
un diletto che non si può afferrare, e può paragonarsi a quello di chi corra
dietro a una farfalla bella e dipinta senza poterla cogliere: e perciò lascia sempre
nell'anima un gran desiderio: pur questo è il sommo de' nostri diletti, e tutto
quello ch'è determinato e certo è molto più lungi dall'appagarci, di questo che
per la sua incertezza non ci può mai appagare.[1]

[The feeling we experience on seeing the countryside or any other thing that
inspires vague and indefinite ideas and thoughts, however extremely delightful
it might be, is like a delight that cannot be captured, and can be compared to
that of someone who chases a beautiful coloured butterfly and is unable to catch
it, and so it always leaves a great yearning in the soul. Yet this is the sum of our
delights, and all that is fixed and certain is much farther from contenting us
than that which, by its very uncertainty, can never content us.]

Beautiful and mottled, ungraspable and hence far more desirable, the butterfly
incessantly flees, as do nymphs, which in classical tradition are *fugitivæ* almost by

definition. No surprise, therefore, if the image of the butterfly recurs several times in Nabokov's book on nymphets, *Lolita*, testifying to the author's entomological interests (he discovered a new species in 1943, which is now called 'Nabokov's Wood-Nymph'), but also echoing the equation between nymph and chrysalis that is implicit in ancient Greek language; nor if Aby Warburg, in his private writings, tends often to equate butterflies and nymphs, moreover developing a veritable obsession for nocturnal butterflies and moths while being convalescent in Ludwig Binswanger's psychiatric hospital.[2]

Let us now connect this fragment to another passage drafted in the *Zibaldone* just one year before, in which Leopardi attempts to analyze the indefinable effect produced by the Greek poet Anacreon on the reader. The passage is centred on an intricate metaphor, and is structured as a single, long sentence:

> Io per esprimere l'effetto indefinibile che fanno in noi le odi di Anacreonte non so trovare similitudine ed esempio più adattato di un alito passeggero di venticello fresco nell'estate odorifero e ricreante, che tutto in un momento vi ristora in certo modo e v'apre come il respiro e il cuore con una certa allegria, ma prima che voi possiate appagarvi pienamente di quel piacere, ovvero analizzarne la qualità, e distinguere perchè vi sentiate così refrigerato già quello spiro è passato, conforme appunto avviene in Anacreonte, che e quella sensazione indefinibile è quasi istantanea, e se volete analizzarla vi sfugge, non la sentite più, tornate a leggere, vi restano in mano le parole sole e secche, quell'arietta per così dire, è fuggita, e appena vi potete ricordare in confuso la sensazione che v'hanno prodotta un momento fa quelle stesse parole che avete sotto gli occhi.[3]

> [In order to express the indefinable effect that the odes of Anacreon have upon us, I can find no better comparison and example than a passing breath of fresh breeze in the summer, fragrant and cheering, that all at once restores you in a way and seems to open your lungs and heart with a kind of gaiety. But before you are able to fully satisfy that pleasure or study its quality and understand why you feel so refreshed, that breath has passed, exactly as happens in Anacreon, for that indefinable sensation is almost instantaneous, and if you want to study its quality it eludes you, you no longer feel it, you return to reading, only the dry words remain in your hand; that little breeze, so to speak, has vanished, and you can barely recall, confusedly, the sensation that the same words in front of your eyes produced just a moment before.]

In the preceding pages, Leopardi had attempted a survey, albeit schematic, of the Italian lyrical canon, which was plausibly meant to pave the way for the composition of his patriotic songs 'All'Italia' [To Italy] and 'Sopra il monumento di Dante' [On the Monument to Dante], which he completed in the same year. Through briefly schematic paragraphs, from pages 23 to 28, Leopardi takes his cue from Petrarch in order to explore a selection of Italian Classicism from the fading propagations of the Baroque to the Academy of Arcadia's rococo taste. After completing his *Discorso di un italiano intorno alla poesia romantica* [Discourse of an Italian on Romantic poetry] in March, Leopardi pursues, we may say, his demystification of the Milanese Romantics by other means, namely by recuperating those eighteenth-century experiences that had sought literary renovation through the emulation (*æmulatio*) of the ancients rather than their imitation (*imitatio*), such as Vincenzo Gravina's theory of poetry and Scipione Maffei's theatre.[4] As far as lyric poetry is concerned, Leopardi approaches at first a still Baroque poet such as Fulvio Testi, moves then to Gabriello Chiabrera's Classicist experiments, and eventually focuses his attention on poets of the Arcadia, including Vincenzo da Filicaia, Alessandro Guidi, Giambattista Felice Zappi, and Eustachio Manfredi. Every author is evaluated through a rapid profile, often supported by short quotations, and dissected through the categories of 'eloquence' (*eloquenza*), 'images' (*immagini*) and 'speech' (*sentenzie*). Leopardi's argumentative strategy and conceptual categories are likely to be derived from the ancient treatise of pseudo-Longinus, *On the Sublime*, which he used to read in Jean Toup's Oxonian edition of 1778.[5] The three categories employed by Leopardi seem to echo the taxonomy of the 'sources' of sublime effects outlined in the eighth chapter of the treatise, in mirroring in the first category what the pseudo-Longinus terms strength in elocution (τῆς ἐν τῷ λέγειν δυνάμεως) and 'innate' poetic abilities; in the second, those skills that can be learned (τῶν σχημάτων πλάσις and γενναία φράσις); and in the third, the synthesis (σύνθεσις) that contains the essence itself of the sublime.[6] The pseudo-Longinus thus provides Leopardi with a model of textual semiotics through which one can produce poetic effects via identifiable techniques. Undertaking a survey of Italian Classicism through this theoretical framework is a form of apprenticeship aimed at acquiring the skills for generating literary pathos.

Within this operation, however, the paragraphs devoted to Zappi seem to describe a different experience in reading. In analyzing this poet, Leopardi seems, in fact, unable to frame the effects engendered by his texts within the fixed categories outlined in the treatise of the pseudo-Longinus. Zappi, Leopardi writes, is rather close to Anacreon; he is even, maybe, the only Italian poet who possesses the 'seeds' (*semi*) of Anacreon (*Zib.* 28), and the only one who is able to engender the same sensation of a refreshing breeze (*Zib.* 31). This kind of poetry eschews the ancient treatise's interpretative grids, indicating a different and still undefined aesthetic experience. Moreover, this strange form of textual enjoyment can only be defined through the limited means of an imaginative simile.

Leopardi's style confirms this impression of immediacy, as if it aimed to capture a fading and indefinable sensation. The fragment shows an asyndetic construction, using no full stops, as if meaning to grasp multiple and concurrent stimuli in which no chronological progression can be detected, nor any further analysis is possible. The effect of Anacreon's poetry cannot be rendered unless by means of negation ('indefinibile') or of adverbial expressions denoting approximation ('in *certo* modo', 'v'apre *come* il respiro', 'una *certa* allegria', '*quasi* istantanea', 'quell'arietta *per così dire*', my emphases). In the same way as happens with the experience of 'suddenness' as defined by Karl Heinz Bohrer, reading Anacreon is an 'epiphany' taking place within the space of an instant, determining a feeling of 'astonishment'.[7] As Bohrer writes, 'the irreality that arises [...] is no psychic project but an event in the transempirical realm. It is covered by the category of the "completely other"', which language is not completely able to render.[8] Several years later, another *Zibaldone* passage reaffirms Leopardi's initial judgement about Anacreon:

> Altrove ho rassomigliato il piacere che reca la lettura di Anacreonte [...] a quello d'un'aura odorifera ec. Aggiungo che siccome questa sensazione lascia

gran desiderio e scontentezza, e si vorrebbe richiamarla e non si può; così la lettura di Anacreonte; la quale lascia desiderosissimi, ma rinnovando la lettura, come per perfezionare il piacere [...], niun piacere si prova, anzi non si vede nè che cosa l'abbia prodotto da principio, nè che ragione ve ne possa essere, nè in che cosa esso sia consistito; e più si cerca, più s'esamina, più s'approfonda, men si trova e si scopre, anzi si perde di vista non pur la causa, ma la qualità stessa del piacer provato, chè volendo rimembrarlo, la memoria si confonde; e in somma pensando e cercando, sempre più si diviene incapaci di provar piacere alcuno di quelle odi, e risentirne quell'effetto che se n'è sentito; ed esse sempre più divengono quasi stoppa e s'inaridiscono e istecchiscono fra le mani che le tastano e palpano p. ispecularle.[9]

[Elsewhere I have compared the pleasure which reading Anacreon gives [...] to that of a scent on a breeze, etc. I would now add, that as this sensation leaves great desire and dissatisfaction, for we should like to recall it but cannot, so too does the reading of Anacreon, which leaves us wanting much more. But in rereading him, as though to perfect the pleasure [...], no pleasure is in fact experienced, indeed we fail to see what it was that produced it in the first place, or what reason there could have been for it, or of what it might have consisted. And the more it is sought, examined, and investigated, the less it is actually found and discovered, indeed, we lose sight not just of the cause but the very quality of the pleasure which we experienced, for in seeking to recall it our mind is confused. In short, as we reason and search, we become increasingly incapable of experiencing any pleasure in those odes, and of feeling again the effect we felt previously, and increasingly they become almost like tow, and grow dry and brittle in the hands of whoever handles and touches them in order to speculate on them.][10]

The asyndetic composition of sentences and the rhetorical use of climax and negation aim to describe something that cannot be told. The conclusion sanctions a sort of failure: this experience cannot be defined 'altrimenti che chiamandola indefinibile, ed esprimendola nel modo ch'ho fatto io con quella similitudine' [in any way other than by saying that it is indefinable, and by expressing it in the way that I did by means of that simile].[10] Anacreon's poetry is an encounter with otherness that only figurative language can perhaps aim to describe, and produces a delight as vain as that of those who chase butterflies without being able to capture them.

Not by chance, in Leopardi's oeuvre Anacreon is systematically mentioned as the most notable example of the constituent untranslatability of ancient poetry.[11] The problem is not uniquely linguistic, but rather tackles the whole relationship entailed by the moderns with classical antiquity. Anacreon is the most untranslatable poet as far as he fully epitomizes the naiveté (*semplicità*) characterizing the ancients.[12] As early as 1815, in an essay on the Greek pastoral poet, Moschus, Leopardi defines Anacreon as 'il vero esemplare dell'antica semplicità, sì facile a perdersi e a disparire' [the true model of that ancient naiveté that can so easily get lost and disappear].[13] Anacreon's naiveté oversteps the merely textual dimension of literary translation. Every translation, Leopardi writes, cannot help but be a paraphrase, but the problem is that 'Una parafrasi di Anacreonte è un mostro in letteratura. Anacreonte parafrasato è un ridicolo: la sua grazia diviene bassezza, la sua semplicità, affettazione: egli annoia e sazia al secondo istante' [a paraphrase from Anacreon is a literary monster. Once paraphrased, Anacreon is ridiculous: his grace becomes shallowness, his naiveté, affectation: he wearies and satiates after a second].[14] The problem posed by Anacreon is therefore a cultural one. His naiveté cannot be translated because of a cultural distance dividing the modern and intellectually sophisticated subject from the simple grace of antiquity.

Framing this consideration within an abstractly Neoclassical paradigm would, however, be misleading. Although moving from a similar acknowledgment of a cultural fracture, Leopardi's answer shows a radical difference from the one, say, of Johann Joachim Winckelmann.[15] Francesca Fedi labels Leopardi's alleged Neoclassicism as an 'optical illusion': although referring to classical antiquity as a constant term of comparison, Leopardi's reflection does not actually share any of the ideological premises of those Italian and European trends stemming from Winckelmann's reflections.[16]

Winckelmann's historical system conceptualizes the relationship of the moderns with classical antiquity as an experience of loss, engrained in a specific concept of history that, for Hayden White, characterizes the modern age:

> The modernity of our epoch differs from all the other modernities of past epochs [...] by virtue of European culture's achievement of 'the concept of history'. While European culture has always been characterized by a sense of history, [...] only in its modern phase — sometime between 1750 and 1850 — did European society begin to think and act as if it existed in history, as if its 'historicity' was a feature, if not the defining feature of its identity.[17]

As Reinhard Koselleck shows by means of the telling example of Friedrich Schlegel commenting on the sixteenth-century painting *Alexanderschlacht*, the Romantic philosopher's modern gaze differs from the concept of history implied by the earlier artwork. Three centuries after the painting's completion, Schlegel shows 'a critical-historical distance' that makes him 'able to distinguish the painting from his own time, as well as from that of the Antiquity it strove to represent'.[18] In modern times, history has undergone a temporalization, through which the past has been distantiated and constructed as a form of alterity. This aspect makes every dream of antiquity, like Winckelmann's art-historical project, an elaboration of mourning. While commenting on a passage from Winckelmann's *History of Ancient Art*, in which the moderns' position is compared to that of an enamoured woman gazing onto the ocean in search of her beloved's sail, Alex Potts borrows an expression from Roland Barthes in terming Neoclassicism 'a lover's discourse': in being grounded in a will of 'animat[ing] the surviving bits and pieces that otherwise would be mere dead fragments', this discourse is unavoidably condemned to delusion, which becomes 'the very essence of history'.[19] As Didi-Huberman points out,[20] Winckelmann's dedication of his book to ancient art is a tribute paid to something that one knows to be dead, so that the *History of Ancient Art* may be seen as the hopeless conjuration (*évocation*) of something lost (*la chose perdue*).[21] Like every elaboration of mourning, this process is, however, rooted in an unresolved ambiguity, oscillating between the 'bringing to life of a lost ideal that was once actually realized' and 'the product of a fevered imagination mourning the loss of what can never be recovered and probably never existed'.[22]

Leopardi's approach to the same problem is different, as Anacreon's example shows. Anacreon's archaic naiveté remains completely unattainable for the modern subject, unless by means of an ineffable instant of graceful enlightenment; still, as Leopardi suggests, this feeling can rather be conceptualized as a consequence of the moderns' distantiated position than as an intrinsic and irrecoverable quality of classical antiquity. In itself, Anacreon is neither naive, nor natural, nor graceful. Only the fracture that separates the modern reader from 'nature' allows us to perceive Anacreon's poetry as an alterity, and so attain a form of enjoyment, even if a fleeting one. Being rooted in a modality of perception, the charm of antiquity is quintessentially relative: antiquity becomes such only when it is constructed as a charming otherness by a subject who is no longer an ancient. This aspect is made evident in a fragment drafted in the *Zibaldone* in 1821:[23]

> quella grazia che deriva dal semplice, dal naturale ec. [...] a noi in tanto par grazioso, in quanto, atteso i nostri costumi e assuefaz. ec., ci riesce straordinario [...]. Diversa è l'impressione che a noi produce la semplicità degli scrittori greci, v. g. Omero, da quella che produceva ne' contemporanei. A noi par graziosa [...] perchè divisa da' nostri costumi, e naturale. Ai greci contemporanei, appunto perchè naturale, pareva bella, cioè conveniente, perchè conforme alle loro assuefazioni, ma non graziosa, o certo meno che a noi. [...] A molte cose può estendersi questo pensiero.[24]
>
> [the grace that derives from the simple, the natural, etc. [...] seems graceful to us to the extent that it comes across to us as extraordinary, taking into consideration our usages and habits, etc. [...]. The simplicity of Greek writers, e.g. Homer, makes a different impression on us than it did on contemporaries. To us it seems graceful [...] because it is distinct from our own customs, and natural. To contemporary Greeks, precisely because it was natural, it seemed beautiful, that is to say, fitting, because it was consistent with what they were accustomed to, but not graceful, or certainly less so than it does to us. [...] This thought may be extended to many topics.]

By inverting the problem, Leopardi goes thus to the core of the unsolvable deadlock engendered by the modern concept of history, centring his analysis on the modern subject rather than on the 'lost' object. As Francesco Erspamer points out, Leopardi perceives the past as a dimension of the present, enacting a strategy of distancing through which the past allows the present to be re-transfigured in a sentimental way.[25] In other words, there is no antiquity but through the acknowledgment of its irremediable absence. Rather than a process of grief, in which the subject mourns the loss of something that once existed, Leopardi's perception of antiquity can therefore be seen as a state of melancholy. Both 'lover's discourses' addressed to an absent object, mourning and melancholy actually differ, in Freudian theory, as far as that in the latter, Giorgio Agamben claims, 'not only is it unclear what object has been lost, it is uncertain that one can speak of a loss at all'.[26]

First and foremost, this experience of alterity is a unique possibility offered to the moderns. 1818 is, from this angle, a crucial year. Leopardi is writing in the midst of the so-called Classicist/Romantic quarrel, a literary debate that engulfs Bourbon Restoration Italy from 1816 until circa 1827. In 1816, Madame de Staël had invited Italian writers to undertake a vast updating of their culture by translating texts from foreign literatures, in order to get rid of the burdens of Classicism.[27] The existence itself of the quarrel raises revealing questions about the possibility of framing Italian experiences within the categories of European Romanticisms, and even about the legitimacy of speaking about an Italian Romanticism at all.[28] Not only is the debate immediately polarized between the Classicists' defence of imitation and the Romantics' total rejection of it, a dichotomy that remains alien to the strong influence of classical antiquity on German and English Romanticisms, but the Italian writers who are the closest to the poetics of European Romanticism choose either not to engage in the quarrel (like Foscolo and Manzoni) or, like Leopardi, to enter the debate from the Classicist side. This discrepancy, as Joseph Luzzi notes, is rooted in a difference in terms of perception: rather than considering 'mythology and classical literature as mere emblems of artistic and cultural authority', Italian writers such as Foscolo and Leopardi view 'the classical heritage [as] a legitimate birthright that enjoined them to ancient Rome, and hence to Troy and ancient Greece'; Foscolo, as Luzzi concludes, 'felt as at home in the temples of Ilium as Wordsworth did in the hills of the Lake District'.[29]

Leopardi's contribution to the quarrel is the discourse on Romantic poetry prepared in the months that precede his survey of Italian Classicism.[30] As François Hartog points out, every 'Quarrel of the Ancients and the Moderns' entails a clash between two different modalities of relationship with time, concretizing into two opposite regimes of historicity.[31] The modern relationship with classical antiquity can therefore either take the shape of the Classicist answer, appealing to a timeless tradition and forcibly stressing the elements of continuity, or result in the Romantic abandonment of every cultural legacy. Although challenging the Romantics' position, Leopardi actually questions both, thus rejecting either the absolute and abstract idealisation of antiquity (as is implicit in every primitivistic dream of earliness), as well as every total abandonment of it. For Leopardi, both options would result in a loss in terms of poetic effect, tending either toward sterile formalism or the paroxysmal pursuit of newness, resulting in other forms of submissive imitation (for example from Ossian).

To borrow an expression from Walter Benjamin's theses 'On the Concept of History', Leopardi's position 'brush[es] history against the grain'.[32] Benjamin opposes this operation to the historicist illusion of a de-subjectivized and impersonal perspective in history-making, which, in the field of Classics, dates back to the eighteenth-century German historian Christian Gottlob Heyne, who asserted the necessity of abandoning every contemporary frame of mind in order to embrace the 'spirit of antiquity' (*Geist des Altertums*) and to evaluate ancient civilizations through conceptual categories of that time.[33] Rather than effacing the historian's point of view as an anachronistic element that would endanger an un-mediated perception of the past, Benjamin constructs it instead as the cornerstone that uniquely makes historical experience possible:

> The Copernican revolution in historical perception is as follows. Formerly it was thought that a fixed point had been found in 'what has been' [*das 'Gewesene'*], and one saw the present engaged in tentatively concentrating the forces of knowledge on this ground. Now this relation is to be overturned, and

what has been is to become the dialectical reversal — the flash of awakened consciousness. [...] The facts become something that just now first happened to us, first struck us; to establish them is the affair of memory. Indeed, awakening is the great exemplar of memory.[34]

In commenting on this passage, Didi-Huberman notes how Benjamin's Copernican revolution undermines the impasse of post-Enlightenment historicism by placing the historian as the addressee and subject of the historical process, rather than its detached observer.[35] For Leopardi, antiquity does not exist equally outside the melancholy of the subject's gaze, which constructs an indefinitely absent sphere of origin for nourishing an incessant nostalgia. Tellingly, the perception of history proposed by Benjamin is rooted in the 'indolence of the heart, that *acedia* which despairs of appropriating the genuine historical image as it briefly flashes up'.[36] This despair comes close to that of Leopardi' subject, intent on analyzing the fleeting glimpse of antiquity that 'flashes up' in the form of a breeze. In the same way as for Benjamin, however, this experience is the only possibility left to the historical subject in order to grasp the past and give it a meaning, without being trapped in the dichotomy between sterile imitation and newness at all costs. The breeze perceived while reading Anacreon is not only the sole form of textual enjoyment left to moderns, but a new and different experience that only modernity can afford. The alleged 'loss' of antiquity determined by modernity's concept of history outlines different possibilities, making of an ostensible defeat the aesthetic foundations of a new kind of poetry.

Whereas the sublime could be systematized within the categories established by the pseudo-Longinus, reading Anacreon reveals therefore to Leopardi another kind of aesthetic pleasure, which is entirely modern and whose alchemy is still undefined. This experience is given the name of grace (*grazia*), and its analysis is progressively systematized as a theory, in the *Zibaldone*, between 1820 and 1828.[37]

Leopardi first encounters the problem of grace while reading Montesquieu's *Essai sur le goût* [Essay on Taste], an unfinished text that was posthumously included in the seventh tome of Diderot and D'Alembert's *Encyclopédie* (1757).[38] One of Montesquieu's chapters was devoted to the 'certain something' (*je ne sais quoi*), an aesthetic notion that enjoyed a peculiar centrality in early modern French culture.[39] Following a persistent usage, however, Leopardi translates the negative structure of the French expression by the positive term of 'grazia'; at the same time, he broadens Montesquieu's aesthetic understanding of the concept to the wider domain of theology: Leopardi's purpose is to analyze grace despite its being 'così astrusa nella teoria delle arti, come quella della grazia divina nella teologia' [just as obscure in artistic theory as divine grace is in theology].[40] Leopardi's inquiry into the concept of grace proceeds therefore in a double direction. On the one hand, it concerns a modern problem, mainly related to the field of aesthetics: the notion of *je ne sais quoi* emerges in the Renaissance, later becoming a crucial category in early modern Europe for denoting a quality that does not identify with any of the categories established by ancient theories of art. On the other hand, the choice of speaking of 'grace' qualifies this aesthetic notion as the afterimage of something that in pre-modern ages used to belong to the sphere of the sacred. The Greek term Χάρις and its Latin translation *gratia*, other than being the names of the sub-divinities known as Graces, denote, from ancient Greek lore to Catholic theology, the glimpse of divinity that shines in the features of earthly creatures.[41] From archaic religion to modern aesthetics, grace is an imperceptible shadow of alterity that insinuates itself within the perimeter of customariness.

Throughout the *Zibaldone*, the notion of grace is identified with the element of alterity that troubles beauty 'to a certain degree'. Grace is naturally connected with foreignness,[42] and can be even identified with an element of ugliness within beauty ('La grazia in somma per lo più non è altro che il brutto nel bello. Il brutto nel brutto, e il bello puro, sono medesimam. alieni dalla grazia' [Grace in short is generally none other than ugliness in beauty. Ugliness in ugliness, and pure beauty, are both alien to grace]).[43] The most recurrent expression for defining grace is, however, 'extraordinary' (*straordinario*).[44] This choice stresses the uncustomary nature of grace, as something that dissolves the boundaries between familiarity and otherness. At the same time, it reveals the intrinsically modern nature of the aesthetic experience that Leopardi is trying to define. As Giorgio Agamben points out, the 'unusual' (*straordinario*) is the value that, in modern societies, has taken the place of 'experience'. In traditional societies, Agamben maintains, 'the everyday — not the unusual — made up the raw material of experience which each generation transmitted to the next'.[45] Whereas, for Leopardi, the ancients rooted their aesthetic enjoyment in the familiarity of the 'everyday' and in a 'beauty' conceptualized as a well-ordered effect grounded in propriety (*convenienza*), once secularized from the sphere of the sacred into that of aesthetics, the extraordinary becomes the main value for intellectually sophisticated societies in search of refined pleasures. The beauty itself of ancient art and poetry acquires its charm once its 'propriety' is no longer attainable, and has therefore become unusual.

For defining grace, Leopardi has recourse once again, in 1823, to the image of the breeze. On 16 August he describes a certain kind of grace as:

> quasi un soave e delicatissimo odore di gelsomino o di rosa, che nulla ha di acuto nè di mordente, o quasi uno spiro di vento che vi reca una fragranza improvvisa, la quale sparisce appena avete avuto il tempo di sentirla, e vi lascia con desiderio, ma vano, di tornarla a sentire, e lungamente, e saziarvene.[46]

> [a kind of sweet and most delicate fragrance, of jasmine or roses, which has nothing sharp or mordant about it, or again, almost like a breath of fresh air that brings with it an unexpected scent, which disappears as soon as you have had time to smell it, and leaves you with the desire, albeit vain, to smell it again, and at length, and to be filled with it.]

The closeness in terms of style and metaphors employed creates an inner reverberation between this passage and the ones describing the effects of Anacreon's poetry. In both cases, grace is a glimpse of otherness that escapes every attempt of analysis; in both passages, the experience of the ineffable is located within a spring-like setting, whose gaiety is doomed to be lost an instant later.

In the *Canti*, spring acts as a polyvalent metaphor, symbolizing the hopes of youth. Like Anacreon's breeze, youth is something ephemeral that only leaves behind the task of recapitulating, in later years, a suddenly lost beatitude. From the ontogenetic sphere of individual lifetime, the metaphor of spring turns into the phylogenetic one of history: the poem 'Alla primavera' employs the image of spring in order to epitomize the age of myths. Both springs are condemned. Youth turns into adult life, whereas every age of mythological illusions is followed by the aridity of civilization. The poem 'Il sabato del villaggio' metaphorizes this decay by the image of Saturday turning into Sunday, with the quivering hope for the festive day giving way to the spleen of Sunday evening, over which the working week already casts its shadow. The ending of the poem openly equates Saturday and youth, as moments when one waits for a feast that must necessarily bring delusion. This phase of expectation is also epitomized by a springlike feminine image: the country girl portrayed in the opening lines of the poem carries a sheaf of grass and 'un mazzolin di rose e di viole' [a bunch of violets and roses],[47] thus being transfigured for an instant into a mythological, Botticelli-like Flora.

It is possible, I think, to develop this connection with Renaissance visual and written sources in a subtler way. In Aby Warburg's degree dissertation, drafted between 1889 and 1891 and published in 1893, Botticelli's *Spring* (c. 1482) and *The Birth of Venus* (c. 1485) are analyzed as re-elaborations of the 'concep[t] of antiquity in Italian Early Renaissance' (*Vorstellungen von der Antike in der italienischen Frühren-aissance*).[48] Warburg's study questions Winckelmann's representation of ancient ideal beauty as 'eine edle Einfalt und eine stille Grösse' [a noble simplicity and a calm grandeur].[49] Whereas the legacy of Winckelmann's writings and of Lessing's *Laokoön* (1766) had promoted an identification of classical visual culture with a noble stillness, Warburg investigates ancient art in search for movement as a device for portraying pathos and creating empathy (*Einfühlung*), a notion borrowed from the writings on art and symbol by the German philosopher Robert Vischer, with the beholder. Warburg's argument is that early Renaissance art does not however refer to human movement in order to render emotional pathos, but rather to a device that he calls 'intensification of outward movement', embodied by the so called 'bewegtes Beiwerk' [accessory forms in motion].[50] The pathos is symbolized by those details, such as draperies, cloths and locks of hair, moved by something defined by Warburg through the French expression *brise imaginaire* [imaginary breeze].[51] This device appears to be always derived from classical sources, and it can be therefore considered as a valuable clue for detecting the influence of ancient iconography.[52] For early Renaissance Italian painters, Warburg asserts, antiquity is not identified with an arbitrarily constructed ideal of calm stillness, but with a moving detail animated by a light breeze. The *brise imaginaire* is the essence of the survival of antiquity, so that 'to take accessory forms in motion as the touchstone of "antique influence"', Warburg concludes, 'may be biased, but is not unjustified'.[53]

What is this imaginary breeze made of? Georges Didi-Huberman analyzes its enigmatic nature, which cannot be reduced to a mere pictorial expedient. In its fluidity, breeze does not only cross the painting's surface, but rather 'touches and alters the very being of what it comes into contact with',[54] sending a multifold 'quiver' that operates through space, time, bodies, and souls: its 'invisible atmospheric displacement — an "outward cause" — serves as a fluid index for the displacement of affects, for "inward causes"'.[55] Recalling André Chastel's studies on

Vasari and Ficino, Didi-Huberman stresses how Quattrocento art theorists adopt air (*aria*) as a polyvalent concept for outlining 'an entire psychology'.[56] The nature of air oscillates between that of 'supernatural substance',[57] showing that a divine intervention is operating, and of 'allegorical fluid',[58] through which to symbolize passions; 'the *aria* follows so closely upon bodily movements that she — air being feminine to the Italian ear — becomes the subtle symptom, almost invisible in her fluidity, of the movements of the *anima*'.[59]

In the same way, the two *Zibaldone* passages on the effects of Anacreon's poetry conjure an imaginary breeze in order to epitomize a perturbation of the soul. Leopardi's breeze is a veritable allegorical fluid which, however, preserves the vestiges of a supernatural substance: the 'parole sole e secche' that alone remain with the reader after the flashing instant of grace sound like the afterimage of a combination of wind and fire, similar to the Holy Ghost of Catholic tradition. Compared to the Quattrocento *aria*, Leopardi's imaginary breeze presents two radical differences. Firstly, the equation between 'air' and 'soul' is declared to be a merely figurative one. As a *Zibaldone* note of February 1821 clarifies, the human mind cannot even conceive anything situated beyond materiality, hence the equation made by the ancients between wind and the human soul in order to get close to the idea of an immaterial substance.[60] Secondly, rather than the externalized air working as an allegory of passions, the Romantic (namely, post-Enlightenment) poet witnesses the interiorization of an 'air-in-motion', thus becoming the passive subject of an action initiated in another and 'foreign' space: as Abrams writes, in Romantic poetry 'the wind is not only a property of the landscape, but also a vehicle for radical changes in the poet's mind'.[61] This swerve affects the process of signification and construction of meaning. In the 1819 poem 'L'infinito' [Infinity], an external wind bursts into the subject's solipsistic meditation, stimulating a reflection on time and the survival of the past:

> E come il vento
> odo stormir tra queste piante, io quello
> infinito silenzio a questa voce
> vo comparando: e mi sovvien l'eterno,
> e le morte stagioni, e la presente
> e viva, e il suon di lei.[62]

[And when I hear the wind stir in these branches, I begin comparing that endless stillness with this noise: and the eternal comes to mind, and the dead seasons, and the present living one, and how it sounds.]

As Gabrielle Sims points out, the presence of gerunds and of the wind signal an intertextual influence from Dante's *Purgatorio*:[63]

> I' mi son un che, quando
> Amor mi spira, noto, e a quel modo
> Ch'e' ditta dentro vo significando.[64]

[I in myself am one who, when Love breathes within me, takes note, and to that measure which he dictates within, I go signifying.]

Between Dante and Leopardi, what declines is this activity of signification, meaning the incessant gloss of the pneumatic and phantasmatic process that for the medieval author connects love, memory, and poetic speech.[65] The experience of the imaginary breeze can no longer be given a proper meaning, and can only be made the object of an interminable process of analysis, entrapped within the threads of figurative language.

In the texts that construct Warburg's reflection, air and grace are often likened to one another. This approach is rooted in theology: divine grace imparts life to inanimate beings, in the same way as the representation of moving air transforms the painting into a 'field of animation'.[66] In Alberti's treatise on painting the effect of grace is retraced 'nei capelli, nei crini, ne' rami, frondi et veste' [in hair, locks, boughs, leafy fronds, and garments].[67] These elements must be animated by 'movimenti moderati et dolci, piu tosto quali porgano gratia ad chi miri, che maraviglia di fatica alcuna' [gentle, moderate movements, appearing to the onlooker as something pleasurable rather than as an effort to be marvelled at];[68] the highest effect of grace will be produced by the representation of wind. The connection is, however, deeper. As Didi-Huberman highlights, in Alberti's text 'the Italian word *ariosa* translates the Latin *grata* so that all grace is seen to participate a certain quality of the "air", whether this word is taken to refer to an appearance or to the atmosphere'.[69] Grace and breeze belong to the same constellation, and both suddenly burst into space like presences from an absolute otherness. While beholding Quattrocento art, the imaginary breeze strikes the beholder by its 'spatial incoherence',[70] appearing regardless of any anti-realistic problem of perspective. This aspect stresses its 'other' nature, coming to signify something that cannot be quantified or defined.

For Warburg, in the same way as for Leopardi, this alterity is the return of antiquity, once it has been constructed as a sphere of origin by the moderns' gaze and therefore manifesting itself as a 'survival' (*Nachleben*). By this term, as we will see more closely in Chapter III, Warburg means something different from the mere 'legacy' of antiquity that was the object of traditional studies in the history of classical tradition. Rather, the notion of *Nachleben* becomes the foundational cornerstone of Warburg's project of science of culture (*Kulturwissensschaft*). Warburg's choice of such an unusual term aims to stress the impure and phantasmatic nature of cultural history and its alinear trajectories made of hidden clues, anachronisms, swerves, and oblique metamorphoses rather than identifiable historical transmissions.[71]

The notion of *Nachleben* allows Warburg, like Leopardi, to brush history against the grain, thus dismantling the linearity of post-Enlightenment historicism. *Nachleben* constructs the perceiver's gaze as the fulcrum of historical knowledge, thus revealing the unconscious dimension of history made of haunting anachronisms and situating antiquity in the sphere of the here-and-now, in the form of a surviving latency. [72] Reading Benjamin's *Arcades Project* in the light of Warburg's *Nachleben*, Didi-Huberman writes, enables the perception of a mythical substrate: the shopgirl is Danaë, the doors of the underground recall those of hell, and the Arc de Triomphe reactivates the unconscious cultural memory of rites of passage.[73] Moreover, the structure of *Nachleben* is close to that of the Freudian symptom, being not only the afterimage of an old thought that troubles new perceptions, but the phantasmal re-staging of an original, traumatic scene — as we will see, the *Urszene* — that may not have taken place at all (and whose actuality is in any case irrelevant). The Freudian symptomatology eschews the distinction between original trauma and its later re-elaboration, in the same way as in Warburg's project, once concretized in the *Bilderatlas Mnemosyne*, 'none of the images', Agamben claims, 'is the original, just as none of the images is simply a copy or repetition. [...] Every photograph is the original; every image constitutes the *archē* and is, in this sense, "archaic"'.[74] In all these cases, what matters is what we do have, in the sphere of the here and now: a symptom, a Danaë-like shopgirl, a montage of images, or the fleeting shadow of grace left by the reading of a Greek poet. In being not perceived as simple afterimages of a lost past, they rather become the only way antiquity can be manifest, insofar as its essence is ultimately that of absence.

As a classical philologist turning to literary writing, Leopardi acknowledges therefore the impossibility of every Classicism, and conceives poetry as the venue of a survival in which antiquity, rather than being a mere referent, is constructed as a melancholy tonality from which a new literary project can be articulated. The following section will analyze the ways in which this quintessentially modern project takes shape.

Flânerie

In September 1823, Leopardi drafts in the *Zibaldone* a fragment on the function of ancient burial practices, a topic that in the early nineteenth century was often employed in order to challenge issues of historical memory, collective and national identity, and the origins of civilization. Such was the case, for instance, of Ugo Foscolo's poem *Dei sepolcri* (1807) [On Tombs], in which the spatial dislocation and rationalization of death imposed by the Napoleonic Edict of St Cloud (1804) was opposed to the role of ancient tombs as catalysts of collective memories, and therefore as venues of social aggregation.[75] Leopardi pivots his argument on the opposition between 'natural' and 'anti-natural': although common sense may bring us to think of burial practices and faith in the afterlife as innate reactions to death that are common to the whole of mankind, he maintains, the only and truly natural response to death would be the identification of the departed one with its remains, and therefore the desire to prolong contact with the corpse. The notion of hereafter, as well as the institutionalization of mourning rites in order to accelerate the transit into the other world, would be cultural (and therefore anti-natural) constructions, created for hygienic and sanitary reasons. The natural man does not believe in a separate soul, and the Homeric poems, Leopardi argues, testify to the fact that in archaic societies the corpse was actually identified with the departed person, in its entireness.[76] As Leopardi notes elsewhere, this has always been the translators' main misunderstanding in rendering the beginning of such an early poem as the *Iliad*: it was not the heroes' bodies that were devoured by dogs following Achilles's rage, but actually the heroes themselves.[77] Faith in other-worldly life, as well as mourning practices, are 'illusions' created in order to cement communities in the early stages of their civilization.[78]

On 15 September 1823, immediately after drafting his reflection on burials and in an apparently disjointed way, Leopardi inserts in the *Zibaldone* a quotation from Francesco Algarotti's *Pensieri* [Thoughts], in which the Venetian essayist noted how the 'ancients' used to tend toward eternity in every aspect of their lives: every event was eternalized by establishing everlasting monuments, while 'moderns' spend all their resources in ephemeral goods.[79] The two reflections cover therefore a similar theme, namely the way ancient civilizations were grounded in 'illusions' and directed toward eternity. Burials and monuments are symptoms of the ancients' and moderns' respectively different attitudes concerning death, collective memory, and the possibility of intellectual legacies. As Leopardi writes, the cityscape of Rome is the most evident epitome of the cultural differences separating ancients and moderns in relation to time, as is evident when comparing the Egyptian obelisk in Piazza del Popolo and the contemporary and endlessly unfinished building sites. The ancients/moderns opposition is framed within a dichotomy between eternity and ephemerality, or, in other words, the tension between posterity and a day-to-day perspective:

> L'immaginazione e le grandi illusioni onde gli antichi erano governati, e l'amor della gloria che in lor bolliva, li facea sempre mirare alla posterità ed all'eternità, e cercare in ogni loro opera la perpetuità, e proccurar sempre l'immortalità loro e delle opere loro. Volendo onorare un defonto innalzavano un monumento che contrastasse coi secoli, e che ancor dura forse, dopo migliaia d'anni. Noi spendiamo sovente nelle stesse occasioni quasi altrettanto in un apparato funebre, che dopo il dì dell'esequie si disfa, e non ne resta vestigio. [...] Le grandi illusioni onde gli antichi erano animati non permettevano loro di contentarsi di un effetto piccolo e passeggero, di proccurare un effetto che avesse a durar poco, instabile, breve; di soddisfarsi d'una idea ristretta a poco più che a quello ch'essi vedevano. L'immaginazione spinge sempre verso quello che non cade sotto i sensi. Quindi verso il futuro e la posterità, perocchè il presente è limitato e non può contentarla; è misero ed arido, ed ella si pasce di speranza [...]. Ma il futuro p. una immaginazione gagliardissima non debbe aver limiti; altrimenti non la soddisfa. Dunque ella guarda e tira verso l'eternità.[80]

> [The imagination and the great illusions by which the ancients were ruled, and the love of glory that seethed within them, meant that they always strove for posterity and eternity, and sought perpetuity in all of their works, and always wanted to procure immortality for themselves and their works. In wishing to honour the dead, they would construct a monument which was able to withstand the centuries and perhaps survives still, after thousands of years. On similar occasions we often spend almost as much on a funerary display that is dismantled the day after the ceremony, and of which no trace remains. [...] The great illusions by which the ancients were moved did not permit them to be content with a small or fleeting effect, with procuring an effect that would not last for long, that would be unstable and short-lived, or to be satisfied with an idea restricted to not much beyond what they themselves could see. The imagination always drives us toward what does not fall within reach of our senses. Therefore, toward the future and posterity, for the present is limited and cannot give satisfaction to the imagination; it is wretched and arid, and the imagination feeds itself on hope [...]. But for a strong imagination the future can have no limits, otherwise it does not satisfy it. Hence the imagination looks and strives toward eternity.]

Interestingly, this reflection is almost immediately projected onto the domain of textuality. The same degeneration of human illusions can be witnessed equally in the domains of burial and mourning rites, of architecture, and of literature. Modernity only knows an ephemeral form of writing that leaves no trace and is dismissed on the following day, in the same way as catafalques are abandoned after the obsequies. The ancients' attitude was different:

> Non s'usavano anticam. le *brochures*, nè gli opuscoli e foglietti volanti, nè scritture destinate a morire il dì dopo nate. E quello ancora che si scriveva per sola circostanza e per servire al momento, scrivevasi in modo ch'e' potesse e dovesse durare immortalmente. Cicerone dopo dato un consiglio al senato o al popolo, da mettersi in opera anche il dì medesimo, dopo perorata e conchiusa una causa, ancor di una piccola eredità si poneva a tavolino, e dagl'informi commentari che gli avevano servito a recitare, cavava, componeva, limava, perfezionava un'orazione formata sulle regole e i modelli eterni dell'arte più squisita, e come tale, consegnavala all'eternità. Così gli oratori attici, così Demostene di cui s'ha e si legge dopo 2000 anni un'orazione per una causa di 3 pecore: mentre le orazioni fatte oggi a' parlamenti o da niuno si leggono, o si dimenticano di là a due dì, e ne son degne, nè chi le disse, pretese nè bramò nè curò ch'elle avessero maggior durata.[81]

> [In ancient times *brochures* were not used, nor pamphlets and leaflets or other forms of writing that were destined to die the day after they were born. And even what was written only for circumstance and to serve the moment, was written in such a way that it could, and indeed should, last immortally. Cicero, after giving counsel to the senate or the people to be implemented even that same day, after pleading and concluding a case even for some small inheritance, would sit down at his desk, and from the shapeless commentaries he had used to recite, derived, composed, refined, perfected an oration based on the eternal rules and models of the most exquisite art, and in this form consigned it to eternity. Thus too the Attic orators, and also Demosthenes, by whom we still have and still read today even 2,000 years later, an oration for a case involving 3 sheep: whereas orations made to parliaments today are either read by no one, or are forgotten in the space of two days and that is what they are worth, nor did the person who uttered them claim, desire, or take care to ensure that they lasted any longer.]

Modern books are therefore doomed to perish and to leave no trace in the memory of descendants. In April 1827, in the days immediately preceding the composition of 'A Silvia', Leopardi notes how the nature of modern books can be compared to that of ephemeral insects, lasting no more than a few days:

> Molti libri oggi, anche dei bene accolti, durano meno del tempo che è bisognato a raccorne i materiali, a disporli e comporli, a scriverli. Se poi si volesse aver cura della perfezion dello stile, allora certamente la durata della vita loro non avrebbe neppur proporzione alcuna con quella della lor produzione; allora sarebbero più che mai simili agli efimeri, che vivono nello stato di *larve e di ninfe* per ispazio di un anno, alcuni di due anni, altri di tre, sempre affaticandosi per arrivare a quello d'*insetti alati*, nel quale non durano più di due, di tre, o di quattro giorni, secondo le specie; e alcune non più di una sola notte, tanto che mai non veggono il sole; altre non più di una, di due o di tre ore.[82]

[Many books today, even when well received, last less than the time that was necessary to collect their material, to arrange them, compose them, and write them. If in addition you wanted to look after the perfection of style, the duration of their life would certainly not be even a fraction of the time it takes to produce them. In such a case they would resemble more than ever the ephemeral creatures that live in the state of *larvae and nymphs* for the space of a year, some for two years, others for three, always striving to arrive at that state of *winged insect*, in which they last for no more than two, three, or four days, according to the species; and some no more than a single night, so that they never see the sun; others live no more than one, two, or three hours.]

Through these reflections, Leopardi challenges a crucial problem of the post-Enlightenment age. The so-called 'second printing revolution', caused by the refinement of printing techniques in the late eighteenth century, has generated a mutated relationship with texts compared to the culture of experience of medieval and early modernity, which was still characterized by continuative and meditative reading and writing practices. As Franco D'Intino notes, Leopardi's intellectual experience takes place between two symbolic dates that can be considered as landmarks of the modern author's increasing attention to the mutated features of cultural production. In 1798, the year of Leopardi's birth, Goethe plausibly writes the 'Prologue in theatre' of the first *Faust*, in which the director of the theatre comments upon the vastness and, at the same time, the superficiality of his audience's knowledge and readings; in 1837, when Leopardi dies in Naples, Balzac publishes the first edition of *Illusions perdues*, being an unmerciful account of the Bourbon Restoration literary scene and of its desperate efforts at teasing the public's immediate taste.[83] Between these two extremes, the experience of the second printing revolution marks intimately Leopardi's oeuvre, through the acknowledgment that a fracture has been produced from which it is impossible to turn back. The strict bond between author and public of traditional societies, in which poetry used to be an element of aggregation, has given place to an impersonal and ephemeral relationship that only knows the 'half-hour' as the maximum time allowed for paying attention to a text.[84] Whereas ancient literatures tended toward eternity, completeness, and durability, modern literary endeavours are doomed to ephemerality, shapelessness, and trendy fatuousness.

As we have seen, Leopardi's confrontation with antiquity is always grounded in the acknowledgment that the culture of experience has declined: for Leopardi, like for Baudelaire, it is 'in the context of th[e] crisis of experience that modern poetry finds its place', so that modern poetry, Agamben writes, can only be founded 'not on new experience, but on an unprecedented lack of experience'.[85] As one of the most notable symptoms of modernity, the vastness of the literary market takes in Leopardi's oeuvre the features of a veritable experience of shock, in the sense given to this expression by Walter Benjamin when commenting on Baudelaire's poetry — namely, as an uninterrupted series of intellectual stimuli from which the decline of experience has left the subject unprotected, thus causing an emotive intensity that overwhelms defences. In the essay 'On Some Motifs in Baudelaire', Benjamin adopts shock as the key notion for understanding modern lyric poetry as a different form of experience 'for which exposure to shock [*Chockerlebnis*] has become the norm'.[86]

With Baudelaire's *Fleurs du mal* and Heine's *Buch der Lieder* the centrality of lyric poetry in the Western canon fades precisely while undergoing an unprecedented success in terms of audience, a consideration that may find its Italian counterpart in the construction of Leopardi's *Canti* as a classic, at the very same moment in which it sanctions the impossibility of writing classic books any longer. For Leopardi, the imperative of thinking in terms of 'half-hours' has made the modern writer lose the authority that ancient cultures connected with authorship: to speak in Benjamin's terms, the modern literary market has therefore produced a phenomenon of 'decadence of the aura' that used to surround the text, thus undermining its uniqueness and authority. In traditional societies, writes Benjamin in his essay on 'The Work of Art in the Age of Its Reproducibility', an object's 'auratic mode of existence is never entirely severed from its ritual function', depending on the labour by which it is brought to life.[87] Cicero's act of sitting and polishing his texts with a view to a posthumous audience, as described in the *Zibaldone*, exemplifies the ritual process that invests the text with an auratic value, which is exactly what the modern proliferation of ephemeral pamphlets has dissolved. This acknowledgment pervades Leopardi's reflection in the course of the years: in the same way as, for Benjamin, the crowd forms the 'hidden figure' that does not appear in any of Baudelaire's poems but actually shapes them like a secret filigree, the crowd of books generated by the second printing revolution proves to be Leopardi's 'phantom crowd', the 'hidden constellation' embodied in those 'words, [...] fragments, [...] beginning of lines, from which the poet [...] wrests poetic booty'.[88]

Seen from this angle, some lexical choices emerging in the *Zibaldone* sound particularly eloquent. In a previously mentioned passage (*Zib.* 3439–40), Leopardi opposes Cicero's polished orations to the shapeless commentaries (*commentari*) from which they had been drafted. In 1821, Leopardi had explored some philological issues concerning Xenophon's *Anabasis* and Julius Caesar's military histories, pointing out how their structure (and hence their literary genre) was not that of historical treatises, but rather of journals ('un Diario o Giornale'):[89] hence their fragmentary nature, the absence of any introduction or preamble, their daily progression, the many enumerations, and above all their characteristic self-presentation as living accounts of first-hand experiences.[90] For these reasons, the genre of these books is rather that of 'Commentario o Memoriale, ossiano ricordi, e materiali' [*Commentary or Memoir, or recollections and materials*].[91] This analysis is interesting, as it sounds like a cryptic self-definition of the very same text of which it forms part: in being structured in a fragmentary and journal-like way, the *Zibaldone* too follows a daily progression, equally indulging in schematism and enumeration, and eventually finding its most specific features in being directly written, without preliminary drafts (*a penna corrente* [with the flow of the pen]).[92] These features are intrinsic to the writing genre labelled in Latin as *commentarium*, an expression that is commonly used to translate the Greek ὑπομνήματον, meaning literally 'aid to memory', and, figuratively, 'note'. In classical literature the notion of *commentarium*/ὑπομνήματον designates the shapelessness and the asystematicity of written notes, opposed to those of βιβλίον [book],[93] or — as happens with the text *On the Sublime* — of σύγγραμμα, implying an idea of systematic treatise opposed to the brief and light collation of notes that the pseudo-Longinus declares to be undertaking (ὑπομνηματίσασθαι).[94] The *commentarium*/ὑπομνήματον genre corresponds to an idea of philosophizing as a living laboratory, characterized by lightness, and to an ideal of empirical philosophy engrained in individual experience, which Michel Foucault connects to the arousal of a 'care for the self' in ancient culture.[95] That of *commentarium*/ὑπομνήματον is by definition a strongly resilient structure, which reveals itself to be particularly apt in investigating the relationships between memory and writing, as well as the 'geographies of knowledge' constructed by their interaction.[96]

The notion of *commentarium* also forms part of the so called *ars excerpendi*, a branch of the art of memory that appears to be strictly connected with the genesis of the *Zibaldone*.[97] The *ars excerpendi* includes a series of techniques aiming at choosing and storing quotations and *loci communes* from books read, in order to re-employ them in future works. Whereas its remotest origins can be found in ancient authors, the *ars* is a typically Classicist technique, inspired by the ideal of the 'bee' that chooses and 'excerpts' from canonically established sources, recomposing and re-actualizing this 'nectar' within a new texture.[98] Moreover, the actual *ars* is an absolutely modern phenomenon, rooted in the proliferation of texts determined by the invention of the press in the fifteenth and sixteenth centuries, and which makes it therefore indispensable to invent new ways of archiving information. The *ars excerpendi* follows the progressive decline of the culture of experience, replacing the mnemotechnique of classical and Renaissance tradition[99] with the elaboration of an artificial memory that takes the shapes of the archive, of the card index, or of the notebook, with the aim of helping the modern subject in orienteering within the vastness of written sources.

The *ars excerpendi* witnesses its zenith between the seventeenth and the eighteenth centuries with the publication of several handbooks across Europe, and proves itself to be influential to such thinkers as Leibniz and Locke, who in 1686 publishes a *Méthode nouvelle de dresser des recueils* [New Method for Making Anthologies] which is directly inspired by the *ars*.[100] As such, this form of knowledge transmigrates into the Recanati of the Bourbon Restoration, conveyed by the Alsatian canon Joseph Anton Vogel,[101] and by Francesco Cancellieri, a Roman erudite who publishes in 1815 a *Dissertazione intorno agli uomini dotati di gran memoria* [Dissertation on Men of Great Memory].[102] Both Vogel and Cancellieri have been considered among the possible influences conveying to Leopardi the notion of 'zibaldone'. This hypothesis is generally questioned, first and foremost because Leopardi employs the expression 'zibaldone' only at a very late stage, when drafting the indexes to the work in 1827,[103] so that it can be said, as Emilio Peruzzi does, that the *Zibaldone* is not born as such, but rather becomes a 'zibaldone', although not in a technical sense.[104] It is, however, worth remarking how both Vogel and Cancellieri insert the notion of 'zibaldone' within a very specific terminological constellation, characterized by the same opposition between shapelessness and perfection that we find in Leopardi's reflections on Xenophon and Caesar. 'Zibaldone' is therefore one of the possible synonyms for the 'informi commentari' from which Cicero used to shape his orations.

In a letter of November 27 1807, Vogel writes to Filippo Solari that the *zibaldoni* are caskets ('scrigni') in which quotations from read books can be included on a daily basis ('di tempo in tempo').[105] The *zibaldoni* can include original thoughts ('pensieri') as well as fragments extrapolated from read books ('estratti'), and can be compared to stocks from which accomplished works may spring almost automatically, assuming that materials have been properly ordered and indexed.[106] The *zibaldoni* are textual objects suspended between the volatile dimension of reading and thinking and the durable one of new written works. One of the possible translations of 'zibaldone', writes Vogel, is 'Caos scritto' [written chaos],[107] so that the *zibaldoni* can be considered as laboratories 'da cui escono alla giornata tante belle opere di ogni genere di letteratura; come dal caos sortirono tempo fa il sole, e la luna e le stelle' [from which there come out, in a day, literary works of every kind, in the same way as long ago the sun, the moon and the stars emerged from chaos].[108] The *zibaldoni* are a specific writing genre that has been named in multiple ways, 'taccuini', 'sottisiers', 'adversaria', 'excerpta', 'pugillares' and 'commentaria'.[109] A similar enumeration can be found in Cancellieri, who mentions Pliny the Younger's *pugillares* and lists, among possible synonyms, 'Memoriali [...] Zibaldoni' (whose Latin translation would be 'adversaria'),[110] 'Diar[i]', 'memorie',[111] 'Promptuarj', and 'Repertorj'.[112]

When giving a working title to his manuscript in 1827, Leopardi therefore goes back to a definition that belongs to the conceptual constellation of the *ars excerpendi*, denoting a sphere of shapelessness and fragmentariness that is opposed to the polished accomplishment that, for ancient writers, used to be the most important value. In other words, with such a choice, Leopardi seems to acknowledge the nature of his manuscript as a huge *commentarium*/ὑπομνήματον, a Protean laboratory that will not plausibly lead to any accomplished work — as it is, already, *the* work, and a definitely modern one. In a letter written from Naples to Charles Lebreton, in 1836, Leopardi eventually confirms the constantly transitory and fragmentarily plural dimension of his own writing, 'je n'ai jamais fait d'ouvrage, j'ai fait seulement des essais en comptant toujours préluder' [I have never produced works, I have only made attempts, reckoning always that they were a starting-point].[113] Peruzzi is right in highlighting how the *Zibaldone* becomes such only at a very late stage, when it proves to be a unique textual object: a shapeless non-book that is not meant for publication and does not consequently envisage any reader except its own compiler;[114] a flowing laboratory of philosophy-making, in which autobiographical and semantic memory are strictly intertwined, constantly tending toward an ideal of philosophical 'system' through, however, a quintessentially asystematic and rhizomatic structure;[115] a portable library, eventually, that embodies and incorporates fragments from a wider one, preluding at the same time a fantastic and ideal library.[116]

In particular, the very essence of the *Zibaldone* tackles the fissure brought by printed culture in terms of production of meaning. As Roger Chartier writes, authors 'do not write books: they write texts that become written objects, which may be hand-written, engraved, or printed [...]. The space between text and object, which is precisely the space in which meaning is constructed, has too often been forgotten'.[117] The only case of identity between 'text' and 'written object' is the 'manuscript book', being, 'in fact, [...] the notarial register or, in

Italy, the *libro-zibaldone*', whose 'unity [...] comes from the fact that its producer is also its addressee'.[118] The *zibaldone* is the genre that allows Leopardi, from 1817 to the cantos of 1828–29, to give a provisional answer to the decline and loss of experience. This task is paradoxically reached through the fragmentariness that belongs to the moderns, who do not have the time (or the will) to undertake any ritual of auratic production, and are therefore unable to polish their notes into any work aiming to become a classic. The shapeless nature of the *commentari* allows the modern writer, however, to elaborate a lighter and more resilient way of producing knowledge, which is maybe better able to grasp the multifold nature of modernity and of its ambiguities. Once again, Leopardi turns the crisis of modernity into opportunity.

Once read from this viewpoint, Leopardi's letter to Lebreton of 1836 does not manifest much resignation about not being able to give birth to any 'work', properly intended, but rather a sort of detached understatement. Four years before, in 1832, Leopardi had drafted the preamble for a never-published magazine, to be titled *Lo Spettatore fiorentino* [The Florentine Spectator].[119] The choice of such a title, Leopardi writes, is to be ascribed to the absence of an Italian equivalent for the French word *flâneur*, being otherwise the perfect definition for a magazine that declares itself to be completely asystematic, politically disengaged and absolutely useless in every civil, social, or pedagogic sense.[120] As for Baudelaire, *flânerie* is Leopardi's final answer to the nineteenth-century commercialization of art, turning the ephemerality of modern culture into elegant lightness, and eliding the philistine values of profit and utility in favour of intellectual wandering.[121] As early as in 1822, Leopardi had written that some poetic effects must be produced 'per mera eleganza, senza necessità veruna' [for the sake of pure elegance, without there being any need].[122]

The 1832 literary manifesto has strong roots in Leopardi's oeuvre, as it is dominated from the beginning by a singular taste for pastiche, dissimulation, and intellectual curiosity. D'Intino compares Leopardi's performance as a public figure to that of Stendhal's Julien Sorel, in that both would be 'Faustian heroes': Bourbon Restoration society compels the hero to dissimulation, cerebral seduction, and self-selling as an ironic performance.[123] Hence Leopardi's fascination, since his erudite experiments of youth (like an apocryphal *Inno a Nettuno* [Hymn to Neptune] of 1816), for a kind of literature that is constantly seen as an artificial and mediated form of writing, finding its outcomes in the adoption of literary disguises and in an experimental pluralism of style that does not disdain the creation of pastiches.[124]

At the same time, Leopardi's attitude seems to reveal deeper roots, namely those of his own aristocratic background. From this angle, Leopardi's *flânerie* and the elegant nonchalance shown by the letter to Lebreton seems to be different from such eminently middle-class figures as Julien Sorel or Baudelaire's *flâneur*, in that they are rooted in the values of the *ancien régime* European aristocracy (probably, the only ones that Leopardi intimately feels to be his own throughout his entire life). With such a set of values Leopardi's *flânerie* finds many points in common, from the ultimate indifference towards any useful or profitable outcome of intellectual activity, to a constantly external and detached perception of society, and ultimately to the systematic dissimulation of one's own emotions, sublimated into the imperative of elegance over affectation. The irony that Leopardi shows in the *Operette morali* or in the preamble to the *Spettatore fiorentino*, which may often sound striking when considering the tragic dimension of his philosophical thought, is rooted in a strategy of dissimulation whose first inspiration is probably Baldassare Castiglione's 1528 *Il Cortegiano* [The Book of the Courtier].[125] The nonchalance of Leopardi's *flâneur* is a nineteenth-century afterimage of Castiglione's ideal of *sprezzatura*, which recuperates a Renaissance paradigm of elegance in order to tackle the specific challenges of post-Enlightenment aesthetics.

Castiglione is a strong influence throughout the reflections on grace articulated in the *Zibaldone*.[126] The *Il Cortegiano* had been one of the key texts of the sixteenth-century debate on *je ne sais quoi*: for Castiglione, grace is the impression of naturalness that must be visible through every act and speech of the gentleman, hiding the apprenticeship that he has undertaken in the art of conversation.[127] This art of concealing art is given the name of *sprezzatura*, which is to be intended as 'the indefinable air of nonchalance that the courtier must affect in order to appear unaffectedly natural'.[128] This notion is notably used by Leopardi in relation to language and style. In March 1823, Leopardi writes that one must always 'usar in ogni cosa una certa sprezzatura, che nasconda l'arte, e dimostri, ciò che si fa, e dice, venir fatto senza fatica, e quasi senza pensarvi. Da questo credo io che derivi assai la grazia' [to use in every thing a certain nonchalance, which conceals art, and demonstrates that what is done and said is done without labour, and almost without thinking about it. From this, I believe, grace derives].[129] On 19 June 1823 (*Zib.* 2797–98), Leopardi moves from Castiglione in order to assert the centrality of style, and one month later he recuperates the notion of *sprezzatura* in order to define the way grace can be reached in the domain of literary writing:

> È bellissima nelle scritture un'apparenza di trascuratezza, di sprezzatura, un abbandono, una quasi noncuranza. Questa è una delle specie della semplicità. Anzi la semplicità più o meno è sempre un'apparenza di sprezzatura [...] perocch'ella sempre consiste nel nascondere affatto l'arte, la fatica, e la ricercatezza. Ma la detta apparenza non nasce mai dalla vera trascuratezza, anzi per lo contrario da moltissima e continua cura e artifizio e studio. [...] la facilità che si dee sentir nelle scritture è la qualità più difficile ad esser loro comunicata. Nè senza stento grandissimo si consegue nè l'abito nè l'atto di comunicarla loro.[130]

> [An appearance in writing of carelessness, nonchalance, abandonment, almost disregard is very beautiful. This is one of the kinds of simplicity. Indeed simplicity is more or less always an appearance of nonchalance [...] because it always consists precisely in hiding the art, the effort, the refinement. But the appearance I speak of is never born out of true carelessness, in fact on the contrary it comes from extensive and continuous care and artifice and study. [...] the facility which we ought to feel in writings is the hardest quality to impart to them. And the aptitude or the practical ability to impart is not acquired without the greatest hardship.]

Grace and *sprezzatura* are therefore intertwined, and both can find an application within the domain of textuality. From the feeling inspired by a text, Anacreon's poems, Leopardi had tried to define the impression of an inexpressible surplus, later ascribed to the aesthetic-theological sphere of grace, which took place beyond the mere texture of rhetorical devices of which the text was made. Whereas Anacreon's simplicity is grounded in a distantiated perception, the reproduction of the same effect must equally enact an oblique move, reaching simplicity by means of technique.

The key notion for understanding this process is that of 'pellegrino', which appears in the *Zibaldone* in 1821 within the framework of the theory of grace, and finally merges into Leopardi's reflections on *sprezzatura* and elegance in the summer of 1823.[131] The word is a Latinism: *peregrinus* literally means 'stranger', and Leopardi himself, when rendering the Latin word *peregrini* in the *Zibaldone*, translates it as 'stranieri, alieni, lontani' [strangers, unrelated or distant].[132] *Pellegrino* denotes therefore the sphere of alterity, encompassing whatever is (or has become) unfamiliar, strange, and even uncanny ('ardito e figurato e non logico' [bold, figurative, and not logical]).[133] As the *Zibaldone* states in a progressively firmer way, the *pellegrino* is the only source of stylistic elegance. In compliance with Leopardi's relativistic thought, it may consist in every element that would sound uncommon in relation to the context's horizon of expectation, and produce an effect of trouble and grace when inserted with unaffected nonchalance.[134] The purpose is to engender a troubling emotion in the audience, which can be identified with the purpose of *movere* of classical rhetoric. In Quattrocento art treatises, the 'accessory forms in motion' used to find their theoretical model in the domain of rhetoric, being the visual counterpart of the *ornatus* that for Quintilian has the task of arousing emotions, so that the Latin terms *perturbatio* (Cicero) and *affectus* (Quintilian) are translated by Alberti in terms of *motus*.[135] 'This effect is termed *movere* in ancient rhetoric and in the interpretation of that tradition at the time of Alberti; it is called *Einfühlung* in the new aesthetics of Aby Warburg's time'.[136] The imaginary breeze is therefore an example of *pellegrino* insofar as it is an out-of-place element aiming to engender surprise and grace. In the generalized sophistication of modern times, when style has reached an unprecedented peak in terms of skilfulness, the effect of *pellegrino* is reached at its best by purity and simplicity. Early writers ('primitivi scrittori'), as Leopardi notes in 1821, are never elegant, but rather ordinarily customary ('ordinariamente familiari'); that very familiarity has, however, become unfamiliar when beheld by the gaze of moderns.[137] The same happens with expressions borrowed from the vocabulary of lower classes, once they are inserted within stylistically refined writing.[138]

This *flânerie* in language must be produced by careful vigilance regarding rhetorical devices and writing techniques, paying attention to the historical development of language and to cultural differences. Philological knowledge becomes consequently crucial in reaching this impression of discreet nonchalance:[139] just like the dandy in the domain of fashion, Leopardi's literary *flâneur* must pay attention to small details, to those imperceptible textual units that produce the effect of grace by engendering irregularity and tension. The *Zibaldone* is the laboratory in which the dissection of the canon allows those expressions that may be able to conjure aesthetic enjoyment to be isolated, within a detailed problematization of poetic effects and a rigorous reflection on the history of languages, on the continuity between ancient and modern ones, and on the possibilities of imitation, translation, and borrowing.

In the *Zibaldone*, these small units are often called 'images' [*immagini*]. Poetry must pay attention to conjuring vague and indefinite images, as is the case of the adverb 'tanto' in two passages from Petrarch and Ippolito Pindemonte compared by Leopardi:

> Le parole che indicano moltitudine, copia, grandezza, lunghezza, larghezza, altezza, vastità ec. ec. sia in estensione, o in forza, intensità ec. ec. sono [...] poeticissime, e così le immagini corrispondenti. Come nel Petr.
>
>> Te solo aspetto, e quel che *tanto* AMASTI,
>> E laggiuso è rimaso, il mio bel velo.
>
> E in Ip. Pindemonte
>
>> Fermossi alfine il cor che BALZÒ *tanto*.
>
> Dove notate che il *tanto* essendo indefinito, fa maggiore effetto che non farebbe *molto, moltiss. eccessivamente, sommamente*. Così pure le parole e le idee *ultimo, mai più, l'ultima volta* ec. ec. sono di grand'effetto poetico, per l'infinità. ecc.[140]
>
> [The words that indicate multitude, abundance, size, length, breadth, height, vastness, etc. etc., whether in extension or in strength, intensity, etc. etc. are [...] highly poetical, and so, too, the corresponding images. As in Petrarch: 'I await only you, and what you *so much* LOVED and has remained below, my lovely veil'. And in Ippolito Pindemonte: 'The heart ceased at last that POUNDED *so much*'. Note here that *so much*, being indefinite, has a stronger impact than *much, very much, excessively, supremely* would do. So too the words and ideas *last, never again, the last time*, etc. etc., have a great poetic impact, because of their infiniteness, etc.]

On the one hand, the philologist-poet's operation must individuate the hidden clues that remain imperceptible to a superficial reading. The *flâneur* is the one who can operate through a paradigm based on clues, thereby individuating the effect-producing detail and re-employing it with skilled nonchalance.[141] As Didi-Huberman writes in relation to Walter Benjamin's approach to history, the task corresponds both to a material archaeology, paying attention to small details seen as the 'waste' of historical development, and to a psychical archaeology that can convert history into memory, shifting from the alleged objectivity of historicism to a way of narrating in which the 'unconscious of history' may find its place.[142] As Leopardi notes, while commenting a passage from Ariosto, the imperfect tense 'soleva' [used to] conjures the idea of vastity 'per la copia delle rimembranze che contiene' [on account of the wealth of memories it contains].[143] The single textual detail is the 'waste' retraced by the philologist-poet, which proves to be an image-symptom of a haunting-like returning memory.

The 'images' isolated within the *Zibaldone* can be therefore seen as 'dialectical images' (*dialektische Bilder*) that may subvert the linearity of historical time by means of vagueness and indefiniteness. As Didi-Huberman writes, the power of Benjamin's dialectical image resides in a feeble equilibrium between 'power' and 'fragility': the image possesses a powerful, enlightening strength, but at the same time is doomed to disappear in the very moment one believes to have grasped it; objects of historical knowledge are 'past' first and foremost because they are 'passing (away)'.[144]

Leopardi's ideal of 'vagueness' and 'indefiniteness' as the ultimate source of poetic grace leads to conceiving poetic texts as montages of dialectical images, characterized by the peculiar indeterminateness that Aby Warburg names *Polarität*.[145] The philologist-poet is the one who is able to perceive the relationship between 'word' and 'image' as a field of tension, and to discern within the grain of language those survivals and fractures that may act as factors of estrangement. By taking as his cornerstones the values of feeling (*sentimento*) and remembrance (*rimembranza*), Leopardi transforms his philological and literary inquiry into a global theory of memory and survival, enacting a Copernican revolution that comes close to Benjamin's in engendering a shift from the point of view of the objective, historicized past to that of the past as a product of memory. As we will see, the adjective/noun 'antico' [ancient/ancientness/antiquity] develops a peculiar flexibility within Leopardi's oeuvre, undergoing a polarization by which it comes to encompass historical ancientness (paradoxically recalled as a memory), and individual memory, in which Leopardi innervates the reminiscence of antiquity. Hence the reason why the intertextual memory of antiquity in the *Canti* is most strongly present where it is least expected, as a skilful concealment of the most cultivated references where the text gives the clearest impression of immediacy and colloquialism.[146] This strategy, Lonardi notes, is already announced in the letter written in 1816 by Leopardi to the periodical *Biblioteca Italiana*, in which translating Homer is made a matter of taste ('sapore') and the translator's task is individuated in paying attention to what seems absolutely irrelevant ('parole che sembrano di niun rilievo').[147]

The idea of antiquity shining through details may bring us again to Warburg. On the one hand, Didi-Huberman stresses that the radicality of Warburg's approach resides in having perceived the symptom-like nature of images. In the same way as Freud sees the hysterical woman's movement as the clue that symbolizes (and conceals) the memory of an original trauma, Warburg analyzes movement as a field of forces in tension: Warburg's images, exactly like the hysterical bodies seen by the young Freud on the stage of the Salpêtrière, 'suffer from reminiscences'.[148] Equally, in Leopardi, language suffers from a double reminiscence: reminiscence of its own history, language being a living organism that witnesses phenomena of continuity, metamorphosis, swerve, or slipping; and reminiscence of the speaker's own past, since well-employed language is a unique factor for the reactivation of memory. A text is therefore poetic when it suffers from reminiscence, since 'quasi tutti i piaceri dell'immaginaz. e del sentim. consistono in rimembranza. Che è come dire che stanno nel passato anzi che nel presente' [almost all pleasures of the imagination and feeling consist of remembering — which is the same as saying that they exist in the past rather than in the present].[149]

On the other hand, this haunting memory takes the shape of determined metrical and linguistic structures, which we may see as veritable formulas of pathos. Speaking of 'A Silvia', Lonardi notes how the text witnesses the return of an ancient pathos conveyed by formal elements, which brings us close to Warburg's *Pathosformeln*.[150]

Moreover, the genealogy of Warburg's notion of *Pathosformel* eschews the bound-aries of art history, and legitimates the possibility of employing it for other kinds of 'images' and 'figures'. In 1948, Ernst Robert Curtius dedicated his *European Literature and the Latin Middle Ages* to the memory of Aby Warburg, thus implying that the study of the survival of antiquity should not be limited to the extra-verbal sphere of visual arts, but could find a profitable field of analysis in the exploration of modalities of survival within τόποι, metaphors, and genres.[151] The definition itself of 'formula' was borrowed from the field of Homeric philology, having been employed by Milman Parry in order to denote the strict conjunction of signified and signifier in determined portions of text, articulated in metre, on which the bard's oral performance was based.[152] The notion of 'formula' is strictly connected with the oral dimension of archaic poetry, and therefore abolishes the cardinal principles of written cultures — authorship, originality, absolute fixedness of texts, distinction between 'original' text and later metamorphoses, silent reading and writing — in favour of the public and performative dimension of ancient singing, in which every execution is the original and there is no fixed boundary between the original-ἀρχή and subsequent re-elaboration. Although taking place before Parry's operation, Leopardi's reflection on Homer's poetry attempts a re-evaluation of the performative aspect of ancient orality, constructed as the term of comparison for a modern poetry that must recuperate an 'epic' dimension, albeit located within a written culture.[153] The reactivation of 'ancient' images within the sphere of poetry, as we will see in more detail in the following chapters, goes consequently in the direction of a decomposition of the text of tradition into 'formulas of pathos' to be surreptitiously re-interwoven within the new performance of modern poetry.

Leopardi is surely aware of the impossibility of fully reproducing the ancient oral dimension in modern times; still, as we have seen, his cultural endeavour aims at paradoxically recuperating antiquity by taking the aporias of modern culture as a starting point. The 1831 edition of Leopardi's poems, grounded in the experience of the cantos of 1828–29, is the most accomplished embodiment of this operation. Unlike the *Zibaldone*, the book of the *Canti* is conceived for the editorial market, and aims therefore at tackling directly the mutated audience determined by the second printing revolution. The title itself is, however, particularly telling. Previous editions of Leopardi's poems had borne technical titles such as *Canzoni* and *Versi*, alluding to the metric genre of poems or to their nature as written compositions: by recuperating the archaic-Homeric idea of 'singing' as an interweavement of *Pathosformeln*, the revolutionary choice of entitling the collection *Canti* shows how the new 'book' tends to an 'ancient' ideal, thus re-conjuring the dimension of pathos that modernity has lost.[154] This radical turn is connected to the mnestic experience of the years 1828–29: as D'Intino writes, the written text of 'A Silvia' is enlivened by the memory of Silvia's voice, so that the poem, although fixed in paper, may be properly defined a *canto*.[155]

The book of the *Canti* is the theatre in which the surviving relics of antiquity are called to play, thereby longing for a new and different form of eternity, which is identified with individual memory. In April 1827, while composing 'A Silvia', Leopardi seems to go back, in order to define his own new poetry, to the purpose that Francesco Cancellieri had assigned to the art of memory and the *ars excerpendi*, namely to build up a 'journal' of one's inner life:

> Viene così a formarsi a poco a poco la nostra *Vita*, e un *Diario* di tutto ciò, che accade di più interessante a' nostri giorni. Se Dio ci fa la grazia di prolungarli, qual compiacenza di riandare nella nostra *Vecchiaja* le memorie della nostra *Gioventù*, di cui, senza quest'ajuto, appena ci rimarrebbe una languida, e confusa idea![156]

> [Little by little there happens therefore to develop our *Life*, and a *Journal* of every interesting thing taking place in these days. If God gives us the grace to prolong them, what satisfaction will it be to go back, during our *Old Age*, to the memory of our *Youth*, of which, without this help, we would keep but a diluted and hazy impression!]

> Uno de' maggiori frutti che io mi propongo e spero da' miei versi, è che essi riscaldino la mia *vecchiezza* col calore della mia *gioventù*; è di assaporarli in quella età, e provar *qualche reliquia de' miei sentimenti passati*, messa quivi entro, per *conservarla* e *darle durata*, quasi in deposito; è di commuover me stesso in rileggerli, come spesso mi accade.[157]

> [One of the greatest fruits that I hope for and expect from my verses is that they will warm my old age with the heat of my *youth*. It is to savour them when I reach that age and to experience *something that remains of my past feelings*, placed there so *it might be kept and last through time*, as though in store. It is to move myself as I reread them, as often happens to me.]

Moreover, the *Canti* enact a 'survival of antiquity' that avoids the 'affectation' of Classicist imitation by opting for a lightness made of dissimulation, intertextual play, and concealed reactivation. Leopardi's book is the outcome of a literate *flânerie* that, behind the apparent peacefulness of small country watercolours ('A Silvia', 'Il sabato del villaggio', 'La quiete dopo la tempesta'), innervates with nonchalance the deeply tragic dimension of one of the most radical experiences of modern philosophy, as well as the erudite density of a laboured philological reflection.

From this angle, the *Canti* are Leopardi's drastic answer to the shock of modernity, pursued through the reactivation of antiquity within the full acknowledgment of the decline of the aura. In the same way as in Baudelaire's poem, 'Le Cygne', the wandering swan evokes the reminiscence of Andromache and of the whole sphere of myth within modern Paris, Leopardi's poems of 1828–29 conjure antiquity in the fullest dimension of the here and now: in the next section we will see one of the shapes that this conjuration takes.

The Misadventures of Virtue

Silvia dies at the threshold of winter, the season of the year, but also that of life, when illusions vanish on entering adult life. The vegetal and seasonal metaphor underlies the poem of 1828, metamorphosing Silvia into Persephone, the girl abducted to Hell who takes away spring.[158] Silvia is a prematurely crushed shoot that will never bloom.[159] Having been murdered while ascending 'il limitare | Di gioventù' [the threshold of youth],[160] Silvia is a fully liminal creature. Once crystallized in a state of unexpressed potentiality — no longer a child, not yet a woman — Silvia is stuck in a liminal state between life and death, as the opening lines show well: 'Silvia rimembri ancora | Quel tempo della tua vita mortale?' [Silvia, do you remember still that moment in your mortal life?].[161]

From the beginning, the poem addresses a presence that is quintessentially made of absence: not a ghost, but rather something close to the semantic constellation encompassed by the Greek word εἴδωλον. As Jean-Pierre Vernant writes, in Homeric Greek the term εἴδωλον condenses the meanings of φάσμα [phantasm, ghost], ὄνειρος [dream, vision, image of dream] and of ψυχή [soul, spirit of a dead person].[162] The εἴδωλον produces the uncanny effect of a presence-in-absence, inscribing emptiness within the very manifestation of the object it simulates. Silvia can therefore be conjured insofar as she belongs to an 'elsewhere', her absence itself being the reason for her haunting return. At the same time, her presence-in-absence mirrors the poetic subject as a living and remembering being, whose hope is however dead: the un-dead Silvia and the poetic 'I' are both liminal subjects, making the poem itself an εἴδωλον in which the extinguished hopes of youth are temporarily brought back to life.

> Tu pria che l'erbe inaridisse il verno,
> Da chiuso morbo combattuta e vinta,
> Perivi, o tenerella. E non vedevi
> Il fior degli anni tuoi;
> Non ti molceva il core
> La dolce lode or delle negre chiome,
> Or degli sguardi innamorati e schivi;
> Né teco le compagne ai dì festivi
> Ragionavan d'amore.
>
> Anche peria fra poco
> La speranza mia dolce.[163]

[You, before winter had withered the grass, stricken then overcome by hidden sickness, died, gentle girl. You did not see your years come into flower. Sweet talk about your raven hair or your beguiling, guarded glance never melted your heart, and on holidays you never talked about love with your friends. Before long, my sweet hope died, too.]

Alessandro Carrera highlights how the use of the verb 'ragionare' at l. 48 sublimates a muttering cluster of country girls into the philosophical speculation on love of medieval and Renaissance poets:[164] the Italian lyric canon is condensed and dissolved in the image of Silvia's friends, investing a rustic scene with a vocabulary that is usually meant to connote a quintessentially aristocratic activity. At the same time, Mario Fubini points out that Leopardi, in a letter to Pietro Giordani of May 1817, had happily remarked how the countrymen of the Marches still employed this verb in its archaic, literate, and Della-Cruscan meaning.[165] The language of the poem engenders thus a paradoxical and reciprocal contamination between the lyric lexicon of Italian tradition and the speech of the lower classes. The same phenomenon can be witnessed in the expression 'sguardi innamorati', which employs the past participle in an active sense, thereby turning the literal meaning of 'innamorati' as 'in love' into that of 'beguiling'. This unusual inversion of the adjective has notable antecedents in the Italian literary canon, first and foremost in Petrarch, but is present in a folksong transcribed by Leopardi in the *Zibaldone* in May 1819, 'Io benedico chi t'ha fatto l'occhi | Che te l'ha fatti tanto 'nnamorati' [I bless him who made your eyes, That he made them so much in love].[166] Both the verb 'ragionare' and the 'sguardi innamorati' engender thus an effect of familiarity and alterity at the same time, making the sphere of the lower classes and popular poetry clash with that of the Italian poetic canon. 'A Silvia' is thus articulated on the tension between two universes that are reciprocally alien to one another, and which collide in the space of the text: the 'high' one epitomized by the poetic subject and the 'innocent' and popular world of the dead girl.

Leopardi begins collecting fragments of popular songs in December 1818, immediately after concluding his recognition of the Italian lyric canon and having described the effects of Anacreon's poetry. The twenty-ninth page of the *Zibaldone* is left blank for further additions, dating respectively to April and May 1819 and May 1820. Leopardi aims to collect some 'Canzonette popolari che si cantavano al mio tempo a Recanati' [Popular songs that were sung in my time in Recanati], thus showing a sort of proto-ethnographic interest in folklore.[167] A subterranean short-circuit seems however to connect these *stornelli*, the sensation of fleeting grace perceived while reading Anacreon, and the remotest seeds of 'A Silvia' and 'Le ricordanze'. In the so called *Vita abbozzata di Silvio Sarno* [Sketched Life of Silvio Sarno], an autobiographical draft of 1819,[168] Leopardi speaks of 'odi anacreontiche composte da me alla ringhiera sentendo [...] cenare allegramente dal cocchiere intanto che la figlia stava male' [Anacreontic odes composed by me at the railing while listening [...] to people dining happily at the coachman's place while his daughter was sick].[169] The coachman's daughter is the prematurely dead Teresa, who will arguably inspire 'A Silvia' and whose death should be incorporated as an episode within the projected novel, 'storia di Teresa da me poco conosciuta e interesse ch'io ne prendeva come di tutti i morti giovani in quello aspettar la morte per me' [story of Teresa whom I did not know well and the interest I used to have for her as for all those who died young while waiting for my own death].[170]

In *Silvio Sarno*, the vicissitudes of Teresa are perceived from a distance, that of the windows of the Leopardi palace that mediate the external world to the secluded subject, isolated within the physical and mental space of the library. From the autobiographical experiment of 1819 to the poems of 1828–29 the window remains a persistent icon in Leopardi's oeuvre, being the only frame through which two such otherwise incommunicable spheres can enter into reciprocal contact, that of the cultivated and aristocratic subject and that of lower-class femininity that still belongs to oral culture.[171] Teresa's crypto-novel is made of fragmentary and mainly auditory impressions of a world that is entirely encompassed within the garden, the small square, and the coachman's house, a micro-universe that also forms the setting for such poems as 'La sera del dì di festa' (1820) [The Evening of the Holiday], 'La quiete dopo la tempesta' and 'Il sabato del villaggio': 'Scena dopo il pranzo affacciandomi alla finestra [...] la porta del cocchiere socchiusa [...] effetti della musica in me sentita nel giardino' [after-lunch scene while overlooking from the window [...] the coachman's door half-closed [...] effects of music on me heard in the garden];[172] 'Canto mattutino di donna allo svegliarmi, canto delle figlie del cocchiere e in particolare di Teresa mentre ch'io leggeva il cimitero della Maddalena' [morning song from a woman while waking up, song of the coachman's daughters and in particular of Teresa while I was reading the cemetery of the Madeleine];[173] the dining family, indifferent to the girl's agony.

The reading and writing male subject is therefore counterpointed by a singing feminine figure: the written culture epitomized by the Anacreontic odes, or by the proto-Romantic sentimentalism of Jean-Joseph Reignault-Warin's Royalist novel *Le Cimetière de la Madeleine* (1800–01), is opposed to the innocent hope expressed in the oral dimension of the song, which hides the incumbent shadow of tragedy. This opposition reappears in Pisa, in 1828, while composing 'A Silvia'. 'Il canto della fanciulla' [The Girl's Song], a poetic fragment that can be dated to April of that year, describes a feminine song resonating in the streets, and which, although joyous (or maybe because of this), inspires in the disenchanted subject the image of broken hopes, 'Or, così lieto, | Al pensier mio sembri un lamento' [Yet though you're happy, you seem like a lament to me].[174] Also in 'A Silvia', the window acts as a point of mediation, in a passage that witnesses the interweaving of subterranean intertextual memories from Homer, echoing, as Lonardi shows, the Chryseis of the *Iliad* and the Penelope of the *Odyssey*:[175]

> Io gli studi leggiadri
> Talor lasciando e le sudate carte
> [...] D'in su i veroni del paterno ostello
> Porgea gli orecchi al suon della tua voce,
> Ed alla man veloce
> Che percorrea la faticosa tela.[176]

[Sometimes I left the cherished books and laboured pages [...] to listen from my father's balcony for the sound of your singing and your swift hand's back- and-forth on the heavy loom.]

The image of the window was already present in the first folksong copied in *Zib.* 29, 'Fácciate alla finestra, Luciola, | Decco che passa lo ragazzo tua' [Come to the window, Luciola, Here's your boyfriend passing by]. In this case, the feminine figure appears at the window, denoting a reciprocated love. The image can be reversed into the one of the dark and empty window, suggesting the absence and death of the beloved, as in this *strambotto* from the Marches traced by Giovanni Battista Bronzini:

> Passo e ripasso e la finestra è chiusa;
> Non ce la vedo più l'innamorata,
> Non ce la vedo più come era prima;
> Quella che cerchi è morta e sotterrata.[177]

[I pass and pass again, and the window is shut; no longer I see there my beloved one, I no longer see her as she used to be, the one you are looking for is dead and buried.]

Bronzini suggests that this folksong may have provided a secret model for the image of Nerina's window as it appears in 'Le ricordanze', in which the subject beholds the window whence the girl used to talk to him and that now, since her death, is shut and dark:

> quella finestra,
> Ond'eri usata favellarmi, ed onde
> Mesto riluce delle stelle il raggio
> È deserta.[178]

[that window where you used to talk to me, and which reflects the sad light of the stars, is empty.]

The image of the alternately lit and dark window is a formula of pathos, derived from folkloric sources, through which is expressed a contrast between joyful youth, made of conversations from window to window, and hopeless maturity, when the interlocutor is voiceless and absent. In one of the most articulated fragments of *Silvio Sarno*, the lit and then extinguished window is an emblem of the dichotomy between life and death, in an episode that anticipates several themes and images of the cantos of 1828–29:

> Giardino presso alla casa del guardiano, io era malinconichiss. e mi posi a una finestra che metteva sulla piazzetta ec. due giovanotti sulla gradinata della chiesa abbandonata [...] sedevano scherzando sotto al lanternone [....] comparisce la prima lucciola ch'io vedessi in quell'anno ec. uno dei due s'alza gli va addosso ec. io domandava fra me misericordia alla poverella l'esortava ad alzarsi ec, ma la colpì e gittò a terra e tornò all'altro ec. intanto la figlia del cocchiere ec. alzandosi da cena e affacciatasi alla finestra per lavare un piattello nel tornare dice a quei dentro = stanotte piove da vero. Se vedeste che tempo. Nero come un cappello. = e poco dopo sparisce il lume di quella finestra ec. intanto la lucciola era risorta ec. avrei voluto ec. ma quegli se n'accorse tornò = porca buzzarona = un'altra botta la fa cadere già debole com'era ed egli col piede ne fa una striscia lucida fra la polvere ec. e poi ec. finchè la cancella. [...] sento una dolce voce di donna che non conoscea né vedea ec..[179]

[Garden next to the surveyor's place, I was most melancholy and I went to a window that overlooked the small square etc. two youths sat joking on the steps of the abandoned church [...] beneath the big lantern [...] there appears the first firefly I saw that year etc. one of the two gets up and sets upon her etc. I begged within myself pity for the poor creature I exorted her to take off etc., but he struck her and threw her to the ground and went back to the other youth etc. in the meantime the coachman's daughter etc. getting up from the dining table went to the window to wash a dish and on her way back says to those inside: — tonight it will rain for sure. if you could see the weather. Dark as a hat. — and soon the light of that window disappears etc. in the meantime the firefly had revived etc. I would have etc. but that one saw what had happened and came back — you fucking bitch — another hit and he makes her fall, feeble as she was, and with his foot he makes of her a luminous line in the dust etc. etc. until he rubs it out. [...] I hear the sweet voice of a woman whom I didn't know nor see etc..]

Teresa shows herself at the window, whose light is suddenly swallowed by the night. Another light is also turned off at the same time, that of the first firefly of the year, murdered by an act of senseless brutality. As D'Intino notes, 'lucciola' [firefly] recalls by homophony the 'Luciola' of the folksong transcribed one year before in the *Zibaldone*.[180] The firefly and Teresa/Luciola are part of the same memorial short-circuit, embedding a window, a feminine voice perceived in the dark and a suddenly extinguished light: a secret connection enthrals Teresa and the luminescent insect, in both being fragile and ephemeral creatures that are doomed to death.[181]

Above all, the respective fates of Silvia and of the firefly are touching in that they are both innocent victims. 'You died, gentle girl' is only a partial translation of the Italian 'perivi, o tenerella',[182] in which the term of endearment reinforces the commiseration for a delicate (*tenero*) being; 'tu, misera, cadesti' [you fell away, poor thing][183] emphasizes the feeling of compassion for a creature that is made to fall by the brutality of the 'hidden sickness'. The firefly is equally named 'poverella', and falls to the ground. Hers is an insensate murder, just as insensate as the infirmity that kills the coachman's daughter:

> Suo bagno cagion del male, suo pianto ch'ella interrogata non sapea renderne ragione ec. ma era chiaro che una giovanetta ec. morire ec., come alcuni godono della loro fama ancora vivente così ella per la lunghezza del suo male sperimentò la consolazione dei genitori ec. circa la sua morte e la dimenticanza di se e l'indifferenza ai suoi mali ec., non ebbe neppure il bene di morire tranquillam. ma straziata da fieri dolori la poverina.[184]

> [Her bath the cause of her sickness, her crying for which, when asked, she couldn't give any explanation etc. but it was clear that a young girl etc. dying etc., in the same way as some people enjoy fame while still living, because of the length of her sickness she experienced her parents' consolation etc. concerning her death and being forgotten and indifference for her sorrows etc., she didn't even have the chance of dying quietly but tormented by cruel pains, the poor one.]

In *Silvio Sarno* Leopardi singularly stresses the aspect of Teresa's virginal innocence, recalling an episode of theft concerning one of her sisters and highlighting how Teresa was not 'avvezza al delitto nè all'obbrobr. ed era toccata dalla confusione della rea cosa orrenda per un innocente' [accustomed to crime nor to terrible things and she was touched by the guilty's confusion, which is a horrible thing for an innocent person].[185] Equally, in 'Il canto della fanciulla', the song is defined 'Canto di verginella' [young girl's song],[186] a 'voce festiva | De la speranza' [joyous voice of hope],[187] in which 'il tempo | Aspettato risuona' [rehearses the expected moment].[188]

Silvia's young age corresponds to a purity of the soul and to a chaste modesty in which hope and uncertainty are confounded. The oxymoron 'lieta e pensosa' [bright and pensive] of the fifth line is one of the many scattered throughout the text ('ridenti e fuggitivi' [smiling, startled], 'innamorati e schivi', 'lacrimata speme' [much-lamented hope]),[189] endorsing the impression that Silvia's nymph-like and undefined nature structures the poem, at a more intimate level, on the 'abstract' theme, as D'Intino claims, of paradox and of the *coincidentia oppositorum*.[190] At the same time, it aims to portray an innocent confusion of thoughts, which may recall the description of Lucia given one year before by Alessandro Manzoni in the first edition of *I promessi sposi* (1827) [The Betrothed], while depicting a similar image of rustic feminine grace:

> Ella si andava schermendo con quella modestia un po' guerriera delle foresi, facendosi scudo alla faccia col gomito, chinandola sul busto, e aggrottando i lunghi e neri sopraccigli, mentre però la bocca si apriva al sorriso. [...] Lucia aveva [l'ornamento] quotidiano d'una modesta bellezza, rilevata allora e accresciuta dalle varie affezioni che le si dipingevano sul volto: una gioia temperata da un turbamento leggiero, quel placido accoramento che si mostra ad ora ad ora sul volto delle spose, e *senza scomporre la bellezza*, le dà un carattere particolare.[191]
>
> [She was defending herself, with the rather aggressive modesty of peasant girls, shielding her face with her elbow, dropping it over her breast, and drawing her long black eyebrows down in a frown, yet with her lips parted in a smile. [...] Lucia had the daily ornament of her modest beauty, heightened and brought out at this moment by the various emotions crossing her face: joy tempered by a slight agitation, and the quiet melancholy which sometimes shows on the faces of brides, and, *without marring their beauty*, gives them an air of their own.][192]

The definition of Lucia's charm mirrors Leopardi's definition of grace as a form of irritation that subtly becomes manifest within beauty, without disturbing its composure. Both Leopardi and Manzoni depict the country-girl's gracious appeal as a contamination between joy and undefined anxiety, opposing it in a more or less explicit way to images of mundane and seductive femininity. In the book of the *Canti*, Silvia is set in opposition to Aspasia, 'dotta | Allettatrice' [expert enticer],[193] who appears as being 'circonfusa | D'arcana voluttà' [veiled in secret sensuality].[194] In *I promessi sposi*, Lucia's naive grace is implicitly opposed to the beauty of the nun Gertrude: in the 1827 edition of the novel, Gertrude's beauty is defined as 'una bellezza sbattuta, sfiorita e, direi quasi, sconcertata' [a worn, faded, and, one might almost say, ravaged beauty],[195] but in the 1840 edition, the opposition is made explicit by an open inversion of the description of Lucia ('una *bellezza* sbattuta, sfiorita e, direi quasi, *scomposta*', my emphases [a worn, faded, and, one might almost say, *marred beauty*]).[196]

The comparison between Leopardi and Manzoni is legitimized by their uniformity in terms of cultural references. On the one hand, eighteenth-century reflections on grace construct the young country-girl — and more specifically the shepherdess, the *bergère* of rococo aesthetics — as the most evident epitome of grace, as is, for instance, evident in Montesquieu, who writes that 'les grandes parures ont rarement de la grace, & souvent l'habillement des bergères en a' [sumptuous robes rarely possess grace, while often the clothes of shepherdesses have it].[197] This charming naiveté is opposed to the sophisticated and overabundant charm of a beauty that is openly connoted in social terms, determining a polarization between 'aristocratic' beauty and 'rustic' (or, better, Arcadia-like, idealized) grace. This dichotomy reverberates in the domain of arts: to Paolo Veronese's elaborate cloths, Montesquieu opposes Raphael as a paradigm of simplicity and of a 'certain something', following a tradition that goes back to Renaissance art treatises.[198] In *Silvio Sarno*, Leopardi accords specific attention to this stereotype of country finesse, describing his 'reverie sopra una giovine di piccola condizione' [daydreams about a lower class young girl].[199] Tellingly, popular innuendo in Recanati had brought this story back to a libertine context, by hypothesizing a child born out of Count Leopardi's courtship games with this girl, Teresa Brini.[200] The idealization of the country-girl or of the shepherdess, as a cultural sublimation of a social power relationship, is a crucial element of the *ancien régime* aristocratic culture, surviving in the fullest of the Bourbon Restoration, which happens to influence Leopardi by the mediation of French literature. Leopardi openly echoes Montesquieu when he notices, in the *Zibaldone*, how a young shepherdess is never ungraceful, unlike a more cultivated and beautiful woman, who always runs the risk of looking affected (*Zib.* 1329–30, 15 July 1821).

On the other hand, the culture both Manzoni and Leopardi are making reference to is the one that, through the 'critical years' of 'European mind' (Paul Hazard) and later through the Enlightenment and in post-revolutionary years, crystallizes the young girl (*la jeune fille*) as an autonomous object of desire, clearly differentiated both from the child and from the adult woman. The 'decline of the accomplished woman' in the decades preceding the French Revolution, as retraced by Laura Kreyder,[201] is counterpointed by the construction of the young girl as an epitome of purity and as a different object of desire for modern male subjectivity, as several historians of sexuality have highlighted.[202] In the literary domain, the type of the naive young girl (the *ingénue*) undergoes a trajectory leading from *ancien régime* libertine literature to such post-revolutionary images of feminine purity as Goethe's Gretchen, one of the models for both Manzoni's Lucia and Leopardi's Silvia.[203] Libertine literature, which shares through the entire eighteenth century the same publishers, shelves, and readers with the philosophers of the Enlightenment, constructs the young maiden's body as a venue of subversion through which the sexual ethics of Christian tradition can be questioned.[204] In late eighteenth-century novels, as expressions of bourgeois Enlightenment, the theme of profaned innocence undergoes a deep metamorphosis, replacing the positive narrative model of the initiation to pleasure with the negative one of seduction.[205] Whilst rooted in middle-class ethics, Enlightenment novels reverse the subversive potential of the aristocratic libertine tradition by constructing the nobleman as the archetype of the seducer, who dishonours lower-class girls through the impunity granted by his privileges.[206] At the same time, bourgeois novels propose a lay afterimage of the formerly Christian virginal taboo, replacing the ideal of physical virginity with the one of a 'purity of the heart' that seduction corrupts in an even more dangerous way: this ideal mirrors such typical middle-class obsessions as the myth of 'naturalness' as a warrant for newness, of security, and of perpetually ensured propriety.[207] The virginal type of the *jeune fille* is therefore opposed to the satanic one of the seducer, thereby re-staging the enmity between the Virgin and the Serpent of Catholic theology. Richardson's *Clarissa* (1748), Lessing's *Emilia Galotti* (1772), Lewis's *The Monk* (1795), the several metamorphoses of Sade's *Justine* (1787, 1791 and 1799),[208] and the first *Faust* by Goethe (1808) can all be seen as different phases — and surely not all — of the popularity of the literary motif of the 'persecuted maiden' between the eighteenth and nineteenth centuries.[209] From this angle, Manzoni's Lucia can be seen as a further metamorphosis of this feminine type, a persecuted anti-Justine who eventually acts as a triumphant agent of conversion in relation to such a figure as the *Innominato* [Unnamed], which is openly modelled on those of Sade's villains.[210]

In 1977, D'Arco Silvio Avalle hypothesized that the secret model of the 'persecuted maiden' narrative structure was the feminine hagiography of Christian tradition.[211] The image of the martyr saint, subject to punishments because of her beauty, is metamorphosed by post-Enlightenment modernity into the Romanesque narration of a virtuous girl undergoing a sort of descent to Hell through a process of seduction. The hagiographic model engenders a complete twist in Sade's *Justine*, which is from its very title intentionally constructed as a reversal of Christian ethics, narrating the misfortunes that unavoidably follow virtuous behaviour. The description of Justine is rooted in the vocabulary of grace, displaying an open opposition with her sister Juliette's sophisticated beauty, marked by coquetry:

> Douée d'une *tendresse*, d'une *sensibilité* surprenantes, au lieu de l'*art* et de la *finesse* de sa sœur, elle n'avait qu'une *ingénuité*, une *candeur* qui devaient la faire tomber dans les pièges. Cette jeune fille à tant de qualités, joignait une *physionomie douce*, absolument différente de celle dont la nature avait *embelli* Juliette; autant on voyait d'*artifice*, de *manège*, de *coquetterie* dans les traits de l'une, autant on admirait de *pudeur*, de *décence* et de *timidité* dans l'autre; *un air de Vierge*, de grands yeux bleus, pleins d'âme et d'intérêt.[212]

> [Full of *tenderness*, endowed with a surprising *sensibility* instead of with her sister's *art* and *finesse*, she was ruled by an *ingenuousness*, a *candour* that were to cause her to tumble into not a few pitfalls. To so many qualities this girl joined a *sweet countenance*, absolutely unlike that with which Nature had *embellished* Juliette; for all the *artifice, wiles, coquetry* one noticed in the features of the one, there were proportionate amounts of *modesty, decency, and timidity* to be admired in the other; *a virginal air*, large blue eyes, very soulful and appealing.][213]

Justine is made an emblem of simple and un-artificial charm. The skilful artifice belongs to the libertine, who therefore beholds the *jeune fille*'s body as a venue of alterity — alterity, for sure, in terms of gender and class, but first and foremost as far as the *jeune fille* epitomizes the simplicity that the mental universe of the libertine perceives as being lost. In other words, the *jeune fille* can be seen as one of the manifestations of *pellegrino*: the libertine's desire for possession arises from distance, and is grounded in the cultural fracture by which modernity has established a fissure between nature and art, illusion and disenchantment, grace and artifice. In the same way as 'ancient' naturalness has become ungraspable for the modern poet, who therefore invents an ideal Greece as an imaginary framework for the tensions of his own time, the libertine constructs the *jeune fille* as the object of his desire insofar as she embodies the lost sphere of origin from which his libertinage itself — as an outcome of civilisation — excludes him. Whereas the modern poet seems entrapped within the dichotomy between revival and a desperate quest for newness, the libertine's desire is split between attraction and a destructive drive toward a grace towhich he feels alien. Within this tension, which is at the same time erotic, aesthetic, and theological, Pierre Klossowski sees the most central paradox of Sade's thought:

> Toute l'œuvre de Sade paraît bien n'être qu'un seul cri désespéré, lancé à l'image de la virginité inaccessible, cri enveloppé et comme enchâssé dans un

cantique de blasphèmes. *Je suis exclu de la pureté, parce que je veux posséder celle qui est pure. Je ne puis ne pas désirer la pureté, mais du même coup je suis impur car je veux jouir de l'injouissable pureté.*[214]

[Sade's entire oeuvre seems to be nothing but a single, desperate cry addressed toward the image of inaccessible virginity, a cry that is enveloped and sort of embedded within a canticle of blasphemies. *I am excluded from purity since I want to possess the one who is pure. I cannot help but desire purity, but at the same time I am impure since I want to enjoy the unenjoyable purity.*]

Exactly like Justine and Gretchen, Silvia and Nerina are two innocent victims, persecuted by an evil and destructive power.[215] D'Intino highlights how the image of Silvia as being overcome by her infirmity transforms her into a Gretchen driven to Hell ('da chiuso morbo combattuta e vinta' [stricken then overcome by hidden sickness]).[216] The warlike metaphor employed here by Leopardi[217] is moreover a direct loan from libertine literature, in which, as Michel Delon notes, a military vocabulary is often used to describe processes of seduction.[218]

A famous passage of the *Zibaldone*, written a few months after 'A Silvia', describes an image of *jeune fille* that can plausibly be connected with the poem's composition:[219]

veram. una giovane dai 16 ai 18 anni ha nel suo viso, ne' suoi moti, nelle sue voci, salti ec. *un non so che* di divino, che niente può agguagliare. [...] quel fiore purissimo, intatto, freschissimo di gioventù, quella speranza vergine, incolume che gli si legge nel viso e negli atti, *o che voi nel guardarla concepite in lei e per lei*; quell'aria d'innocenza, d'ignoranza completa del male, delle sventure, de' patimenti; quel fiore insomma, quel primissimo fior della vita; tutte queste cose, *anche senza innamorarvi, anche senza interessarvi,* fanno in voi un'impressione così viva, così profonda, così *ineffabile,* che voi *non vi saziate* di guardar quel viso, ed io non conosco cosa che più di questa sia capace di elevarci l'anima, di trasportarci in un altro mondo, di darci un'idea d'angeli, di paradiso, di divinità, di felicità. Tutto questo, ripeto, *senza innamorarci, cioè senza muoverci desiderio di posseder quell'oggetto.*[220]

[in truth a young woman of 16 to 18 years has about her face, her gestures, the tones of her voice, her movements, etc., *something of the* divine which nothing can equal. [...] that purest, intact, freshest flower of youth, that virgin unblemished hope which can be read in her face and in her demeanour, *or which you conceive in her, and for her, as you look at her*; that air of innocence, of complete ignorance of evil, of misfortune, of suffering; that flower, that very first flower of life; all of these things, *even if they do not make you fall in love with her, even if they do not interest you,* make so keen, so deep, so *inexpressible* an impression upon you *that you can never tire* of gazing upon that face; and I know of nothing which is more able to raise our spirit, to transport us into another world, to give us an idea of angels, of paradise, of divinity, of happiness. All this, I repeat, *without making us fall in love, that is, without being moved by a desire to possess that object.*]

The image of the teenage girl is here openly connected with the culture of grace. Still, exactly in the same way as happens with the grace of antiquity, this is not an intrinsic peculiarity of the object, but rather the outcome of a subjective perception. The young girl, Leopardi writes, is an 'object', which, in itself, is completely unaware of its own condition. The hope itself that can be perceived in her face does not belong to her, but is conceived by the beholder's gaze. Only through a confrontation with his own impurity can the subject conceptualize the purity of the *jeune fille* as a form of inspiration, and only the comparison between her innocence and the misadventures that follow adult life can provide her with her oblique charm:

> La stessa divinità che noi vi scorgiamo, ce ne rende *in certo modo alieni*, ce lo fa riguardar come di una sfera diversa e superiore alla nostra, *a cui non possiamo aspirare*. [...] Del resto se a quel che ho detto [...] si aggiunga il pensiero dei patimenti che l'aspettano, delle sventure che vanno ad oscurare e a spegner ben tosto quella pura gioia, della vanità di quelle care speranze, della *indicibile fugacità di quel fiore*, di quello stato, di quelle bellezze; si aggiunga il *ritorno sopra noi medesimi*; e quindi un sentimento di compassione per quell'angelo di felicità, per noi medesimi, per la sorte umana, per la vita, [...] ne segue un affetto il più vago e il più sublime che possa immaginarsi.[221]

> [The very divinity which we perceive in it in *some way estranges* us, makes us look on it as though it were from a different and higher sphere than our own, *to which we cannot aspire*. [...] Moreover, if we add to what I said [...] the thought of the suffering that awaits her, the misfortunes that will soon obscure and extinguish that pure joy, the vanity of those fervent hopes, *the inexpressible transience of that flower*, that state, that beauty; if we add our *turning back upon ourselves*; and therefore a feeling of compassion for that angel of happiness, for ourselves, for human destiny, for life, [...] the effect is the most beautiful and the sublimest feeling that can be imagined.]

We can perhaps understand better why Leopardi, in writing to his sister from Pisa, speaks of 'A Silvia' as of 'versi veramente all'antica'.[222] This expression should not be intended in the sense of 'old-fashioned', but as referring to a sphere of archaicity that can uniquely be thought of from a modern perspective. On the one hand, to behold the lower-class girl's activities means accessing a world that is situated beyond historical time, in which antiquity veritably survives — in the same way as Petrarchan expressions resurface in the common language of country people. In *Silvio Sarno*, Leopardi had made explicit how the German country girls described in Goethe's *Die Leiden des jungen Werthers* (first published in 1774) [The Sorrows of Young Werther] did not actually do anything but repeat gestures that could be found in the most archaic Greek writers: 'lettura di Senofonte [...] notato quel luogo delle fanciulle persiane che cavano acqua comparato cogl'inni a Cerere di Callimaco e Omero ec. e Verter lett. 3' [reading Xenophon [...] noticed that passage about Persian girls pumping water compared with Callimachus's hymns to Ceres and Homer etc. and Werther 3rd letter].[223] On the other hand, the modern and historicized subject — Werther, Leopardi — is condemned, although noticing these phenomena of survival and continuity, to the production of a *modern* work, 'all'antica', but not ancient at all: Silvia's beauty itself, her 'negre chiome' [raven hair],[224] fully belongs to the present time, if black eyes and hair have only become charming for the moderns: 'Occhi azzurri belli tra' greci: neri tra noi. Capelli biondi belli in Italia nel 500. neri al presente' [Beautiful eyes: blue for the Greeks, black for us. Blond hair beautiful in Italy in the sixteenth century: now black].[225]

Gradiva

The poetry of the 'canti pisano-recanatesi' is constructed as a field of tension, by which alterity is incorporated within the text as a survival. The space of poetry allows the conjuration of εἴδωλα (the un-dead girls, the hopes of youth, the grace of ancients), halting for a moment their inexorable escape and thereby allowing their preservation as fossils. This consideration may allow us to understand better why, in the *Canti*, the caducity of Silvia and Nerina is expressed through images of physical motion, as if meant to highlight their passing transience. Silvia is portrayed while climbing and passing the *limen* that separates infancy from youth. Nerina's life is compared to a rapid, dancing gait:

> Ma rapida passasti; e come un sogno
> Fu la tua vita. Ivi danzando; in fronte
> La gioia ti splendea, splendea negli occhi
> Quel confidente immaginar, quel lume
> Di gioventù.[226]

[But you passed quickly; and your life was like a dream. You danced; joy glistened on your forehead, and that confident imagining, that light of youth, shone in your eyes.]

Both girls are depicted in the act of 'passing'. In 'A Silvia', the subject laments how the girl is 'past', although the Italian verb 'passare' evokes the image of a physical passing (over), 'Ahi come, | Come *passata* sei' [Ah, how *truly past* you are].[227] In 'Le ricordanze' the verb 'passare' forms a rhythmic counterpoint in the final stanza, being repeated four times in a remote past tense as if to underline Nerina's irremediable absence:

> Altro tempo. I giorni tuoi
> Furo, mio dolce amor. *Passasti*. Ad altri
> Il *passar* per la terra oggi è sortito,
> E l'abitar questi odorati colli.
> Ma rapida *passasti* [...].
> Ahi tu *passasti*, eterno
> Sospiro mio: *passasti*[228]

[Another time. Your days are over, my sweet love. *You passed away*. Others *pass on* the earth today and live in these fragrant hills. But *you passed* quickly [...]. *You have passed away*, lifelong regret of mine, *you have passed away*.]

Silvia's and Nerina's 'passare' is first of all a euphemism for 'dying'. At the same time, the verb conjures the Christian image of human life as a pilgrimage through earthly Babylon, an image which sounds, however, more terrible once it is emptied of every theological and salvific implication by Leopardi's materialism. As Michel de Certeau summarizes, Christian medieval art used to portray cities from above, thereby transforming the spectator into a 'celestial eye'; once seen from the detached perspective of Nature, the passing movement of every living being, makes Leopardi's gaze, 'like Schreber's God, kno[w] only cadavers'.[229] In 'La sera del dì di festa', a song heard during the night after a country feast evokes the idea of the general caducity of human matters, which is similarly expressed by the verb 'passare':

> E fieramente mi si stringe il core,
> A pensar come tutto al mondo *passa*,
> E quasi *orma* non lascia. Ecco è *fuggito*
> Il dì festivo, ed al festivo il giorno
> Volgar succede, e se ne porta il tempo
> Ogni umano accidente.[230]

> [and my heart is stricken to think how everything in this world *passes* and barely leaves *a trace*. Look, the holiday *is gone*, the workday follows, and time makes off with every human thing.]

Everything 'passes' and 'escapes'. Growing up means seeing everything pass away, namely becoming 'past': like Benjamin's angel of history, rather than a process of becoming, Leopardi's speaking subject sees in the process of time a landscape of ruins. The innocence of youth is consequently identified with the absence of any past and with the privilege of not having beheld the cycle of destruction to which every living being is condemned. In October 1820, plausibly in the same months when he is drafting 'La sera del dì di festa', Leopardi notes in the *Zibaldone* that:

> Il giovane non ha *passato*. Tutto quello che ne ha, non serve altro che ad attristarlo e *stringergli il cuore*. Le *rimembranze* della fanciullezza e della prima adolescenza, dei godimenti di quell'età *perduti* irreparabilmente, delle *speranze fiorite*, delle *immaginazioni ridenti*, dei disegni aerei di prosperità futura, di azioni, di vita, di gloria, di piacere, *tutto svanito*.[231]

> [A young person does not have *a past*. What little he has serves only to sadden him and *strike his heart*. *Remembrances* of childhood and early adolescence, the delights of that age now irreparably *lost*, the *flowering of hopes*, *imagined joys*, flights of fancy about future prosperity, action, life, glory, pleasure, *all vanished*.]

The connection between 'passare'/'passato' and the feeling of 'stringere il cuore' establish a close relationship between this passage and the poem, as well as an underlying, semantic short-circuit that reverberates into 'A Silvia': in the poem of 1828, the adjective 'ridenti' couples with 'fuggitivi' in a hendiadys that aims at describing the eyes of the passing girl. The term 'fuggitivi', translated by Galassi as 'startled' but actually meaning 'fleeting', 'fugitive', or 'fleeing', fully embodies the vague nature of grace as defined through the philological reflection of the *Zibaldone*: while literally referring to a modest girl's elusive gaze, it secretly alludes to the ephemeral and transitory dimension of her earthly passing, as well as to the fact that the light of those eyes — like that of the window in *Silvio Sarno* and 'Le ricordanze' — is doomed to be switched off. Both Silvia and Nerina are described through a luminescence that shines in their eyes or on their brow:

> Quando beltà splendea
> Negli occhi tuoi ridenti e fuggitivi.[232]

> [When beauty shimmered in your smiling, startled eyes.]

> Ivi danzando; in fronte
> La gioia ti splendea, splendea negli occhi

Quel confidente immaginar, quell lume
Di gioventù, quando spegneali il fato,
E giacevi.[233]

[You danced; joy glistened on your forehead, and that confident imagining, the light of youth, shone in your eyes, till fate extinguished them and you fell.]

Since ancient Greek poetry, χάρις/*gratia* is associated with light, as a luminescence that erupts from a visible being, alluding to the dimension of transcendence: in Sappho's poems the verb μαρμαίρω alludes both to the shimmering of Anactoria's eyes and to the rapidity of her movement, thus connecting grace both to motion and to a luminous aura.[234] Didi-Huberman speaks of a 'woman-brilliance' (*femme-éclat*), making the luminous quality of the object and the subject's wondering gaze inextricably intertwined: when Freud introduces his theory of fetishism, he writes that he does so with the expression 'Glanz auf der Nase' [sparkle on the nose], in which the German word 'Glanz' evokes the English 'glance', encompassing subjective gaze, haunting detail, and the inexplicable brilliance, by means of assonance.[235] First and foremost, this luminescence is associated with nymphs, as divinities that become manifest in the shimmering surface of waters, and in which the connection between movement and light seems to be most strong. Eloquently, Leopardi employs therefore the adjective 'fuggitivi' in order to describe Silvia's eyes, nymphs being characterized since ancient poetry by their fleeing and, at the same time, fleeting nature. The choice of such an adjective signals a *fil rouge* running throughout the whole parabola that I am attempting to reconstruct, from the reflections on Anacreon's poetry to the 'canti pisano-recanatesi'. In the discourse on Moschus of 1815, Leopardi quotes an idyll inspired by Anacreon and entitled 'Amor fuggitivo';[236] the same title belongs to the poem by Torquato Tasso that Leopardi reads in September 1829, shortly before composing 'Le ricordanze', and which is moreover the presumed epilogue of the *Aminta*, from which the names Silvia and Nerina are borrowed.[237] The conjunction between the verb 'passare' and the adjective 'fuggitivo' encompasses therefore a whole constellation of ephemerality and virginal modesty, of χάρις and nymph-like nature, oscillating between a metaphorical understanding of transience and a more literal one, embodied by the physical movement of passing. Silvia's and Nerina's pace is a *Pathosformel* that embodies, in the lightness of their *gestus*, a universal meditation on the frailty of the human condition.

After completing his dissertation on Botticelli in 1900, Aby Warburg gives birth to a very odd narrative experiment with a friend, the Dutch scholar André Jolles: a fictive exchange of letters about a feminine figure appearing in Domenico Ghirlandaio's frescoes in the Cappella Tornabuoni in Florence, that they decide to name 'the Nymph'. In the painting showing the nativity of the Baptist, 'there runs,' Jolles writes, with a climax of verbs and an oxymoron, 'no, that is not the word, there flies, or rather there hovers — the object of my dreams, which slowly assumes the proportions of a charming nightmare'.[238] This 'fantastic figure', 'a servant girl, or a classical nymph', is characterized by a peculiar aerial nature and levity, embodied by, Jolles writes, a 'lively, light-footed and rapid gait', an 'irresistible energy' and a 'striding step' ('Diese lebendig leichte, aber so höchst bewegte Weise zu gehen; diese energische Unaufhaltsamskeit, diese Länge vom Schritt'); it seems, Jolles continues, 'as if the servant girl rushed with winged foot through the clear ether [*mit beflügelten Füssen den hellen Äther durchschnellt*] instead of running on the real ground'.[239] The question is who she is: 'As a real being of flesh and blood', Warburg replies, 'she may have been a freed slave from Tartary ... but in her true essence [*ihrem wirklichen Wesen*] she is an elementary sprite, a pagan goddess in exile [*ein Elementargeist, eine heidnische Göttin im Exil*]'.[240] The nymph is a supernatural being, who manifests her true nature in the act of walking: the aerial grace of her step shows her as an ancient presence, resurfacing in the Renaissance fresco. Three years later, in 1903, the German author Wilhelm Jensen writes *Gradiva*, a short novel inspired by a neo-attic Roman bas-relief and nowadays mostly known because Sigmund Freud, in 1907, analyzed it from a psychoanalytical viewpoint: although nymphs are not explicitly mentioned, the connection between the step, walking, and supernatural nature of a feminine figure is the same:

> [...] a complete female figure in the act of walking [*im Schreiten*]; she was still young, but no longer in childhood [*nicht mehr im Kindesalter*] and, on the other hand, apparently not a woman, but a Roman virgin [*Virgo*] about in her twentieth year. [...] In her was embodied something humanly commonplace [...] as if the artist [...] had fixed her in a clay model quickly, from life, as she passed in the street [*sie auf der Straße im Vorübergehen rasch nach dem Leben im Tonmodell festgehalten haben*] [...]. So the young woman was fascinating. Not at all because of plastic beauty of form, but because she possessed something rare in antique sculpture, a realistic, simple, maidenly grace [*eine naturwahre, einfache, mädchenhafte Anmut*] which gave the impression of imparting life [*Leben einzuflößen*] to the relief. This was effected chiefly by the movement [*die Bewegung*] represented in the picture. [...] The left foot had advanced, and the right, about to follow, touched the ground only lightly with the tips of the toes, while the sole and heel were raised almost vertically. This movement produced a double impression [*Doppelgefühl*] of exceptional agility and of confident composure, and the flight-like poise [*flugartiges Schweben*], combined with a firm step, lent her the peculiar grace [*eigenartige Anmut*]. [...] he had called it to himself Gradiva, 'the girl splendid in walking' [*die Vorschreitende*].[241]

In Warburg and Jensen, the passing nymph is the embodiment of surviving antiquity, which becomes manifest in a dancing gait. As Didi-Huberman highlights, the Quattrocento debate on movement is directly influenced by gestural arts, showing a strong connection between the artists' reflections on grace and the vocabulary of treatises about dance: in both cases, 'bodily movements along with the "accessories" that invariably attached to them, were perceived as the *indexes of a soul*'.[242] 'Air', 'grace' and 'suavity' form part of the same constellation that reverberates in both the domains of visual arts and dance.[243] At the same time, the lightness of movement is connected to the domains of memory and time. By quoting the Quattrocento choreographer, Domenico da Piacenza, Didi-Huberman notes how motion is connected to the definition of *fantasma* [phantasm], so that 'in the suspense of immobility and motion, the dancer must suddenly become a "phantasmal shadow" (*ombra phantasmatica*)'.[244] By 'phantasm', Aristotelian philosophy conceptualizes the process of memory: recollection is produced by the 'phantasm' of a past perception,

as an εἴδωλον conjured in the absence of its referent. This consideration opens the
possibility of rethinking Warburg's notion of *Pathosformel* in the light of this bond
between movement, grace, and memory. In quoting the same source, Giorgio
Agamben writes that Warburg's *Pathosformeln* belong to the sphere of time and
can therefore be identified with Domenico's 'phantasms': they are 'crystals of
historical memory'.[245] The fleeting and gracious step of the nymph transforms
her into a surviving 'phantasm', an εἴδωλον: through her movement, the nymph,
like Quattrocento dancers, 'escapes gravity and the earthly condition; she becomes
a semblance of the ancient gods, an airy creature of dreams and after-life, a
revenant: an embodiment of *Nachleben*'.[246] This is why Warburg dedicates his atlas
of *Pathosformeln* to the Greek personification of memory, Mnemosyne; in the same
way Leopardi embodies his depiction of the passing nymph in a poem dedicated
to Mnemosyne, and therefore entitled 'Le ricordanze', meaning 'recollections' or
'memories'.

'A Silvia' and 'Le ricordanze' are therefore the enchanted frame within which
the conjuration of the two past girls takes place, crystallized as εἴδωλα in their
liminal status between life and death and portrayed as joyously stepping toward
dissolution. Already in the poem, 'All'Italia', Leopardi had evoked the battle of
Thermopylae by depicting the Spartans while running 'ridenti' [smiling][247] toward
the tearful 'passo' [passing]:[248] 'Parea ch'a danza e non a morte andasse | Ciascun
de' vostri, o a splendido convito' [It appeared that each of you was going to a dance
or splendid banquet, not to death].[249] In the poem, 'Sopra un bassorilievo antico
sepolcrale', composed in the early 1830s, Leopardi similarly takes as his theme
the depiction of the instant of death, 'una giovane morta è rappresentata in atto
di partire, accommiatandosi dai suoi' [On an Ancient Funeral Relief in Which a
Dead Young Woman Is Represented in the Act of Leaving, Bidding Farewell to
Her Own]. [250] By capturing Silvia and Nerina in a gracious movement of passing,
soon to be halted and turned into fall, these poems delineate a *Pathosformel* that
embodies liminality in the gesture's tensive asymmetry. Both in Warburg's Nymph
and Jensen's Gradiva, the light graciousness of walking epitomizes a form of survival
beyond death: their movement, as Didi-Huberman writes, betrays their nature
as surviving anachronisms.[251] As Carlo Ginzburg shows by comparing several
Euroasian myths, 'peculiarities connected with walking' often signal a connection
with the world of the dead:[252] liminal subjects, who know both realms, show a trace
of their 'double nature' (*Doppelnatur*)[253] in asymmetries of walking.

This is why lightness (*levitas*) is a quality that eminently belongs to Persephone/
Proserpina, a maiden (the other name of Persephone, Κόρη, is also a synonym for
'young girl') who — like Silvia and Nerina — belongs both to the earth and to
the underworld, thereby fully embodying the bipolarity between mortality and
immortality, death and resurrection. As D'Intino notes, the ending of 'A Silvia' can
be read in a double sense:

> e con la mano
> La fredda morte ed una tomba ignuda
> Mostravi di lontano.[254]

[and from afar you pointed out cold death and a naked grave.]

The literal reading shows Silvia's gesture as a *memento mori*; her act of pointing out the grave evokes however an image of rebirth, echoing, on the one hand, the *Noli me tangere* of Christian iconography and the resurrected Jesus outside the empty sepulchre, and, on the other, the victorious image of Persephone reborn.[255] Silvia-Κόρη conceals therefore a divine and immortal nature, heralding one of the names given by the Asian shepherd to the moon in the 'Canto notturno': by addressing the moon as 'giovinetta immortal' [immortal maiden],[256] Leopardi invests it with the double aspect of Κόρη as both a mythical figure and as an actual girl.[257] Moreover, as we have seen, the term 'giovinetta' may be a cryptomnesia from the Greek word νύμφη and the entire expression perfectly echoes an epithet given to Zeus in the already mentioned *Hymn to Zeus*, 'ἄφθιτος[...] νύμφη' [immortal maiden].[258] Like Persephone, Silvia and Nerina are κόραι surviving through death, whose joyous naiveté, albeit echoing libertine literature, is rooted in the *levitas* [lightness] and *simplicitas* [simplicity] that classical sources assign to the girl abducted by Hades. By recapitulating the history of Persephone's metamorphoses between Ovid, D'Annunzio, Braque, Kokoschka, and Merini, Roberto Deidier reads Persephone's *levitas* as the sign of her mobility that, preserving her from the *gravitas* [heaviness] of Hell, condemns her to a double return, and to a double nostalgia.[259] At the same time, like Silvia and Nerina, Persephone is above all a figure of absence: as Claudian writes in his unfinished poem, *De raptu Proserpinæ* [Rape of Proserpine], 'Persephone nusquam' (III, l. 244) [Persephone was/is nowhere].[260]

In the space of the poem, this 'nowhere' becomes a 'somewhere'; the gracious image of the dead girl permits a balancing of the *gravitas* of Leopardi's philosophical nihilism with the *levitas* of poetry. As Didi-Huberman writes, both Warburg's Nymph and Jensen's Gradiva display a gesture ('geste') and make a different perception of time emerge; both, moreover, demand a different style of knowledge ('style de connaissance') and a new interpretative practice ('une pratique nouvelle de l'interprétation').[261] In the same way, the gesture of Silvia and Nerina enacts a reconfiguration of time, turning into a new and different style of knowing, interpreting, and speaking — something close, I argue, to the state of he whom Greek lore used to name νυμφόληπτος, the one possessed and made a fool of by the nymphs.

Leopardi's reflection on poetry, orality, and written cultures is widely indebted to Plato's *Phaedrus*, a dialogue in which the renowned myth of Theuth and the Egyptian king Thamus tackles the problems of memory, writing, and forgetting, providing a conceptual framework for Leopardi's writing project itself.[262] One passage in particular of the *Phaedrus* leaves a persistent trace in Leopardi's oeuvre, a passage in which the notion of nympholepsy — the state of being νυμφόληπτος — is tellingly mentioned. The text begins with Socrates and his disciple Phaedrus who decide to depart from Athens, and walk along the Ilissos river. Phaedrus proposes to sit under a plane tree, where, he says, 'There is shade there and a moderate breeze [πνεῦμα μέτριον], and grass to sit on'.[263] As Socrates notes, that must be a holy place, 'it seems to be a sacred place of some nymphs and of Achelous, judging by the figurines and statues. Then again, if you please, how lovely and perfectly charming the breeziness [τὸ εὔπνουν] of the place is! And it resounds with the shrill summer music [θερινόν τε καὶ λιγυρὸν] of the chorus of cicadas'.[264] The summerlike breeze signals the presence of nymphs: the expression 'alito passeggero di venticello fresco nell'estate odorifero e ricreante' (*Zib.* 30) sounds like a maybe unconscious translation of this Platonic passage, obliquely conjuring the presence of Greek nymphs with the image of a physical and supernatural πνεῦμα. First and foremost, as in Leopardi, this holy πνεῦμα produces a perturbation of the mind, which affects the subject's speech. When Phaedrus notes that Socrates has 'an unusual fluency', the philosopher answers that this is because 'the place seems filled with a divine [θεῖος] presence; so do not be surprised if I often seem to be taken by the nymphs [νυμφόληπτος] as far as my discourse progresses, for I am already almost uttering dithyrambics [διθυράμβων φθέγγομαι]'.[265] In the fullest heat of midday, the imaginary breeze-nymph subdues the subject's mind, engendering a possession that becomes a new way of speaking. The speech of the νυμφόληπτος can no longer be prosaic, or explanatory, but rather takes the shape of a flowing of words articulated in metre. Nympholepsy, in other words, causes the subject to speak poetically.

Notes to Chapter 1

1. *Zib.* 75.
2. On Nabokov's discoveries, see Francesco M. Cataluccio, 'Farfalle russe', in *Vladimir Nabokov*, ed. by Maria Sebregondi and Elisabetta Porfiri (Milan: Marcos y Marcos, 1999), pp. 244–46. On nymphs and butterflies in Warburg's oeuvre, see Salvatore Settis's remarks in his presentation to Jean Seznec, *La sopravvivenza degli antichi dei. Saggio sul ruolo della tradizione mitologica nella cultura e nell'arte rinascimentali* (Turin: Bollati Boringhieri, 1990), pp. vii–xxix (pp. xv–xvi). On Warburg's obsession with butterflies and moths, see Ludwig Binswanger and Aby Warburg, *La guarigione infinita: Storia clinica di Aby Warburg*, ed. by Davide Stimilli (Vicenza: Neri Pozza, 2005), pp. 77 and 79. Echoing the double meaning of the Greek word for 'butterfly', ψυχή, Rosita Copioli speaks of a 'butterfly-psyche' that constantly and unavoidably escapes the chaser's hand: see her introduction to Giacomo Leopardi, *Discorso di un italiano intorno alla poesia romantica*, ed. by Rosita Copioli (Milan: Rizzoli, 1997), pp. 5–36 (p. 21).
3. *Zib*, pp. 30–31.
4. Both Gravina and Maffei are subterranean presences in the first pages of the *Zibaldone*: Gravina is quoted several times as an authority in aesthetics (*Zib.* 16, 25 and 32), whereas Maffei's *Merope* is declared the only truly artistic work of the Italian eighteenth century (*Zib.* 3). This choice, in terms of canon, confirms how Italian eighteenth-century Classicism paves the way for later aesthetic experiences: see the new periodization proposed by Giovanna Scianatico, *La questione neoclassica* (Venice: Marsilio, 2010), pp. 16–22, who stresses the continuity between the Classicism of Arcadia and Foscolo's and Leopardi's reconfigurations of European Neoclassical trends.
5. Longinus, *Dionysii Longini quæ supersunt latine et græce*, ed. by Jean Toup (Oxford: Clarendon Press, 1778). On the identification of Leopardi's source with Toup's edition, I agree with Raffaele Gaetano, *Giacomo Leopardi e il sublime* (Soveria Mannelli: Rubbettino, 2002), pp. 111–16.
6. Longinus, 'On the Sublime', in *The Poetics, On the Sublime, On Style*, by Aristotle, Longinus and Demetrius, ed. and transl. by W. Hamilton Fyfe (London: Heinemann, 1946), pp. 119–254 (pp. 140–41). For a detailed analysis of Leopardi's linguistic calques from the treatise 'On the Sublime' in the *Zibaldone* see my 'Lo pseudo-Longino, Montesquieu e l'alchimia dell'effetto poetico nello *Zibaldone*', in *Leopardi e la traduzione: Teoria e prassi* (forthcoming).
7. Karl Heinz Bohrer, *Suddenness: On the Moment of Aesthetic Appearance*, transl. by Ruth Crowley (New York: Columbia University Press, 1994), p. 60.

8. Ibid.

9. *Zib.* 3441–42, 16 September 1823.

10. *Zib.* 3443.

11. On the problem of Anacreon's untranslatability see Franco D'Intino, 'Il gusto dell'altro: La traduzione come esperienza straniera in Leopardi', in *Hospes: Il volto dello straniero da Leopardi a Jabès*, ed. by Alberto Folin (Venice: Marsilio, 2003), pp. 147–58.

12. *Zib.* 20.

13. TPP, p. 413.

14. TPP, p. 414.

15. On this aspect Mario Andrea Rigoni's 1976 essay 'L'estetizzazione dell'antico' is still relevant in many ways (Mario Andrea Rigoni, *Il pensiero di Leopardi* (Rome: Aragno, 2010), pp. 3–40).

16. See Francesca Fedi, *Mausolei di sabbia: Sulla cultura figurativa di Leopardi* (Lucca: Pacini Fazzi, 1997), p. 119. Fedi's comparison of Leopardi's position with that of Neoclassical aesthetics concerns, however, the sole conceptualizations of nature, ideal beauty, educational and civil aims of art, and the relationship of poetry with the visual arts (p. 120). Her analysis does not therefore cover Winckelmann's paradigms of historicity, nor the Neoclassical awareness (which is the same as Leopardi's, although giving birth to a radically different answer) about the distance separating the modern subject from classical antiquity.

17. Hayden White, foreword to *The Practice of Conceptual History. Timing History, Spacing Concepts*, by Reinhart Koselleck, transl. by Todd Samuel Presner and others (Stanford: Stanford University Press, 2002), pp. ix-xiv (p. x). On the construction of modern conceptualizations of history, see also Hayden White's *The Historical Imagination in Nineteenth-Century Europe* (Baltimore and London: Johns Hopkins University Press, 1973).

18. Reinhart Koselleck, *Futures Past: On the Semantics of Historical Time*, transl. by Keith Tribe (New York: Columbia University Press, 2004), p. 10.

19. Alex Potts, *Flesh and the Ideal: Winckelmann and the Origins of Art History* (New Haven and London: Yale University Press, 1994), pp. 47–50 (p. 49).

20. Didi-Huberman, *L'Image survivante*, p. 16.

21. Ibid., p. 17.

22. Potts, *Flesh and the Ideal*, p. 49.

23. This reflection recurs several times in the summer of 1821: see for instance *Zib.* 1325, 14 July, and pp. 1579–80, 28 August. See also *Zib.* 1689, 13 September 1821, 'La semplicità d'oggi è diversissima da quella d'allora [di Senofonte, o de' nostri trecentisti], e di un grado molto minore. Cosa che non s'intende da coloro che raccomandano l'imitazione degli antichi' [The simplicity of today is very different from the simplicity of the time of Xenophon, or that of our writers of the fourteenth century, and much lower in degree. Something that is not understood by those who urge us to imitate the ancients].

24. *Zib.* 1366, 21 July 1821.

25. Francesco Erspamer, *La creazione del passato* (Palermo: Sellerio, 2009), p. 72.

26. Giorgio Agamben, *Stanzas: Word and Phantasm in Western Culture*, transl. by Ronald L. Martinez (Minneapolis and London: University of Minnesota Press, 1993), p. 20.

27. Germaine de Staël, 'Sulla maniera e l'utilità delle traduzioni', in *Discussioni e polemiche sul romanticismo (1816–1826)*, ed. by Egidio Bellorini, 2 vols. (Bari: Laterza, 1943), I, 3–9. See Joseph Luzzi, *Romantic Europe and the Ghost of Italy* (New Haven and London: Yale University Press, 2008), pp. 222–23 note 2.

28. Luzzi, *Romantic Europe and the Ghost of Italy*, pp. 25–52.

29. Ibid., p. 35.

30. On the quarrel, and on the specificity of Leopardi's position, see my *Classicism and Romanticism in Italian Literature: Leopardi's 'Discourse on Romantic Poetry'* (London: Pickering & Chatto, 2013).

31. François Hartog, 'Il confronto con gli antichi', in *I greci: Storia, cultura, arte, società*, ed. by Salvatore Settis, 4 vols. (Turin: Einaudi, 1996), I, 3–37 (p. 11).

32. SW, IV, 392.

33. See Marianne Heidenreich, *Christian Gottlob Heyne und die alte Geschichte* (Munich: Saor, 2006), p. 387. Heyne was fascinated by Winckelmann's theories on ancient art and published in 1778 a text entitled *Lobschrift auf Winckelmann* [In Praise of Winckelmann].

34. Benjamin, *Arcades Project*, pp. 388–89.

35. Didi-Huberman, *Devant le temps*, p. 100.

36. SW, IV, 391.

37. On Leopardi's theory of grace, see Gaetano, *Giacomo Leopardi e il sublime*, pp. 371–94.

38. For the elaboration and the editorial history of the text, see the critical edition by Charles-Jacques Beyer (Geneva: Droz, 1976), p. 98 note.

39. See Richard Scholar's reconstruction, *The Je-Ne-Sais-Quoi in Early Modern Europe: Encounters with a Certain Something* (Oxford and New York: Oxford University Press, 2005). See also Paolo D'Angelo and Stefano Velotti, *Il 'non so che': Storia di un'idea estetica* (Palermo: Aesthetica, 1997).

40. *Zib.* 198, 4–9 August 1820.

41. See Martino Rossi Monti's analysis of the constellation χάρις/gratia, *Il cielo in terra: La grazia fra teologia ed estetica* (Turin: Utet, 2008). On the etymology of the Latin word *gratia* and its reverberations in the domains of theology and aesthetics, see Claude Moussy, *Gratia et sa famille* (Paris: Presses Universitaires de France, 1966). On the divinities known as Χάριτες [Graces], see Erkinger Schwarzenberg, *Die Grazien* (Bonn: Habelt, 1966), Karl Deichgräber, *Charis und Chariten, Grazie und Grazien* (Munich: Heimeran, 1971), and Bonnie MacLachlan, *The Age of Grace* (Princeton: Princeton University Press, 1993).

42. *Zib.* 4293, 21 September 1827.

43. *Zib.* 4416, 25 October 1828.

44. For instance in *Zib.* 2831–32, 27 June 1823.

45. Giorgio Agamben, *Infanzia e storia. Distruzione dell'esperienza e origine della storia* (Turin: Einaudi, 2001), p. 6; *Infancy and History: The Destruction of Experience*, transl. by Liz Heron (London and New York: Verso, 1993), p. 14.

46. *Zib.* 3179.

47. Leopardi, 'Il sabato del villaggio', l. 4.

48. Aby Warburg, 'Sandro Botticelli's *Birth of Venus* and *Spring*: An Examination of Concepts of Antiquity in the Italian Early Renaissance', in *The Renewal of Pagan Antiquity*, by Aby Warburg, ed. by Gertrud Bing with Fritz Rougemont, transl. by David Britt (Los Angeles: Getty Research Institute for the History of Art and the Humanities, 1999), pp. 89–156 (p. 89). See also Kurt W. Forster's introduction to *The Renewal of Pagan Antiquity*, pp. 1–75 (pp. 10–19).

49. See Potts, *Flesh and the Ideal*, p. 1.

50. Warburg, 'Sandro Botticelli's *Birth of Venus*', p. 89.

51. See Georges Didi-Huberman, 'The Imaginary Breeze: Remarks on the Air of the Quattrocento', *Journal of Visual Culture*, 2 (2003), 275–89 (p. 277).

52. Warburg, 'Sandro Botticelli's *Birth of Venus*', p. 108.

53. Ibid., p. 104.

54. Didi-Huberman, 'The Imaginary Breeze', p. 275.

55. Ibid., pp. 277–78.

56. Ibid., p. 278.

57. Ibid.

58. Ibid., p. 279.

59. Ibid., p. 280.

60. *Zib.* 601–02, 4 February 1821. See also *Zib.* 1054, 15 May 1821, 'Non solo la greca parola Ψυκή […] deriva da *spirare* ec. ma anche la latina *animus* e quindi *anima* da ἄνεμος *vento*' [Not only does the Greek word Ψυκή […] derive from *spirare*, etc., but the Latin *animus* and hence *anima* from ἄνεμος, wind]. In this passage Leopardi also quotes his own *Saggio sopra gli errori popolari degli antichi* [Essay on the Popular Errors of the Ancients], of 1815, 'La voce *anima* presso gli scrittori latini è spesse volte sinonima di vento. […] Forse questo costume di scrivere *anima* per *vento* ebbe origine dalla conformità della voce *anima* colla parola ἄνεμος che in greco vale *vento*; come par che supponga Servio. Forse anche l'error popolare, che attribuiva l'anima ai venti, derivò in parte dalla medesima origine. In greco la voce πνεῦμα vale al tempo stesso *spirito* e *vento*' (TPP, pp. 918–19) [in Latin writers, the term *anima* is often a synonym for wind. […] Maybe this habit of writing *anima* in order to mean *wind* was inspired by the closeness of the word *anima* to ἄνεμος, meaning *wind* in Greek; as Servius seems to hypothesize. Maybe even the superstition of

assigning a soul to the winds derived to some extent from the same origin. In Greek, the term πνεῦμα means at the same time *spirit* and *wind*]. On these passages see Copioli's introduction to *Discorso di un italiano intorno alla poesia romantica*, by Giacomo Leopardi, ed. by Rosita Copioli (Milan: Rizzoli, 1997), pp. 23–26.

61. See M.H. Abrams, 'The Correspondent Breeze: A Romantic Metaphor', in *The Romantic Breeze: Essays on English Romanticism*, by M.H. Abrams (New York and London: Norton, 1984), pp. 25–43 (p. 26).

62. Leopardi, 'L'infinito', ll. 8–13.

63. Gabrielle Sims, 'Speaking about Infinity without Recourse to Fragments: Leopardi's "L'infinito" as a Challenge to the Sublime Ellipsis' (2010), <http://www.birmingham.ac.uk/Documents/college-artslaw/lcahm/leopardi/fragments/leopardi/paper-sims.pdf>, p. 7 [accessed 28 May 2013].

64. *Purg.*, XXIV, 52–55. For the English translation I refer to Dante Alighieri, *Purgatorio*, ed. and transl. by Robert M. Durling (New York and Oxford: Oxford University Press, 2003).

65. See Agamben, 'Eros at the Mirror', in *Stanzas*, pp. 73–89. I will analyze this aspect more closely in the second section.

66. Didi-Huberman, 'The Imaginary Breeze', p. 281.

67. Warburg, 'Sandro Botticelli's *Birth of Venus*', pp. 95–96.

68. Ibid.

69. Didi-Huberman, 'The Imaginary Breeze', p. 285.

70. Ibid., p. 279.

71. Didi-Huberman, *L'Image survivante*, pp. 51–60, and 'The Surviving Image: Aby Warburg and Tylorian Anthropology', *Oxford Art Journal*, 25, 1 (2002), 61–69.

72. Didi-Huberman, *Devant le temps*, p. 92.

73. Ibid., pp. 92–93.

74. Agamben, *The Signature of All Things*, p. 29.

75. See Tom O'Neill, *Of Virgin Muses and Of Love: A Study of Foscolo's 'Dei Sepolcri'* (Dublin: Irish Academic Press, 1981). On Foscolo's poem, tombs, civilisation, and Italian national identity, see also Luzzi, *Romantic Europe and the Ghost of Italy*, pp. 5–11.

76. *Zib.* 3430–32, 15 September 1823.

77. *Zib.* 4305–06, 10 May 1828.

78. The notion of 'illusion' (*illusione*) is central to Leopardi's thought. On this topic, see Arturo Mazzarella, *I dolci inganni: Leopardi, gli errori e le illusioni* (Naples: Liguori, 1996), and Rolando Damiani, 'Le "credenze stolte": Leopardi e gli errori popolari', in *L'impero della ragione: Studi leopardiani*, by Rolando Damiani (Ravenna: Longo, 1994), pp. 7–55.

79. *Zib.* 3439.

80. *Zib.* 3435–37.

81. *Zib.* 3439–40.

82. *Zib.* 4271–72, 2 April 1827.

83. D'Intino, *L'immagine della voce*, p. 77.

84. Michael Caesar, '"Mezz'ora di nobiltà": Leopardi e i suoi lettori', in *Leopardi a Firenze*, ed. by Laura Melosi (Florence: Olschki, 2002), pp. 461–72 (p. 465). See also D'Intino, *L'immagine della voce*, pp. 9 and 189.

85. Agamben, *Infancy and History*, p. 41.

86. SW, IV, 318.

87. SW, III, 105.

88. Benjamin, 'On Some Motifs in Baudelaire', SW, IV, 321.

89. *Zib.* 466, 2 January 1821

90. *Zib.* 466–68.

91. *Zib.* 467, my emphasis.

92. *Zib.* 95. Franco D'Intino too notes this coincidence, highlighting how Leopardi employs Xenophon in order to construct a canon of 'non-literary literature' that privileges 'direct observations over reasonings, actual data over conceptual superstructures and stylistic artifice': Leopardi, *Volgarizzamenti in prosa*, pp. 62–63.

93. Rudolf Pfeiffer, *Storia della filologia classica. Dalle origini alla fine dell'età ellenistica*, ed. by Marcello

Gigante, transl. by Marcello Gigante and Salvatore Cerasuolo (Naples: Macchiaroli, 1973), p. 79.

94. Longinus, 'On the Sublime', pp. 122–23.

95. Michel Foucault, 'Self Writing', in *Ethics: Subjectivity and Truth*, by Michel Foucault (New York: New Press, 1997), pp. 207–21.

96. See for instance Bernard Stiegler, 'Anamnesis and Hypomnesis', *Ars Industrialis*, <http://arsindustrialis.org/anamnesis-and-hypomnesis> [accessed 28 May 2013].

97. The *ars* has always been quickly dismissed by Leopardi-related criticism, see for example Fabiana Cacciapuoti, *Dentro lo 'Zibaldone': Il tempo circolare della scrittura di Leopardi* (Rome: Donzelli, 2010), p. 28. See Lucia Marinelli, '*Ars memoriae* e *Ars excerpendi*: le alternative del ricordare', in *I libri di Leopardi*, by Maria Gabriella Mansi and other (Naples: De Rosa, 2000), pp. 131–58.

98. See Marc Fumaroli, 'Les abeilles et les araignées', in *La Querelle des anciens et des modernes XVIIe-XVIIIe siècles*, ed. by Anne-Marie Lecoq (Paris: Gallimard, 2001), pp. 7–220 (pp. 216–18). By inheriting the bee/spider opposition from Aesop, the image of the bee as an emblem of Classicism is opposed in Jonathan Swift's *Battle of the Books* (1697) to that of the spider as an epitome of the modern writer, whose pride goes to the point of weaving its web out of its own excrement.

99. On the art of memory see Frances Yates, *The Art of Memory* (Chicago: Chicago University Press, 1966), Mary Carruthers, *The Book of Memory: A Study of Memory in Medieval Culture* (Cambridge: Cambridge University Press, 1990), and Lina Bolzoni, *The Gallery of Memory: Literary and Iconographic Models in the Age of the Printing Press*, transl. by Jeremy Parzen (Toronto: University of Toronto Press, 2001).

100. For a history of the *ars* see Alberto Cevolini, *De arte excerpendi: Imparare a dimenticare nella modernità* (Florence: Olschki, 2006), pp. 113–29, and pp. 429–33 for a comprehensive list of related sources.

101. See Marcello Verdenelli's introductory essay to *Epistolario*, by Giuseppe Antonio Vogel, ed. by Marcello Verdenelli (Ancona: Transeuropa, 1993), pp. 5–33, and Vogel's biographical profile on pp. 34–36.

102. Francesco Cancellieri, *Dissertazione intorno agli uomini dotati di gran memoria ed a quelli divenuti smemorati con un'appendice delle biblioteche degli scrittori sopra gli eruditi precoci, la memoria artificiale, l'arte di trascegliere e di notare ed il giuoco degli scacchi* (Rome: Bourlie, 1815).

103. A general reconstruction of the quarrel can be found in Marcello Verdenelli, 'Cronistoria dell'idea leopardiana di "Zibaldone"', *Il Veltro. Rivista della civiltà italiana*, 5–6 (1987), 591–620.

104. See Leopardi, *Zibaldone di pensieri*, ed. by Emilio Peruzzi, 10 vols (Pisa: Scuolo Normale Superiore, 1989–94), I, xxii.

105. See Vogel, *Epistolario*, pp. 92–98 (p. 92).

106. Ibid., pp. 94–95.

107. Ibid., p. 92.

108. Ibid., pp. 92–93.

109. Vogel, *Epistolario*, p. 92.

110. Ibid., p. 107.

111. Ibid., p. 111.

112. Ibid., p. 112.

113. E, II, 2073.

114. See Leopardi, *Zibaldone di pensieri*, ed. by Giuseppe Pacella, 3 vols. (Milan: Garzanti, 1991), I, pp. xxx-xxxi.

115. On the peculiarities of the *Zibaldone* and its structure, see: Prete, *Il pensiero poetante*, p. 196; Luigi Blasucci, 'Quattro modi di approccio allo *Zibaldone*', in *I tempi dei 'Canti'*, by Luigi Blasucci (Turin: Einaudi, 1996), pp. 229–42; Marco Riccini, 'Lo *Zibaldone di pensieri*: progettualità e organizzazione del testo', in *Leopardi e il libro nell'età romantica*, ed. by Michael Caesar and Franco D'Intino (Rome: Bulzoni, 2000), pp. 81–104; the several contributions included in *Lo 'Zibaldone' cento anni dopo. Composizione, edizioni, temi*, ed. by Ronaldo Garbuglia, 2 vols. (Florence: Olschki, 2001), especially those by Fabiana Cacciapuoti ('La scrittura dello *Zibaldone* tra sistema filosofico ed opera aperta', I, 249–56) and Antonio Prete ('Sulla scrittura dello *Zibaldone*: la forma dell'*essai* e i modi del *preludio*', I, 387–94); Cacciapuoti, *Dentro lo 'Zibaldone'*.

116. Antonio Prete, 'Un anno di Zibaldoni e altre meraviglie' (2004), <http://www.zibaldoni.it/comunicato_stampa/index_frascati_a.htm> [accessed 28 May 2013].

117. Roger Chartier, *The Order of Books: Readers, Authors and Libraries in Europe between the Fourteenth and Eighteenth Centuries*, transl. by Lydia G. Cochrane (Stanford: Stanford University Press, 1994), p. 10.

118. Ibid., pp. 55–56.

119. TPP, pp. 1032–33. See Michele Monserrati, *Le 'cognizioni inutili': Saggio su 'Lo Spettatore fiorentino' di Giacomo Leopardi* (Florence: Firenze University Press, 2005).

120. TPP, p. 1032.

121. For a convincing comparison between Leopardi's and Baudelaire's notions of *flânerie* see Cosetta Veronese, 'Fleetingness and Flâneurie [sic]: Leopardi, Baudelaire and the Experience of Transience' (2010), <http://www.birmingham.ac.uk/Documents/college-artslaw/lcahm/leopardi/fragments/leopardi/paper-veronese.pdf> [accessed 28 May 2013].

122. *Zib.* 1336, 17 July 1822.

123. Franco D'Intino, 'Leopardi, Julien Sorel e il diavolo: Il gioco sottile dell'eroe faustiano nell'epoca della Restaurazione', *Igitur*, 3 (1991), pp. 23–47.

124. Giulio Bollati, introduction to Leopardi, *Crestomazia italiana*, p. lxxvii.

125. See Uberto Motta, 'Nel nome della grazia: Leopardi e Castiglione', in *Leopardi e il '500*, ed. by Paola Italia (Pisa: Pacini, 2010), pp. 185–204. On Castiglione's *Book of the Courtier*, elegance and 'je ne sais quoi' see also Carlo Ossola, *Dal 'Cortegiano' all''Uomo di mondo'. Storia di un libro e di un modello sociale* (Turin: Einaudi, 1987).

126. See Gaetano, *Giacomo Leopardi e il sublime*, pp. 382–86.

127. See Rossi Monti, *Il cielo in terra*, pp. 119–22

128. Scholar, *The Je-Ne-Sais-Quoi in Early Modern Europe*, p. 191.

129. *Zib.* 2682, 14 March 1823.

130. *Zib.* 3050–51, 27 July 1823.

131. In the *Zibaldone*, the expression 'non so che' is often used in relation to the *pellegrino*. In *Zib.* 1336 Leopardi speaks of 'quell'aria di pellegrino, e quel non so che di temperatamente inusitato, e diviso dall'ordinario costume, da cui deriva l'eleganza' (14 July 1821) [that air of unfamiliarity and that indefinable something of of the mildly unusual, set apart from ordinary custom, from which elegance derives]; in 2505 he defines 'pellegrino' in language as endowing speech with 'un non so che di raro, ch'è insomma l'eleganza' (29 June 1822) [something rare, which is what in short elegance is]; in 3372–73 he translates the Latin expression *quiddam* with 'non so che' ('*pingue quiddam sonantibus atque peregrinum.* [...] solamente macchiati d'un non so che di pingue e di peregrino', 6 September 1823) [in their sounds somewhat gross and strange. [...] tainted with the occasional gross or strange element].

132. *Zib.* 541, 22 January 1821.

133. *Zib.* 2131, 20 November 1821.

134. 'Come è mutabile l'idea della convenienza,' Leopardi notes on 29 June 1822, 'così è variabile il pellegrino, e quindi è variabile l'eleganza reale, effettiva e concreta, benchè l'eleganza astratta sia invariabile' (*Zib.* 2513) [just as the idea of propriety is changeable, so the unfamiliar is variable, and hence real, effective, concrete elegance is variable, although abstract elegance is invariable]. The *pellegrino* is an element whose irregularity is always grounded in distantiation, be it historical, cultural, or geographical (*Zib.* 1337, 17 July 1821).

135. Rossi Monti, *Il cielo in terra*, p. 142.

136. Didi-Huberman, 'The Imaginary Breeze', p. 283.

137. *Zib.* 1818, 30 September 1821.

138. *Zib.* 2542–43, 30 June–2 July 1822.

139. Antonio Prete speaks of a 'fantastic philology', highlighting how Leopardi's philological apprenticeship is always connected with creation, pastiche-making, and writing direct action, 'Filologia fantastica', pp. 29–38.

140. *Zib.* 1825–26, 3 October 1821.

141. My notion of paradigm based on clues (*paradigma indiziario*) is based on Ginzburg, 'Morelli, Freud and Sherlock Holmes'.

142. Didi-Huberman, *Devant le temps*, pp. 103–04.

143. *Zib.* 1789, 25 September 1821.
144. Didi-Huberman, *Devant le temps*, p. 116.
145. Ibid., pp. 90–92, for montage, polarity, and the dialectical image.
146. Lonardi, *L'oro di Omero*, pp. 9–56.
147. TPP, p. 940. See Lonardi, *L'oro di Omero*, p. 10.
148. Didi-Huberman, *L'Image survivante*, pp. 307–14. The expression is coined by Freud and Josef Breuer in the 1893 'Preliminary Communication' to the *Studies on Hysteria*: 'Hysterics suffer mainly from reminiscences', SE, II, pp. 3–17 (p. 7).
149. *Zib.* 4415, 22 October 1828.
150. Lonardi, *L'oro di Omero*, p. 146.
151. Ernst Robert Curtius, *European Literature and the Latin Middle Ages*, transl. by Willard R. Trask (Princeton: Princeton University Press, 1990), p. 1. On the relationship between Curtius and Warburg, see also Silvia De Laude, *Continuità e variazioni fra Curtius e Warburg* (Naples: Inprint, 2005).
152. For the comparison Warburg-Parry see Agamben, 'Nymphs', p. 64. Parry's works are collected in Milman Parry, *The Making of Homeric Verse: The Collected Papers*, ed. by Adam Parry (Oxford: Clarendon Press, 1971).
153. See D'Intino, *L'immagine della voce*, pp. 161–201.
154. On the poignancy of Leopardi's choice of titling his book as *Canti*, see Luigi Blasucci, 'Sul libro dei *Canti*', in *Leopardi e il libro nell'età romantica*, pp. 213–36.
155. D'Intino, *L'immagine della voce*, p. 173.
156. Cancellieri, *Dissertazione*, p. 111.
157. *Zib.* 4302, 15 April 1828, my emphases.
158. See Franco D'Intino, 'I misteri di Silvia'. The Persephonean element in 'A Silvia' was suggested for the first time by Cesare Galimberti, 'Di un Leopardi "patrocinatore del circolo"', *Sigma*, 8 (1965), pp. 23–42, and later discussed by Claudio Colaiacomo, *Camera obscura: Studio di due canti leopardiani* (Naples: Liguori, 1992), pp. 139–46.
159. The images of death at a tender age and prematurely dead plants are often interconnected in Leopardi's oeuvre. See the following passages from the autobiographical sketch *Vita abbozzata di Silvio Sarno*, 'mio dolore in veder morire i giovini come a veder bastonare una vite carica d'uve immature ec. una messe ec. calpestare' (SFA, p. 99) [my sorrow in seeing young people die, just like in seeing an unripe grapevine being thrashed etc. corn etc. being trampled]; 'così mi duole veder morire un giovine come segare una messe verde verde o sbattere giù da un albero i pomi bianchi ed acerbi' (SFA, p. 107) [seeing a young person dying hurts me like seeing some green green corn being cut, or seeing some still white and unripe pommels being thrown out from a tree]. On this aspect, see D'Intino, 'I misteri di Silvia', p. 219.
160. Leopardi, 'A Silvia', ll. 5–6.
161. Ibid., ll. 1–2.
162. Jean-Pierre Vernant, 'Psuche: Simulacrum of the Body or Image of the Divine?', in *Mortals and Immortals: Collected Essays*, by Jean-Pierre Vernant, ed. by Froma I. Zeitlin (Princeton: Princeton University Press, 1991), pp. 186–92 (pp. 186–87).
163. Leopardi, 'A Silvia', ll. 40–50.
164. Alessandro Carrera, introduction to *Giacomo Leopardi: Poeta e Filosofo*, ed. by Alessandro Carrera (Fiesole: Cadmo, 1999), pp. xi-xviii (p. xii).
165. Quoted in Sebastiano Timpanaro, '"Gli sguardi innamorati e schivi" (A Silvia, 46)', in Id., *Aspetti e figure della cultura ottocentesca* (Pisa: Nistri-Lischi, 1980), pp. 277–85 (p. 283). Timpanaro reproduces here the postscript added by Fubini to the first publication of his essay, in 1961.
166. *Zib.* 29. The active sense of the past participle was highlighted for the first time by Timpanaro, '"Gli sguardi innamorati e schivi" (A Silvia, 46)'. See also Fubini's footnote *ad locum* in his edition of Leopardi's *Canti*, p. 168 note 46.
167. See Giovanni Battista Bronzini, *Leopardi e la poesia popolare dell'Ottocento* (Naples: De Simone, 1975).
168. SFA, pp. 45–122. For a general introduction to this text see ibid., pp. xliv-xcvii.
169. SFA, p. 87.
170. SFA, pp. 87–88.
171. On the window as a persistent image in Leopardi's oeuvre, see Franco Ferrucci, *Il formidabile deserto: Lettura di Giacomo Leopardi* (Rome: Fazi, 1998), pp. 94–96.

172. SFA, pp. 54–55.

173. SFA, p. 92.

174. Leopardi, 'Il canto della fanciulla', ll. 9–10. The girl sings 'da *chiuso* ricetto' [from a *hidden* room] (l. 2, my emphasis). The adjective returns in a very different acceptation in 'A Silvia', 'da *chiuso* morbo combattuta e vinta' [stricken then overcome by *hidden* sickness] (l. 41, my emphasis).

175. See Lonardi, *L'oro di Omero*, pp. 166–69.

176. Leopardi, 'A Silvia', ll. 15–16 and 19–22.

177. Bronzini, *Leopardi e la poesia popolare*, p. 92.

178. Leopardi, 'Le ricordanze', ll. 141–44.

179. SFA, pp. 108–11.

180. SFA, pp. 110–11, note 203.

181. I will return to the image of the firefly in the Conclusion.

182. Leopardi, 'A Silvia', l. 42.

183. Ibid., l. 61.

184. SFA, pp. 97–98.

185. SFA, p. 97.

186. Leopardi, 'Il canto della fanciulla', l. 1.

187. Ibid., ll. 6–7.

188. Ibid., ll. 7–8.

189. Leopardi, 'A Silvia', l. 55.

190. D'Intino, 'I misteri di Silvia', p. 242.

191. Alessandro Manzoni, *I promessi sposi (1827)*, ed. by Salvatore Silvano Nigro (Milan: Mondadori, 2002), p. 47, my emphasis.

192. Alessandro Manzoni, *The Betrothed*, transl. by Archibald Colquhoun (London: J.M. Dent, 1951), pp. 27–28, my emphasis.

193. Leopardi, 'Aspasia', ll. 20–21.

194. Ibid., ll. 19–20.

195. Manzoni, *I promessi sposi (1827)*, p. 179.

196. Alessandro Manzoni, *I promessi sposi (1840)*, ed. by Salvatore Silvano Nigro (Milan: Mondadori, 2002), p. 170; *The Betrothed*, p. 124 (adapted to my own purpose). On the description of Gertrude, see Verina R. Jones, 'Le *Dark Ladies* manzoniane', in *Le Dark Ladies manzoniane e altri saggi sui 'Promessi sposi'*, by Verina R. Jones (Rome: Salerno, 1998), pp. 90–108 (pp. 98–100).

197. Charles Secondat de Montesquieu, *Œuvres* (Amsterdam, 1781), p. 395. See also the description of a young shepherdess in the *Temple de Gnide*, a text included in the same volume of Montesquieu's works: the girl 'a quelque chose de si naïf, qu'il semble qu'elle ne parle que le langage du cœur. Tout ce qu'elle dit, tout ce qu'elle fait, a les charmes de la simplicité; vous trouvez toujours une bergère naïve. Des graces si légères, si fines, si délicates, se font remarquer, mais se font encore mieux sentir', pp. 339–40 [has something so naif that it seems that she does not speak but the language of heart. Everything she says, everything she does possesses the charms of simplicity; you will always find a candid shepherdess. Such impalpable, fine, gentle charms are to be noticed, but far more to be felt].

198. See Scholar, *The 'Je-Ne-Sais-Quoi' in Early Modern Europe*, p. 28. One of the first attestations of the Italian expression 'non so che' is to be found in Lodovico Dolce's 1557 *Dialogo della pittura* [Dialogue on Painting], referring to Raphael's skilfulness in exciting feelings (*movere*): see Rossi Monti, *Il cielo in terra*, pp. 142–45 and 150.

199. SFA, p. 79.

200. Rolando Damiani, *All'apparir del vero: Vita di Giacomo Leopardi* (Milan: Mondadori, 1998), pp. 115–17.

201. Laura Kreyder, *La passion des petites filles: Histoire de l'enfance féminine de la Terreur à Lolita* (Arras: Artois Presses Université, 2003), pp. 14–35.

202. Solange Petit-Skinner notes that the seventeenth and eighteenth centuries witness a remarkable demand for young virgins in the prostitution market, 'L'Homme et la sexualité', in *Histoire des moeurs*, ed. by Jean Poirier, 6 vols. (Paris: Gallimard), ii, 929–71 (p. 937). At the same time, several European legislatures start to distinguish the abuse of minors as an aggravation of the crime of rape: see Georges Vigarello, *Histoire du viol XVIe-XXe siècle* (Paris: Seuil, 2000), p. 67.

203. On Silvia and Gretchen, see Franco D'Intino, 'Il monaco indiavolato. Lo *Zibaldone* e la tentazione faustiana di Leopardi', in *Lo 'Zibaldone' cento anni dopo. Composizione, edizioni, temi*, ed. by Rolando Garbuglia, 2 vols. (Florence: Olschki, 2001), II, 467–523.

204. See Robert Darnton, *Édition et sédition: L'Univers de la littérature clandestine au XVIIIe siècle* (Paris: Gallimard, 1991), and Jean-Marie Goulemot, *Ces livres qu'on ne lit que d'une main: Lecture et lecteurs de livres pornographiques au XVIIIe siecle* (Aix-en-Provence: Alinea, 1991).

205. See Pierre Saint-Amand, *Séduire ou la passion des Lumières* (Paris: Klincksieck, 1987), p. 7.

206. See Pierre Fauchery, *La Destinée féminine dans le roman européen du dix-huitième siècle 1713–1807: Essai de gynécomythie romanesque* (Paris: Armand Colin, 1972), p. 310, and Petit-Skinner, 'L'Homme et la sexualité', p. 937.

207. See Pierre Fauchery, *La Destinée féminine*, pp. 309–10, and Paul Hoffmann, *La Femme dans la pensée des Lumières* (Paris: Ophrys, 1977), p. 383.

208. Respectively, the tale, *Les Infortunes de la vertu*, the novel, *Justine ou les malheurs de la vertu*, and the rewriting known as *La Nouvelle Justine*.

209. This connection was first hypothesized by Mario Praz in *The Romantic Agony*, transl. by Angus Davidson (Oxford: Oxford University Press, 1970), p. 172 (first published in 1930).

210. On Lucia as an agent of conversion, see Arcangelo Leone De Castris, *Il problema Manzoni* (Palermo: Palumbo, 1990), pp. 88–95. The Unnamed's castle described in the twentieth chapter of *I promessi sposi* can be seen as a veritable example of a 'castle of subversion', following Annie Le Brun's definition, *Les Châteaux de la subversion* (Paris: Pauvert & Garnier Frères, 1982).

211. D'Arco Silvio Avalle, 'Da Santa Uliva a Justine', in *La fanciulla perseguitata*, by Aleksandr N.J. Veselovskij and Sade, ed. by D'Arco Silvio Avalle (Milan: Bompiani, 1977), pp. 7–33.

212. Sade, *Œuvres*, ed. by Michel Delon, 3 vols. (Paris: Gallimard, 1990–98), II, 133, my emphases.

213. Sade, *Justine, Philosophy in the Bedroom and Other Writings*, ed. and transl. by Richard Seaver and Austryn Wainhouse (London: Arrow Books, 1991), p. 459, my emphases.

214. Pierre Klossowski, *Sade mon prochain* (Paris: Seuil, 1947), pp. 108–09.

215. On the affinities between Leopardi and Sade in the conceptualization of a world tended toward evil, see Mario Andrea Rigoni, 'Leopardi, Sade e il dio del male', in *Il pensiero di Leopardi*, by Mario Andrea Rigoni, pp. 111–20.

216. Leopardi, 'A Silvia', l. 41. See D'Intino, 'I misteri di Silvia', p. 215.

217. D'Intino, 'I misteri di Silvia', pp. 225–26 and note 70.

218. Michel Delon, *Le Savoir-vivre libertin* (Paris: Hachette, 2000), pp. 51–66.

219. See also D'Intino, 'Il monaco indiavolato', p. 478.

220. *Zib.* 4310–11, 30 June 1828, my emphases.

221. *Zib.* 4311, my emphases.

222. E, II, 1480.

223. SFA, p. 70.

224. Leopardi, 'A Silvia', l. 45.

225. *Zib.* 8, c. 1817. On Silvia's black hair see D'Intino, 'I misteri di Silvia', pp. 228–29 and note 77. In speaking of the sixteenth century, Leopardi is clearly evoking the centrality of blonde hair in the Italian lyric canon, for which see Giovanni Pozzi, 'Il ritratto della donna nella poesia d'inizio Cinquecento e la pittura di Giorgione', *Lettere italiane*, XXXI, 1 (January March 1979), 3–30, and Alessandra Paola Macinante, '*Erano i capei d'oro a l'aura sparsi*': *Metamorfosi delle chiome femminili tra Petrarca e Tasso* (Rome: Salerno, 2011). Leopardi's operation parallels the deconstruction of the lyric feminine ideal pursued in Manzoni's *I promessi sposi*, in which Lucia is equally dark-haired: see Jones, 'Le *Dark Ladies* manzoniane', pp. 90–96.

226. Leopardi, 'Le ricordanze', ll. 152–56.

227. Leopardi, 'A Silvia', ll. 52–53, my emphasis.

228. Leopardi, 'Le ricordanze', ll. 148–52 and 169–70, my emphases.

229. Michel de Certeau, 'Walking in the City', in *The Practice of Everyday Life*, by Michel de Certeau, transl. by Steven Rendall (Berkeley: University of California Press, 1984), pp. 90–110 (pp. 92–93).

230. 'La sera del dì di festa', 28–33, my emphases;

231. *Zib.* 278, 16 October 1820, my emphases.

232. Leopardi, 'A Silvia', ll. 3–4.

233. Leopardi, 'Le ricordanze', ll. 153–57.

234. Rossi Monti, *Il cielo in terra*, pp. xxxiii–xxxiv.

235. Didi-Huberman, *La Peinture incarnée, suivi de Le Chef-d'œuvre inconnu par Honoré de Balzac* (Paris: Minuit, 1985), pp. 85–87. See Freud, 'Fetishism' (1927), SE, XXI, 147–57 (p. 152): 'The "shine on the nose" [in German "*Glanz auf der Nase*"] — was in reality a "*glance* at the nose". The nose was thus the fetish, which, incidentally, [the patient] endowed at will with the luminous shine which was not perceptible to others'.

236. TPP, p. 411.

237. Torquato Tasso, *Opere*, ed. by Bortolo Tommaso Sozzi, 2 vols. (Turin: Utet, 1964), II, 161–67. *Amor fuggitivo* is absent from all editions of the *Aminta* published during the author's lifetime, with the exception of the Baldiniana edition of 1581, and later appears in a 1622 posthumous edition of the pastoral fable: see p. 161. In the *Discorso sopra Mosco*, Leopardi also mentions Tasso's poem (TPP, p. 410).

238. André Jolles-Aby Warburg, 'Fragment on the *Nympha*', quoted in *Aby Warburg: An Intellectual Biography*, by Ernst Gombrich, p. 107.

239. Ibid., pp. 107–08.

240. Ibid., p. 124.

241. Wilhelm Jensen, *Gradiva: A Pompeian Fancy* (1903), in *Delusion and Dream: An Interpretation in the Light of Psychoanalysis of 'Gradiva', a Novel, by Wilhelm Jensen*, by Sigmund Freud, transl. by Helen M. Downey (New York: Moffat, Yard & Co., 1917), pp. 3–125 (pp. 3–5); Sigmund Freud, *Der Wahn und die Träume in W. Jensens 'Gradiva' mit dem Text der Erzählung von Wilhelm Jensen*, ed. by Bernd Urban and Johannes Cremerius (Frankfurt am Main: Fischer, 1986), pp. 23–24.

242. Didi-Huberman, 'The Imaginary Breeze', p. 284.

243. Ibid., p. 285.

244. Ibid., p. 286.

245. Agamben, 'Nymphs', p. 65; on Warburg and Domenico da Piacenza, see pp. 63–65.

246. Didi-Huberman, 'The Imaginary Breeze', p. 286.

247. Leopardi, 'All'Italia', l. 92.

248. Ibid., l. 93.

249. Ibid., ll. 94–95.

250. See Fedi, *Mausolei di sabbia*, pp. 102–17, for a close discussion of the iconographic models of this poem.

251. Didi-Huberman, *L'Image survivante*, p. 344.

252. Carlo Ginzburg, 'Bones and Skin', in *Ecstasies*, by Carlo Ginzburg, pp. 226–95 (p. 230).

253. Jensen, *Gradiva*, p. 103; Freud, *Der Wahn und die Träume in W. Jensens 'Gradiva'*, p. 77.

254. Leopardi, 'A Silvia', ll. 61–63.

255. D'Intino, *L'immagine della voce*, p. 172 note, and 'I misteri di Silvia', pp. 270–72.

256. Leopardi, 'Canto notturno', l. 99.

257. Guido Ceronetti, 'Intatta luna', *Belfagor*, 25 (1970), 97–103 (p. 99).

258. Porfirio, *Sui simulacri*, pp. 70–71.

259. Roberto Deidier, introduction to *Persefone: Variazioni sul mito*, ed. by Roberto Deidier (Venice: Marsilio, 2010), pp. 7–33 (p. 13).

260. Claudian, 'Rape of Proserpine', in *Claudian*, ed. and transl. by Maurice Platnauer, 2 vols. (London: Heinemann, 1922), II, 292–377 (p. 363).

261. Didi-Huberman, *L'Image survivante*, p. 244.

262. On Leopardi and the *Phaedrus*, see D'Intino, *L'immagine della voce*, pp. 28–32, and Brozzi, 'I demoni di Leopardi', p. 456, and, in general, the whole essay for the notion of demonic enthusiasm in Leopardi's oeuvre. According to Sebastiano Timpanaro (*La filologia di Giacomo Leopardi* (Bari: Laterza, 1997), pp. 102–03), Leopardi would have read the *Phaedrus* for the first time in 1823, but the connection with the passage on Anacreon of 1818 may allow us to backdate this experience. In the Recanati library, Leopardi had a Latin edition of Plato's works by Marsilio Ficino published in Lyon in 1590.

263. Plato, *Euthyphro, Apology, Crito, Phaedo, Phaedrus*, ed. and transl. by Harold North Fowler (London: Heinemann, 1913), pp. 418–19 (229b).

264. Ibid., pp. 422–23 (230b–c).

265. Ibid., pp. 446–47 (238c–d): Fowler translates νυμφόληπτος as 'in a frenzy'.

CHAPTER 2

Melancholy

'La crainte de l'effondrement est la crainte d'un effondrement qui a été déjà éprouvé (*primitive agony*) [...] et il y a des moments où un patient a besoin qu'on lui dise que l'effondrement, dont la crainte mine sa vie, a déjà eu lieu'. De même, semble-t-il, pour l'angoisse d'amour: elle est la crainte d'un deuil qui a déjà eu lieu, dès l'origine de l'amour. Du moment que j'ai été ravi, il faudrait que quelqu'un puisse me dire, 'Ne soyez plus angoissé, vous l'avez déjà perdu(e)'.

['The clinical fear of breakdown is the fear of a breakdown which has already been experienced (*primitive agony*) [...] and there are moments when a patient needs to be told that the breakdown, fear of which is wrecking his life, has already occurred'. Similarly, it seems, for the lover's anxiety: it is the fear of a mourning which has already occurred, at the very origin of love, from the moment when I was first 'ravished'. Someone would have to be able to tell me, 'Don't be anxious any more — you've already lost him/her'.]

ROLAND BARTHES, *Fragments d'un discours amoureux*, 'Agony',
translated by R. Howard

The Noonday Demon

A British poet who has gone into voluntary exile in Majorca realizes, while finalizing his attempt to carve a 'historical grammar of poetic myth', that every discourse on mythology must necessarily confront the legacy of Socrates. The introduction to Robert Graves's second edition of *The White Goddess* challenges with a discreet amount of irony the quick liquidation of myth operated by the Greek philosopher in the *Phaedrus*. There would be no point, Socrates argues, in speculating about the fate of the girl Orithya, whether she was kidnapped by Boreas, or simply fell from a cliff because of a gust of northern wind, later personified as such by popular imagination; or where it happened, or when. This would be 'the province of a very curious, painstaking, and not very happy man', who, after having solved this riddle, should then plunge into such problems as 'the form of the Hippocentaurs, and then as [...] that of the Chimaera'; unavoidably, Socrates continues, 'there [would] pou[r] in upon him a crowd of similar monsters, Gorgons and Pegasus, and other monstrous creatures, incredible in number and absurdity'.[1] Socrates has instead 'no leisure at all for such matters', and this is because he is not yet able to know himself, following the precept of the Delphic oracle: 'it appears to me', he concludes, 'to be ridiculous, while I am still ignorant of this, to busy myself about matters that do not concern me'.[2]

For Graves, Socrates's statement conceals, however, a secret fascination for the very object it refuses. 'Myths', he writes, 'frightened or offended him'; his 'petulant tone' testifies, however, to the fact that 'he had spent a long time worrying about the Chimaera, the horse-centaurs and the rest', but had decided to repress the charm they possessed upon him 'because he was no poet and mistrusted poets, and because [...] he was a confirmed townsman who seldom visited the countryside'.[3] Moreover, Graves explains, 'though "a very curious and painstaking person" I cannot agree that I am any less happy than Socrates was, or that I have more leisure than he had, or that an understanding of the language of myth is irrelevant to self-knowledge'.[4]

Like Nietzsche had done a few decades before, Graves turns therefore to Socrates in order to individuate the remotest origins of the fissure that has been established between λόγος and μῦθος, as well as between philosophy and poetry, and between critical analysis and illusion.[5] The dialogue between Socrates and Phaedrus stages this discordance in a theatrical fashion. Socrates, as we have seen, is about to be possessed by the nymphs in the stillness of noonday; he deliberately chooses to turn to dialogical speculations, but, in the end, he feels obliged to pay his duty to the very divinities of poetry and possession that he mistrusts. Hence the prayer he addresses to the nymphs of the sacred country place. By such means, apparently, Socrates manages to escape from the charming fascination of noonday.

What is the risk that Socrates fears? Giorgio Agamben, who — although from a different perspective than that of Graves — devotes his 1977 book *Stanzas* to recomposing the discord between poetry and critical-philological disciplines,[6] evokes the 'scourge' known through the Middle Ages under the various names of '*Acedia* (sloth), *tristitia* (sorrow), *tædium vitæ* (weariness, loathing of life), and *desidia* (idleness)'.[7] This constellation, corresponding to the medical symptomatology of melancholy as described since antiquity, and which also leaves persistent traces in Freud's 1917 essay 'Mourning and Melancholia', is traditionally connected with noonday, and corresponds to the creature known by patrology as 'the noonday demon' (*demonius meridianus*). This definition comes from the Bible, and more precisely from Psalm 90:5–6, '[non timebis] A sagitta volante in die a negotio | perambulante in tenebris ab incursu et dæmonio meridiano' [you shall not be afraid for the arrow that flies by day, for the pestilence that walks in the darkness and for the demon that wastes at noonday]. Notwithstanding the Biblical reference, however, the noonday demon of medieval authors is a survival of archaic Greek lore, and Agamben points out that, according to Erwin Rohde, a friend of Nietzsche and the author of *Psyche* (1890–94), it can be considered as 'a reincarnation of Empusa, one of the ogress figures in the spectral retinue of Hecate, which appears, in fact, at noon'.[8] The nympholepsy that is about to seize Socrates the philosopher on the banks of the Ilissos comes close to this haunting retinue of nymph-like and demonic creatures, chased away through the recourse to scientific thinking. Dismissing the inspiration provided by the nymphs means dispelling myth, possession, and the poetic frenzy inspired by gods (θεῖα μανία) as forms of knowledge, which is the most compelling prerequisite for the new, rational subject theorized by Socrates.

The temptation feared by medieval monks and hermits belongs to a similar constellation. The subject dominated by the melancholy humour, as medieval and

Renaissance sources agree, is unstable, temperamental, and dismal; he is inclined to vain and changeable desires, and is first and foremost unable to fix his thoughts on a single object, as is required by prayer, meditation, and scientific thinking. Nympholepsy and melancholy share thus a common feature: possessed subjects (both states are perceived as external forces that seize the human mind in moments of weakness and distraction) cannot focus their thought, which rather takes erratic and vague routes. This is why 'an ancient tradition associated the exercise of poetry, philosophy, and the arts with this most wretched of all humors'.[9] It is no surprise that Nietzsche's attempt of defining a new figure of 'philologist-poet', at the chronological height of the *Birth of Tragedy* and of the *Untimely Meditations*, must needs confront Socrates's refusal of poetry, nor that the activity of the so-called 'Basel Circle' (*der Baseler Kreis*) — namely, those scholars working in late nineteenth-century Basel, such as Nietzsche, Rohde, Johann Jakob Bachofen, and Jacob Burckhardt — goes in the direction of a re-evaluation of the Greek irrational, through an analysis of myth and of the attention paid to pre-classical and pre-Socratic aspects of Greek civilization, an approach that will also prove itself to be seminal for Freud's understanding and use of ancient myths.[10]

Leopardi devotes to the noonday demon the seventh chapter of his 1815 *Saggio sopra gli errori popolari degli antichi* [Essay on the Popular Errors of the Ancients]: interestingly, this erudite work of the young Leopardi is the only reference provided by Agamben for a definition of this phenomenon.[11] Leopardi's overview of classical sources concerning the demon is philologically exhaustive, and particularly telling as it comes from an author who often describes himself, and is described, as affected by melancholy,[12] and by a deep fascination for the charming laziness of noonday.[13]

A point raised by Socrates in the *Phaedrus* sounds particularly meaningful in understanding and problematizing the impact of melancholy and of the classical notion of poetic frenzy on Leopardi's oeuvre. To what extent does nympholepsy — intending by such a term a constellation of melancholy humour, dithyrambic speech, and inclination to reverie — represent an obstacle to the construction of subjectivity underlying the self-knowledge claimed by Socrates as the principal goal of philosophy? The Delphic oracle's precept, Socrates reminds us, suggests one know one's self before undertaking any other speculative endeavour. Still, as Roberto Calasso writes, Greek thought contemplates a form of knowledge that does not stem from rational self-inquiry, but rather from divine or demonic possession.[14] The possession operated by the nymphs is characterized by the irruption of a form of alterity that produces a different kind of knowledge, working through frenzy and uncontrolled speech and identified by Aristotle with πάθος.[15] The self-knowledge brought by the nymphs belongs thus to an entirely different sphere from that of Socrates's rationalism, by determining an alogical and emotional form of introspection made of πάθος, or, to speak in Leopardi's terms, of 'feeling' (*sentimento*) and 'remembrance' (*rimembranza*).[16] As such, nympholepsy happens also to affect the way the subject narrativizes itself — in other words, the way one writes about one's self, a practice commonly labelled as *autobiography*.

Leopardi's relationship with the autobiographic genre is a peculiarly ambivalent one. Leopardi conceives from a very early stage the project of writing an autobiographical novel, a genre to which he was attracted after reading two such seminal works of European pre-Romanticism as Goethe's *Werther* and Ugo Foscolo's *Ultime lettere di Jacopo Ortis* [Last Letters of Jacopo Ortis], published in various forms between 1798 and 1817.[17] This project is variously concretized, over the course of years, through several drafts, sharing as a common feature the attempt to portray the 'story of a soul', as Leopardi synthesizes in the previously mentioned letter to Pietro Colletta of March 1829.[18]

From the beginning, although these works generally remain as drafts, Leopardi's autobiographism displays three immediately evident characteristics: an almost totally inner development of narrative action, by which external events are usually made absent or irrelevant; the central position assumed by the main character's subjective perspective; and the retroactive point of view, which lets narration follow the rhythms of memory rather than those of the diachronic development of events. In other words, Leopardi's autobiographical subject is characterized by performing an almost uninterrupted monologue that suppresses every logical and temporal connection, which is also one of the reasons why, Alessandro Carrera argues, Leopardi is overall incapable of writing a novel: Leopardi's *Bildungsroman*, he points out, does not involve any other figures or voices than Leopardi himself.[19] The comparison with Stendhal proposed by Franco D'Intino is, from this angle, extremely interesting: whereas the novelist's writing implies a plural, social, and empathic experience of the world, whose knowledge is propaedeutic to the novel's polyphony, Leopardi's self-seclusion and its neurotic manifestations — such as both the graphic and orthographic perfection of the written page — signal a centrality of subjective perspective that excludes any other point of view, and therefore any possibility of narrating other experiences.[20] As has often been noted, and most recently by Luigi Blasucci[21] and Alberto Folin,[22] 'Le ricordanze' is the final accomplishment of this project of writing the 'story of a soul': the floating superimposition of images and recollections in the poem of 1829 individuates in a structure detached from every logical progression, as we will see, the most suitable genre for articulating the subject's self-narratization. By excluding the ordered and teleological orientation of prosaic autobiography, 'Le ricordanze' aims to reproduce mimetically the mechanisms of involuntary memory, and to portray a split subjectivity which is literally possessed by the irruption of a haunting past. The cantos of 1828–29 definitely fix Leopardi's autobiographical discourse in the dimension of poetic speech, conceived and composed for the subject's sake only:

> Uno de' maggiori frutti che io mi propongo e spero da' miei versi, è [...] di assaporarli [nella mia vecchiezza], e provar qualche reliquia de' miei sentimenti passati, messa quivi entro, per conservarla e darle durata, quasi in deposito; è di commuover me stesso in rileggerli.[23]

> [One of the greatest fruits that I hope for and expect from my verses is [...] to savour them [in my old age] and to experience something that remains of my past feelings, placed there so it might be kept and last through time, as though in store. It is to move myself as I reread them.]

Thus, the mnestic experience of 1828–29 re-activates a pre-Socratic modality of subjective self-inquiry, in which the spheres of μῦθος and λόγος are not yet disjointed, nor is the dithyrambic speech determined by the noonday demon's possession alien to a certain kind of self-knowledge. By re-polarizing and condensing into the dimension of poetry the reflection developed in the prosaic writing of the preceding years — from the erudite writings of youth to the *Operette morali*, and through the *Zibaldone* — the experience of nympholepsy underlying the cantos of these years happens to recompose the fracture between philosophy and poetry, that is to say, in the words of Giorgio Agamben, 'the very schizophrenia of Western culture'.[24]

The way Leopardi re-stages the conflict between μῦθος and λόγος, enacting a regression to a poetic and melancholy monologism questioning the logical linearity of prosaic autobiography, may also echo a specific mechanism, outlined by contemporary psychoanalytical theory. In fact, several features of Leopardi's autobiographism — centrality of the subject, exclusion of the external world, choice of a centrifugal and fragmented form of writing, melancholy disposition of mind — could be interpreted as the outcomes of an unresolved relationship with the symbolic order in the Lacanian sense, bearing significant consequences in terms of construction of subjectivity and the way it articulates and narrativizes itself. As we will see, Julia Kristeva's analysis of melancholy individuates the roots of melancholy and depressive drives in the subject being stuck in a pre-symbolic (which we may also label as *mythical*) stage, at the threshold between the attachment with the nursing body — the original, lost state termed 'the Thing' — and the irruption of the paternal (and Socratic) λόγος by which it is made to enter into the symbolic order, driving the subject towards abstraction and rational thinking, and towards a modality of signification rooted in fixed relationships between signifier and signified.[25] Thus, following the theory of language developed by Kristeva in her *La Révolution du langage poétique* of 1974,[26] we can interpret Leopardi's turning to a poetic form of autobiography as the re-emergence of the 'semiotic' sphere that, for Kristeva, precedes the symbolic one, and 'which designates', as Sara Fortuna and Manuele Gragnolati synthesize, 'a pre- or proto-linguistic mode of signification that takes place in the body':

> Kristeva associates the *semiotic* with the intermediate condition that in *Timæus* Plato calls the '*chora*'. [...] Kristeva characterizes *chora* as the form of multiple signification expressed in vocal and rhythmic motility that precedes and underlies adult verbal language. Although Kristeva claims that the semiotic *chora* is lost in the symbolic order of adult verbal language, [...] she argues that a form of poetic praxis can subvert this order at all its levels (morpho-syntactic, semantic, and phonologic) and let the *semiotic* re-emerge.[27]

The progressive re-emergence of the semiotic *chora* is not diachronically linear in the autobiographical experiments undertaken by Leopardi in the course of his oeuvre, and demonstrates, in particular, two significant exceptions. On the one hand, there are the fragments of the *Zibaldone* later indexed under the label 'Memorie della mia vita' [Memoirs of my Life]. These are generally passages which, while moving away from autobiographical anecdotes, result in considerations on human nature as a whole, and which can therefore be considered as experiments in self-knowledge in a Socratic sense, attempting a negotiation — to speak in Kristeva's terms —

with the symbolic order. On the other hand, such texts as the *Memorie del primo amore* (1817) [Memoirs of the First Love] and the *Storia di un'anima scritta da Giulio Rivalta* (c. 1825) [Story of a Soul Written by Giulio Rivalta][28] are intermittent and rhapsodic attempts aimed at crystallizing the autobiographical discourse in a more traditional form, and, particularly in the second case, at moving from a fragmentary and drafted writing to more established editorial conventions.[29] From the first manifestations of Leopardi's autobiographism to its end, however, the specificity of those cases in which an apparently chaotic fragmentation has taken the upper hand over logical order seems to be associated with moments of peculiar tension in writing, which even reverberates into the material aspects of the manuscripts. In the draft of the *Vita abbozzata di Silvio Sarno*, writing is continuous, dense, without any punctuation except for a few isolated commas; almost completed in haste, and in a very short while — about three months in the Spring of 1819 — the manuscript of *Silvio Sarno* seems to testify to the attempt of grasping an isolated and very private moment of writing *jouissance*.[30] The external aspect of the *Silvio Sarno* draft is even more surprising if we consider Leopardi's spasmodic and paroxysmal care for graphic neatness, and may evoke two writing practices that seem to be strictly interconnected, given also the fact that both have nineteenth-century roots. Both the automatic writing of Spiritualism (with its literary repercussions, from Rimbaud and Lautréamont to the French Surrealists, namely in the course of what Kristeva labels the 'revolution in poetic language') and Freud's method of free association, developed in the course of his analysis of hysterical patients in the 1890s, attempt to unchain language from logic and diachronic connections in order to allow the eruption of alterity, be it a supernatural one or the arousal of the unconscious.[31] Equally, in 'Le ricordanze' — exactly ten years later — Leopardi adopts a strategy of composition that is remarkably different from that of his previous poetic works. The manuscript of the poem gives a strong impression of immediacy. The stanzas (which Luigi Blasucci vaguely defines as 'lasse', thus stressing the indeterminacy of this poem with respect to the conventional metric rules of Italian literary tradition)[32] are already defined in the hand-written draft. Moreover, for the first time in the laboratory of the *Canti*, variants are not sketched in the margins of the page, but are incorporated directly into the text within brackets, so as to suggest a more fluid process of composition, grounded in semantic associations and affinities in sound, which deliberately accepts fragmentariness and disconnection as its dimension.[33]

The time-span between *Silvio Sarno* and 'Le ricordanze' shows how the return to a form of automatic writing is not grounded in a pre-conceived project, but rather in the final acknowledgment, determined by the mnestic experience that forms the backbone of the poems of 1828–29, that no other discourse about the self is any longer possible, and that the self-representation of subjectivity can only be given by means of poetry and by freeing speech from the boundaries of prosaic autobiographism. From this angle, Kristeva's notion of semiotic *chora* can also be helpful in understanding the principal innovation in poetry adopted by Leopardi between Pisa and Recanati at the end of the 1820s. Since the first canzoni, 'All'Italia' and 'Sopra il monumento di Dante', Leopardi's poetic parabola can be seen as a struggle with the metric conventions of literary tradition, concretized into manifold experiments, and finally finding its most suitable dimension in the so-called *canzone libera*, arguably borrowed from the Arcadia poets explored in 1818. The *canzone libera* is made of hendecasyllables and *settenari* alternated without a pre-fixed structure, and constitutes the very personal metric scheme adopted by Leopardi from the 'canti pisano-recanatesi' onwards. Somehow, the tension towards the *canzone libera* can thus be seen as a progressive shifting from the 'symbolic' dimension of established literary conventions to the 'semiotic' subversion of that same tradition through a metric structure that is aimed at rendering the scattered dimension of mnestic and emotional associations, a pattern that Kristeva identifies, in the transition from nineteenth-century Romanticisms to twentieth-century avant-gardes, as the progressive establishment of the poetic text as a 'semiotic device' (*dispositif sémiotique*).[34] Not accidentally, alongside the so-called 'grandi idilli' [great idylls] of 1828–29 that are grouped together in the *Canti* ('A Silvia', 'Le ricordanze', 'Canto notturno', 'La quiete dopo la tempesta', and 'Il sabato del villaggio'), the other two examples of 'canzone libera' placed elsewhere in the collection are two poems that are directly connected, as we will see, with the tradition of melancholy humour conveyed to Leopardi by medieval and Renaissance sources, 'Alla sua Donna' [To His Lady], the hymn of 1823 that challenges the courtly notion of the object of desire as an image (*imago*) and a phantasm (*fantasma*) beholden by the melancholy speculation of the idolatrous lover, and 'Il passero solitario' [The Solitary Thrush] (date uncertain, but plausibly composed after 1828), being the allegorical portrayal of the fissure that has originally separated the melancholy subject from human collectivity.

Moreover, Leopardi's poetic research constantly tends toward a recuperation of the physical dimension that, for him, used to characterize archaic epic poetry, determining an empathic adhesion of audiences through the magical enchantment of musical and rhythmic patterns, concretizing itself into corporeal responses.[35] Ancient audiences would differ from modern readers in that they used to physically and mimetically identify themselves with the 'passions' evoked by the bard's voice. This fissure would be rooted in Socrates's (or, better, Plato's) mistrust for poetry as expressed in the *Republic*, which, as D'Intino synthesizes, concerns the very form of poetical communication: Plato's philosophy evaluates critical detachment over empathic and physical transport, analysis over (prose) μίμησις, writing over poetic speech.[36] Thus, in a long fragment drafted in the *Zibaldone* in January 1829, Leopardi hypothesizes an archaic phase of Greek literature in which language still preserved the features of its earlier oral stage, such as irregularities and inconsistencies in terms of orthography, syntax, and grammar, later normalized by the intervention of those grammarians that he names (with a term borrowed from Sanskrit philology) 'diascheuasti'. This original shape of Greek literature can now only be suggested by isolated and scarce examples, such as Democritus's fragments, in which:

> Una stessa cosa si ripete in uno stesso periodo, non vi è quasi sintassi, parole necessarie, ed intere frasi o periodi, si omettono e sottintendono, l'un membro del periodo non ha corrispondenza coll'altro, il discorso procede p. via di quelle forme che i greci chiamano anacoluti [...], cioè *inconseguenti*, che è quanto dire senza forme.[37]

[One and the same thing is repeated in the same sentence; there is hardly any syntax; essential words and entire phrases and sentences are omitted and implied; one part of the sentence does not agree with another; the discourse proceeds by way of those forms which the Greeks call anacolutha [...], i.e., *non-sequiturs* which is the same as saying without form.]

A transition is here narratized at multiple levels, from corporeality to intellectual speculation, from grammatical irregularity to normativity, and from poetry to philosophy. This transition invests the erasure of ancient epic poetry by Socrates's choice for dialectics and critical analysis, but is at the same time interiorized within the subject's individual experience, as the *Zibaldone* makes explicitly clear:

Nella carriera poetica il mio spirito ha percorso lo stesso stadio che lo spirito umano in generale. Da principio il mio forte era la fantasia, e i miei versi erano pieni d'immagini [...]. Io era bensì sensibilissimo anche agli affetti, ma esprimerli in poesia non sapeva. Non aveva ancora meditato intorno alle cose, e della filosofia non avea che un barlume [...]. Sono stato sempre sventurato, ma le mie sventure d'allora erano piene di vita [...]. In somma il mio stato era allora in tutto e per tutto come quello degli antichi. [...] La mutazione totale in me, e il passaggio dallo stato antico al moderno, seguì si può dire dentro un anno, cioè nel 1819, dove [...] cominciai ad abbandonar la speranza, a riflettere profondamente sopra le cose [...], a divenir filosofo di professione (di poeta ch'io era), a sentire l'infelicità certa del mondo, in luogo di conoscerla, e questo anche per uno stato di languore corporale, che tanto più mi allontanava dagli antichi e mi avvicinava ai moderni. Allora l'immaginazione in me fu sommamente infiacchita, e quantunque la facoltà dell'invenzione allora appunto crescesse in me grandemente, anzi quasi cominciasse, verteva però principalmente, o sopra affari di prosa, o sopra poesie sentimentali. E s'io mi metteva a far versi, le immagini mi venivano a sommo stento, anzi la fantasia era quasi disseccata [...]. Così si può ben dire che in rigor di termini, poeti non erano se non gli antichi, e non sono ora se non i fanciulli, o giovanetti, e i moderni che hanno questo nome, non sono altro che filosofi.[38]

[In its poetic career, my spirit has followed the same course as the human spirit in general. At the beginning, my strength lay in fantasy, and my verses were full of images [...]. I was indeed very sensitive to feelings, too, but I did not know how to express them in poetry. I had not yet meditated on things, and as for philosophy, I had only the merest glimmer [...]. I have always been unfortunate, but my misfortunes at that time were full of life [...]. In short, my condition then was exactly the same as the ancients. [...] The total transformation that took place in me, my passing from ancient to modern, happened, you might say, in the space of a single year, that is, in 1819, when [...] I began to abandon hope, to reflect deeply on things [...], to become a professional philosopher (instead of the poet I was before), to feel the incontrovertible unhappiness of the world, rather than knowing about it, in part also because of a state of bodily languor, which removed me even further from the ancients and brought me close to the moderns. At that point, imagination in me was greatly enfeebled, and although the faculty of invention grew in me enormously, indeed that was almost its beginning, it was mainly directed either to works in prose or to sentimental poems. And if I set to writing verse, images came to me with the greatest difficulty, indeed my imagination had almost dried up [...]. So, we could well say that, strictly speaking, the only poets were the ancients, and the only ones now are children, or young people, while the moderns who go by the name of poets are really philosophers.]

The fact that Leopardi is speaking about the transition from orality to writing, and from grammatical irregularity to fixed norms, is quite telling when we consider the humanist tradition in which Leopardi's intellectual experience is fully inserted. In a book of 2003, Gary Cestaro analyzes how Dante, in accordance with 'the larger collective imagination of his day', precisely narrativizes the exile from the sphere of the maternal (or of the nurse's) breast into the paternal one of discipline and normalization as a transition from lallation to grammatical regularity, a both real and symbolic fracture that only the extinction of language in the final vision of *Paradiso* will heal, by making the subject return to a baby-like form of speech. Medieval grammar schools, characterized by the omnipervasive presence of the *magister* as a model of authority, symbolize for Dante the abandonment of the nursing body and the entrance into a masculine mode of signification:

> The adolescent must leave behind childhood desires and submit to paternal discipline, just as earlier the infant had first seized upon, but then turned away from, the breast, as soon as the first glimmer of reason appeared [...]. The symbolic father-*magister* stands at the opposite pole from the mother's body, whose lacteal flow spells peril.[39]

No different are the manifold transitions portrayed by Leopardi, as an heir of the same humanistic tradition, throughout his oeuvre, always opposing an original and 'maternal' moment of freewheeling imagination, multiple and inconstant desires, corporeal strength, to a later and 'paternal' one characterized by disenchantment, rigorous thinking, intellectualism, and physical weakness. In the same way, grammatical normalization becomes the emblem of an exile from an original state of grace in which children and ancients are homologized, so that the problem, for Leopardi, is whether and how this ancient *and* infantile disposition of mind can be retrieved — regaining Paradise, we may say, after and notwithstanding the Fall, and moreover after having been deprived of Dante's theological and religious apparatus. Leopardi's answer is that the venue for this operation to be undertaken is the praxis of modern lyric poetry. A fragment of the *Zibaldone* drafted between 29 and 30 March of 1829, states that lyric is the only form of poetry left to moderns, through which they can paradoxically attain a 'primitive' effect:

> Da queste osservaz. risulterebbe che dei 3 generi principali di poesia, il solo che veram. resti ai moderni, fosse il lirico; (e forse il fatto e l'esperienza de' poeti moderni lo proverebbe); genere, siccome primo di tempo, così eterno ed universale, cioè proprio dell'uomo perpetuam. in ogni tempo ed in ogni luogo, come la poesia; la quale consistè da principio in questo genere solo, e la cui essenza sta sempre principalm. in esso genere, che quasi si confonde con lei, ed è il più veram. poetico di tutte le poesie, le quali non sono poesie se non in quanto son liriche. [...] Ed anco in questa circostanza di non aver poesia se non lirica, l'età nostra si riavvicina alla primitiva.[40]

> [The outcome of these observations would seem to be that, of the 3 main kinds of poetry, the only one that truly remains to the moderns is the lyric; (and perhaps what is done and experienced by modern poets would be evidence); the

genre which, as it was the first in time, so it is proper to mankind in perpetuity, in every time and every place, like poetry itself; which from the beginning consisted in this genre alone, one that is almost indisguishable from it, and is the most truly poetic of all kinds of poetry, which are not poetry, except insofar as they are lyrical. [...] And also in this situation of having only lyric poetry, our age is moving closer to primitive times.]

The 'canzone libera' is the peculiar shape that this absolutely modern, and at the same time most ancient, poetic genre takes within Leopardi's oeuvre. As such, it must confront the anxiety of influence represented by Petrarch, whose *Canzoniere* had been the most influential model for the Italian, but also European, lyrical canon: through the 'canzone libera', Leopardi inserts his work within the conventions of Petrarchist tradition, at the same time subverting them in metric, lexical, and thematic aspects. Moreover, Petrarch must be challenged in that the *Canzoniere* constitutes an inescapable paragon of self-narratization. As Nicola Gardini argues, Dante's *Vita nova* and the *Canzoniere* respectively provide the twentieth-century Italian literary canon with two models of poetic book: the 'psychological novel' and the 'psychoanalytic monologue'.[41] From his pre-Freudian perspective, Leopardi employs the *Canzoniere* as a model for interrogating the Ego's mutability, the tensions it engenders with time and history, and its mnestic processes, by means of fragmentariness.[42] Leopardi's recuperation of Petrarch is far more meaningful if we consider how the *Canzoniere* had constructed a form of post-medieval subjectivity that had survived in European literary tradition up to the eighteenth century. We can therefore say that Leopardi's confrontation with Petrarch takes place when that very same subjectivity is questioned by the post-Enlightenment fracture, and the Ego discovers itself to be no longer 'master in its own house'.[43] This defamiliarization and splitting of modern subjectivity is interrogated in the nineteenth century by going back to the foundational texts of Western authorship — *Confessiones*, *Vita Nova*, *Canzoniere*: Leopardi employs therefore Petrarch's vernacular poetry as a flexible structure, in which to frame and articulate those very tensions of the modern subject later to be explored by psychoanalysis as a discursive practice.[44]

Through his several experiments of autobiographical narration, Leopardi meaningfully repudiates Petrarch's lyric poetry while drafting the *Memorie del primo amore*, probably, as D'Intino notes, in order not to fall into affectation.[45] He recuperates this influence, however, while analyzing the Italian lyric canon in 1818 and while drafting *Silvio Sarno* in 1819. At this point, Petrarch's poetry is consciously employed as a model for Leopardi's prose, as far as its influence allows him to circumvent the threats of an excessively neat and accurate style, and the 'story of a soul' to bypass the cold descriptivism that uniquely prosaic paragons would inspire.[46] The fragmentariness of *Silvio Sarno* is thus only apparently 'Romantic': through a paradoxically anti-modern move, Leopardi roots his literary experiment in a post-medieval example of fragmentary narration of a soul's vicissitudes.[47] The discontinuous and floating rhythm of the *Canzoniere* reverberates into that of *Silvio Sarno*: both texts, indeed, require an oscillating and undulating reading process, in which returns, pauses, and echoes follow the same alinear structure of the processes of memory and desire.[48]

The confrontation with Petrarchist and courtly tradition allows Leopardi to represent an inner experience from which actuality is elided, and whose poetic vagueness, the meticulous care for affinities in sound, and the deconstruction of traditional metric forms consent to the unchaining of a different logic. By entangling the reader within a series of unexpected rhymes and timbric returns, Leopardi's *canzone libera* — from 'Alla sua Donna' to the 'Canto notturno di un pastore errante dell'Asia' — exploits the ambiguities of language in order to enact an almost incessant production of meaning. Thus, Leopardi questions the teleological orientation and chronological linearity of autobiographical narrations: the 'story of a soul' cannot be a 'history', but rather, speaking in Benjamin's terms, a 'memory', meaning by this term a form of writing in which the past is not reconstructed through a linear progression of events, but rather as a messianic revelation arising from the deflagration of disjointed and fragmentary images. As Georges Didi-Huberman points out, the fracture produced by Benjamin's thought in contemporary historiography stems from his replacing history with memory, since only memory can purify (*décanter*) the past from its exactness, thereby humanizing time through its 'essential impurity'.[49] The mnestic experience of 1828–29 enables Leopardi's writing to recompose the fracture between critical analysis and poetry, and his self-narration to attain that very melodious and 'dithyrambic' vagueness that had scared Socrates on the banks of the Ilissos. Unlike Socrates, however, through the parabola leading from *Silvio Sarno* to 'Le ricordanze', Leopardi comes to acknowledge that the possessed speech is not unrelated to self-knowledge, but rather allows a different (and more poetic) form of narrating one's self. If, as Agamben claims, 'psychoanalysis appears to have reached conclusions very similar to those intuited by the church fathers' as far as the knot between loss, mourning, melancholia, and speech is concerned,[50] Leopardi seems to have understood how the noonday demon, with its cohort of nymphs, can perhaps be the only way for the subject to re-access a pre-logical, pre-Socratic, and pre-symbolic sphere, in which the exactness of rational thinking is mitigated and humanized by regaining a domain labelled by psychoanalytical theory as the semiotic order, and by archaic Greek thought as possession. In all cases, the conscious acceptance of melancholy fantasizing allows writing to recuperate the empathic, corporeal, and emotional effects lost in the process of disenchantment, and to reproduce mimetically a 'time of the soul' that gives an account of its ambiguities, of its fragmentary nature, and of its umbrae.

The Woman (That) Does Not Exist

When talking about dreams, Leopardi seems often to refer to Petrarch's intertextual influence. Dream is intended here in a literal sense — namely, denoting the oneiric activity as it is commonly understood — but also as diurnal fantasy: daydream, in other words, thanks to an ambiguity that is present in most European languages (Italian: *sogno/sogno a occhi aperti*; French: *rêve/rêverie*), which, as we will see, forms the backbone of Freud's analysis of daydreaming (although in German *Traum* stems from a different etymology from *Phantasie*).

As we have seen, one of the most accomplished narrative cores of *Silvio Sarno* is the story of the protagonist's love games with a country girl named Teresa Brini. In relating these fleeting encounters in the streets of Recanati, Leopardi employs stylistic and thematic features borrowed from the Dolce Stil Novo and Petrarchan traditions, his main sources for the conventions and practices of medieval courtly love.[51] One episode relates a dream, experienced by the subject after the girl greets him in the street:

> Sogno di quella notte e mio vero paradiso in parlar con lei ed esserne interrogato e ascoltato con viso ridente e poi domandarle io la mano a baciare ed ella torcendo non so di che filo porgermela guardandomi con aria semplicissima e candidissima e io baciarla senza ardire di toccarla con tale diletto ch'io allora solo in sogno per la primissima volta provai che cosa sia questa sorta di consolazioni con tal verità che svegliatomi subito e riscosso pienamente vidi che il piacere era stato appunto quale sarebbe reale e vivo e restai attonito e conobbi come sia vero che tutta l'anima si possa trasfondere in un bacio e perder di vista tutto il mondo come allora proprio mi parve e svegliato errai un pezzo con questo pensiero e sonnecchiando e risvegliandomi a ogni momento rivedevo sempre l'istessa donna in mille forme ma sempre viva e vera ec. in somma il sogno mio fu tale e con sì vero diletto ch'io potea proprio dire col Petrarca In tante parti e sì bella la veggio *Che se l'error durasse altro non chieggio*.[52]

> [Dream of that night and real heaven for me in talking to her, and her asking me questions and listening to me with a joyful expression, and then me asking for her hand to kiss, and her, while pulling I don't know which string, lending her hand to me, looking at me with a most naive and chaste behaviour, and me kissing her hand without daring to touch her, and with such a delight that only then, in dreams, for the very first time I experienced what this kind of consolation is, with such an impression of truth that, having suddenly reawakened and fully rekindled, I saw that the pleasure had precisely been the way it would have been if it were true and vivid, and I was astonished, and I acknowledged how it is true that all the soul can be poured into a single kiss and lose sight of the entire world, in the way it seemed to me in that very moment, and when I was awake I wandered for a while with this thought, and while drowsing and waking up at every moment, I always saw that very woman in a thousand shapes, but always alive and true etc. In short, my dream was of such a kind, and of such delight, that I could truly repeat Petrarch's words: in many places I see her, so lovely *that all I ask is that my error last*.]

The quotation from Petrarch aims at stressing the choice for a form of love whose dimension is uniquely solipsistic: not by chance, as Nicola Gardini highlights, the choice of Petrarchism generally signals, within the Italian canon, the opting for a de-corporealized, cerebral, and anti-penetrative eroticism.[53] Leopardi describes an experience of dreaming that overlaps and replaces reality: not only is the physical enjoyment induced by the dream absolutely equal to the one granted by actual sexual intercourse ('vidi che il piacere era stato appunto quale sarebbe *reale e vivo*', my emphasis), but also the dream persists in producing its effects in full wakefulness, allowing the subject to see the object of desire as if it were actually present ('a ogni momento rivedevo sempre l'istessa donna in mille forme ma sempre *viva e vera*', my emphases).[54] In other words, the Brini episode confirms the philosophical position reached by Leopardi in late 1819 and symbolically sanctioned, through a lapidary aphorism, at the bottom of page 99 of the *Zibaldone*, just before starting the new, self-conscious structure of his intellectual journal with page 100: 'Pare un assurdo, e pure è esattamente vero che tutto il reale essendo un nulla, non v'è altro di reale nè altro di sostanza al mondo che le illusioni' [It seems absurd and yet it is absolutely true that, since all reality is nothing, there is no other reality or other substance in the world but illusions].

This position remains unchanged in Leopardi's reflections throughout the following years, at least until his decision to turn to the search for 'truth' ('il vero') announced in a letter to Giordani of 6 May 1825 and in the poetic epistle 'Al conte Carlo Pepoli' [To Count Carlo Pepoli], composed in March 1826.[55] At this stage, however, the main problem dominating Leopardi's inquiry is that of the actuality of illusions, and of the ways in which a fervent imagination can give them a concreteness, albeit provisional. The Brini episode confirms this theory, showing how oneiric fantasy can burst into everyday life in the form of daydreaming, without losing any of its pleasantly deceiving powers. This aspect is also present in the poem 'Il sogno' [The Dream], arguably inspired by the previously quoted passage of *Silvio Sarno*, in which the subject meets, in dreams, the 'simulacro' [image][56] of his dead beloved: once the dream is broken, the poem concludes, 'Ella negli occhi | Pur mi restava, e nell'incerto raggio | Del Sol vederla io mi credeva ancora' [But she was there in front of me, and in the sun's veiled light I kept on believing I could see her].[57] The two endings of the poem and of the Brini episode definitely take the side of illusion against reality, and through the very acknowledgment of its deceiving nature ('io mi credeva'; 'error'). Thus, both texts outline a process of desire that leaves aside its actual object — the woman — by rather being pivoted on the subject's wandering imagination, which is not only able to produce a 'simulacro' of the desired object in its absence, but *because* of this very absence.

Other than Petrarch, another intertextual source is at play here. In Torquato Tasso's dialogue *Il Messaggiero* [The Messenger], written in 1580 and variously re-elaborated until 1587, the protagonist converses with a 'spirito amoroso' [amorous spirit].[58] In the dialogue the protagonist and the spirit debate the same problem that lies at the core of Leopardi's reflection, namely whether diurnal imagination possesses the same strength and illusionary force of nocturnal dreams.[59] By quoting Petrarch, Virgil, Horace, and Dante, the protagonist argues about the existence of some mental alienation ('alienazione di mente'), suspended between actual disease ('infirmità di pazzia') and divine possession ('divino furore'): this 'alienation' would make the subject able to give provisional concreteness to unreal things in the same way as dreams ('è tale che può non meno rappresentar le cose false per vere di quell che faccia il sogno'), and can be perhaps identified with the 'excessive melancholy' ('soverchia maninconia') described by ancient sources. Melancholy is identified with an overabounding imagination ('fa[re] imagini e sogni infiniti'), which, unlike folly, does not lead to self-forgetting; it can lead to suicide, the protagonist continues, and sometimes to insanity ('pazzia'); still, it is often connected with a remarkable intelligence, so that melancholy subjects have often been excellent in philosophy, politics, and poetry ('sono stati di chiaro ingegno ne gli studi de la filosofia e nel governo de la republica e nel compor versi'), and even heroes have been haunted by melancholy ('gli eroi [...] sono infestati dal medesimo vizio').[60]

Even at a superficial glance, Tasso's description of the symptomatology of melancholy shows a remarkable similarity to the way in which Leopardi relates the Brini episode in *Silvio Sarno*. The subject's desires are changeable and contradictory, constantly shifting between exaltation and deception in a way that completely leaves aside actual facts; the 'furore' aroused by Brini's greeting is fully a form of *amor hereos*, in that it encompasses a compulsion to write ('mio innalzamento d'animo elettrizzamento furore e cose notate ne' pensieri'), a stimulus to heroic actions, and suicidal drives ('conobbi che l'amore mi avrebbe proprio eroificato e fatto capace di tutto e anche di uccidermi'). First and foremost, *Il Messaggiero* proves itself to be a strong influence on Leopardi's text in that it addresses the relationship between dream and fantasy, and outlines a definition of the melancholy disposition as a propensity to daydream and to the possession of an object of desire situated outside the domain of actuality. Interestingly, in answering the protagonist, the spirit quotes the very same lines from the *Rerum vulgarium fragmenta* cited by Leopardi,[61] in order to assert the temporary and fleeting effect of imagination: however strong fantasy can be, he says, 'l'error de la imaginazione non dura' [the imagination's mistake does not last for long],[62] hereby preluding his final explanation, in which he employs the neo-Platonic tradition to explain the influence of demons on the human mind.[63]

The influence of *Il Messaggiero* problematizes Leopardi's use of Petrarch in *Silvio Sarno*, in that the quotation from *RVF* CXXIX is, if we consider both sources, at least a double quotation — that is, from Petrarch, and from Tasso citing Petrarch. This ambiguity connects the conflict between dream and reality analyzed by Tasso to the problems of love and of the actuality of the object of desire raised by courtly tradition, and finally reverberates in the 'Dialogo di Torquato Tasso e del suo Genio familiare' [Dialogue of Torquato Tasso and his Guardian Spirit] of the *Operette morali*, written in 1824. This dialogue can be seen as Leopardi's very personal re-elaboration of *Il Messaggiero*, and one of the most accomplished analyses of the melancholy temperament attempted by Leopardi in his oeuvre. In a note to the dialogue, Leopardi explains how:

> Ebbe Torquato Tasso, pel tempo dell'infermità della sua mente, un'opinione simile a quella famosa di Socrate; cioè credette vedere di tratto in tratto uno spirito buono ed amico e avere con esso lui molti e lunghi ragionamenti. Così leggiamo nella vita del Tasso scritta dal Manso: il quale si trovò presente a uno di questi o colloqui o soliloqui che noi li vogliamo chiamare.[64]

> [Torquato Tasso, during the time of his infirmity of mind, had a conviction similar to that famous one of Socrates; that is, he thought that from time to time he saw a good and friendly spirit, and with him held many and lengthy conversations. This is what we read in the life of Tasso written by Manso, who happened to witness one of these dialogues, or monologues, if we prefer.]

Hence, the text portrays Tasso's split subjectivity, disguised as a dialogue between the subject, secluded in the Sant'Anna hospital in Ferrara, and a spirit that lives 'in qualche liquore generoso' [in some strong spirits].[65] Through his imaginary conversation,

Tasso comes to the conclusion that, every joy being expected or remembered, but never present, there is no substantial difference between being imprisoned or free: as the satisfaction of all desires can only take place in the imagination, the only possibility of *jouissance* is relegated to dreaming or daydreaming, or to a sort of alienation induced by alcohol or drugs. These considerations are particularly relevant as far as the problem of love is concerned:

> TASSO: Oh potess'io rivedere la mia Leonora. Ogni volta che ella mi torna alla mente, mi nasce un brivido di gioia, che dalla cima del capo mi si stende fino all'ultima punta dei piedi; e non resta in me nervo nè vena che non sia scossa. Talora, pensando a lei, mi si ravvivano nell'animo certe immagini e certi affetti, tali, che per quel poco tempo, mi par di essere ancora quello stesso Torquato che fui [...]. Io mi maraviglio che il pensiero di una donna abbia tanta forza, da rinnovarmi, per così dire, l'anima, e farmi dimenticare tante calamità. E se non fosse che io non ho più speranza di rivederla, crederei non avere ancora perduta la facoltà di essere felice.
> GENIO: Quale delle cose stimi che sia più dolce: vedere la donna amata, o pensarne?
> TASSO: Non so. Certo che quando mi era presente, ella mi pareva una donna; lontana, mi pareva e mi pare una dea. [...] Con tutto questo, io mi muoio dal desiderio di rivederla, e di riparlarle.
> GENIO: Via, questa notte in sogno io te la condurrò davanti: bella come la gioventù; e cortese in modo, che tu prenderai onore di favellarle molto più franco e spedito che non ti venne fatto mai per l'addietro: anzi all'ultimo le stringerai la mano; ed ella guardandoti fiso, ti metterà nell'animo una dolcezza tale, che tu ne sarai sopraffatto; e per tutto domani, qualunque volta ti sovverrà di questo sogno, ti sentirai ballare il cuore dalla tenerezza.
> TASSO: Gran conforto: un sogno in cambio del vero.[66]

[TASSO: O, if only I could see my Leonora again. Every time she comes to mind I feel a shudder of joy from the crown of my head to the very tips of my toes; and there is not a nerve or a vein in my body that is not shaken by it. Sometimes, when I think of her, such images and emotions are rekindled in my mind, that for a little while I feel once more the Torquato I used to be [...]. Indeed, I am astonished that the thought of a woman has such power to restore my soul, as it were, and make me forget so many calamities. And if it were not for the fact that I have no more hope of seeing her again, I would think I had not yet lost the ability to be happy. SPIRIT: Which of these things do you esteem the sweeter: to see your beloved woman, or to think about her? TASSO: I don't know. Certainly when she was with me she appeared to be a woman; but far away she seemed, and still seems, a goddess. [...] Despite all this, I am half dead with longing to see her again, and talk to her. SPIRIT: Well then, tonight in your dreams I will bring her before you; as beautiful as youth; and so gracious, that you will pluck up the courage to chat with her far more openly and fluently than you ever did in the past; indeed, in the end you will grasp her hand; and she will gaze at you, and put such sweetness in your soul, that you will be overcome by it; and all day tomorrow, every time you remember this dream, you will feel your heart leap with tenderness. TASSO: That's a great comfort: a dream in exchange for truth.]

This passage shows strong affinities with the Brini episode of *Silvio Sarno*. Here too, the dimension of dream is highly eroticized; moreover, the oneiric deception leaves persistent traces on the following day, in the same way as the dream of Teresa Brini had haunted the subject even in his diurnal imagination. In addition, another quotation from Petrarch is perhaps here at play, in this case the fourth line from *Rerum vulgarium fragmenta* CCCII. The Leonora appearing in dreams, 'beautiful as youth; and gracious', can arguably be seen as an afterimage of the dead Laura portrayed in Petrarch's poem as being 'più bella et meno altera' [more lovely, less proud] than she had been on earth:

> Levommi il mio penser in parte ov'era
> quella ch'io cerco, et non ritrovo in terra:
> ivi, fra lor che 'l terzo cerchio serra,
> la rividi più bella et meno altera.
> Per man mi prese, et disse: — In questa spera
> sarai anchor meco, se 'l desir non erra:
> i' so' colei che ti die' tanta guerra,
> et compie' mia giornata inanzi sera.
> Mio ben non cape in intelletto humano:
> te solo aspetto, et quel che tanto amasti
> e là giuso è rimaso, il mio bel velo.
> Deh perché tacque, et allargò la mano?
> Ch'al suon de' detti sí pietosi et casti
> poco mancò ch'io non rimasi in cielo.[67]

[My thought lifted me up to where she was, the one I seek and cannot find on earth; there among those enclosed in the third sphere she looked more lovely, less proud than before. She took my hand and said, 'Here in this sphere, desire unerring, you'll be with me again; I am the one who made you fight so hard and who ended my day before night came. My bliss no human mind can comprehend; I only wait for you and what you loved so much, and is down there, my lovely veil'. Ah, why did she stop speaking and drop my hand? For with the sound of words so kind and chaste I came quite close to never leaving Heaven.]

There is constant reference to this poem in Leopardi's oeuvre: as well as quoting it in a passage of the *Zibaldone* of 3 October 1821 as a particularly strong example of vagueness, Leopardi makes it the subject of one of his literary projects, probably drafted in the late 1810s or early 1820s. In this very short text, Leopardi establishes an opposition between the oneiric Laura, whose beauty and courtesy are revived by the satisfaction of desires granted by the dreamlike dimension, and the real Laura beheld by Petrarch, in the afterlife, appearing exactly as she had been in her mortal life:

> Incontro di Petrarca morto, con Laura p. la prima volta. Ella era la stessa *neanche più bella* di quel che fosse in terra, ma in nulla mutata. Anche l'accrescimento della bellezza pregiudica al sentimento e alla rimembranza, cosa non intesa dai nostri poeti, neppur dal Petrarca che disse: La rividi più bella e meno altera.[68]

[The dead Petrarch meeting Laura for the first time. She was the same one, *not even more beautiful* than she had been on earth, and had not changed at all. Even the increase in beauty jeopardizes feeling and remembrance, something not understood by our poets, including Petrarch, who said: She looked more lovely, less proud than before.]

In addressing the same issues about loss, mourning, the hereafter, and its relationships of continuity or metamorphosis with earthly life, this literary draft engenders a deviation from its source, which can be seen as a clue to the more general deviation which intervened between medieval and post-Enlightenment subjectivities in relation to the themes of death and memory. Petrarch portrays a mourning fantasy in which the subject witnesses the sublimated and transfigured retrieval of the lost object. The notion of sublimation should be intended in a double sense, denoting, on the one hand, a spatial displacement of the object from a downward to an upward dimension ('fra lor che 'l terzo cerchio serra'), and, on the other, its refinement in terms of beauty and courtesy ('più bella et meno altera'). By eliding the heavenly context, Leopardi displays instead an 'a-theologized' hereafter, whose nature shifts from the domain of metaphysics into that of aesthetics (the 'sentimento' and the 'rimembranza'), and which is situated in a position of substantial contiguity with earthly life.

Compared to this project, the dialogue between Tasso and the spirit undertakes a further manipulation of its source: unlike Laura, Leonora is the product of a dreamy imagination propitiated by melancholy and alcohol, and, what is more, her increase in beauty and grace makes this oneiric imagining far more pleasing than the actual woman. By echoing Petrarch's sonnet ('più bella'-'bella come la gioventù'; 'meno altera'- 'cortese in modo, che tu prenderai onore di favellarle molto più franco e spedito che non ti venne fatto mai per l'addietro'), the dialogue definitely chooses deception over reality, by outlining the process of love as a meditation on absence, and grounding desire in a solipsistic relationship between the melancholy subject and a purely mental image.

From this angle, the dialogue between Tasso and the spirit can be compared with the song-hymn 'Alla sua Donna', composed one year before, in 1823, and anticipated, as a sort of manifesto, by a letter in French that Leopardi sent to his Belgian friend André Jacopssen on 23 June of the same year.[69] In this letter, Leopardi states how his way of loving has never been that of 'les âmes vulgaires' [ordinary souls].[70] He has rather experienced a far more refined and deep form of enjoyment, which is however doomed by the fact of necessarily being fleeting and momentary ('un seul instant de ravissement et d'émotion profonde'): how would it be possible, Leopardi asks, to make this feeling last for longer ('que ce sentiment soit durable'), or to reproduce it at will ('qu'il se renouvelle souvent dans la vie')? His provisional answer follows the strictest clichés of the so-called courtly or Platonic love: the object of desire must not be physically approached, but only beheld in the imagination:

> Plusieurs fois j'ai évité pendant quelques jours de rencontrer l'objet qui m'avait charmé dans un songe délicieux. Je savais que ce charme aurait été détruit en s'approchant de la réalité. Cependant je pensais toujours à cet objet, mais je ne le considérais d'après ce qu'il était; je le contemplais dans mon imagination, tel qu'il m'avait paru dans mon songe. Était-ce une folie? suis-je romanesque? Vous en jugerez.

> [Several times I have avoided for several days meeting the object which had charmed me in a delightful dream. I knew that charm would have been

destroyed approaching the reality. Yet I thought continually of that object, but
I did not consider it as it was in itself; I contemplated it in my imagination, as
it had appeared to me in my dream. Was that a folly? Am I a romantic? You
be the judge.]

Up to this point, in other words, Leopardi conceptualizes love within the strictest
bonds of the tradition of courtly love, that 'highly refined way', to put it in Jacques
Lacan's terms, 'of making up for [*suppléer à*] the absence of the sexual relationship, by
feigning that we are the ones who erect an obstacle there too'.[71] The Lady (Teresa
Brini, the dead beloved of 'Il sogno', Leonora, the 'object' evoked in the letter to
Jacopssen) still exists, somewhere; at the same time, she is elided and avoided by the
'romanesque' subject who chooses, as the dialogue between Tasso and the Spirit
synthesizes, 'a dream in exchange for truth'.

In September 1823, Leopardi composes 'Alla sua Donna', which can be considered,
as Carrera remarks, a sort of poetic rewriting of the themes raised in the letter to
Jacopssen.[72] At the same time, the poem enacts a significant deviation from the
approach adopted in the letter, in a way that Leopardi formalizes as follows, in the
famous note written in 1824 for the first publication of the poem in the Milanese
magazine, *Nuovo ricoglitore*:

> La canzone che s'intitola *Alla sua Donna* [...] è la più breve di tutte, e forse
> la meno stravagante, eccettuato il soggetto. La donna, cioè l'innamorata,
> dell'autore, è una di quelle immagini, uno di quei fantasmi di bellezza e virtù
> celeste e ineffabile, che ci occorrono spesso alla fantasia, nel sonno e nella
> veglia, quando siamo poco più che fanciulli, e poi qualche rara volta nel sonno,
> o in una quasi alienazione di mente, quando siamo giovani. Infine, è *la donna
> che non si trova*. L'autore non sa se la sua donna (e così chiamandola, mostra di
> non amare altra che questa) sia mai nata finora, o debba mai nascere; sa che ora
> non vive in terra, e che noi non siamo suoi contemporanei; la cerca tra le idee
> di Platone, la cerca nella luna, nei pianeti del sistema solare, in quei de' sistemi
> delle stelle.[73]

> [The song entitled *To His Lady* [...] is the shortest, and maybe the least eccentric,
> of all, except for its subject. The lady, so to say the beloved of the author, is
> one of those images, one of those phantasms of celestial and ineffable beauty
> and virtue that often come to our fantasy, dreaming or awake, when we are a
> little more than children, and then, far less often, while dreaming or in a sort
> of mental alienation when we are young. In the end, she is *the lady that cannot be
> found*. The author does not know whether his lady (and by naming her as such
> he shows that he loves none other but her) has ever been born, or is to be born
> at all; he knows that she does not live on earth at present, and that we are not
> her contemporaries; he looks for her amidst Plato's ideas, he looks for her in the
> moon, in the planets of the solar system and in those of the stars.]

In this passage, Leopardi specifies again how the object of love is nothing but an
'image' and a 'phantasm', conjured by a melancholy disposition of mind.[74] The
note stresses how the communion with the Lady can only take place, exactly like
the evocation of Leonora in the dialogue between Tasso and the spirit, in such
states of regression from rational consciousness that pertain to the melancholy
subject as dream, diurnal fantasy, and the 'alienazione di mente' mentioned in *Il*

Messaggiero; this expression is literally re-evoked in the 'Elogio degli uccelli' [In Praise of Birds] of the *Operette morali*, written in the same year, 1824, as one of the ways men can re-access the lost world of illusions. The most important element of this note, however, is that it directly faces the courtly and Petrarchist tradition of love poetry in that it brings the problem of the object of love to its degree zero. Adelia Noferi highlights how 'Alla sua Donna' is symbiotically linked to Petrarch's intertextual memory, by reactivating both Petrarch's constitutive structures of the desiring process and the linguistic dimension — in rhythm, syntax, and vocabulary — through which desire is articulated; at the same time, she argues, Leopardi's operation repolarizes the Petrarchist tradition by stressing and bringing to its most extreme consequences the opposition between 'presence' and 'absence' left by the *Canzoniere* as a legacy to Western culture as a whole.[75] From this angle, Leopardi would constitute a significant turning-point in what Agamben terms the 'poetic process whose emblematic temporal extremes are Petrarch and Mallarmé', in which:

> The essential textual tension of Romance poetry [...] displac[es] its center from desire to mourning: Eros [...] yield[s] to Thanatos its impossible love object so as to recover it, through a subtle and funereal strategy, as lost object, and the poem [...] becom[es] the site of an absence yet nonetheless draws from this absence its specific authority.[76]

In particular, while speaking of 'Alla sua Donna', Luigi Blasucci notes that the poem recuperates a metrical and lexical Petrarchism with a double effect of sublimation and estrangement.[77] This peculiarity can be individuated, following Leopardi's note, in a tension between the conventionality of the poem from a structural angle ('maybe the least eccentric of all') and the eccentricity (*stravaganza*) of its subject, which evokes the lost and imagined, but always actual, woman of Petrarchist tradition while replacing her with a purely intellectual phantasm that is basically defined by means of negation — '*la donna che non si trova* [...] ora non vive in terra [...] noi non siamo suoi contemporanei'.

Negation appears thus as the pre-eminent rhetorical strategy by which Leopardi, after the letter to Jacopssen, problematizes and reassesses the Petrarchist themes of loss and retrieval of the object of love, sanctioning its ultimate extraneity with respect to the domain of reality. In other words, negation is the only resource that, by moving from the limitedness of sensory experience, allows for the possibility of further and unlimited aesthetic enjoyment, be this the contemplation of the indefinitely absent lady or the perception of the 'interminati | Spazi' [unending spaces] of the 1819 idyll 'L'infinito'.[78] In the latter, the contemplation of a hedgerow cuts off the view of the landscape, thereby reproducing the rhetorical structure of litotes and allowing the subject to imagine an endless beyond in which rational thought is wrecked ('annega' [sinks] and 'naufragar' [foundering]).[79] According to Jacques Derrida, the condition for the production of the sublime is the establishment of a limiting frame, which he labels *parergon*:[80] as Mark Cheetham comments, for Derrida 'the experience and pleasure of the sublime does not stem from the promise of something noumenal, outside a given frame, but rather from the perpetual, yet always provisional, activity of framing itself, from the *parergon*'.[81] Equally, in

'L'infinito' and 'Alla sua Donna', the imagined beyond and the beloved Lady do not have any actual (namely, noumenal) existence, but can be conjured only through the construction of a physical or rhetorical *parergon* — the hedgerow, or the structure of negation that locates the Lady outside every possibility of embodying her in any actual woman. Thus can the melancholy subject attain his or her *jouissance*: as Jean-François Lyotard writes, the feeling of the beyond 'can only "take place" or find its occasion at the price of suspending th[e] active power of the mind',[82] a moment of 'bliss' that — exactly like Tasso's melancholy 'alienazione di mente' — grasps its peculiar enjoyment by suspending the activity of rational consciousness and giving provisional concreteness to the products of fantasy.

The way Leopardi frames the problem of love within the rhetorical structure of negation has also strong psychoanalytical resonances. In psychoanalysis, negation (*Verleugnung*) is the token of repression, the rhetorical structure that embodies the tension between positive experience and the irreducible alterity of the original 'Thing'. Acting as a 'negative reference',[83] negation 'alludes constantly beyond itself to something that can never be really possessed',[84] and is therefore the only device by which the aporias of language can be circumvented, allowing the unconscious to express itself. Thus, in 'Alla sua Donna', negation does not uniquely denote the actual inexistence of the Lady, but rather provides the only possible premises for evocation of her presence-in-absence.

Carrera has reconstructed the way Leopardi's 'loving degree zero' has open antecedents in the Occitan corpus of courtly love poetry, and most notably, as is obvious, in the medieval legend of Jaufre Rudel and its theme of 'love from afar' (*amor de lonh*).[85] Moreover, as far as the expression 'donna che non si trova' is concerned, Mario Andrea Rigoni has convincingly proven how Saint-Evremond's short text *Idée de la femme, qui ne se trouve point, et qui ne se trouvera jamais* [Idea of the Woman who Cannot Be Found, and Who Will Never Be Found], read in the original French or through the mediation of Lorenzo Magalotti, is the literal source that Leopardi quotes in his 1824 note, although without declaring it.[86] Still, it seems to me that the ultimate roots of the deviation which intervened between June 1823, when Leopardi writes to Jacopssen about the courtly strategies he adopts in order to preserve his illusions in an untouched and pure form, and September 1823, when he writes 'Alla sua Donna' with the idea of the 'donna che non si trova' in his mind, are to be retraced to another source, accessed in summer 1823. Leopardi's lists of read books attest to the reading of Plato's *Sophist* during those months.[87] That of the presence of Platonism in 'Alla sua Donna' and within Leopardi's oeuvre more generally, is a widely debated question in Leopardi-related criticism.[88] Still, as far as the poem of 1823 is concerned, no one seems to have recognized how Plato's presence should not be identified so much in the theme of disincarnate love, which is more plausibly borrowed from the courtly and Petrarchist tradition, as in the function of negation as outlined in the *Sophist*, a dialogue that precisely poses the problem of the ontological status of 'non-being': 'When we say not-being [τό μή ὤν], we speak [...] not of something that is the opposite of being, but only of something different [τί ἕτερον μόνον]'.[89]

This 'difference' allows us to reassess the problem of negation in 'Alla sua

Donna', in that it denotes — for Leopardi, as it will for Freud — the irreducible doubleness of the present/absent object, the 'Thing' that the melancholy-phantasmal speculation incessantly attempts to grasp. Once interpreted through Plato's definition of negation, Leopardi's expression 'donna che non si trova' does not signal the Lady's antithetical position against actuality, in that negation does not denote the 'opposite' of the denied thing: it rather stresses the gap separating the two, so that the Lady is indefinitely situated beyond every possible, positive incarnation. The 'actual woman' can only have, as Leopardi will sanction in 'Aspasia' (1834), a 'dolce somiglianza' [sweet resemblance][90] with the Lady, a sort of phantasmal affinity that does not mitigate the Lady's absolute alterity. To speak in Lacan's terms, Leopardi's lover's discourse incessantly repeats to the beloved, '*I love you, but [...] inexplicably I love in you something more than you* [*j'aime en toi quelque chose en plus que toi*]'.[91] The 'quelque chose' is the *objet a*, namely the glimpse of alterity that obliquely alludes to the Other from the surface of the actual other that the lover is addressing — similarly to the way in which the χάρις-*je ne sais quoi* shines from the surface of visible objects, alluding to an ungraspable (and divine) beyondness. Lacan's 'quelque chose' is equivalent to Plato's τί ἕτερον, thus outlining a process of desire that is grounded in absence, and polarized towards melancholy as the only strategy for granting possession. Longing for its celestial phantasm, Leopardi's negation *mutilates* — this expression, again, is Lacan's[92] — the actual woman, who is always and only but a shadow of 'something different', 'questa [il rapito amante] non già, ma quella, ancora | Nei corporali amplessi, inchina ed ama' [yet it's not she whom the enraptured lover reveres and loves, even as he holds her, but the other].[93] By using negation as a device for bypassing the reality/imagination dichotomy, Leopardi reactivates the courtly theme of the Lady as a mental *imago*, while at the same time acknowledging its absolutely fictitious nature and ultimately accepting the irremediable absence of the 'Thing'. The phantasmal image beheld in states of more or less voluntary vanishing of rational consciousness — dream, daydreaming, 'alienazione di mente', or when the subject is half-asleep — is taken as the only object of love and of poetic discourse, inasmuch as its absence constitutes the only means for it to be present.

Nevermore

In a letter to Giuseppe Melchiorri of 5 March 1824, Leopardi declines the offer of writing poems to order. As far as poetic composition is concerned, Leopardi writes, he is different from everyone else. In the letter, Leopardi openly employs the vocabulary of demonic possession, which perhaps echoes the readings from Plato undertaken in these years:

> Io non ho scritto in mia vita se non pochissime e brevi poesie. Nello scriverle non ho mai seguito altro che un'ispirazione (o frenesia), sopraggiungendo la quale, in due minuti io formava il disegno e la distribuzione di tutto il componimento. Fatto questo, soglio sempre aspettare che mi torni un altro momento, e tornandomi (che ordinariamente non succede se non di là a qualche mese), mi pongo allora a comporre, ma con tanta lentezza, che non mi è possibile di terminare una poesia, benché brevissima, in meno di due o tre

settimane. Questo è il mio metodo, e se l'ispirazione non mi nasce da sé, più facilmente uscirebbe acqua da un tronco, che un solo verso dal mio cervello.[94]

[In my life I've written only a very small number of short poems. In writing them I've never followed anything but an inspiration (or frenzy); when it came on me, in two minutes I formed the outline and plan of the whole composition. When that is done, it is always my habit to wait for another moment to come, and when it does come (which normally happens only a few months later), then I set about composing, but so slowly, that it is not possible for me to finish a poem, even a very short one, in less than two or three weeks. This is my method, and if inspiration does not come of its own accord, it would be easier for water to come from a tree trunk than a single line from my brain.]

This letter is of 5 March 1824, and therefore belongs to the most intensive phase of Leopardi's endeavour to engage in prose writing, mainly concretized in the *Operette morali*. Leopardi feels unable, he writes, to write poetry: surely, as we know, because his project is, at this stage, a different one; but also because poetry comes from an outer space, outside the subject's control, and inspiration cannot be evoked on command. It is clear that Leopardi is torn by the very discord between poetry and philosophy, inspiration and rational thinking, which will not be resolved until the cantos of 1828–29. Poetic inspiration belongs to a sphere that cannot be accessed, and which is perhaps forever lost.

Between the end of October and the beginning of November 1824 Leopardi composes, however, the 'Elogio degli uccelli', to be included in the *Operette morali*. In analyzing this writing, Franco D'Intino argues that the contrast between the sitting philosopher Amelio and the flying birds may be intended as a way of metaphorizing the contrast between the cultivated subject's bookish and scriptural form of knowledge and the joyously purposeless and *oral* dimension of birds, intent on singing;[95] in the same way, as we have seen, the 'story of Teresa', from *Silvio Sarno* to 'A Silvia', opposed the subject at the library windows and the innocent, singing girl. Still, D'Intino suggests, Amelio's envy of the freedom of birds is perhaps nothing but the desire to return to a state to which he himself used to belong: the writing's closure, with Amelio declaring that 'io vorrei, per un poco di tempo, essere convertito in uccello, per provare quella contentezza e letizia della loro vita' [I would like, for a little while, to be transformed into a bird, to experience the joy and contentment of their life],[96] should be read as the longing to re-access a once known, and later lost and forgotten, paradise. Amelio's fantasy would reproduce, through an allegorical narration, the nostalgia for the inaccessible and repressed sphere of childhood, whose corporeal freedom, wandering imagination and games deprived of every practical purpose have been traumatically replaced, at a later stage, by physical constriction and solitary study:[97]

Gli uccelli [...] pochissimo soprastanno in un medesimo luogo; vanno e vengono di continuo *senza necessità veruna*; usano il volare *per sollazzo* [...]. Anche nel piccolo tempo che soprasseggono in luogo, tu non li vedi *mai fermi* della persona; sempre si volgono qua e là, sempre si aggirano, si piegano, si protendono, si crollano, si dimenano; con quella vispezza, quell'agilità, quella prestezza di modi indicibile.[98]

[Birds [...] remain very briefly in one place; they come and go continually *without the least necessity*; they make use of flight *for diversion* [...]. Even in the little while they do remain in one place, you *never see them keeping still*; they are forever looking this way and that, forever turning, bending, leaning forward, shaking themselves and fidgeting; with that liveliness, that agility of theirs, that indescribable swiftness of motion.]

In particular, D'Intino's analysis focuses on the fracture that separates the child's fancy, made of continuous distractions and characterized by the absence of any speculative goal, and the need for attention of dialectical thinking, which fixes one's mind on a single and specific object.[99] This would be the main fissure that divides the adult subject from the lost sphere of infancy, the traumatic turning towards a logical and rational way of posing problems that dissolves the freewheeling imagination of children, and which can be considered the equivalent — in the history of the subject's development — of the turning from μῦθος to λόγος invoked by Socrates in the *Phaedrus*. At the same time, we should not fail to notice how the corporeal dimension of birds, opposed to Amelio's purely intellectual speculation, reproduces Kristeva's distinction between semiotic and symbolic. The *chora* finds its referent in bodily movements, and is associated with rhythm and tonality — in other words, with singing:

Per ogni diletto e ogni contentezza che hanno, [gli uccelli] cantano; e quanto è maggiore il diletto o la contentezza, tanto più lena e più studio pongono nel cantare. E cantando buona parte del tempo, s'inferisce che ordinariamente stanno di buona voglia e godono. E se bene è notato che mentre sono in amore, cantano meglio, e più spesso, e più lungamente che mai; non è da credere però, che a cantare non li muovano altri diletti e altre contentezze fuori di queste dell'amore.[100]

[With every pleasure and every satisfaction the birds feel, they sing; and the greater the pleasure or satisfaction, the more zest and study they put into their song. And as they sing a good deal of the time, we may infer that they are normally in good heart and enjoying themselves. And though it has been noted that when they are in love, they sing better, and more often, and for longer than ever; it is not therefore to be thought, that they are not moved to songs by pleasures and satisfactions other than those of love.]

Birds are located in a dimension that precedes desire, because, having experienced no loss, they do not look for any fulfilment. Amelio's position, as an adult, civilized, and intellectual subject, is remarkably different: he perceives an absence, which is not recognized as a loss, and therefore fantasizes about being metamorphosed into a bird, yet describing a stage to which he himself has once belonged.

As I have anticipated, it seems as if this original loss, this fall from an original grace, pre-exists and provides a narrative structure to all the manifold losses complained of by Leopardi throughout his entire oeuvre. In other words, all the irrecoverable transitions from a previous state of innocence to a phase of disenchantment and waste that dominate Leopardi's reflection on cultural history and the human nature — from antiquity to modernity, from youth to adulthood, from the oral dimension of ancient epos to the ephemerality of modern scriptural culture, from irregularity to grammatical normalization — would be ways of metaphorizing that initial fissure, which is unmentionable insofar as it has been repressed by rational consciousness. From the beginning, Leopardi seems to be dominated by a neurotic obsession with loss, which results in paroxysmal strategies of self-protection. The terror of irretrievable loss leads the subject to consider every encounter as if it were the last, so as to anticipate and mitigate the possible abandonment through the adoption of an already posthumous gaze:

> Io [...] da fanciullo aveva questo costume. Vedendo partire una persona, quantunque a me indifferentissima, considerava se era possibile o probabile ch'io la rivedessi mai. Se io giudicava di no, me le poneva intorno a riguardarla, ascoltarla, e simili cose, e la seguiva o cogli occhi o cogli orecchi quanto più poteva, rivolgendo sempre fra me stesso, e addentrandomi nell'animo, e sviluppandomi alla mente questo pensiero: *ecco l'ultima volta, non lo vedrò mai più, o, forse mai più*. E così la morte di qualcuno ch'io conoscessi, e non mi avesse mai interessato in vita, mi dava una certa pena, non tanto per lui, o perch'egli mi interessasse allora dopo morte, ma per questa considerazione ch'io ruminava profondamente: *è partito per sempre — per sempre? sì: tutto è finito rispetto a lui: non lo vedrò mai più: e nessuna cosa sua avrà più niente di comune colla mia vita*. E mi poneva a riandare, s'io poteva, l'ultima volta ch'io l'aveva o veduto, o ascoltato ec. e mi doleva di non avere allora saputo che fosse l'ultima volta, e di non essermi regolato secondo questo pensiero.[101]

> [As a child [...] I had this habit. When I saw a person leave, and no matter how indifferent I was to him, I wondered if it was possible or probable that I would ever see him again. If I judged that I would not, I hung around looking at the person, listening to him, and things like that, and followed him around with my eyes and ears as much as I could, all the time turning over, and absorbing, and developing this thought in my mind, 'this is the last time, you will never see him again, or maybe never again'. And thus the death of someone whom I knew, and who had never been of any interest to me in life, caused me a degree of distress, not so much for his sake, or because after his death he might then be of interest to me, but for the following reason, which I pondered at length, 'he has gone forever — forever? yes — it's all over for him. I shall never see him again. And nothing of his will any longer have anything in common with my own life'. And I set about rehearsing, if I could, the last time I had either seen or listened to him, etc., and it pained me that I had not known then that it was the last time, and that I had not acted on this thought.]

Hence, we return to the Lady who cannot be found and her genealogy from *Silvio Sarno* onwards, Leopardi's algid eroticism, and its withdrawing into the dimension of fancy and dream, which denies the very existence of the object of desire so as to protect the subject from its expected loss. Julia Kristeva notes that this is precisely the strategy of the melancholy subject, 'far from repressing the trouble that the loss of the object entails (whether archaic or present loss), melancholy persons settle the lost Thing or object within themselves, identifying with the loss's beneficial features on the one hand, with its maleficent ones on the other'.[102] This is what happens in the 'Elogio degli uccelli': while beholding the singing birds, the subject does not realize how he is merely recalling, in a nostalgic way, a state that once was his own; still, his nostalgia concretizes in a process of fantasizing, which reproduces, in its erratic style, the purposeless and wandering movements of birds. As D'Intino notes, birdsong makes Amelio turn from silent reading to a slow process of introspection, which gives birth to the 'praise', 'a poco a poco datosi ad ascoltare e pensare, e lasciato il leggere; all'ultimo pose mano alla penna' [little by little beginning to listen and ponder, and leaving off reading; he finally took his pen in hand].[103] The text represents the very 'instalment' of 'the Thing' within the subject's self, in that it unconsciously replicates the lost state in its double, beneficial and malign, aspect: the enjoyment caused by daydreaming and writing is inexorably bound with the bitter statement that the birds' joy is not (or, rather, no longer) accessible.

In his 1908 writing on 'Creative Writers and Day-dreaming',[104] Freud notes that fancy and daydreaming (*Phantasie*) are nothing but the afterimages of children's games, repressed in the transition to adulthood:

> As people grow up [...] they cease to play, and they seem to give up the yield of pleasure which they gained from playing. But whoever understands the human mind knows that hardly anything is harder for a man than to give up a pleasure which he has once experienced. Actually, we can never give anything up; we only exchange one thing for another. What appears to be a renunciation is really the formation of a substitute or surrogate. In the same way, the growing child, when he stops playing, gives up nothing but the link with real objects; instead of *playing*, he now *phantasies*. He builds castles in the air and creates what are called *day-dreams*.[105]

Both play and *Phantasie* share, according to Freud, the structure of dreams,[106] being situated in a visual and extra-linguistic dimension at the centre of which, in a dominating position, there always stands the subject. The *Phantasie* is therefore a melancholy enjoyment by which introspective self-withdrawing allows the construction of a scene in which the satisfaction of desire may take place. However, the awareness of its illusionary nature contaminates the scene, projecting onto it the depressive feeling of inanity. Two passages from *Silvio Sarno* show this oscillation between enjoyment and depression. The subject, intent on a cosmic meditation or on recreational activities is abruptly reawakened by a sudden irruption from the external world; in both cases, we witness an analogous frustration, which brings the subject to a melancholy-depressive gaze on existence, which is seen as being 'nothing':

> Mie consideraz. sulla pluralità dei mondi e il niente di noi e di questa terra e sulla grandezza e la forza della natura che noi misuriamo coi torrenti ec. che sono un nulla in questo globo ch'è un nulla nel mondo e risvegliato da una voce chiamantemi a cena onde allora mi parve un niente la vita nostra e il tempo e i nomi celebri e tutta la storia ec.[107]

> [My considerations about the plurality of the worlds and the nothingness of us and of this earth, and on the greatness and force of nature that we measure with streams etc. which are nothing in this globe, which is nothing in the universe, and then, awoken by a voice calling me to dinner, then everything seemed nothing to me, our life, and time, and famous names, and all history, etc.]

> Come quando essendo fanciullo io era menato a casa di qualcuno per visita ec. che coi ragazzini che v'erano intavolava ec. cominciava ec. e quando i genitori sorgevano e mi chiamavano ec. mi si stringeva il cuore ma bisognava partire lasciando l'opera tal quale nè più nè meno a mezzo e le sedie ec. sparpagliate

e i ragazzini afflitti ec. come se non ci avessi pensato mai così che la nostra esistenza mi parve veramente un nulla.[108]

[Like when, as a child, I was brought to visit someone etc., and with the children who were there I started etc. and began etc. and then, when my parents emerged and called me etc., my heart was stricken, but I had to leave, and leave the work as it was, nothing more nor less, with the chairs all scattered and the children troubled etc. as if I had never thought about it, so that our existence seemed to be truly nothing to me.]

By comparing these two passages, D'Intino notes how, for Leopardi, daydreaming and play are systematically approached, in that they both belong to an infantile and preschool dimension, and are therefore alien to rational dialectics, which — irrupting from outside in the shape of a 'voice' — breaks the rhapsodic oscillation of reverie.[109] If we consider these passages in the light of Freud's writings on daydreaming, we may, however, hypothesize that these conscious recollections of interrupted and lost states of grace allude to a remoter and repressed interruption and loss, of which they constitute the later, symbolic afterimage. Psychoanalytical theory has confirmed how the concealed object of repression symbolically reverberates in the very means of its return. The unmentioned lost object of Leopardi's *Phantasie* may be therefore seen as a moment of fusion and unending imagination, interrupted by a 'voice' that breaks this harmony by throwing the subject into the sphere of distinction, causal relations, and logical thinking.

This original moment corresponds to what Kristeva terms 'the Thing', namely the state of attachment with the maternal body that precedes the entrance of the subject into the (paternal) domain of the symbolic, so to say the point of departure for the concurrent construction of language and subjectivity. From this angle, 'the Thing' is, by definition, lost, and the difference between those who exploit 'the Thing' and the melancholy-depressive subjects is that, while the former elaborate their mourning by committing their 'matricide', and are therefore able to find a replacement for the lost object in alternate signifiers, thus denying the loss, the latter deny that very negation, reaching 'the impression of having been deprived of an unnameable, supreme good, of something unrepresentable, that [...] no word could signify'.[110] The melancholy subject would therefore suffer from an 'initial deprivation', which is not 'the deprivation of a "property" or "object" constituting a material, transferable heritage, but the loss of an unnameable domain, [...] the secret and unreachable horizon of our loves and desires [which] assumes, for the imagination, the consistency of an archaic mother, which, however, no precise image manages to encompass'.[111] Quite interestingly, in the 'Elogio degli uccelli', Leopardi mentions the original bond between mother and child, characterized by laughter ('riso') and enjoyment, namely the state of innocent happiness to which birds belong. Still, the 'negation of the negation', to speak in Kristeva's terms, is so strong that the mother-child link, for Leopardi, is connected to weeping rather than joy, and that the happiness of children is a mere result of civilization and of the imitation of others:

Io sono di opinion che il riso, non solo apparisse al mondo dopo il pianto, della qual cosa non si può fare controversia veruna; ma che penasse un buono spazio di tempo a essere sperimentato e veduto primieramente. Nel qual tempo, né la madre sorridesse al bambino, né questo riconoscesse lei col sorriso, come dice Virgilio. Che se oggi, almeno dove la gente è ridotta a vita civile, incominciano gli uomini a ridere poco dopo nati; fannolo principalmente in virtù dell'esempio, perchè veggono altri che ridono.[112]

[I am of the opinion that laughter not only appeared in the world after weeping, as to which there can be no argument at all; but that it languished for a good while before being for the first time attempted and observed. During which period, neither did the mother smile at the child, nor the child recognize her with a smile, as Virgil puts it. For if today, at least where people have got used to civilized life, men begin to laugh soon after birth; they do so principally by virtue of example, because they see others smiling.]

The subject's inability to acknowledge the loss is the root of the fracture that divides the melancholy subject from the symbolic order, the fundamental lack that has determined his irremediable isolation from the community of others. This self-exclusion, bearing the stigmata of melancholy disposition of mind, has been notably portrayed by Leopardi in 'Il passero solitario': again, birds are employed as powerful emblems of the subject's current or desired condition. In this poem, what separates the thrush from the other birds is an inexplicable difference; an original deprivation, we may argue, which, not having been consciously recognized as such, has left 'the Thing' as an unmentionable and ungraspable emptiness, and the subject stuck in a melancholy nostalgia for something that cannot be conceptualized:

> D'in su la vetta della torre antica,
> Passero solitario a la campagna
> Cantando vai finché non more il giorno;
> [...]
> Gli altri augelli contenti, a gara insieme
> Per lo libero ciel fan mille giri,
> Pur festeggiando il lor tempo migliore:
> Tu pensoso in disparte il tutto miri;
> Non compagni, non voli,
> Non ti cal d'allegria, schivi gli spassi;
> Canti, e così trapassi
> Dell'anno e di tua vita il più bel fiore.[113]

[High on the rooftop of the ancient tower, solitary thrush, you keep on singing to the countryside till the day dies. [...] The other birds compete in happiness, taking a thousand turns in the wide sky, exulting in their best of times. Pensive and apart, you watch it all. No comrades and no flights, no happiness for you. You shun their games; you sing, and so you spend the high time of the year and of your life.]

Still, while stating the bitterness of the subject's condition, this poem outlines the possibility of an answer. The subject — the thrush — 'sings', and the act of singing is actually the peculiarity that characterizes him, compared to the other birds' physical (and pre-linguistic) joys. This corresponds to the way in which, for Kristeva, poetry can be seen as a sublimating way to assure the melancholy subject a form of retrieval of the lost Thing: 'through melody, rhythm, semantic polyvalency, the so-called poetic form, which decomposes and recomposes signs, [sublimation] is the sole "container" seemingly able to secure an uncertain but adequate hold over the Thing'.[114] Thus, exactly as in the 'Elogio degli uccelli', in 'Il passero solitario' the melancholy subject's erratic speech skims over the borders of its unmentionable object, recuperating and re-staging it in the form of a reverie-like writing (like Amelio's 'praise', drafted by following his daydreaming in the countryside), or of an unending song.

As we had noted, 'Il passero solitario' is arguably composed after 1828, and is therefore to be inserted within the discovery of the *canzone libera* as the most suitable form for reproducing the rhythms and erratic movements of memory and desire.[115] In publishing his poems in 1831 (although, in this edition, 'Il passero solitario' is still not present), Leopardi gives them the collective title of *Canti*. The implicit evocation of the oral dimension of singing aims at stressing the negotiation that his new kind of poetry has enacted between the lost, pre-scriptural dimension of the 'ancients' and the editorial conventions of intellectual modernity: again, Leopardi's strategy recuperates its lost object by an oblique process of retrieval, at the very moment in which it laments its loss. The word 'canto' is also present in the title of the poem that, in the book's sequence, immediately follows 'A Silvia' and 'Le ricordanze': inspired by a passage from the Russian baron Meyendorff, read by Leopardi in 1826 and quoted in the *Zibaldone* two years later,[116] the 'Canto notturno di un pastore dell'Asia', drafted at the end of 1829, explicitly evokes the dimension of orality, fictively dissimulating itself as the transcription of a song.

In analyzing this poem, criticism has often spoken of an evolution of Leopardi's poetics, moving from the autobiographical dimension of memory — as happens in 'A Silvia', 'Le ricordanze', and, to some extent, in 'Il passero solitario' — to a global reflection on the general unhappiness of the entire creation that leaves aside the author's subjective position, and, under the fictive mask of the Asian shepherd, gives birth to a 'universal' poem. Still, the 'Canto notturno' seems rather the final outcome of Leopardi's poetics of melancholy, and as such is more closely related than would seem at a first glance to the trajectory that I have attempted to reconstruct in this chapter. This point is already clear in the quotation from Meyendorff's *Voyage d'Orenbourg à Boukhara* [Journey from Orenburg to Bukhara] transcribed in the *Zibaldone*:

> Les Kirkis (nazione *nomade*, al Nord dell'Asia centrale) ont aussi des chants historiques (*non scritti*) qui rappellent les hauts faits de leurs héros [...]. Plusieurs d'entre eux (d'entre les Kirkis) [...] passent la nuit assis sur une pierre à *regarder la lune*, et à *improviser* des *paroles assez tristes* sur des *airs* qui ne le sont pas moins.[117]

> [The Khirkiz (*nomadic* nation, in the North of Central Asia) also have historical songs (*not written*) which recall the brave deeds of their heroes [...]. Several of them (of the Khirkiz) [...] pass the night sitting on a stone and *looking at the moon*, and *improvising quite sad words* to *tunes* that are no less so.]

The Khirkiz are a nomadic people, a feature that is echoed by the adjective 'errante' in the title of Leopardi's poem (the manuscript includes the variation 'vagante' [rambling]); their culture is an oral one, and, most importantly, their songs are improvised, gathering sad words accompanied by sad music. The wandering shepherd of the 'Canto notturno' bears therefore the stigmata of the melancholy symptomatology, the nomadic nature of his life mirroring the erratic dimension of his improvised song. Certainly, the 'Canto notturno' exhibits a strong deviation from the 'Elogio degli uccelli'. In the poem of 1829 even birds are no longer exempted from universal misery, nor would (perhaps) the transformation into a bird be of any help for the subject:

> Forse s'avess'io l'ale
> Da volar su le nubi,
> E noverar le stelle ad una ad una,
> O come il tuono errar di giogo in giogo,
> Più felice sarei, dolce mia greggia,
> Più felice sarei, candida luna.
> O forse erra dal vero,
> Mirando all'altrui sorte il mio pensiero:
> Forse in qual forma in quale
> Stato che sia, dentro covile o cuna,
> È funesto a chi nasce il dì natale.[118]

[Maybe if I had wings to fly above the clouds and count the stars out one by one, or, like thunder, wander from peak to peak, I would be happier, my gentle flock, happier, bright moon. Or maybe my mind is straying from the truth, imagining the destiny of others. Maybe in whatever form or state, be it in stall or cradle, the day we are born is cause for mourning.]

The portrayal of cosmic unhappiness allows, however, the subject to grasp a form of *jouissance*, albeit oblique. Already in *Silvio Sarno*, as we have seen, Leopardi had described an experience of daydreaming, in which the subject's freewheeling imagination encompassed the totality of the universe. Although sorrowful, this fantasizing imagination conveyed, however, an embryonic pleasure, abruptly interrupted by a voice coming from an external place. It is clear, then, how *jouissance* was not engrained in the *content* of the subject's meditation, which — in the same way as the 'Canto notturno' — was a bitter statement of the 'nothingness' of everything, but in its formal structure, mimetically reproducing and alluding to the very object of the original loss. In problematizing the Freudian notion of fantasy, Jean Laplanche and Jean-Bertrand Pontalis have pointed out how 'fantasy [...] is not the object of desire':

> In fantasy the subject does not pursue the object or its sign: he appears caught up himself in the sequence of images. He forms no representation of the desired object, but is himself represented as participating in the scene although, in the earliest forms, of fantasy, he cannot be assigned any fixed place in it [...]. As a result, the subject, although always present in the fantasy, may be so in a desubjectivized form, that is to say, in the very syntax of the sequence in question. On the other hand, to the extent that desire is not purely an upsurge of the drives, but is articulated into the fantasy, the latter is a favoured spot for the most primitive defensive reactions, such as turning against oneself, or into an opposite, projection, negation.[119]

'The Thing', in other words, is retrieved through the process itself of fantasy, which, in the case of the 'Canto notturno', becomes the structure itself of the poem, both in terms of its formal aspects and of its all-encompassing oscillations between micro- and macrocosm. The subject being lost 'in the very syntax' of images, the form of the 'canzone libera' reproduces what Kristeva terms:

> A rhythmic space, which has no thesis and no position, the process by which significance is constituted. Plato himself leads us to such a process when he calls this receptacle or *chora* nourishing and maternal, not yet unified in an ordered whole because deity is absent from it. Though deprived of unity, identity, or deity, the *chora* is nevertheless subject to a regulating process (*réglementation*), which is different from that of symbolic law but nevertheless effectuates discontinuities by temporarily articulating them and then starting over, again and again. The *chora* is a modality of significance in which the linguistic sign is not yet articulated as the absence of an object and as the distinction between real and symbolic.[120]

In a series of poetic projects plausibly drafted in 1819, Leopardi had foreseen the possibility of writing a poem out of a dream, 'Luna caduta secondo il mio sogno' [Fallen Moon, According to my Dream].[121] In the same year, he had also composed the fragment known as 'Odi, Melisso' [Listen, Melisso], previously entitled 'Il sogno' [The Dream] or 'Lo spavento notturno' [The Nocturnal Terror]. In this poem, the shepherd Alceta relates how, in a dream, he has seen the moon falling from the sky:

> Allor mirando in ciel, vidi rimaso
> *Come un barlume, o un'orma,* anzi *una nicchia,*
> Ond'ella [la luna] fosse svelta; in cotal guisa,
> Ch'io m'agghiacciava; *e ancor non m'assicuro.*[122]

> [Then, looking up in the sky, I saw something still there, *a glimmer* or a *shadow,* or *the niche* that the moon had been torn away from, which made me cold with fear. *And I am still anxious.*]

It is as if the omnipresent moon of the 'Canto notturno', referent and addressee of another shepherd's song, replaced the empty space left in the sky in the subject's (or Alceta's) anxious dream. Gary Cestaro records the medieval identification between *Gramatica* and *Luna*, highlighting how it 'represents a primal feminine presence who at once holds out hope for an original unity of language and experience while forever foreclosing to humans complete access'.[123] As such, *Luna* is present in Dante's oeuvre both as 'The waxing and waning moon evok[ing] [...] the unending variability of the temporal, sublunar world' and as the 'bulbous, milky presence in the night sky harbour[ing] associations via Diana with an alluring female corporeality both pure and unattainable'.[124] Both elements are also present in Leopardi's poem, alternately depicting the moon as 'solinga, eternal peregrina' [eternal solitary wanderer],[125] and as 'Vergine luna' [virgin moon][126] and 'giovinetta immortal' [immortal maiden].[127] Perhaps it would not, therefore, be improper to see the double and intangible moon of the 'Canto notturno' as the emblem of a similar 'original unity of language and experience' whose loss the canto aims to deny. Once transposed to the plains of central Asia, and in the night-time when no voice coming from an outer space can interrupt the subject's melancholy speech, the process of fantasy can be released, by re-staging a scene in which no fracture has yet been experienced, and the moon is still in place.

Notes to Chapter 2

1. Quoted in Robert Graves, *The White Goddess: A Historical Grammar of Poetic Myth* (London: Faber & Faber, 1959), pp. 10–11.
2. Ibid., p. 11.
3. Ibid.
4. Ibid.
5. See the classic work by Wilhelm Nestle, *Vom Mythos zum Logos: Die Selbstentfaltung des griechischen Denkens von Homer bis auf die Sophistik und Sokrates* (Stuttgart: Metzler, 1940). The strictness of such distinction between λόγος and μῦθος has been widely re-problematized by recent studies in classical anthropology: for a general orientation, see Paul Veyne, *Les Grecs ont-ils cru à leurs mythes?* (Paris: Seuil, 1983).
6. Agamben, *Stanzas*, pp. xv-xix.
7. Ibid., p. 3.
8. Ibid., p. 8 note 2.
9. Ibid., p. 12.
10. See Michael Worbs, *Nervenkunst: Literatur und Psychoanalyse im Wien der Jahrhundertwende* (Frankfurt am Main.: Athenäum, 1988), p. 275, and Yamina Oudai Celso, *Freud e la filosofia antica: Genealogia di un fondatore* (Turin: Bollati Boringhieri, 2006), p. 27. See also Richard H. Armstrong, *A Compulsion for Antiquity: Freud and the Ancient World* (Ithaca: Cornell University Press, 2005).
11. Agamben, *Stanzas*, p. 8 note 2.
12. On Leopardi and melancholy, see: Neuro Bonifazi, *Leopardi e l'immagine antica* (Turin: Einaudi, 1991); Alberto Folin, *Leopardi e la notte chiara* (Venice: Marsilio, 1993), pp. 69–95; Elio Gioanola, *Leopardi: La malinconia* (Milan: Jaca Book, 1995); and Novella Bellucci, *Il 'gener frale': Saggi leopardiani* (Venice: Marsilio, 2010), pp. 29–63.
13. See Brozzi's essay, 'I demoni di Leopardi', for an exhaustive overview of the theme of noonday in Leopardi's oeuvre.
14. Calasso, *La follia che viene dalle ninfe*, p. 27.
15. Ibid., p. 28.
16. *Zib.* 4415, 22 October 1828.
17. Leopardi probably reads both novels at the beginning of 1819, as D'Intino argues in SFA, p. xliv.
18. E, II, 1634.
19. Carrera, introduction, pp. xiii-xiv.
20. Franco D'Intino, 'Errore, ortografia e autobiografia in Leopardi e Stendhal', in *Memoria e infanzia tra Alfieri e Leopardi*, ed. by Marco Dondero and Laura Melosi (Macerata: Quodlibet, 2004), pp. 167–83.
21. Luigi Blasucci, 'I tempi dei "Canti"', pp. 177–218 (pp. 202–03).
22. Alberto Folin, *Leopardi e il canto dell'addio* (Venice: Marsilio, 2008), p. 94 note.
23. *Zib.* 4302, 15 April 1828.
24. Agamben, 'Warburg and the Nameless Science', p. 100.
25. Julia Kristeva, *Soleil noir: Dépression et mélancolie* (Paris: Gallimard, 1987); *Black Sun: Depression and Melancholia*, transl. by Leon S. Roudiez (New York: Columbia University Press, 1989).
26. Julia Kristeva, *La Révolution du langage poétique. L'Avant-garde à la fin du XIXe siècle: Lautréamont et Mallarmé* (Paris: Seuil, 1974); *Revolution in Poetic Language*, transl. by Margaret Waller (New York: Columbia University Press, 1984).
27. Sara Fortuna and Manuele Gragnolati, 'Between Affection and Discipline: Exploring Linguistic Tensions from Dante to *Aracoeli*', in *The Power of Disturbance: Elsa Morante's 'Aracoeli*, ed. by Sara Fortuna and Manuele Gragnolati (Oxford: Legenda, 2009), pp. 8–19 (pp. 8–9).
28. See SFA, pp. 161–66.
29. SFA, p. xvi.
30. SFA, p. lxvii.
31. Robert Douglas-Fairhurst, *Victorian Afterlives: The Shaping of Influence in Nineteenth-Century*

Literature (Oxford: Oxford University Press, 2002), has shown how nineteenth-century conceptualizations of literary influence are often expressed with metaphors that echo the notion of haunting, outlining influence as the re-emergence of a subterranean alterity that erupts in the subject's writing outside the control of consciousness ('detecting another hand in one's writing', p. 5). On automatic writing between spiritualism, psychoanalysis, and Surrealism, see Rachel Leah Thompson, 'The Automatic Hand: Spiritualism, Psychoanalysis, Surrealism', *Invisible Culture: An Electronic Journal for Visual Culture*, 7 (Spring 2004), <http://www.rochester.edu/in_visible_culture/ivchome.html> [accessed 28 May 2013].

32. Blasucci, 'I tempi dei "Canti" ', p. 203.

33. This peculiarity of the 'Le ricordanze' had already been highlighted by Francesco Moroncini: see Emilio Peruzzi, in *Canti*, by Giacomo Leopardi, ed. by Emilio Peruzzi (Milan: Rizzoli, 1998), pp. 471–72 note.

34. Kristeva, *La Révolution du langage poétique*, pp. 210–20. The second and longest part of the book, which is devoted to the analysis of the ways texts are progressively constructed as 'semiotic devices' in the course of the 'revolution in poetic language' by means of subversion of established lyric conventions, is absent from the English translation.

35. See the survey of this theme throughout Leopardi's entire oeuvre made by D'Intino in *L'immagine della voce*, pp. 165–69.

36. Ibid., pp. 167–68. See also Eric A. Havelock, *The Muse Learns to Write: Reflections on Orality and Literacy from Antiquity to the Present* (New Haven: Yale University Press, 1986).

37. *Zib.* 4436.

38. *Zib.* 143–44, 1 July 1820.

39. Gary P. Cestaro, *Dante and the Grammar of the Nursing Body* (Notre Dame, IN: University of Notre Dame Press, 2003), pp. 49–51.

40. *Zib.* 4476–77.

41. Nicola Gardini, 'Considerazioni sullo stilnovismo novecentesco: Il modello della *Vita nova*', *Italianistica*, 29, 3 (September-December 2000), 445–50 (p. 446).

42. Andrea Torre, *Petrarcheschi segni di memoria: Spie, postille, metafore* (Pisa: Edizioni della Normale, 2007), p. xiv.

43. This very famous expression is used by Sigmund Freud in the 1917 essay 'A Difficulty in the Path of Psychoanalysis', SE, xvii, 135–44 (p. 143).

44. See Natasha Distiller, 'Petrarchism and Psychoanalysis', in *Desire and Gender in the Sonnet Tradition*, by Natasha Distiller (Basingstoke and New York: Palgrave Macmillan, 2008), pp. 21–42 (p. 21, 'The imbrication of psychoanalytic discourse in Renaissance literature has implications for the theorisation of the modern subject the former has enabled. [...] I suggest that psychoanalytic models for subjectivity can be seen to have a relation to the subject of Petrarchan poetry').

45. SFA, p. liv.

46. SFA, pp. liv-lv.

47. See Marco Santagata, *I frammenti dell'anima: Storia e racconto nel Canzoniere di Petrarca* (Bologna: Il Mulino, 1992).

48. SFA, pp. xcii-xciii.

49. Didi-Huberman, *Devant le temps*, p. 37.

50. Agamben, *Stanzas*, p. 20.

51. Leopardi knew little of Occitan courtly tradition, and themes and motifs of courtly love are uniquely conveyed, in his oeuvre, by Italian sources. See Alessandro Carrera's convincing reconstruction in *La distanza del cielo: Leopardi e lo spazio dell'ispirazione* (Milan: Medusa, 2011), p. 126.

52. SFA, pp. 119–201.

53. Nicola Gardini, 'Considerazioni sullo stilnovismo novecentesco', and 'Dante as a Gay Poet', in *Metamorphosing Dante: Appropriations, Manipulations, and Rewritings in the Twentieth and Twenty-First Centuries*, ed. by Manuele Gragnolati, Fabio Camilletti and Fabian Lampart (Vienna and Berlin: Turia + Kant, 2010), pp. 61–74 (p. 62).

54. See also the *Memorie del primo amore*, 'tra il sonno e la veglia spontaneamente m'è passata innanzi alla fantasia la desiderata immagine vera e viva, onde io immediatamente riscosso e spalancati gli occhi, subito le son corso dietro colla mente', SFA, pp. 29–30 [while half-asleep, spontaneously

there passed before my imagination the desired image, true and alive, whence I, having suddenly waken up and opened my eyes, immediately started running behind her with my mind].

55. See Carrera, *La distanza del cielo*, p. 121.

56. Leopardi, 'Il sogno', l. 7.

57. Leopardi, 'Il sogno', ll. 98–100.

58. Torquato Tasso, 'Il Messaggiero', in Id., *Dialoghi*, ed. by Giovanni Baffetti, 2 vols. (Milan: Rizzoli, 1998), I, 305–83.

59. Ibid., p. 323.

60. Ibid., pp. 325–26.

61. Petrarch, *Rerum vulgarium fragmenta*, CXXIX.

62. Ibid., p. 327.

63. Also 'Il sogno' openly evokes Tasso's text in its opening lines, 'Era il mattino, e tra le chiuse imposte | Per lo balcone insinuava il sole | Nella mia cieca stanza il primo albore; | Quando in sul tempo che più lieve il sonno | E più soave le pupille adombra | Stettemi allato e riguardommi in viso | Il simulacro di colei che amore | Prima insegnommi, e poi lasciommi in pianto', ll. 1–8 [It was morning, and the sun's first light was filtering into my dark room through the closed shutters; at the time when sleep most lightly, gently veils the eyes, the image of the woman who first showed me love, then left me in tears, stood next to me, staring into my eyes]. *Il Messaggiero* begins, 'Era già l'ora che la vicinanza del sole comincia a rischiarare l'orizonte, quando a me, che ne le delicate piume giaceva co' sensi non fortemente legati dal sonno, ma così leggiermente che il mio stato era mezzo fra la vigilia e la quiete, si fece a l'orecchio quel gentile spirito che suole favellarmi ne le mie imaginazioni' [It was already the time when the closeness to the sun begins to light up the horizon, when there came to my ear, while I was lying in my soft bed with my senses not strongly bound by sleep, but in a such way that my state was almost half-awake, that gentle spirit that tends to talk to me in my imagination].

64. TPP, p. 529 note.

65. TPP, p. 532.

66. TPP, pp. 529–30.

67. Petrarch, *The Canzoniere, or Rerum Vulgarium Fragmenta*, ed. and transl. by Mark Musa (Bloomington and Indianapolis: Indiana University Press, 1999), pp. 422–23.

68. TPP, p. 1111. The date is uncertain. However, the presence, in the same list, of a project that anticipates the poem 'Bruto minore' [Brutus], of 1821, may allow us to put this date as a *terminus ad quem*.

69. E, I, 722–25.

70. E, I, 723.

71. Jacques Lacan, *On Feminine Sexuality: The Limits of Love and Knowledge, The Seminar Book XX: Encore 1972–1973*, transl. by Bruce Fink (New York and London: Norton, 1998), p. 69.

72. Carrera, *La distanza del cielo*, p. 121.

73. TPP, p. 222.

74. See the notion of 'immagine-fantasma' [image-phantasm] in Adelia Noferi, 'Petrarca in Leopardi e la funzione di un commento', in *Il gioco delle tracce: Studi su Dante, Petrarca, Bruno, il neo-classicismo, Leopardi, l'informale*, by Adelia Noferi (Florence: La Nuova Italia, 1979), pp. 299–328.

75. Ibid., p. 327.

76. Agamben, *Stanzas*, p. 129.

77. Luigi Blasucci, 'Petrarchismo e platonismo nella canzone "Alla sua Donna"', in *I tempi dei 'Canti'*, (Turin: Einaudi, 1996), pp. 62–80 (p. 76).

78. Leopardi, 'L'infinito', ll. 4–5. On the rhetorical structure of negation and the image of the hedge in 'L'infinito', see Cesare Galimberti, 'Modi della negazione nei "Canti"', in *Linguaggio del vero in Leopardi*, by Cesare Galimberti (Florence: Olschki, 1959), pp. 68–95, and Luigi Blasucci, 'Petrarchismo e platonismo nella canzone "Alla sua Donna"', pp. 66–67.

79. Leopardi, 'L'infinito', ll. 14–15.

80. Jacques Derrida, *The Truth in Painting*, transl. by Geoffrey Bennington and Ian McLeod (Chicago and London: University of Chicago Press, 1987).

81. Mark A. Cheetham, *Kant, Art, and Art History: Moments of Discipline* (Cambridge: Cambridge University Press, 2001), p. 107.

82. Jean-François Lyotard, *The Inhuman: Reflections on Time*, transl. by Geoffrey Bennington and Rachel Bowlby (Cambridge: Polity Press, 1991), p. 140.
83. Agamben, *Stanzas*, p. 32.
84. Ibid., p. 33.
85. Carrera, *La distanza del cielo*, pp. 122–29. See also my ' "On pleure les lèvres absentes". "Amor di lontano" tra Leopardi e Baudelaire', *Italian Studies*, 64, 1 (2009), 77–90.
86. Mario Andrea Rigoni, 'Post Scriptum: Sulla fonte della canzone *Alla sua Donna*', in Id., *Il pensiero di Leopardi*, pp. 57–59.
87. TPP, p. 1115.
88. See, among the most recent contributions, Massimo Natale, *Il canto delle idee. Leopardi fra 'Pensiero dominante' e 'Aspasia'* (Venice: Marsilio, 2009), and D'Intino, *L'immagine della voce*, p. 13.
89. Plato, *Theaetetus, Sophist*, ed. and transl. by Harold North Fowler (London: Heinemann, 1961), pp. 414–15.
90. Leopardi, 'Aspasia', l. 87.
91. Jacques Lacan, *The Four Fundamental Concepts of Psychoanalysis. The Seminar Book XI*, ed. by Jacques-Alain Miller, transl. by Alan Sheridan (New York and London: Norton, 1998), p. 268; *Le Séminaire livre XI: Les Quatre Concepts fondamentaux de la psychanalyse*, ed. by Jacques-Alain Miller (Paris: Seuil, 1973), p. 241.
92. Lacan, *The Four Fundamental Concepts of Psychoanalysis*, p. 268.
93. Leopardi, 'Aspasia', ll. 44–45.
94. E, I, 792–93.
95. D'Intino, *L'immagine della voce*, pp. 19–76.
96. TPP, p. 574.
97. D'Intino, *L'immagine della voce*, pp. 59–60.
98. TPP, p. 573, my emphases.
99. D'Intino, *L'immagine della voce,*, pp. 59 and 206.
100. TPP, p. 571.
101. *Zib.* 644–46, 11 February 1821.
102. Kristeva, *Black Sun*, pp. 166–67.
103. TPP, p. 571.
104. SE, IX, 141–53.
105. SE, IX, 145.
106. 'Our dreams at night are nothing else than phantasies like these', SE, IX, 148.
107. SFA, pp. 71–72.
108. SFA, pp. 100–01.
109. D'Intino, *L'immagine della voce*, p. 206.
110. Kristeva, *Black Sun*, p. 13. As Kristeva specifies some pages later, 'Signs are arbitrary because language starts with a *negation (Verneinung)* of loss, along with the depression occasioned by mourning. "I have lost an essential object that happens to be, in the final analysis, my mother", is what the speaking being seems to be saying. "But no, I have found her again in signs, or rather since I consent to lose her I have not lost her (that is the negation), I can recover her in language". Depressed persons, on the contrary, *disavow the negation*: they cancel it out, suspend it, and nostalgically fall back on the real object (the Thing) of their loss, which is just what they do not manage to lose, to which they remain painfully riveted', pp. 43–44. On the matricide as a 'vital necessity' see pp. 27–28.
111. Ibid., p. 145.
112. TPP, p. 572.
113. Leopardi, 'Il passero solitario', ll. 1–3 and 9–16. Franco D'Intino has noted how, in Cesare Ripa's *Iconologia*, a 'passero solitario' accompanies the allegorical representation of the melancholy subject: see *L'immagine della voce*, p. 23.
114. Kristeva, *Black Sun*, p 14.
115. See Ugo Dotti, 'La poesia leopardiana', in *Canti*, by Giacomo Leopardi, ed. by Ugo Dotti (Milan: Feltrinelli, 1993), pp. 9–150 (pp. 89–92).
116. *Zib.* 4399–400, 3 October 1828.
117. *Zib.* 4399–400, 3 October 1828, my emphases.

118. Leopardi, 'Canto notturno', ll. 133–43.
119. Jean Laplanche and Jean-Bertrand Pontalis, 'Fantasy and the Origins of Sexuality', in *Formations of Fantasy*, ed. by Victor Burgin, James Donald and Cora Kaplan (London and New York: Routledge, 1986), pp. 5–34 (pp. 26–27).
120. Kristeva, *Revolution in Poetic Language*, p. 26.
121. TPP, p. 459.
122. Leopardi, 'Odi, Melisso', ll. 17–20, my emphases.
123. Cestaro, *Dante and the Grammar of the Nursing Body*, p. 57.
124. Ibid.
125. Leopardi, 'Canto notturno', l. 61.
126. Ibid., l. 37.
127. Ibid., l. 99.

CHAPTER 3

Uncanny

Appliquant l'*analogie* de l'être à sa méfiance, intrigué par les diverses phases de
son démon tutélaire, et bientôt décidé à fonder une secte sur le tempérament
lunatique — ambitieux jusqu'à vouloir faire figure de jaloux hérésiarque au sein
de l'orthodoxie *éphésienne*, [Actéon] avait décelé dans une locution aussi banale
que: *les chiens hurlent à la lune* comme le vestige d'une vérité secrète.

[By applying the *analogy* of being to his mistrust, mystified by the diverse phases
of his tutelary daemon and forthwith resolved to found a sect on the *lunatic*
temperament — as well as ambitious enough to want to appear as a jealous
heresiarch in the very bosom of the *Ephesian* orthodoxy — [Actaeon] had
uncovered, in as a banal an expression as *the dogs howl at the moon*, something
like the vestige of a secret truth.]

PIERRE KLOSSOWSKI, *Le Bain de Diane*, pp. 18–19,
translated by S. Sartarelli

Got to keep movin', I've got to keep movin'
Blues fallin' down like hail, blues fallin' down like hail
And the day keeps on worrin' me, there's a hellhound on my trail
Hellhound on my trail, hellhound on my trail

ROBERT JOHNSON, *Hellhound on My Trail* (1937)

The Palace of Memory

After physically returning to his family house in 1829, Leopardi gives birth to
'Le ricordanze', a poem in which the 'return home' catalyzes the unexpected
reawakening of long-gone memories. By alternately shifting between physical and
poetic 'stanzas', those of the Leopardi palace and those of the poem, 'Le ricordanze'
displays an oscillatory movement between physical and mental spaces; through a
complex game of refractions, fantasy, actuality, and recollection are superimposed
one over the other, mirrored by the floating interweavement of verbal tenses
— present, historical past, and *imperfetto*. The memories conjured by the family
house are almost immediately converted into the poetic undulations of the text,
through a freewheeling monologue aimed at rendering the indistinguishable
juxtaposition of past and present. The contrast between the hopes of childhood
and the disenchantment of maturity is rendered by juxtaposing recollections and
current sensations, thereby polarizing the activity of memory between sweetness
and sorrow.[1]

Which is the 'home' the subject has returned to? The poem begins with an apostrophe addressed to the stars of the Great Bear:

> Vaghe stelle dell'Orsa, io non credea
> Tornare ancor per uso a contemplarvi
> Sul paterno giardino scintillanti
> E ragionar con voi dalle finestre
> Di questo albergo ove abitai fanciullo.[2]

[Shimmering stars of the Bear, I never thought that I would be back again to see you shine over my father's garden and talk with you from the windows of this house where I lived as a child.]

The act of customarily talking to the stars signals how the return home mirrors the return to another and infantile state of mind, an unforeseen resurfacing of memories that, as Alberto Folin argues, should be seen as the re-activation of a 'mythical' modality of seeing the world.[3] The acknowledgment of being 'back again' to see the stars announces the amazement of rediscovering one's self as still able to feel the charming power of illusions in the way young children do, condensed and symbolized by the act of addressing speech to inanimate lights perceived in the sky. As Alessandro Carrera notes, the dialogue with celestial bodies often reproduces, in Leopardi's oeuvre, a relationship between child and object that, in infantile psychology, precedes the articulation of language, resulting in a crucial step in the progressive self-construction of subjectivity.[4] The regression portrayed in the opening lines of 'Le ricordanze' therefore signals the return, albeit fleeting, to a pre-symbolic dimension of perception, namely — as we have seen — the return to the maternal *chora* that takes the vague and undefined shape of poetry by subverting the paternal and patriarchal speech. Carrera points out that this phase corresponds to an anthropological condition, rather than to an ontological one:[5] while perceiving the stars in a way that once used to be customary and familiar, the adult and enlightened subject can momentarily re-access a 'savage' frame of mind,[6] a modality of perception through which the dialogue with lifeless objects is unexpectedly possible once again.

Animistic belief and the tendency to personify abstract entities lie at the innermost core of Leopardi's anthropological thought, and as such they form the backbone of the 'mythological system' [sistema [...] mitologico], outlined in the *Zibaldone* while discussing the problem of Romanticism.[7] For Leopardi, Romantic poetry tends to construct skilful and artificial personifications in order to replace the mythological figures inherited by literary tradition, which unavoidably dooms it to kitsch and affectation. Human nature tends instead, in a spontaneous way, to 'dare agli oggetti inanimati, agli Dei, e fino ai propri affetti, pensieri e forme e affetti umani' [bestow human thoughts and forms and emotions upon inanimate objects, Gods, and even feelings]; true mythology is not an artificial construction, but rather an intrinsic drive of human nature. Whereas Madame de Staël had exhorted Italian writers to abandon their Greek and Latin 'fables' (*favole*) as untimely residues of an outworn literary tradition,[8] Leopardi shows, instead, how their survival in Western culture cannot be reduced to the mere survival of literary clichés. For Leopardi, ancient myths correspond to the antiquity of everyone's own development; that is to say, those beliefs of childhood that have been later surmounted by adult disenchantment. A proper use of myths possesses therefore the power of reactivating an infantile (and quintessentially poetic) feeling.

In Leopardi's oeuvre, this association between 'children' and 'ancients' is constantly asserted by stressing how they both share an animistic frame of mind, and tend to attribute human qualities and thoughts to inanimate beings. In a page of the *Zibaldone* drafted in 1819, which we may consider as the first elaboration of themes later explored in the 1822 poem 'Alla primavera', Leopardi compares infantile beliefs to early Greek religion:

> Che bel tempo era quello nel quale ogni cosa era viva secondo l'immaginazione umana e viva umanamente cioè abitata o formata di esseri uguali a noi, quando nei boschi desertissimi si giudicava per certo che abitassero le belle Amadriadi e i fauni e i silvani e Pane ec. ed entrandoci e vedendoci tutto solitudine pur credevi tutto abitato e così de' fonti abitati dalle Naiadi ec. e stringendoti un albero al seno te lo sentivi quasi palpitare fra le mani credendolo un uomo o donna come Ciparisso ec. e così de' fiori ec. come appunto i fanciulli.[9]

> [What a marvelous time it was when everything was alive, according to human imagination, and humanly alive, in other words inhabited or formed by beings like ourselves; when it was taken as certain that in the deserted woods lived the beautiful Hamadryads and fauns and woodland deities and Pan, etc., and, on entering and seeing everything as solitude, you still believed that everything was inhabited and that Naiads lived in the springs, etc., and embracing a tree you felt it almost palpitating between your hands and believed it was a man or a woman like Cyparissus, etc., and the same with flowers, etc., just as children do.]

This reflection was already present in the discourse on Romantic poetry, in which Leopardi asserts that:

> Quello che furono gli antichi, siamo stati noi tutti, e quello che fu il mondo per qualche secolo, siamo stati noi per qualche anno, dico fanciulli e partecipi di quella ignoranza e di quei timori e di quei diletti e di quelle credenze e di quella sterminata operazione della fantasia; quando il tuono e il vento e il sole e gli astri e gli animali e le piante e le mura de' nostri alberghi, ogni cosa ci appariva o amica o nemica nostra, indifferente nessuna, insensata nessuna; quando ciascun oggetto che vedevamo ci pareva che in certo modo accennando, quasi mostrasse di volerci favellare; quando in nessun luogo soli, interrogavamo le immagini e le pareti e gli alberi e i fiori e le nuvole, e abbracciavamo sassi e legni, e quasi ingiuriati malmenavamo e quasi benefiziati carezzavamo cose incapaci d'ingiuria e di benefizio.[10]

> [What the ancients were, so have we all been, and what the world was for centuries, so were we for some years, and that is, children: participants in that ignorance and in those fears and delights and beliefs and in that excessive fantasizing that belongs to childhood; when the thunder and the wind and the sun and stars and animals and plants and the very walls of our houses, all things, were either friends or enemies but never indifferent or meaningless for us; when every object that we saw seemed to be trying to tell a story; when we were never alone and we interrogated the painted walls and the trees and flowers and the clouds, and when we embraced stones and trees, and as though offended we punished, or as though blessed we cherished, things incapable of inflicting injury or conferring bliss.]

In this passage, the sphere of ontogenesis is superimposed on and fused with that of phylogenesis: infancy is assimilated to antiquity, which is seen as the 'infancy of humanity' through an 'organicistic' way of narrating historical progression.[11] The alinear mechanics of subjective memory enlighten cultural ones and vice versa, outlining — as we shall see — a model for interpreting the history of culture in an equally disrupted and intermittent way, characterized by phenomena of repression, survival, and unexpected return.

We should not fail to notice how Leopardi's superimposition between psychological structures of childhood and ancient beliefs is grounded in a very specific paradigmatic framework, namely the evolutionary scheme employed in cultural history since the eighteenth century. The encounter with non-European cultures following the colonization of the Americas had since the sixteenth century led to the progressive erosion of the Biblical and theological hypothesis of single and unique linear descent, paving the ground for an evolutionary way of interpreting the history of civilization. The reflection on origin creates an equation between children, 'ancients', and the 'primitives' as homologous subjects that shed reciprocal light upon each other, thus bridging such differentiated forms of knowledge as anthropology, psychology, ethnography, and antiquarian philology. This common paradigmatic frame is perfectly epitomized by the frontispiece of the French Jesuit Joseph-François Lafitau's *Mœurs des sauvages amériquains comparés aux mœurs des premiers temps* [Customs of the American Primitives Compared to the Customs of Antiquity], published in 1724. In this artwork the geographical and cultural alterity of native Americans is conceptualized through a historical perception that implies the construction as an otherness of Mediterranean antiquity itself: statues, medals, and fragments of ancient art are amassed like 'obsolete objects' on the ground, while the angel of history addresses the writing muse's gaze to the Eden-like purity of 'primitives' that are portrayed as veritable living fossils.[12] The last stanza of Leopardi's 'Inno ai patriarchi, o de' principii del genere umano' [Hymn to the Patriarchs, or on the Origins of the Human Race], of 1822, reproduces the same connection, by comparing the ancients to the 'beata prole' [blessed race][13] born in the 'vaste californie selve' [boundless California forests].[14]

No differently did Aby Warburg think, while adding as an epigraph to his conference paper on the 'Serpent Ritual' an ironic rephrasing of a quotation from Goethe's *Faust*, 'It is an old book to be leafed through | Athens-Oraibi, all kinsfolk' ('Es ist ein altes Buch zu blättern: | Athen-Oraibi, alles Vettern').[15] In this text, presented at the Kreuzlingen mental clinic in 1923 but only posthumously published in 1939, Warburg outlines the possibility of interpreting Pueblo religion in the light of Greek myths and vice versa, thus bypassing the philological need for direct and documentable connections in order to assert cultural kinships. In doing this, Warburg was freely re-elaborating several influences absorbed in his youth, from the writings of the Italian philosopher Tito Vignoli on myth, science, and evolution, to the seminars on cultural science and the history of religion that he had attended in 1886–88 at the University of Bonn, in which scholars such as Hermann Usener and Karl Lamprecht had asserted the need for a comparative study of religion grounded in a synergy between philology and anthrophology.[16]

Usener's comparative approach, as well as Vignoli's and Lamprecht's evolutionist theories on the history of human culture, thus brought Warburg to understand the lore of the Pueblos as a living 'survival of antiquity', shedding direct light on the mythological frame of mind of earlier stages of cultural development. Moreover, even if native American cultures are undergoing a process of secularization as a consequence of colonialism, this survival cannot be completely lost, as the example of children tellingly demonstrates. When asked to sketch the scene of a storm described in a fairy tale, Warburg says, some Pueblo schoolboys drew lightning bolts in a Western fashion; however, two children portrayed them in the very same way their ancestors would have, namely in the shape of snakes.[17] This experience locates the *Nachleben der Antike* at the intersection between ontogenesis and phylogenesis, promoting a psychological reading of history (and, vice versa, a historical-evolutionist understanding of human development); at the same time, it constructs the 'mythological view' as a form of knowledge that survives underneath (and despite) the secularization promoted by modern culture.[18] 'The Indian,' Warburg writes, 'stands midway between logic and magic, and his instrument of orientation is the symbol. Between the primitive man who snatches the nearest booty, and the enlightened man who plans and awaits the result of his action, is the man who interposes symbols between himself and the world'.[19] Like Leopardi, Warburg is extremely critical of the advantages of post-Enlightenment rationalistic overcoming of ancient 'illusions': even if technological development has mitigated the 'fears' of natural elements that are characteristic of 'primitive' cultures, Warburg writes, 'we should be loth to decide whether this emancipation from the mythological view really helps mankind to find a fitting answer to the problems of existence'.[20] Notwithstanding, mythology survives and resurfaces within the fullest of modernity, even if its presence has become unperceivable and undefined: as children perceive the world or in the smallest details of images, in which 'ancient' formulas of pathos are re-activated. For Warburg, images possess an unconscious, which corresponds to a demonic and subterranean dimension — the very plates of the *Bilderatlas Mnemosyne* have been seen as an afterimage of ritual Hopi altars, in which images convey the actual presence of demons.[21] The post-Enlightenment perception of the universe, in surmounting the 'poetic mythology'[22] of children and of ancient civilizations, constrains it to resurface obliquely from the unconscious of culture, producing a feeling of estrangement. The conference paper on the 'Serpent Ritual', read by Warburg while he himself was a clinical patient, can be seen as a negotiation with one's own personal demons: the clash between post-Enlightenment rationalism and symbolic and mythological thought stems from Warburg's own experience of mental disease, which is equally grounded in a tension between rationality and the resurfacing of an 'irrational' that modern psychiatric knowledge has relegated to the domain of psychosis. Exactly in the same way as the 'imaginary breeze' of Renaissance painters epitomized, in Warburg's essay on Botticelli, the survival of antiquity in the form of an erupting otherness, the 'Serpent Ritual' paper deals with the alienating return of something allegedly buried that unexpectedly and troublingly reappears.

Parallel with Warburg's operation, another intellectual experience of the early twentieth century challenges similar questions, although via a completely different route: not from myth to infancy, but the other way round. Written in 1919, Freud's essay on 'The Uncanny'[23] establishes a close connection between childhood omnipotence and magical-supernatural beliefs: the uncanny comes to the fore when the adult and rational subject encounters something 'that ought to have remained ... secret and hidden but has come to light',[24] either being a residual of childhood impressions or the survival of mythical-superstitious beliefs inherited from the 'infancy of humanity'.[25] The ambiguity between ontogenesis and phylogenesis remains unresolved in Freud's text. The two possibilities are superimposed one upon the other, making it impossible to draw a clear distinction between individual and collective memory:

> We — or our primitive forefathers — once believed that these possibilities were realities [...]. Nowadays we no longer believe in them, we have *surmounted* [*überwunden*] these modes of thought; but we do not feel quite sure of our new beliefs, and the old ones still exist within us [*die alten leben noch in uns fort*] [...]. As soon as something *actually happens* in our lives which seems to confirm the old, discarded [*abgelegten*] beliefs we get a feeling of the uncanny.[26]

Moreover, Freud conceptualizes the equation between children, ancients, and 'primitives' by referring to animism and to the personification of abstract entities. This element was already present in Ernst Jentsch's article of 1906, 'On the Psychology of the Uncanny', in which it is noted how, 'among all the psychical uncertainties' that may arouse uncanny feelings, the only one presenting 'a fairly regular, powerful and very general effect' is the '*doubt as to whether an apparently living being is animate and, conversely, doubt as to whether a lifeless object may not in fact be animate*'.[27] Freud quotes this passage in 'The Uncanny', adding that a stronger feeling of the uncanny is given by 'the impression made by waxwork figures, ingeniously constructed dolls and automata [*Wachsfiguren, kunstvollen Puppen und Automaten*]',[28] in which the uncanny may be seen as the afterimage of the sacred supernatural that used to be anciently connected with idols.[29] The beliefs of children and those of ancients/primitives share therefore, for Leopardi, Warburg, and Freud, a common structure, blurring the borders between individual and collective psychology. In his essay, Freud connects the definition of 'omnipotence of thoughts', which he had coined for the case of the 'Rat-Man', with the religious beliefs of animism. The passage shows striking similarities with Leopardi's description of children's 'ancient' state of mind, and it is therefore necessary to quote it in its entirety:

> Our analysis of instances of the uncanny has led us back to the old, animistic conception of the universe. This was characterized by the idea that the world was peopled with the spirits of human beings; by the subject's narcissistic overevaluation of his own mental processes; by the belief in the omnipotence of thoughts and the technique of magic based on that belief; by the attribution to various outside persons and things of carefully graded magical powers, or 'mana'; as well as by all the other creations with help of which man, in the unrestricted narcissism of that stage of development, strove to fend off the manifest prohibitions of reality. It seems as if each one of us has been passing through a phase of individual development corresponding to this animistic stage in primitive men, that none of us has passed through it without preserving

certain residues and traces of it which are still capable of manifesting themselves, and that everything which now strikes us as 'uncanny' fulfils the condition of touching those residues of animistic mental activity within us and bringing them to expression.[30]

Once read in the light of this paradigm, the opening lines of 'Le ricordanze' display a tension between a once familiar and disregarded magical perception and the disenchanted gaze of the modern and adult subject, a tension that is rooted in the same oscillation between homeliness and unhomeliness underlying Freud's analysis of the uncanny. This reading of 'Le ricordanze' through Freud's essay of 1919 is further confirmed by considering a crucial element of the poem. As we have seen, 'Le ricordanze' articulates a two-fold meaning of return: the return to a mythical-mythological way of seeing the world and of speaking with inanimate objects, and the νόστος to a physical space that is transfigured in a mythical way.[31] In both cases, we have a 'return home', namely to places that used to be familiar, and, more generally, to the sphere of the customary and the habitual.

Although the construction of the poem as a flow of loose hendecasyllables aims to highlight the rhapsodic movement of thought, incorporating the dancing movement of bundled memories, it is worth remarking that one of the motifs that emerges from the text is that of places, being at the same time physical *loci* and *loci memoriæ* around which the process of recollection coalesces. The overview of the palace starts from the garden ('sul paterno giardino' [over my father's garden])[32] and the windows ('dalle finestre | Di questo albergo' [from the windows of this house])[33] and then moves to the 'voci' [voices][34] coming from beneath; it widens towards the horizon, 'la vista | Di quel lontano mar, quei monti azzurri' [the sight of that far sea, those blue mountains],[35] before returning to the 'buia stanza' [dark room][36] from which the subject hears 'il suon dell'ora | Dalla torre del borgo' [the hour that tolls from the town tower].[37] It enters the house, 'Quella loggia colà' [that loggia there],[38] 'queste dipinte mura, | Quei figurati armenti, e il Sol che nasce | Su romita campagna' [these painted walls, those pictured herds, and the Sun that rises over lonely country];[39] it follows 'queste sale antiche' [these ancient rooms][40] and walks alongside 'queste | Ampie finestre' [these wide windows];[41] it eventually points 'colà [...] la fontana' [that fountain [...] there][42] while recalling suicidal fantasies, before turning to Nerina's places, the 'colli' [hills],[43] 'ogni fiorita | Piaggia' [each blooming hill],[44] and the window that is now 'deserta' [empty].[45]

'Le ricordanze' is a poem about 'coming back home': as Jacques Lacan suggested while commenting Freud's 'The Uncanny', the word 'home' (*maison*) should be invested with all possible resonances, including astrological ones.[46] The 'home' is a familiar place connected to infancy and origin (what Lonardi terms Leopardi's 'luoghi primi' [primal places]),[47] which is best expressed in German by the word *Heim*, whose linguistic analysis forms the backbone of Freud's interpretation of the uncanny. The *Heim* is actually more than a physical space: it is essentially an affective perimeter, the field of 'homeliness' and the place where the Ego feels 'home', which explains why it forms the root of the German word for 'uncanny', *das Unheimliche*. As Anthony Vidler writes, 'the word *heimlich* is [...] linked to domesticity (*Häuslichkeit*), to being at home (*heimatlich*) or being neighborly (*freundnachbarlich*)'.[48]

First and foremost, the *Heim* is constructed as a familiar place insofar as it is invested and inextricably connected with memory. To speak in Leopardi's terms, the *Heim* is the place where 'non è cosa | Ch'io vegga o senta, onde un'immagin dentro | Non torni, e un dolce rimembrar non sorga' [There's nothing here I see or feel but that some image does not live in me again, some sweet memory come to light].[49] The *Heim* is a setting in which every sign denotes a specific meaning, according to an established semiotic code.

At the same time, the *Heim* also possesses an ambiguous and troubling aspect, which may lead us to problematize Leopardi's understanding of returning 'home' further. While questioning Breme's praise of Romanticism in the *Zibaldone*, Leopardi had tried to enumerate the elements that could form a hypothetical 'sentimental landscape', 'la campana del luogo natio, (così dic[e Breme]) e io aggiungo la vista di una campagna, di una torre diroccata ec. ec.' [the bells of the place where one was born (as Breme says) and I add the sight of a country landscape, a ruined tower, etc. etc.].[50] What Leopardi is actually asserting is that what excites feeling is nature, 'purissima, tal qual'è, tal quale la vedevano gli antichi' [nature, in its purest form, as it is, as the ancients saw it], 'per propria forza insita in lei, e non tolta in prestito da nessuna cosa' [by its own inherent force, not borrowed from any other thing].[51] If the adjective 'natio' (which could be perfectly translated as *heimlich*) surreptitiously introduces the shadow of subjective recollection, it is worth remarking how Leopardi's addition — which is completely pleonastic (and hence far more important from the point of view of unconscious memory) — takes as its chosen examples such pivotal elements of Leopardi's imagery as the 'tower' and the 'country'. The tower had been constructed as a typical icon of the eighteenth-century sublime through Edmund Burke's *Philosophical Enquiry into the Origin of our Ideas of the Sublime* (1757).[52] The two terms appear however to be strictly related in Leopardi's oeuvre, as happens in the poem 'Il pensiero dominante' (c. 1830–32) [The Dominant Idea], in which the persistent thought of love is compared to a '*torre* | In solitario *campo*' [*tower* in an empty *field*],[53] as well as in the initial couplet of 'Il passero solitario', 'D'in su la vetta della *torre* antica, | Passero solitario, alla *campagna*' [High on the rooftop of the ancient *tower*, Solitary thrush, to the *countryside*].[54] Moreover, several passages of the *Zibaldone* couple the terms 'torre' and 'campagna', always in connection with the themes of 'vagueness' and 'indefiniteness'.[55]

As Freud maintains, the uncanny (*Unheimliche*) is rooted in the sphere of familiarity (*Heimlichkeit*): the uncanny is the form of anxiety that becomes manifest in the field of homeliness, either when something homely presents itself in a slightly distorted shape or when something extraneous and de-familiarizing bursts into the 'homely' space of the 'house of the Ego'. From this angle, the opening lines of 'Le ricordanze' display an apostrophe, addressed to the stars of the Bear, whose actual meaning is the intimate acknowledgment of the return to an 'ancient' state of mind. Alberto Folin reconstructs this process as the veritable acknowledgment of something that once used to be familiar and then, apparently forgotten, unexpectedly returns, 'rather than as an invocation, the appellation "Shimmering stars of the Bear" sounds more as the identification of someone who once used to be familiar, and who — as such — suddenly reappears, inviting to greet'.[56] This process is not much different from that of the Freudian uncanny, described in the essay of 1919 as 'something which is familiar and old-established in the mind and which has become alienated from it only through the process of repression [*etwas dem Seelenleben von alters her Vertrautes, das ihm nur durch den Prozeß der Verdrängung entfremdet worden ist*]'.[57] The feeling engendered by this unforeseen return — a mixture of joy and surprise — is surely different from the vague disease caused by the experience of the uncanny. Still, the tension between familiarity and unexpectedness is very close, grounding the feeling that gives rise to poetic speech in the unpredicted return of an animistic frame of mind. The stars greeted by the subject at the very beginning of the poem signal that we are entering another sphere from the one of diurnal logic — the one of memory, dreams, and the return of the repressed.

In being an aesthetic experience rooted in a tension between homeliness and unhomeliness, as well as between proximity and distance, the uncanny presents a remarkable closeness to Leopardi's reflection. If the poetic of 'vagueness' and 'indefiniteness' itself is articulated in a shift between familiarity and non-familiarity, the discussion led by Leopardi in the *Zibaldone* about such concepts as those of grace and the sublime seems to situate aesthetical enjoyment in a liminal zone between pleasure and pathos, individuating the poetic effect in practices of distancing within the familiar or in a search for familiarity in otherness.

As far as the first kind of experience is concerned, Leopardi's aesthetic reflection, as we have seen, seems systematically to evaluate a form of oblique perception, the only one that can grant the experience of an aesthetic shudder, as happens with grace. A passage of the *Zibaldone* drafted in 1818 anticipates an image returning, more than ten years later, in 'Le ricordanze'. The solely auditory perception of the town tower's watch determines a feeling of estrangement, enhanced by the isolation of the subject in his dark room:

> Sento dal mio letto suonare (battere) l'orologio della torre. Rimembranze di quelle notti estive nelle quali essendo fanciullo e lasciato in letto in camera oscura, chiuse le sole persiane, tra la paura e il coraggio sentiva battere un tale orologio. Oppure situazione trasportata alla profondità della notte, o al mattino.[58]

> [From my bed I hear the ringing (striking) of the tower clock. Memories of those summer nights when I was a child left in bed in a dark room, with only the shutters closed, and suspended between fear and boldness hearing the striking of such a clock. Or the situation transferred to the dead of night, or the morning.]

In the same way, in 'L'infinito', the experience of bliss is located in a familiar space, in which the hedgerow that obstructs the sight of the horizon becomes the vehicle, as we have highlighted, for the conjuration of alterity. The opening line of the poem, 'Sempre caro mi fu quest'ermo colle' [This lonely hill was always dear to me], marks a strong caesura with the tradition of the sublime, turning from the wild landscapes of the iconographic tradition to the most familiar of all settings. The feeling of terror engendered by the sublime does not stem from objective features of the place, but from an inner experience that transfigures the familiarity of the 'dear' hill into a mental construction 'ove per poco | Il cor non si spaura' [till what I feel is almost fear].[59] The homeliness of the place is not merely a variation in the aesthetics of the sublime, but rather appears as a crucial element for the feeling of fear to be induced, as if Leopardi had acknowledged how the true *Unheimliche* could only stem from the familiarity of the *Heim*.

At the same time, Leopardi seems often to engender a subtle game of associations that transfigures uncustomary spaces into familiar echoes. In the letter sent to his sister on 25 February 1828, only the convergence created by the subject's fantasizing imagination between Pisa's unfamiliar cityscape and the familiar memory of Recanati can allow the experience of recollection and poetry-making:

> Io sogno sempre di voi altri, dormendo e vegliando: ho qui in Pisa una certa strada deliziosa, che io chiamo *Via delle Rimembranze*: là vo a passeggiare quando voglio sognare a occhi aperti. Vi assicuro che in materia d'immaginazioni, mi pare di esser tornato al mio buon tempo antico.[60]

> [I'm always dreaming about you all, asleep or awake: here in Pisa I have a delightful street, which I call *Street of Memories*: that is where I go to walk when I want to day-dream. I assure you that where imagination is concerned, I seem to be back to my good, ancient times.]

The same tension seems to be fully articulated in 'Le ricordanze', literally shaping the structure of the poem in a subterranean and intimate way. In defining the uncanny, Freud borrows a quotation from Schelling, 'everything is *unheimlich* that ought to have remained secret and hidden but has come to light [*alles, was ein Geheimnis, im Verborgenen bleiben sollte und hervorgetreten ist*]'.[61] This definition is singularly flexible, and actually opens several possibilities of interpretation. Freud's text itself seems to follow two separate lines of analysis that determine the peculiar ambiguity — and the charming newness — of his essay. On the one hand, the uncanny operates in the sphere of the subject's own development, as the return of a repressed memory that belongs to childhood. The feeling of *déjà vu* would for example be the unconscious recollection of 'the entrance to the former *Heim* (home) of all human beings, to the place where each one of us lived once upon a time and in the beginning. [...] In this case [...] the *unheimlich* is what was once *heimisch*, familiar; the prefix '*un*' ('un-') is the token of repression'.[62] On the other hand, the process of repression is projected onto a cultural scale, a path of inquiry that — moving on from Freud's essay — is developed with great finesse, for example, by Michel de Certeau:[63] 'an uncanny effect is often and easily produced when the distinction between imagination and reality is effaced, as when something that we have hitherto regarded as imaginary appears before us in reality, or when a symbol takes over the full functions of the thing it symbolises, and so on', namely when the 'civilized' culture of modernity finds itself trapped in a magical and mythical frame of thought.[64] Indeed, this ambiguity underlies Leopardi's 'Le ricordanze' too: 'ancient' beliefs (either in the form of childhood memories or of the illusions of the 'ancients') undergo a process of burial, and their return engenders a feeling of wonder and surprise that produces a both personal and universal, inner and historical meditation. Leopardi's ambiguity is the same as Freud's, first and foremost because their respective cultural backgrounds are rooted in the Enlightenment.[65] By this term, I do not mean to evoke the monolithic construction hypothesized, for instance, by Horkheimer and Adorno's *Dialectic of Enlightenment* (1947), but rather to speak of a critical modality of analysis directed against 'errors' and 'prejudices' retraced in the text of tradition, which is exactly the cultural perspective from which the young Leopardi operates while writing the *Saggio sopra gli errori popolari degli antichi*:

> [Questa operetta] non è inutile, benché non abbia per oggetto che i *pregiudizi degli antichi* [...]. Per renderla ancor più profittevole, ho cercato spesso [...] di *paragonare gli antichi coi moderni*, e di far vedere che taluno degli errori, dei quali avea parlato, *sussisteva tuttora nel popolo*. [...] Uno degli oggetti che si sono proposti alcuni tra quelli che hanno scritto degli errori popolari, è stato quello di confutarli. Scrivendo *in un secolo illuminato* ho creduto quasi inutile il farlo. Nondimeno, *poiché molti degli errori communi una volta agli antichi non sono ancora distrutti*, ho stimato bene di far parola di tratto in tratto anche di quegli scrittori antichi, che hanno condannata qualche falsa opinione, adottata generalmente nel loro secolo.[66]

> [This little work is not useless, although it only takes as its subject *the prejudices of ancients* [...]. In order to make it more profitable, I have often tried [...] *to compare the ancients with the moderns*, and to show how some errors that I had treated *still survive in people's beliefs*. [...] Some who wrote on popular errors have had the aim of confuting them. Because I live *in an enlightened age*, I thought that doing so would be quite useless. Still, *given that many errors that once were common for the ancients have not yet been destroyed*, I thought better to mention, from time to time, those ancient writers who had condemned some false beliefs that their age used generally to accept.]

As Francesco Orlando highlights, the perspective of the Enlightenment's demystification of 'errors' is exactly the same as the one that structures Freud's essay on the uncanny. By broadening the structure of unconscious processes to phenomena of cultural history, Freud's essay of 1919 legitimates the extension of the notion of 'repression' (*Verdrängung*) outside the sphere of psychoanalysis, establishing an analogy between the repression of childhood beliefs on the basis of the individual's intellectual development and the surmounting of 'irrational' beliefs on a cultural scale. This hesitating ambiguity of Freud's text justifies, as Orlando notes, the possibility of employing the structure of the repression process to phenomena of cultural fracture, and most notably to that of the Enlightenment: the emergence of fantastic literature and its stress on the uncanny in the post-Enlightenment age is to be intended as a 'return of the surmounted' (*ritorno del superato*), in which themes that were once familiar, in that they used to belong to the sphere of the sacred supernatural, are metamorphosed into an obliquely fearful otherness.[67] Like Warburg and Benjamin, Freud comes close to a conceptualization of historicity that necessarily implies the theorization of an 'unconscious of time': the analysis of phenomena of fracture, repression, and survival in cultural history makes the task of the historian a sort of interpretation of dreams.[68]

If we return to the quotation from Schelling employed by Freud, we should consequently acknowledge that what 'ought to have remained secret and hidden but has come to light' denotes both an autobiographical memory connected to infancy and a semantic-anthropological memory connected to the 'infancy of humanity'. As we have seen, in Leopardi, Warburg, and Freud the same ambiguity is evident: the individual 'spirit' that 'ha percorso lo stesso stadio che lo spirito umano in generale' [has followed the same course as the human spirit in general],[69] embodies the very same duplicity that we find in the 'Serpent Ritual' and 'The Uncanny'. The uncanny feeling stems from the sudden and disturbing encounter with something 'past', which the philosophical development of both subject and society has surmounted.

The uncanny — as the return of a mythological frame of mind — can therefore be defined as the return of an 'error', of an incorrect belief that contrasts with a (collective and individual) cultural maturity. It is useful to note how this is exactly Leopardi's understanding of the Greek notion of μῦθος. Carlo Ginzburg has shown in detail how this word is often connoted, in Western tradition, by the sense of 'fable' as an 'untrue' discourse, and therefore opposed to λόγος.[70] This analysis was however already developed by Leopardi in the *Zibaldone*, following a cultural tradition that, within the Italian milieu, goes back to Vico's *Scienza nuova* [New Science].[71] In Leopardi, the terms 'mito' and 'favola' are often confused and superimposed in that they both refer to the sphere of the 'untrue', an association that is justified in the *Zibaldone* through etymological considerations:

> l'antico e il primitivo significato di *fabula*, non era *favola*, ma *discorso*, da *for faris*, quasi *piccolo discorso*, onde poi si trasferì al significato di *ciancia nugae*, e finalmente di *finzione* e *racconto falso*. Appunto come il greco μῦθος nel suo significato proprio, valeva lo stesso che λόγος, [...] e da Omero non si trova, cred'io, adoperato se non in questa o simili significazioni [...]. Poi fu trasferito alla significazione di *favola*.[72]

> [The ancient and original meaning of *fabula* was not *fable* but *speech*, from *for faris*, something like a *short speech*, whence it acquired the meaning of *idle talk*, *chitchat*, and finally that of *fiction* and *false account*. Precisely like the Greek μῦθος, which in its proper meaning is the same as λόγος, [...] and from Homer onward is not found, or so I believe, save with this or similar meanings [...]. Then it acquired the meaning of *fable*.]

We witness here a semantic constellation in which the notions of myth, fairy tale or fable, error, prejudice, falsity, and illusion undergo a meaningful process of interchangeability. In Leopardi, the 'illusion' is always intrinsically, and even etymologically, a 'myth', which partially explains Leopardi's very personal use of explicit mythological sources.[73] In the *Canti*, openly mythical images are always declared as illusory, as happens in 'Alla primavera':

> Già di candide ninfe i rivi albergo,
> Placido albergo e specchio
> Furo i liquidi fonti. Arcane danze
> D'immortal piede i ruinosi gorghi
> Scossero e l'ardue selve (oggi romito
> Nido de' venti): e il pastorel ch'all'ombre
> Meridiane incerte ed al fiorito
> Margo adducea de' fiumi
> Le sitibonde agnelle, arguto carme
> Sonar d'agresti Pani
> Udì lungo le ripe; e tremar l'onda

Vide, e stupì, che non palese al guardo
La faretrata Diva
Scendea ne' caldi flutti, e dall'immonda
Polve tergea della sanguigna caccia
Il niveo lato e le verginee braccia.[74]

[Bright nymphs walked on your shores once, your clear springs were their tranquil home and mirror. Hidden dancing of immortal feet beat on the ruined heights and in the impenetrable forests (distant nest for winds today). And the shepherd boy who led his thirsty lambs among the fleeting noontime shadows and the flowering banks could hear the shrills of woodland Pans piping on the shores and saw the water's surface shimmer and, in amazement, watched the arrow-bearing Goddess enter the warm waves unrecognized to wash the foul dust of the bloody hunt from her snow-white sides and virgin arms.]

Leopardi's semantic extension of the notion of 'myth' to the broader sphere of 'untruth' legitimates however the possibility of perceiving mythical structures and mythologems, in the sense defined by Jung and Kerényi, in more subterranean veins of his oeuvre. In the poem 'Alla sua Donna', for instance, Cesare Galimberti has retraced a subterranean Gnostic shadow between the lines of an *excusatio non petita*.[75] In the notes to the poem Leopardi overjustifies his employing of the article in the expression 'L'una' in line 46, suggesting that behind the literal meaning ('the one and only') homophony may suggest the hidden presence of the moon-goddess (*Luna*). Often, a mythical element resurfaces beneath a *lapsus calami* or in the form of an unperceivable intertextual echo, which makes it difficult to identify its actual intention. For example, while elaborating his own 'sistema di belle arti' in the first pages of the *Zibaldone*, Leopardi proposes a terminological triad ('Passioni morti tempeste ec. piacciono egregiamente benchè sian brutte per questo solo che son bene imitate' [Passions, deaths, storms, etc., give us great pleasure in spite of their ugliness for the simple reason that they are well imitated])[76] that structurally echoes a passage from the *Saggio sopra gli errori popolari degli antichi*, 'la voluttà, la libidine, il pallore, la febbre, la tempesta, ebbero tempii ed incensi' [pleasure, lust, paleness, fever, and storm, had temples and religious honours].[77] 'Volontà' and 'libidine' are subsumed under the general term 'passioni', the illness ('febbre') directly turns to 'morti', while the 'tempesta' remains unaltered, although becoming plural. The echo between the two passages, although probably unconscious, confirms how the 'favole antiche', retraced in the wide corpus of the classical irrational, are assimilated as literary expedients, thus confirming their common nature as illusions. If 'myth' is, for Leopardi, the frame of mind that everybody shares in childhood, and into which one can fall again through the momentary suspension of disbelief granted by art or by a certain disposition to fantasy (as is the case of the beginning of 'Le ricordanze'), then the 'semantic memory' of the 'favole antiche' and the autobiographical memory of infantile illusions may collide and interact.

The 'cheating' nature of myth, although explicitly denied by rational thinking, casts thus an umbra back onto the text, determining an undecidability that comes close to that of the fantastic, as defined by Tzvetan Todorov. Albeit 'repressed' and 'surmounted' by Leopardi's rationalistic modality of thought, myth is re-activated at the moment in which this thought decides to turn to poetry and to a figurative and connotative language that chooses, rather than the paternal/patriarchal λόγος of philosophical discourse and argumentative rigour, the semiotic *chora* of emotionality, vagueness, and rhythmic patterns. It can be therefore said that, with the cantos of 1828–29, Leopardi consciously regresses from the diurnal and logical structures of language to a nocturnal, symbolic, and figurative alternate logic, a pre-verbal state of mind that forces the boundaries of speech in order to regain access to an allegedly forgotten perimeter of 'homeliness'. Returning to poetry means returning home, to a maternal womb in which language is dissolved and sublimated into music, and into a kaleidoscopic interweavement of *images*.

Ghost-Stories for Adults

In 'Le ricordanze', as we have seen, the mnestic process is activated by the mediation of images, corresponding to the physical places or *loci* of the house transfigured into as many *loci memoriæ*. The tradition of the 'art of memory', elaborated in classical antiquity and later refined through the Middle Ages and the Renaissance, is given by Leopardi a final concretization and a significant twist: on the one hand, whereas classical mnemonics recommended the mental composition of a fairly ordered 'palace of memory' as a visual embodiment of an organized mnemonic structure, 'Le ricordanze' reifies the imagined palace of tradition into the actuality of the Leopardi family house; on the other, the memories conjured up by this process are situated, as we have seen, on an ambiguous ridge between familiarity and estrangement, suggesting a passive position of the subject which is literally no longer 'master in its own house'.[78] The 'images' perceived in the space of the 'house'/*Heim* catalyze the unexpected resurfacing of memories, creating an indistinguishable superimposition between visual and actual images and the inner-standing point from which they are perceived. The images evoked in 'Le ricordanze' are therefore φαντάσματα in the fullest Greek and Aristotelian acceptation of the word, as far as they are external perceptions impressed by the mediation of the eye, invested with desire, transmitted to phantasy, and possessed by memory; as Giorgio Agamben synthesizes, in Aristotle's theory 'there is no memory without a phantasm'.[79] The process of memory on which 'Le ricordanze' is articulated is therefore a complex game of phantasmal elaboration:

> Qui non è cosa
> Ch'io vegga o senta, onde un'immagin dentro
> Non torni, e un dolce rimembrar non sorga.
> Dolce per se; ma con dolor sottentra
> Il pensier del presente, un van desio
> Del passato, ancor tristo, e il dire: io fui.
> Quella loggia colà, volta agli estremi
> Raggi del dì; queste dipinte mura,
> Quei figurati armenti, e il Sol che nasce
> Su romita campagna, agli ozi miei
> Porser mille diletti allor che al fianco
> M'era, parlando, il mio possente errore
> Sempre, ov'io fossi.[80]

[There is nothing here I see or feel but that some image does not live in me again, some sweet memory come to light. Sweet in itself; but knowledge of the present replaces it with pain, and a vain desire for the past, however sad, and the wish to say: I was. That loggia there, which faces the day's last rays, these painted walls, those pictured herds, and the Sun that rises over lonely countryside, offered a thousand pleasures as I lay with my omnipotent imagination, ever eloquent and always with me.]

Poetic writing dissolves the borders between actuality and imagination: real places, situated in the present, become indistinguishable from the mental images preserved by memory and charged with affection and desire. This ambiguity shares a structural proximity with the most crucial impasse of psychoanalysis, namely the impossibility to draw a final distinction between reality and phantasm. Intersecting the very origins of psychoanalysis as a scientific discourse, this impasse remains unresolved throughout Freud's entire intellectual development. The scenes of paternal seduction that Freud initially believed to be actual recollections of his hysterical patients turn out to be phantasms, obliging Freud to admit, in a letter to Wilhelm Fliess of 21 September 1897, that — when speaking about the unconscious — it is impossible to properly distinguish ('unterscheiden') between truth ('die Wahrheit') and emotional fiction ('die mit Affekt besetzte Fiktion').[81] More than twenty years later, in *Beyond the Pleasure Principle* (1920), Freud eventually admits the irremediably provisional nature of every psychoanalytical, conceptual, and linguistic means: the often 'bewildering and obscure' ('befremdende und unanschauliche') nature of psychoanalytical vocabulary is due to to its being obliged to employ a 'figurative language' ('Bildersprache').[82] The necessity of adhering to the actuality of phenomena is consequentially hampered by the impossibility of neglecting its fictional aspects; psychoanalytical writing cannot help but being intrinsically hybrid, as well as rooted in an unresolved undecidability between fact and fiction. Moreover, this aspect possesses strong implications from a cultural angle. If, as we have seen, the notion of 'fiction' is encompassed within the semantic constellation of μῦθος as referring to the sphere of whatever is untrue, the eruption of a figurative and connotative *Bildersprache* within the scientific discourse echoes the resurfacing of the mythological sphere within post-Enlightenment secularization, namely the cultural process in which the uncanny is rooted.

As Anneleen Masschelein has highlighted, the essay on 'The Uncanny' does not, curiously, leave explicit traces in Freud's later oeuvre:[83] however, this consideration of *Beyond the Pleasure Principle*, written one year later, seems to stem obliquely from a passage in the previous text. In 'The Uncanny', Freud establishes a comparison between psychoanalysis and fantastic literature, both being rooted in an undecidability between rationalistic instances and the resurfacing of 'bewildering and obscure' drives. 'The Middle Ages', writes Freud, 'attributed all these manifestations of sickness [...] to the influence of demons', so that he would not be surprised 'to hear that psychoanalysis, which seeks to uncover these secret forces, [has] for this reason itself come to seem uncanny to many people'.[84] As Erik Midelfort points out, 'Sigmund Freud and other founders of psychoanalysis spoke often of the devil and of subterranean forces', so that, 'instead of asking how psychoanalysis can be used to investigate the history of witchcraft, [it seems useful] to ask rather how the history of witchcraft can illuminate the origins of psychoanalysis'.[85] This ambiguity does not only haunt psychoanalysis as a form of knowledge, but actually pervades the whole culture of the post-Enlightenment age. The demolition of 'illusions' promoted by rationalism in the course of late-modern European thought casts an umbra back onto rationalism itself, as far as it is obliged to deal with figurative language and therefore to obliquely re-conjure the very chimeras, μῦθοι, it consciously aims to deny. As Jean Starobinski writes, while using myth in order to interpret phenomena of the subject's unconscious life, Freud's writing engenders the unpredictable effect of operating a 're-mythologization' of medical-psychological language:[86] re-activating myth in an age of disenchantment means, however, turning it into an uncanny presence. To quote a text by Heine that Freud much loved, the unconscious has become the uncanny Olympus of 'Gods in Exile', the venue of a troubling and estranged 'survival of antiquity'.

Leopardi's choice of poetry and its indefinite vagueness goes in the same direction, by employing figurative language in order to render the peculiar undecidability of mnestic processes, the superimposition between actual recollections and affective, retroactive constructions, and the ultimately pre-linguistic and visual dimension of the unconscious. If we return to the previously quoted lines from 'Le ricordanze', we note that the expression 'immagin dentro' is not merely a synonym for 'recollection'. Literally, the adverb 'dentro' is linked to the verb 'torni'; the enjambment, however, casts it back onto 'immagine', thus echoing the notion of the 'image in the heart' of classic mnemonics, a paradigm of visual thinking that is rooted in the Aristotelian theory of memory, and that reverberates in Freudian psychoanalysis[87] and its 'emphasis on the visual'.[88] As Didi-Huberman writes, 'the royal road to the unconscious' is identified by Freud in the:

> work of *figurability* that gives to dreams, symptoms, and phantasms their paradoxical visual quality, their dissemblant semblances. These semblances are always displaced, inextricably tied up with one another, touched by the great wind of the *Unheimliche*, and always condemned to become something other than what they are, to mingle with everything else, or even to disappear into obscure places below [...]. Every image is offered only as a maddening, often sublime, intensity of simultaneous contradictions, a meeting of heterogeneous orders that move unhindered between thing-representations and word-representations.[89]

'Le ricordanze' demonstrates this 'visual quality', through an underlying game of refractions that oscillates from actual *loci* and images to mnestic images that erupt 'within', and which are ultimately embodied by the 'figurability' of Leopardi's *Bildersprache*. Equally, the image does not present itself as a univocal object of interpretation, but as a set of simultaneous and contradictory stimuli tending towards both past and present, sweetness and pain. Already in *Silvio Sarno* the painted walls of the Leopardi palace and their 'pictured herds' would unchain a series of free associations in which memories of childhood were suffused with such obsessive themes as the sense of duty, paternal expectations, and infantile terrors:[90] 'Canto dopo le feste; Agnelli sul cielo della stanza, suono delle navi, Gentiloni (otium est pater ec.), Speziali (chierico), dettomi da mio padre ch'io dovea essere un dottore, Paure disciplinazione notturna dei missionari' [singing after festive days; Lambs on the room's sky, sound of ships, Gentiloni (otium est pater etc.), Grocers (cleric), my father telling me that I should become a doctor, Fears nocturnal flagellation of the missionaries].[91]

In this passage, the painted image fully coincides with the mental one: here, as Didi-Huberman would put it, 'image' is 'something completely different from a *picture*, a figurative illustration', but 'first of all a *crystal of time*, both a construct and a blazing shape, a sudden shock'.[92] Leopardi's *Bildersprache* incorporates past illusions and their affective connections within the object itself of recollection, through such devices as metonymy ('sky' for 'ceiling') or synaesthesia (the 'sound' of painted ships): thus, by skipping uniquely ekphrastic praxes, figurative language manages to come close to the process by which 'the dynamic unconscious often "sees" with clarity what conscious perception — grounded in merely "descriptive" faculties — obscures'.[93] These memories conceal, however, a deep feeling of terror connected with the night. In the expression 'Paure disciplinazione notturna dei missionari', the adjective 'notturna' is referred to 'disciplinazione', but taints at the same time the preceding significant. The passage can be therefore read as the kernel of the night-terrors evoked in 'Le ricordanze':

> Era conforto
> Questo suon, mi rimembra, alle mie *notti*,
> Quando fanciullo, nella buia stanza,
> Per assidui *terrori* io vigilava,
> Sospirando il mattin.[94]

[This sound, I can remember, was a comfort to my nights, when as a child I lay in my dark room prey to unrelenting *terrors*, sighing for morning.]

Biographers usually connect the 'Paure disciplinazione notturna dei missionari' of *Silvio Sarno* with a passage of Monaldo Leopardi's memoirs.[95] This is a short text written by Leopardi's father in July 1837 after his son's death, and which was meant to provide useful information for future critics. Relating Leopardi's childhood, Monaldo highlights a specific episode in order to stress his son's strong imagination ('fantasia'):

Da bambino [Giacomo] fu docilissimo, amabilissimo, ma sempre di una fantasia tanto calda apprensiva e vivace, che molte volte ebbi gravi timori di vederlo trascendere fuori di mente = Mentre aveva 3 o quattro anni si diedero qui le missioni; e i missionarii nei fervorini notturni erano accompagnati da alcuni confrati vestiti col sacco nero e col cappuccio sopra la testa. Li vidde e ne restò così spaventato che per più settimane non poteva dormire, e diceva sempre di temere i *bruttacci*. Noi tememmo allora molto per la sua salute, e per la sua mente.[96]

[As a child, Giacomo was very obedient and lovely, but always had such an excited, anxious and lively imagination that many times I feared to see him lose his mind. When he was three or four years old we hosted here some missionaries; during their nocturnal exhortations they were followed by some brothers of the same order, who were dressed with black habits and wearing cowls on their heads. He saw them, and took such fear that for several weeks he could not sleep, and always said he was scared by the *bruttacci* [the ugly ones]. We feared much, then, for his health and his mind.]

It is possible that the missionaries were hosted in a specific room of the Leopardi palace, the recently discovered 'night alcove' concealed by some shelves of the library since at least 1813, when Leopardi was already fifteen. This hypothesis is merely speculative, although charming: the repressed memory of the night-terrors would reverberate into the Leopardi palace constructed as a mnestic topography, with its secret rooms and hidden corners. Still, the 'night alcove' presents interesting elements, first and foremost since its painted walls are covered with symbols connected with the semantic areas of night and sleep: a soldier portrayed while inviting silence with the lifted finger in front of his nose, a resting lion, a painted landscape, an owlet. Moreover, one of the scrolls painted on the walls is inscribed with a verse from Psalm 90:5, which is widely used in evening prayers and liturgy and which provides further evidence to link the room to the 'night-terrors' of 'Le ricordanze', 'non timebis a timore nocturno' [Thou shalt not be afraid of the terror by night].

In connecting the notions of 'night' and fear-terror, this Biblical passage may be considered as the root of the 'nocturnal terrors' that systematically resurface in Leopardi's oeuvre. Alongside *Silvio Sarno* and 'Le ricordanze', we may recall how the original title of the fragment 'Odi, Melisso' is 'Lo spavento notturno', which openly echoes the passage from the psalm: interestingly, in the manuscript Leopardi had used it in order to replace the previous one, 'Il Sogno', suggesting a substantial interchangeability between nightmare and dream.[97] In the *Saggio sopra gli errori popolari degli antichi*, Leopardi speaks of those ancient gods who 'passeggia[vano] di notte e prende[vano] sollazzo in ispaventar chi dormiva' [used to wander at night and took amusement in scaring those who slept]:[98] the expression 'passeggiare di notte' can be seen as an oblique translation of the verse immediately following the one of the 'terror by night' in Psalm 90, '[non timebis] a negotio perambulante in tenebris' [Thou shalt not be afraid of the pestilence that walketh in darkness]. First and foremost, the eighth chapter of the *Saggio* is entitled 'Dei terrori notturni' [The Nocturnal Terrors]: Leopardi collects there ancient superstitions concerning the night, deliberately employing the Biblical verse as a collective definition for all the phenomena of the classical irrational described in the section.

Quite eloquently, however, in titling the eighth chapter of the *Saggio*, Leopardi decides to translate the psalmist's expression *timor* [fear] with the Italian one *terrore* [terror]. This choice is particularly meaningful, especially if we consider how the notion of 'timore' had been crucial in the Enlightenment's anthropological reflection (notably by Vico) in order to describe the psychological processes of ancient civilisations, whose invention of polytheistic religions was grounded in their fear of inexplicable natural phenomena.[99] In the *Zibaldone*, years later, Leopardi establishes a clear distinction between the expressions 'timore' and 'terrore'. The former pertains to the ancients–'primitives' and to children, following the association that we have already analyzed, as far as both are frightened by phenomena that they are unable to understand scientifically:

Lascio stare il timore e lo spavento proprio di quell'età (per mancanza di esperienza e sapere, e per forza d'immaginazione ancor vergine e fresca): timor di pericoli di ogni sorta, timore di vanità e chimere proprio solamente di quell'età, e di nessun'altra; timor delle larve, sogni, cadaveri, strepiti notturni, immagini reali, spaventose per quell'età e indifferenti poi, come maschere ec. ec. [...] Quest'ultimo timore era così terribile in quell'età, che nessuna sventura, nessuno spavento, nessun pericolo per formidabile che sia, ha forza in altra età, di produrre in noi angosce, smanie, orrori, spasimi, travaglio insomma paragonabile a quello dei detti timori fanciulleschi. L'idea degli spettri, quel timore spirituale, soprannaturale, sacro, e di un altro mondo, che ci agitava frequentemente in quell'età, aveva un non so che di sì formidabile e smanioso, che non può esser paragonato con verun altro sentimento dispiacevole dell'uomo. Nemmeno il timor dell'inferno in un moribondo, credo che possa essere così intimamente terribile. Perchè la ragione e l'esperienza rendono inaccessibili a qualunque sorta di sentimento, quell'ultima e profondissima parte e radice dell'animo e del cuor nostro, alla quale penetrano e arrivano, e la quale scuotono e invadono le sensazioni fanciullesche o primitive, e in ispecie il detto timore.[100]

[To say nothing of the fear and terror typical of that age (due to a lack of experience or knowledge, and to the power of our imagination, still fresh and virgin): fear of dangers of every kind; fear of figments and chimeras typical of that age alone, and of no other; fear of ghosts, dreams, dead bodies, noises in the night and real images that frighten us at that age and later become of no account, such as masks, etc. etc. [...] This last fear was so terrible at that age that no misfortune, no fear, no danger, however tremendous, has the power, in later life, to produce anguish, agitation, dread, torments, in a word agony comparable to the agony of those childhood fears. The idea of spectres, that spiritual, supernatural, sacred, otherworldly fear, which frequently gripped us at that age, had something so dreadful and frenzied about it that it cannot be compared to any other unpleasurable feeling felt by human beings. Not even the fear of Hell in a dying man, I think, can be so profoundly terrible. For childhood or primitive sensations, and this fear in particular, reach, assail, penetrate, and overwhelm the ultimate and deepest part and root of our mind and heart, which reason and experience render inaccessible to any kind of feeling.]

'Terrore' is instead the form of fear that is felt by the enlightened and rational subject, who theoretically would not have grounds for being scared, but is. As Leopardi states as far back as in the *Saggio*, even Voltaire, 'quel banderaio degli spiriti forti, quell'uomo sì ragionevole e sì nemico dei pregiudizi, tremava nelle tenebre come un fanciullo' [that flag-bearer of the brave, that man who was so rational and so hostile against prejudices, used to shiver like a child in the dark], in the same way as the bravest soldiers 'hanno ceduto al timore degli spiriti' [have surrendered to the fear of ghosts].[101] 'Terrore' is identified with this kind of fear, as two eloquent passages of the *Zibaldone* clearly demonstrate:

Lo spavento e il terrore sebbene di un grado maggior del timore, contuttociò bene spesso sono molto meno vili, anzi talvolta non contengono nessuna viltà: e possono cadere anche negli uomini perfettamente coraggiosi, al contrario del timore. [...] Lo spavento degli spiriti, così puerile esso, e fondato in opinione così puerile, è stato (ed ancora è) comune ad uomini coraggiosissimi.[102]

[Fright and terror, although of a greater magnitude than fear, are nevertheless very often much less cowardly, and sometimes not cowardly at all. They can affect even the most courageous people, unlike fear. [...] The fear of ghosts, so childish, and based on such a childish notion, was very common (and remains so) among very courageous people.]

Altro è il timore altro il terrore. Questa è passione molto più forte e viva di quella, e molto più avvilitiva dell'animo e sospensiva dell'uso della ragione, anzi quasi di tutte le facoltà dell'animo, ed anche de' sensi del corpo. Nondimeno la prima di queste passioni non cade nell'uomo perfettamente coraggioso e savio, la seconda sì. Egli non teme mai, ma può sempre essere atterrito. Nessuno può debitamente vantarsi di non poter essere spaventato.[103]

[Fear is one thing but terror quite another. The latter is a much more powerful and more intense passion than the former, and humbles the mind far more and is far more likely to cause the use of reason to be suspended, indeed, than almost all of the faculties of the mind, and also of the senses of the body. Nonetheless the first of these passions does not occur in a wholly courageous or wise man, but the second does. He is never afraid but he can always be terror-struck. No one can justifiably boast of not being able to be frightened.]

It may be therefore hypothesized that the 'nocturnal terror' of the Bible, inscribed in the physical space of the 'night alcove', acts as a pre-logical and infantile reminiscence. As Claudio Colaiacomo points out, in the *Zibaldone* Leopardi theorizes how the first recollections of childhood ('le più antiche reminiscenze') are particularly strong insofar as they correspond to the moment when the child starts connecting visual perceptions with language: 'la prima mia ricordanza è di alcune pere moscadelle che io vedeva, e sentiva nominare al tempo stesso' [my first memory is of some musk pears I saw, and heard being named at the same time].[104] Similarly, it may be argued, the visual memory of the Biblical verse intersects the aural one of liturgies, establishing a connection between night and fear that finds its setting within the emotional topography of the *Heim*, and which will be later systematized and given a rational-theoretical frame from the *Saggio* to the *Zibaldone*.

In the *Saggio*, Leopardi deals extensively with infantile terrors, assimilated to those that used to haunt the 'ancients'. Whereas philosophy has destroyed superstitions on a cultural scale, a particularly lasting survival of ancient prejudices can be found in the stories that are still employed in order to scare children:

Muove la bile del filosofo il vedere con quanta cura s'istruisca un fanciullo intorno alle favole più terribili, e alle chimere più atte a fare impressione sulla sua mente. Egli sa appena balbettare [...] che la storia dei folletti e delle apparizioni ha già occupato il suo luogo nel di lui intelletto pauroso e stupefatto. Alquanto inquieto, perchè vivace, egli era forse molesto ad una allevatrice impaziente [...]. La novella degli spiriti fu lo specifico sicuro per liberarla dalle importunità del fanciullo. Eccolo infatti divenuto attonito e timoroso; riguardare l'avvicinarsi della notte come un supplizio, i luoghi tenebrosi come caverne spaventevoli; palpitare nel letto angosciosamente; sudar freddo; raccogliersi pauroso sotto le lenzuola; cercar di parlare, e nel trovarsi solo inorridire da capo a piedi. L'allevatrice ha perfettamente ottenuto il suo intento. Il fanciullo durante il giorno non dimentica i suoi terrori notturni.[105]

[It disappoints every philosopher to see how meticulously children are instructed with the most scary stories, and with those fancies that are most apt to frighten their minds. As soon as a child can babble [...], already have stories about ghosts and goblins taken their place in his frightened and bewildered imagination. Restless, only because he was lively, he was perhaps annoying an impatient nurse [...]. Ghost-stories were the sure remedy for freeing her from the child's troublesome behaviour. And so he has become petrified and full of fears; he sees the approaching of the night as a torture, every dark place as a dreadful cavern; he quivers in his bed, full of anxiety; he is in a cold sweat; he huddles fearful underneath his bed sheets; he tries to speak, and when he finds himself alone he is horrified from head to foot. The nurse has perfectly achieved her goal. During the day, the child does not forget his night terrors.]

I will return to the nurses' frightening stories in the following section. For now, let us remark how, by drawing a distinction between 'timore' and 'terrore', Leopardi challenges one of the most crucial impasses of post-Enlightenment culture, namely the arousal of a different and subtler form of fear — taking the several names of 'uncanny', *Unheimliche*, *inquiétante étrangeté*, *perturbante*, *siniestro* — from the secularization itself of culture and society, the 'secolo illuminato' [enlightened age][106] that has freed Western culture from 'prejudices'. The possibility of interpreting Leopardi's 'terrore' as a notion close to the Freudian one of the uncanny is justified by the fact that both are helpless and inexplicable forms of fear affecting the post-Enlightenment subject, the 'homm[e] éclair[é]' [enlightened man] who, for Madame de Staël, was fascinated by ghosts (*revenants*) though not rationally believing in them.[107] Exactly like the Freudian uncanny, Leopardi's 'terrore' is a 'toxic side effect' of the Enlightenment,[108] clearly differentiated from the neurotic fear of ancients, 'primitive' peoples, and of children: once denied by rational consciousness, 'terrore' bursts into the familiar perimeter of the adult-enlightened subject's paradigmatic frame as a form of alterity, which is the more frightening in as much as it arises from the inexplicable. The feeling it engenders is a contradictory and undefined one: like grace, 'terrore' may only emerge from the distantiated perspective of a loss of innocence. As something that was once familiar and that unexpectedly presents itself again, the 'terrore' determines an ambiguous feeling of surprise and shock — in the same way, we may hypothesize, as the unexpected return of a mythological and symbolic frame of mind makes the subject surprised at being able to talk with the stars once more.

From this angle, 'Le ricordanze' is a poem about the uncanny return of the past which questions historicism's linear and teleological conceptualization of time. The poem pivots the recollection of the past on the current, grown up, and disenchanted subject, thus 'brushing history against the grain' and bypassing the autobiographical and historicist quest for an objective representation of the past. The poem's strategy, in subjectivizing the past as a recollection (*ricordanza*), dissolves the borders between actuality and phantasmal re-elaboration, constructing the past as a resurfacing and uncanny otherness that contrasts with the subject's present and rational acknowledgment of 'truth':

> con dolor sottentra
> Il pensier del presente, un van desio
> Del passato, ancor tristo, e il dire: io fui.[109]

[knowledge of the present replaces [some sweet memory] with pain, and a vain desire for the past, however sad, and the wish to say: I was.]

However, it is important to highlight how the tension between 'knowledge of the present' and 'vain desire for the past' does not uniquely refer to the subject's disenchantment. The entire modern invention of history is at stake here, as far as it is grounded on the construction of the past as an otherness, an aspect highlighted by Leopardi's choice of employing, here, the past historic tense ('il dire: io fui'). The 'vain desire for the past' alludes therefore not only to the speaking subject's infancy, but to the broader project of reanimating the past that underlies eighteenth- and nineteenth-century dreams of antiquity. As we have seen, the Neoclassical discourse on ancient civilisation is but a 'lover's discourse' addressed to an absence: the 'vainness' stressed by Leopardi sounds then like a lucid acknowledgment that antiquity (like infancy) is over and dead, and actually killed off by the process itself that has constructed it as an object of historical knowledge. As Georges Didi-Huberman argues, while literally inventing art history as a form of knowledge that is clearly separated from the 'chronic' model of Pliny the Elder and Giorgio Vasari, Winckelmann happens to conjure (évoquer) the past at the very moment he realizes its definitive loss.[110] The answer to this position of stalemate relies on reversing the perspective. The celebrated 'Angel of History', identified by Walter Benjamin in a drawing by Paul Klee, beholds the past retrospectively, perceiving 'one single catastrophe, which keeps piling wreckage upon wreckage', rather than the chain of events implied by the organicist model of historicism, poised between 'greatness' and 'decadence'.[111] Similarly, the subject of 'Le ricordanze' looks backward, beholding the scattered and fragmented illusions of youth. These ruins, however, may talk again, once they are incorporated within the subject's poetic speech: to paraphrase a biblical expression from the Book of Habakkuk employed by Freud in 'The Aetiology of Hysteria' (1896), the unexpected mnestic process makes the past live again, albeit fleetingly, and the 'stones talk' (saxa loquuntur).[112]

The centrality of subjectivity in 'Le ricordanze' transforms, then, the objectivity of autobiographical writing into a 'hauntology' (hauntologie), a term, as is well known, introduced by Jacques Derrida in Spectres of Marx (1993) in order to label the self-definition of the present in relation to the past's ghost-like presence-absence.[113] The modern conceptualization itself of history, in constructing the past as an irremediable otherness, polarizes the relationship between the historical subject and the past in the terms of a dialogue with the dead, making historiography a spiritualist-like conjuration of something 'that ought to have remained ... secret and hidden but has come to light'. This aspect is extremely clear to Friedrich Schlegel, who, in his Geschichte der epischen Dichtkunst der Griechen [History of Epic Poetry of the Greeks] comments that all ancient literary works are, to some extent, lost, since we have lost their most inner meaning, 'all antiquity [...] is forever lost, and only within the hearts of a few chosen spirits can it, feebly, come to life again [das gesammte Alterthum [...] auf ewig untergegangen ist, und nur in dem Innern auserwählter Geister schwächer wieder aufleben kann]'.[114] Like Warburg's expression, Nachleben, Schlegel's terminology constructs the survival of antiquity as a form of posthumous life that comes close to the feeble existence of ghosts. Making cultural history consequently entails dealing with such ethereal presences: a note taken by Warburg on 2 July 1929 for the *Bilderatlas Mnemosyne* project defines the object of the analysis as the 'influence [*Einfluss*] of antiquity'; making this 'history' (*Geschichte*) is, however, a sort of fairy-tale operation (*Märchenhaft*), and can be defined as a 'ghost-story for adults [*Gespenstergeschichte f[ür] ganz Erwachsene*]'.[115] For Warburg, the modern historiographer is suspended between two poles, acting as two modalities of being clairvoyant (*Sehertypus*) epitomized respectively by Jacob Burckhardt and Friedrich Nietzsche: on the one side, the Enlightener (*Aufklärer*), who conjures the survivals of the past but is not overwhelmed by their uncanny return, rather beholding them with scientific detachment; on the other, the necromancer (*Nekromant*), who deals with the dead and becomes possessed by them.[116]

The uncanny ghost-story provides thus the model for the 'nameless science' that early twentieth-century German-Jewish thought tries to construct in order to question the aporias of historicism. It can even be said that fantastic literature is the embryonic expedient by which the nineteenth century attempts to explicate the feeling of estrangement engendered by modernity. From this angle, the ghost can be seen to epitomize the survival of a past that has been unavoidably confined in the sphere of alterity, in the same way as the literary theme of the 'haunted house' expresses the tension between the modern subject and a space of homeliness that has become uninhabitable, the house in which the Ego feels no longer master and comfortable. In other words, this is the fear, at once 'spatial' and 'temporal', described by Anthony Vidler:

> [The space of the uncanny] was [...] an interior, but now the interior of the mind, one that knew no bounds in projection or introversion. Its symptoms included spatial fear, leading to paralysis of movement, and temporal fear, leading to historical amnesia. In each case, the uncanny arose, as Freud demonstrated, from the transformation of something that once seemed homely into something decidedly not so, from the *heimlich*, that is, into the *unheimlich*.[117]

As such, the ghost-story anticipates and metaphorizes this new form of fear, and consequently provides a narrative model that both Freud and Warburg, probably not by chance, happen to challenge. Alongside Freud's explicit analyses of fantastic tales — Hoffmann's *Der Sandmann* in 'The Uncanny', Jensen's *Gradiva* in the eponymous essay of 1907 — the narrative structure of Freud's clinical cases seems widely indebted to such nineteenth-century genres as those of the ghost-story and the detective fiction: psychoanalysis, as a form of knowledge, states since its inaugural act, the *Studies on Hysteria* (1895), that mental patients 'suffer mainly from reminiscences',[118] so that analysis must be constructed as a progressive and narratively calibrated unveiling of some buried secret.[119] As far as Warburg is concerned, the aborted project of the fictive exchange of letters with André Jolles on Domenico Ghirlandaio's Nymph can easily be compared to fin de siècle narrative experiments about 'uncanny portraits', conducted through an epistolary style.[120]

Themes and topics of fantastic literature seem to be singularly absent from Leopardi's poetics. In the fourth of the *Pensieri*, Leopardi tells a story which occurred in Florence in 1831, when people had believed an apron and a distaff, seen from a window, to be a ghost (*fantasima*). The apologue, Leopardi concludes, is not only funny, but rather quite telling about the way civilizations that are supposed to be advanced are still entrapped within 'primitive' superstitions:

> [Può] essere non inutile alla critica storica ed alla filosofia sapere che nel secolo decimonono, nel bel mezzo di Firenze, che è la città più culta d'Italia, e dove il popolo in particolare è più intendente e più civile, si veggono fantasmi, che sono creduti spiriti, e sono rocche da filare. E gli stranieri si tengano qui di sorridere, come fanno volentieri delle cose nostre; perchè troppo è noto che nessuna delle tre grandi nazioni che, come dicono i giornali, *marchent à la tête de la civilisation*, crede agli spiriti meno dell'italiana.[121]

> [It may be not unuseful for historical criticism and philosophy to know that in deepest nineteenth-century Florence, which is the best-educated Italian city and whose citizens are in particular the most rational and civilized, ghosts are seen that are believed to be spirits of the dead, and are actually distaffs. Still, foreigners should refrain from smiling at this, as they are wont to about our business: as is well known, among the three nations that — as newspapers say — *marchent à la tête de la civilisation*, none believes in ghosts less than the Italian one.]

Moreover, it is enough to highlight the very peculiar use the late Leopardi makes — in the *Paralipomeni della Batracomiomachia* (1831–37) [Paralipomena of the Batrachomyomachia] and 'La Ginestra' (1836) [The Broom] — of such a recurrent setting for fantastic literature as that of Pompeii,[122] namely one of the most visible embodiments of the post-Enlightenment uncanny relationship with the historical past: as Vidler summarizes, 'Of all sites, that of Pompeii seemed to many writers to exhibit the conditions of unhomeliness to the most extreme'.[123]

The impression of an absence of elements borrowed from fantastic literature in Leopardi's oeuvre is not, however, due to a lack of sensitivity for such themes, but rather because Leopardi's thought, in pointing to the most inner core of the uncanny relationship of modernity with the past, does not seem to need to metaphorize this tension by referring to the literary devices of the fantastic. 'Le ricordanze', as we have seen, depicts the eruption of the *Unheimlichkeit* within the homely perimeter of the *Heim*, a process that is structurally close to the Gothic and Romantic theme of the 'haunted house': still, for Leopardi, the haunted house is the 'house of the Ego', and ghosts reveal themselves to be 'ricordanze' and childhood memories. In other words, we see here the very same process that structures Jensen's *Gradiva*, in which the feminine figure, believed by the protagonist to be the ghost of a Roman girl who died in the destruction of Pompeii, is revealed to be a flesh-and-blood woman, and Norbert Hanold's fascination for a Roman bas relief is actually rooted, rather than in some uncanny reminiscence, in the recollection of that very same girl, known in childhood and later, consciously, forgotten. By dissolving the clichés of fantastic literature, Leopardi and Jensen, as Freud would put it, 'presen[t] us with a perfectly correct psychiatric study, on which we may measure our understanding of the mind — a case history and the history of a cure'.[124]

Ghosts, previously placed by the subject's delirium within the (more emotional than historical) sphere of 'antiquity', reveal their actual nature as recollections: the historical subject suffers from reminiscences, namely from 'after-images of [old] thoughts' which 'trouble new perceptions'.[125] 'Le ricordanze' is therefore a process of psycho-analysis, by which images from the past, which have resurfaced within the perimeter of the here-and-now, shift from being beheld — as Georges Didi-Huberman would put it — as 'ghost-images' (*image-fantôme*) to being analyzed as 'symptom-images' (*image-symptôme*).[126] The neurotic symptom, as Freud acknowledges in witnessing the hysterics at the Salpêtrière, is the symbolization of a past trauma, a sort of rebus or puzzle to be interpreted by the analyst-reader, in order to be reassessed within the continuum of memory. With Freud, Didi-Huberman writes, the hysterical symptom is no longer seen as part of an iconographical system, but rather as a clue.[127] According to Freud's studies on hysteria of the 1890s, the hysterical symptom is articulated upon a concurrent process of both 'dissociation', through which the traumatic 'impression' is disjointed from its symptomatic outcome, and of a 'return of what is buried' (*retour de l'enfoui*).[128] This double process of abstraction (from the original trauma to its symbolization) and of reification/concretization (of symbolization into symptom) corresponds to the double movement of extraction and displacement that characterizes the rhetorical structure of metaphor, so that, as Jacques Lacan puts it, 'the symptom *is* a metaphor, whether one likes to admit it or not, just as desire *is* a metonymy, even if man scoffs at the idea'.[129] By rendering, and consequently by metaphorizing, the processes of memory by means of linguistic constructions, the text itself of 'Le ricordanze' happens therefore to be, in Slavoj Žižek's terms, a 'return of the living dead' which is 'the reverse of the proper funeral rite. While the latter', Žižek continues, 'implies a certain reconciliation, an acceptance of loss, the return of the dead signifies that they cannot find their proper place in the text of tradition'.[130] 'Le ricordanze' attempts a symptomatology and a psycho-analysis of mnemonical processes, through which poetry-making is constructed, at the same time, as a therapeutic, historical, and demonic operation: as Douglas-Fairhurst concludes, 'once the past ha[s] been put in its place, the present c[an] be made surprising again'.[131]

'Le ricordanze' is therefore a 'ghost-story for adults', in which the illusions of childhood can come momentarily back to life, despite and because of the violent caesura operated by reason. As Leopardi had outlined as far back as 1820, art can become the venue for ghosts to be conjured back:

> Hanno questo di proprio le opere di genio, che quando anche rappresentino al vivo la nullità delle cose, quando anche dimostrino evidentemente e facciano sentire l'inevitabile infelicità della vita, quando anche esprimano le più terribili disperazioni, tuttavia ad un'anima grande che si trovi anche in uno stato di estremo abbattimento, disinganno, nullità, noia e scoraggiamento della vita, o nelle più acerbe e *mortifere* disgrazie (sia che appartengano alle alte e forti passioni, sia a qualunque altra cosa); servono sempre di consolazione, raccendono l'entusiasmo, e non trattando né rappresentando altro che la morte, le rendono, almeno momentaneamente, quella vita che aveva perduta.[132]

> [It is a property of works of genius that, even when they represent vividly the nothingness of things, even when they clearly show and make you feel the inevitable unhappiness of life, even when they express the most terrible despair, nevertheless to a great soul that finds itself in a state of extreme dejection, disenchantment, nothingness, boredom, and discouragement about life, or in the most bitter and *deathly* misfortune (whether on account of lofty, powerful

passions or something else), such works always bring consolation, and rekindle enthusiasm, and, though they treat and represent nothing but death, they restore, albeit momentarily, the life that it had lost.]

These lines construct the artistic process as a vampiric operation, by which dead beings can attain a corporeality, albeit fleeting. This is what happens in 'Le ricordanze', in which the process itself that has distantiated memories of childhood permits their oblique recovery. With 'Le ricordanze', as we have seen, Leopardi's poetry ceases to long for an autobiographical dimension; also, the composition of the poem corresponds temporally to the interruption — with the exception of a few pages, fragmentarily drafted in the following years — of the writing of the *Zibaldone*, as if the ὑπομνήματον, as an aid to memory, must necessarily leave room for the sudden and direct resurfacing of the recollection (μνήμη). To some extent, it may be said that the writing experiment begun in 1817 is at this stage exhausted. It would therefore be useful to go back to that inaugural act, to see where Leopardi's project had found its beginning, an aspect to which the following, and final, section will be devoted.

Urszenen

> You see! — a dog, and not a ghost, is here.
>
> JOHANN WOLFGANG VON GOETHE, *Faust* I, l. 1163,
> translated by J. S. Blackie

In July or August 1817, Giacomo Leopardi drafts three isolated fragments that will constitute the embryo of the *Zibaldone*. The handwriting, an elaborate cursive in which different writing tools and kinds of ink can be detected, testifies to three independent phases of elaboration,[133] which give the page the structure of a palimpsest. As a 'self-reflexive home for diverse models of psychological, historical, and social integration, and poetic shorthand for a shadowy archaeology of memory and desire',[134] this palimpsest-like stratification embodies the most distant genealogy of Leopardi's project, which is grounded in such an intertwinement of memory, desire, and private writing. Entering the *Zibaldone*, one can already recognize the features that will characterize Leopardi's journal as a unique textual object in Western cultural modernity: chronological sequence, fragmentariness, inner reverberations, pluristylism, polyphony.[135] An approximate dating, plausibly added in January 1820,[136] proves the function of this page as an archaeological space of origin for Leopardi's project. From page 100 onwards, following a taste for numerical symbolism, Leopardi starts dating his fragments: the original loose-leaf manuscript progressively reveals its nature as an autonomous work, adhering to the chronological structure of ancient ὑπομνήματα and thus becoming what Carlo Ossola terms a 'livre d'heures'.[137] It is not by chance that Leopardi feels the need to return to his original notes at this stage, historically constructing them as the beginning of his intellectual endeavour.

Three fragments, then: a brief description in prose, presumably the subject for a poem but already articulated in metre (three quinaries and a *settenario*, or two quinaries and an hendecasyllable);[138] a poetical sketch in six lines; and the paraphrase of a Latin text, Avianus's fable *De nutrice et infanti* [The Wet Nurse and the Child], which Leopardi read in an edition of 1721.[139] Although other fragments follow on the same page, the date, later placed at the end of the third fragment, encloses these three as an autonomous set:

> Palazzo bello. Cane di notte dal casolare, al passar del viandante.
> Era la luna nel cortile, un lato
> Tutto ne illuminava, e discendea
> Sopra il contiguo lato obliquo un raggio...
> Nella (dalla) maestra via s'udiva il carro
> Del passegger, che stritolando i sassi,
> mandava un suon, che precedea da lungi
> Il tintinnio de' mobili sonagli.

Onde Aviano raccontando una favoletta dice che una donna di contado piangendo un suo bambolo, minacciogli se non taceva che l'avrebbe dato mangiare a un lupo. E che un lupo che a caso di là passava, udendo dir questo alla donna credettele che dicesse vero, e messosi innanzi all'uscio di casa così stette quivi tutto quel giorno ad aspettare che la donna gli portasse quella vivanda. Come poi ristesse tutto quel tempo e la donna non se n'accorgesse e non n'avesse paura e non gli facesse motto con sasso o altro, Aviano lo saprà che lo dice. E aggiugne che il lupo non ebbe niente perchè il fanciullo s'addormentò, e quando bene non l'avesse fatto non ci saria stato pericolo. E fatto tardi, tornato alla moglie senza preda perchè s'era baloccato ad aspettare fino a sera, disse quello che nell'autore puoi vedere. (Luglio o Agosto 1817).

[Palazzo bello. Dog in the night from the farmhouse, as the wayfarer goes by. The moon shone in the yard, one side in its full light, and a moonbeam slanting obliquely down the next... On (from) the highway you could hear the traveler's carriage crunching on the stones, and before that, from a long way off, the jingling of harness bells. And so Avianus tells a story about a country woman who threatened her crying child that if he didn't quieten down she would feed him to a wolf. And by chance a wolf was passing by and heard her. He thought she meant what she said, so he sat down in front of the door of the house and stayed there all day waiting for the woman to bring him his food. How he stayed there all that time without the woman noticing him, or being afraid, or chasing him off with a stone or anything, only Avianus can explain. And he adds that the wolf didn't get anything because the child fell asleep, and even if he had not, he wouldn't have come to any harm. And when it got late, and the wolf went back to his wife without any prey, because he had wasted the whole day waiting, he said what you can read in the story.]

The relationship between these three textual units has always seemed enigmatic, and criticism has in fact more or less always tended to dissolve it. The connection between the first and the second fragments is generally accepted, given the clear thematic association between the two: they would both form the initial subject matter of a nocturnal idyll, taking place between 'Palazzo bello' and the main road, and focused on the dog, the 'viandante'/'passegger' and the moon.[140] The connection with the third fragment is, however, far more problematic, most of all because of the puzzling adverb 'onde', so perplexing that, when first publishing the *Zibaldone* in 1898, editors decided to suppress it,[141] and in 1909 Giulio Augusto

Levi argued that it should not be considered as a part of the *Zibaldone* at all.[142] Levi asserted that the paraphrase belonged to a projected rewriting of the *Saggio sopra gli errori popolari degli antichi*, 'onde' would therefore refer back to another text, thereby disconnecting Avianus's fable from the rest of the page.

This possibility cannot of course be excluded, but some elements make it unlikely (although its validity is in any case irrelevant to this analysis). The beginning of a rewriting of the essay was presumably drafted between 1815 and 1817.[143] It should be noted, however, that this date has in fact been surmised from the *Zibaldone*, as well as from a letter to Pietro Giordani of 5 December 1817, in which Leopardi wrote that 'il Luglio passato, la lettura de' trecentisti m'invogliò di scrivere un trattato del quale anni sono avea preparati e ordinati e abbandonati i materiali. Ne scrissi il principio', Leopardi concluded, 'e poi lo lasciai per miglior tempo' [Last July, reading fourteenth-century writers made me want to write a treatise for which I had prepared and ordered and abandoned the material years ago. I wrote the beginning of it and then I put it aside till a more favourable time].[144] This treatise could certainly be the rewriting of the *Saggio*, although this hypothesis also raises difficulties: it is unlikely that fourteenth-century writers would be connected to an essay on ancient superstitions, and in any case the *Saggio* was definitely more than a mere collection of later abandoned materials (although at this stage the manuscript was no longer in Leopardi's possession, since the only copy had been sent unsuccessfully to the Milanese publisher Stella in 1816).[145] The redrafting of the *Saggio* is instead explicitly mentioned several years later, when Leopardi, in 1826, includes among his future plans a 'Trattatello degli errori popolari degli antichi Greci e Romani' [Small Treatise on the Popular Errors of Ancient Greeks and Romans].[146] Most significantly, there is a striking dissonance between the style of the *Zibaldone* paraphrase and that of the new beginning: not only does 'onde' appear not to correspond to any passage of the surviving text, but the ironic and colloquial tone of the fragment can hardly be reconciled with the formal, bookish one of the rewriting.

In 1990, however, Neuro Bonifazi proposed a comprehensive re-reading of the page, in which 'onde' was interpreted as logically consequential to the first two fragments.[147] Bonifazi's hypothesis is that 'onde' connected the paraphrase to the description and poetical sketch, with the dog and the wagon's noise inspiring in the countrywoman the idea of the wolf. By depicting a nocturnal scene dominated by the woman's menace, Bonifazi argues, the page alludes to Leopardi's memories of the terrors that he experienced as a child, with the effect that he unconsciously identifies himself with the 'bambolo'. This interpretation is ingenious, and curiously enough precisely this term has been used in order to reject it, first by Pacella ('Personalmente non condivido la ricostruzione del Bonifazi, pur riconoscendone l'ingegnosità' [personally, I do not agree with Bonifazi's reconstruction, although acknowledging its ingenuity])[148] and then by Felici ('la tesi troppo ingegnosa — sorretta da una lettura psicoanalitica — di Neuro Bonifazi' [Neuro Bonifazi's excessively ingenious argument, supported by a psychoanalytical reading]).[149] More specifically, this rejection has focused on two evident mistakes made by Bonifazi: the definition of the fragments as the 'proem' (*proemio*) of the *Zibaldone*, grounded in a misreading of *Silvio Sarno*;[150] and the identification of 'Palazzo bello' with the Leopardi palace, given that a 'Palazzo bello' actually exists — on the 'maestra via' leading to Recanati — and was, as Pacella notes, a very familiar place for the poet (probably, as we shall see, the only thing that matters).[151] These errors, however, do not affect the main core of Bonifazi's hypothesis: the dismissal of his interpretation, a leitmotif of almost every reading of the first page of the *Zibaldone* in the past twenty years, should therefore be read as a symptom of the irreducible anti-Freudism of Italian literary criticism.[152]

This phenomenon is even more remarkable when we consider that the Freudian flavour of Bonifazi's analysis is merely superficial and limited to a few terminological allusions ('riaffiora[re]', 'simbolo', 'sostituto'),[153] thus making the censorship of alternative keys to interpretation even more eloquent. My hypothesis is, instead, that the deepest substratum of the opening page of the *Zibaldone* can be read through the dream logic described by Freud in *The Interpretation of Dreams* (1900), and subsequently extended — in the *Psychopathology of Everyday Life* (1901 and 1904) and the essay on *Jokes* (1905) — to phenomena of diurnal life. The internal reverberations between the three fragments can be understood, I argue, through recourse to a 'Freudian rhetoric',[154] thus meaning that an ambiguous and stratified discourse works as the 'compromise formation' of cultural tension. The internal reverberations that structure Leopardi's page give birth to the mechanics of displacement and condensation, crystallizing themselves into textual units, like 'onde', whose logical explanation seems ultimately ungraspable. The critical debate surrounding this passage, more or less always intended to defuse its ambiguity, is the most eloquent symptom of its puzzling nature, and of its need for different analytical tools.

Avianus's fable had already been quoted by Leopardi in the eighth chapter of the *Saggio*, devoted to 'Nocturnal Terrors': 'Si minacciava pure i bambini di farli divorare da qualche mostro, o da qualche fiera. Nella prima favola di Aviano si legge quel distico: "Rustica deflenti puero iuraverat olim | Ni taceat, rabido quod foret esca lupo"' [People used also to threaten children with the menace of letting them be devoured by some monster or animal. In the first of Avianus's fables we read the famous distich: Once upon a time, a countrywoman swore to a child who was crying that, if he did not stop, she would give him to a wolf as a meal].[155] In the same chapter, Leopardi analyzes some superstitions concerning Hecate:

> Ecate metteva urli e schiamazzava *per le strade* in un modo infernale: '*Nocturnisque* Hecate *triviis* ululata per urbes' dicea Didone presso Virgilio: ed Apuleio invocando *la Luna*, 'Regina del cielo', esclamava, 'o tu sii Cerere inclita madre delle messi... o la sorella di Febo... o Proserpina terribile per gli urli *notturni*'. Una maga, presso Teocrito, dice alla Luna, 'Su via, splendi più bella, affin che teco | favellar possa, e con Ecate inferna, | che *a' pavidi cagnuoli* orrore ispira, | quando *di notte*, d'atre faci al lume, | va per le tombe degli estinti e il sangue'. [...] Per ammansire la terribile Ecate, se gli davano per cena, dice lo Scoliaste di Teocrito, *dei cani* ancor teneri [...] Volendo dopo cena tornare a casa, prendeano gli antichi [...] un tozzo di pane [...] e lo recavano seco per preservarsi dai terrori notturni, che poteano sorprenderli *nella strada*. [...] Aggiunge Eustazio che questi terrori credevasi cagionati da Ecate. Certamente [...] la precauzione

usata dagli antichi di portar seco del pane nell'*andar vagando di notte*, era molto opportuna a causa dei *cani che infestavano le strade.*[156]

[Hecate used to scream and made noise *in the streets* in a hellish way; 'Hecate howled, in cities, *at midnight crossways*', said Dido through Virgil; while invoking *the Moon*, Apuleius exclaimed, 'O Queen of Heaven — whether thou art Ceres, the illustrious mother of the harvest, or the sister of Phoebus or Proserpine, dreaded in cries that pierce the *night*'. By Theocritus, a sorcerer says to the Moon, 'So shine out fair, so that I can talk to you, and to the infernal Hecate, who inspires terror in *the fearful dogs*, while *at night*, enlightened by dreadful torches, she haunts, stained with gore, the mansions of the dead'. [...] In order to placate the terrible Hecate, according to the scholiast of Theocritus, people used to give her young *dogs* as a meal. [...] In case they had to return home after dinner, the ancients used to carry [...] a morsel of bread with them [...] in order to be safe from the night-terrors that could seize them while *on the road*. [...] Statius adds that these terrors were believed to be caused by Hecate. Certainly [...] the caution of carrying some bread *while wandering at night* was definitely appropriate because of *the dogs that used to haunt the roads*.]

The same passage from Virgil had been quoted by Leopardi in the earlier treatise *Storia dell'astronomia* (1814) [History of Astronomy], in which he highlighted the ancient identification of Hecate with the moon:

> Lo scoliaste di Aristofane asserisce che *Ecate anticamente detta era la stessa che la luna* e Diana, e veneravasi nei trivi; perloché Virgilio: 'Nocturnisque Hecate triviis ululata per urbes.' Afferma Porfirio, presso Eusebio, che la luna era detta Ecate per la varietà de' suoi aspetti e delle sue forze.[157]

> [The scholiast of Aristophanes asserts that, *in ancient times, Hecate meant exactly the moon*, and was worshipped at crossroads; which explains Virgil's line: 'Hecate howled, in cities, at midnight crossways'. According to Eusebius of Caesarea, Porphyry affirms that the moon was called Hecate because of the variety of her aspects and of her forces.]

These passages cast an evident shadow on the first page of the *Zibaldone*. The 'viandante' of the *Zibaldone*, whose image is situated within the present, finds himself trapped in the same situation as ancient night-wanderers, scared by a dog howling at the crossroads: above shines the moon, 'anticamente' connected to Hecate, thus explaining the ferocity of stray dogs through the influence of celestial bodies. The rational explanation is hence intertwined with the supernatural one, making myth shine through the page's subterranean texture. The very sentence 'Cane di notte dal casolare, al passar del viandante' is ambiguous: 'di notte' surely has an adverbial function, but at the same time contaminates 'cane', conjuring up the infernal dogs of Hecate's cult and of the Wild Hunt (the Welsh *cum Annwm*, 'the "Hounds of Hell" with white bodies and red ears' mentioned by Robert Graves, the equivalent of the English 'Yell Hounds, Yeth Hounds, Wish Hounds, Gabriel Hounds, or Gabriel Ratchets').[158] The connection between dog and wanderer transfigures the main road near 'Palazzo bello' into a Grecian crossroads, while the dog implicitly evokes Aviano's wolf, confusing time.[159]

The image of barking dogs recurs with singular frequency in Leopardi's oeuvre. In a letter written by Leopardi to Giordani on 6 March 1820 we witness the same connection between country landscape and resurfacing mythical elements:

> Poche sere addietro, prima di coricarmi, aperta la finestra della mia stanza, e vedendo un cielo puro e un bel *raggio di luna*, e sentendo un'aria tepida e *certi cani che abbaiavano da lontano*, mi si svegliarono alcune *immagini antiche*, e mi parve di sentire un moto nel cuore, *onde* mi posi a gridare come un forsennato, domandando misericordia alla natura, la cui voce mi pareva di udire dopo tanto tempo. [...] E in quel momento dando uno sguardo alla mia condizione passata, [...] m'agghiacciai dallo *spavento*, non arrivando a comprendere come si possa tollerare la vita senza illusioni e affetti vivi, e senza immaginazione ed entusiasmo, delle quali cose un anno addietro si componeva tutto il mio tempo.[160]

> [A few evenings ago, before going to bed, I opened the window of my room, and seeing a clear sky and *bright moonlight*, and feeling the warm air and hearing *some dogs barking in the distance*, there stirred within me certain *ancient images*, and I thought I felt an impulse in my heart, and so I set to yelling like a madman, begging nature for mercy — nature, whose voice I seemed to be hearing after so long a time. [...] And at that moment, casting a glance at the state I'd been in, [...] I felt an icy *fear*, not being able to understand how life can be endured without illusions and intense feelings, and without imagination and enthusiasm, things which a year ago took up all my time, and made me so blissfully happy in spite of my troubles.]

What does Leopardi mean exactly by 'immagini antiche'? The adjective 'antico' is remarkably flexible in Leopardi's works. 'Le parole *lontano*, *antico*, e simili', he writes on 25 September 1821, 'sono poeticissime e piacevoli, perchè destano idee vaste, e indefinite, e non determinabili e confuse' [the words *distant*, *ancient*, and the like are very poetic and pleasurable because they evoke vast, and indefinite, and interminable, and indistinct ideas].[161] This consideration, alongside the analysis made above about the superimposition of the ontogenetic and phylogenetic spheres in Leopardi's conceptualization of time, seem to legitimate a semantic extension and to individuate at least two possible readings of the adjective, interwoven in the 'undefined' nature of the signifier.

The first possibility is to read 'antico' as referring to the sphere of history, 'immagini antiche' would then refer to the mythological associations reactivated by the connection between moon and dogs. Moreover, the image of Leopardi crying out to the moon, begging nature for mercy, recalls Lucius's prayer in the eleventh book of Apuleius's *Metamorphoses*, already quoted by Leopardi in the *Saggio*:

> At about the first watch of night I was awakened by a sudden fright [*pavore subito*] and I saw the full orb of the moon gleaming radiantly with splendid sheen [...] Now that fate [...] was offering, though late [*licet tardam*], a hope of deliverance, I decided to address in prayer the sacred image of the goddess now present in person [*augustum specimen deae praesentis statui deprecari*]. 'O Queen of Heaven — whether thou art Ceres [...] or [...] Venus [...] or the sister of Phoebus [...] or [...] Proserpine, dreaded in cries that pierce the night [*nocturnis ululatibus horrenda Proserpina*] [...] whoever thou art, illumining all city walls with that womanly light [*ista luce femminea conlustrans cuncta moenia*][...] help me now in the depth of my trouble [...] Remove the cruel four-footed form, restore me to the sight of my loved ones, restore me to my own self as Lucius [*redde me meo Lucio*].[162]

The first hours of the night, the moon shining on a wall, the 'spavento'-*pavor* and the prayer seem to suggest an intertextual influence. The goddess worshipped by Lucius is a personification of nature, whom he beseeches to give him back his human shape, invoking her manifold names. In the same way, in the letter, Leopardi contrasts his current, dehumanized nature to a time in the past when he was still able to feel emotions, 'ora [...] nessuna passione trova più l'entrata di questa povera anima', and he has become 'stecchito e inaridito come una canna secca' [Now I am stiff and withered like a dry reed, and [...] no feeling finds its way into this poor soul].[163] Like in Apuleius, the act of gazing at the moon-goddess allows a fleeting metamorphosis, suddenly turning into a terrified meditation on the emptiness of the subject's present condition.

This consideration lets another kind of memory emerge, suggesting a different interpretation of 'immagini antiche': the adjective refers in this case to an autobiographical or 'episodic memory', strictly interwoven with the 'semantic' memory of classical mythology.[164]

In the letter to Giordani, the connection between moon and dogs therefore reawakens these dual 'immagini antiche', in which infantile beliefs and classical myth are confused. The superimposition of episodic and semantic memories causes a perception of reality that is anchored in an abstract sphere of origin ('antico') to resurface. The structure of the first page of the *Zibaldone* is internally articulated, it can be argued, via a similar connection: the howling dog, perceived in the nocturnal space illuminated by the moon, produces a memorial short-circuit in which episodic and semantic memory collide, by association conjuring up both the wolf and the terrifying stories of countrywomen.

Structured around this tension — past-present, as well as mythical-rational — the page becomes an open text, in which associations operate below the surface, without any explicit logical connection. These features legitimate the possibility of interpreting it as an oneiric construction, shaped by the concurrent processes of condensation (*Verdichtung*) and displacement (*Verschiebung*): as Nicolas Abraham and Maria Torok would put it, 'we see here a genuine dream process in full wakefulness'.[165] On the one hand, as Freud writes in *The Interpretation of Dreams*, 'dreams are brief, meagre and laconic': once transcribed, a dream 'may perhaps fill half a page'.[166] On the other hand, 'the dream is, as it were, differently centred',[167] thus indefinitely deferring the appearance of its real object through the production of a chain of alternative signifiers (the nocturnal scene, the reference to Avianus). Dreams tend eventually to reproduce '*logical connection* by *simultaneity*',[168] meaning by this both temporal concurrence and spatial coexistence. Speaking from a meta-textual perspective, the co-presence of the three fragments in the same graphical space indicates that we may perceive a logical connection between them. By delineating this space, the date seems to reveal a later acknowledgment of this implicit connection.

Moreover, the three fragments describe a scene that is characterized by such a spatial and chronological contiguity: palace, dog, wanderer, moonlight, courtyard, and wagon coexist within the same space; almost simultaneously, without the possibility of distinguishing any temporal sequence, we hear howling and the noise of wheels and tinkling bells. 'Onde' can therefore be interpreted as the key to understanding the logical connection between these occurrences, as is confirmed by the *Saggio*: the dog howls, the wagon squeaks, and *hence* countrywomen, now as in ancient times, admonish children with scary stories.

Franco D'Intino highlights how 'the key element of the scene [...] is the sensation of terror that forms the fable's core, the child being threatened to be given to the wolf as a meal'.[169] The 'immagin[e] antic[a]' of childhood terror invests an apparently innocent landscape with a mythical quality, the howling dog evoking the big bad wolf of fairy tales. If we consider the sequence of the fragments we note that, from this perspective, the page does no more than follow the structure of dreams, which 'for representing *causal relations* [...] introduce the dependent clause as an introductory dream and [...] add the principal clause as the main dream'. This temporal sequence, Freud adds, 'may be reversed' although 'the more extensive part of the dream always corresponds to the principal clause'.[170] The principal clause would be the paraphrase from Avianus, which has undergone a process of both causal and temporal inversion. The ambiguity of 'onde' (causal and/or consecutive) would therefore be close to that of symptom in the repression process (*Verdrängung*), in which both the repressive drive and the repressed element are condensed into a multistable signifier. This hypothesis is confirmed by another passage from the *Interpretation of Dreams*, in which Freud writes that another 'method of representing a causal relation [...] consists in one image in the dream [...] being transformed into another': in any case, '*causation* is represented by temporal sequence'.[171] The dog metamorphosed into a wolf and the moon implicitly transformed into Hecate show therefore that a causal relation is in operation, acting in two concurrent and opposite directions: while the dog conjures up Avianus's wolf (a connection situated within the present), nothing but the fear of the wolf, which has re-emerged from the sphere of origin, allows the subject to comprehend the connection between the howling and the moon, and its simultaneously infantile and mythical resonances. The dog and the wolf work as equivalent subjects, given that in dream logic 'similarity, consonance, the possession of common attributes' — in this case the act of howling — 'are represented in dreams by unification'.[172]

The presence of an 'archaic' sensation of terror in the first page of the *Zibaldone* is confirmed most of all by the fact that, while quoting Avianus's fable, Leopardi seems to fall into a systematic misunderstanding of the text. As Bonifazi has already highlighted, the fable was originally a humorous apologue: it depicts a gullible wolf who believes that the woman will act on her threats to throw her child to him, and so patiently waits to be brought this meal.[173] In both the *Saggio* and the *Zibaldone*, however, Leopardi systematically elides this aspect of the story, leaving only the countrywoman's menacing behaviour, and using it to epitomize those 'night terrors' in which the 'ancients' believed, to which peasants continue to refer in their superstitions, and which still scare children in the greatest age of human reason: 'Non sembra egli di ravvisare nei costumi degli antichi il ritratto dei nostri?' [Do not ancient customs seem to mirror our own?].[174]

The paraphrase from Avianus is therefore a mutilated quotation, the partial retention of a text preserved by memory in an erroneous and incomplete way: the focus is displaced onto a facet that was only marginally present in the original text, thus putting the quotation to new uses. Needless to say, misunderstanding is always — from a Freudian point of view — the symptom of repression. In speaking of such processes of reading and quoting, and by evoking the Freudian notion of 'screen memory' (*Deckerinnerung*), Pierre Bayard recently coined the term 'screen books' (*livres-écrans*), arguing that:

> We do not retain in memory complete books [...], but rather fragments surviving from partial readings, frequently fused together and further recast by our private fantasies [*nos fantasmes personnels*]. In the end we are left with falsified remnants of books, analogous to the screen memories discussed by Freud, whose principal function is to conceal others.[175]

From this angle, the incomplete and tendentious quotation from Avianus surely hides the semantic memory of other texts, namely those mentioned in the *Saggio*. Still, perhaps not only semantic memory is in play here. Freud had conceptualized the notion of 'screen memories' in the *Psychopathology of Everyday Life*: screen memories 'are substitutes [...] for other impressions which are really significant', which 'a resistance prevents [...] from being directly reproduced'.[176] Like in dreams, a process of displacement (*Verschiebung*) gives birth to a compromise formation, grounded in an 'associative relation' with the repressed content.[177] Would Leopardi's misquotation work as a screen memory? This is possible, although indemonstrable: Freud himself, in an essay of 1913 on 'The Occurrence in Dreams of Material from Fairy Tales',[178] pointed out how 'in a few people a recollection of their favourite fairy tales takes the place of memories of their own childhood; they have made the fairy tales into screen memories'.[179] Still, if the hypothesis that a repressed memory accounts for the peculiarities of the first page of the *Zibaldone* remains speculative, we can perhaps explore in greater depth the image of the wolf and its uncanny presence in these opening fragments.

In his essay of 1913, Freud introduced his preliminary observations regarding the dream of a patient whom he had been treating since 1910: in 1918, with the publication of the results of the analysis, this patient would become universally known by his clinical pseudonym, 'The Wolf-Man', inspired by this childhood nightmare.[180] In the dream, the patient was lying in bed when the window suddenly opened. 'I was terrified [*mit großen Schrecken*]', he related, 'to see that some white wolves were sitting on the big walnut tree in front of the window. [They] looked more like foxes or sheep dogs [*Schäferhunde*] [...]. In great terror, evidently of being eaten up by the wolves [*von den Wölfen aufgefressen zu werden*], I screamed'.[181] Freud connected the dream to a fairy tale recounted by the patient's grandfather and to a picture book of *The Wolf and the Seven Little Goats*. The patient's zoophobia was therefore grounded, as Freud remarked, in cultural impressions rather than in direct experience: his phobia-inducing animal was 'known to him only from stories and picture books'.[182]

The superficial resonances between the Wolf Man's dream and Leopardi's description — the window (explicitly mentioned in the letter to Giordani, and implicit in the 'luna nel cortile' of *Zib.* 1), the underlying terror, the superimposition of dog and wolf, the fear of being devoured — are immediately evident. I would not however suggest that we limit ourselves to these observations. On the one hand, both Leopardi and the Wolf-Man may be unconsciously recollecting specific iconographic material: the tarot's eighteenth major arcana, 'The Moon', shows just such a wolf and domesticated dog, respectively emblems of primitive instinctivity and civilization, howling at the moon, an image that is sometimes interpreted as representing Hecate; in the background there stand two 'towers in an empty field',[183] whereas, at the bottom of the card, a crab (Cancer was Leopardi's astrological sign) is slowly emerging from a pond, symbolizing concealed memories resurfacing from the depths of the unconscious. On the other hand, the connection between wolf and dog is also legitimated by folklore, since '[i]n fable the wolf appears, often with emphasis on its cunning, and often too being presented in contrast with the dog'.[184] It is consequently possible that folkloric beliefs resurface in both scenes: Carlo Ginzburg suggests that, since the 'Wolf Man', Sergei Pankeiev, was of Russian heritage, the phobic image of the wolf should be connected to the werewolves of Slavic folklore. Pankeiev was born with the caul on Christmas day, and 'there is an obvious cultural homogeneity between these facts and the infantile dream focused on the appearance of the wolves'.[185] Equally, superstitions concerning werewolves are a strong presence in the folklore of Leopardi's region, the Marches, the result of Slavic influences or of the Grecian cultural substratum of the Ancona area.[186] Furthermore, most interestingly for our purposes, 'the intermediary between the sphere of folkloric beliefs connected with werewolves and Freud's future patient, who belonged [...] to an upper-middle-class family', must have necessarily been 'the nurse, the *njanja*'.[187]

For Pankeiev, therefore, exactly as for Leopardi, the nurse-'donna di contado' (Avianus's *rustica*), traditionally connected with witchcraft, is the link with the folkloric world of the lower classes, and with ancient beliefs metamorphosed into popular superstition. The nurse's body, from which the child has been exiled by the paternal and normative sphere of the symbolic, epitomizes the world that rational and modern thinking has erased, in that, by 'purvey[ing] both physical nourishment and the beginnings of symbolic language', it 'harbour[s] a potential conflict by confusing the corporeal and the mental',[188] as well as, we may add, error and truth. Avianus's fable, whose moral is that men say one thing and do something else, tellingly stages this ambiguity underlying the nurse as a figure deeply embedded in the collective imaginary. Thus the countrywoman is the intermediary for a fabulous (and, therefore, intrinsically false) imaginary that Leopardi does not hesitate to associate with a dream of his own while sketching the topic for a potential poem in 1819: 'Luna caduta secondo il mio sogno. Luna che secondo i villani fa nere le carni, *onde* io sentii una donna che consigliava per riso alla compagna sedente alla luna di porsi le braccia sotto il zendale' [Fallen moon, according to my dream. The moon, which peasants believe turns the skin black, *so that* I once heard a woman who jokingly suggested to her friend, who was sitting under the moon, to hide her arms under her apron].[189] Most significantly, for both Leopardi and Pankeiev, superstition clashes with post-Enlightenment rationalism, sublimating the conflict into a cultural compromise formation. Once 'subjected to opposing cultural pressures', writes Ginzburg — the nurse and his own cultural milieu — Sergei Pankeiev becomes 'a neurotic on the brink of psychosis', in whose dreams elements of the folkloric sphere, with which he had brief contact during his early childhood, resurface.[190] Trapped within a similar conflict, but one intensified by the cultural stimulus of classical philology, Leopardi envisages a close relationship in identity between 'antichi', children, and 'villani', thus investigating within the classical irrational the very same marvels and anxieties that he recalls from his own childhood and which resurface in his dreams. In both childhood memories and the countryside of the Marches, a mythical frame of mind survives, to which even the adult and enlightened subject can momentarily gain access, as to a lost homeland. One of these moments structures the first page of the *Zibaldone*, in which the tensions between past and present, and between rationalism and the underlying presence of myth, engender a set of ambiguous signifiers that obliquely make the image of 'Ecate inferna' resonate behind the nocturnal landscape.

This fluctuation between childhood and cultural memories is also present, although obliquely, in the Wolf Man's case, written just one year before the essay on 'The Uncanny'.[191] As is well known, in this text Freud interprets the dream of white wolves as an unconscious re-elaboration of the 'primal scene' (*Urszene*), the coitus between his parents allegedly witnessed by Pankeiev in his earliest childhood. Ginzburg, however, has highlighted how this term was by no means new to Freud's work, although previously employed in a different way. In a letter to Wilhelm Fliess of 2 May 1897, Freud used the term *Urszenen* to define the episodes of paternal seduction that he had made resurface while analyzing his hysterical patients.[192] As is the case in the essay on the uncanny, doubt is expressed about the reality (*Realität*) of the 'scene', heralding the final abandonment of the seduction hypothesis in September 1897, on the basis of Freud's own self-analysis.[193] Mirroring the uncanny, the *Urszene* of paternal seduction (or of the parents' coitus) is an image possessing the same emotional intensity as a real experience, but through a psychical reality (*psychische Realität*) rather than actuality. The notion of *Urszene* therefore dissolves the boundaries between reality and imagination, as well as those between actual recollection and afterwardsness (*Nachträglichkeit*),[194] and, as such, has been proposed by Ned Lukacher as an 'interpretive strategy' answering to the problem of the ungraspability of origin within modernity:

> It is with regard to this conjunction of literature/philosophy/psychoanalysis and the ensuing revelation/concealment that I propose the notion of the primal scene as a trope for reading and understanding. For this purpose I do not restrict 'primal scene' to the conventional psychoanalytic understanding of the term: the child's witnessing of a sexual act that subsequently plays a traumatic role in his or her psychosexual life. In my use of the term it becomes an intertexual event that displaces the notion of the event from the ground of ontology. It calls the event's relation to the Real into question in an entirely new way. Rather than signifying the child's observation of sexual intercourse, the primal scene comes to signify an ontologically undecidable intertextual event that is situated in the differential space between historical memory and imaginative construction, between archival verification and interpretive free play. [...] I propose this definition of the primal scene as a step toward solving the crisis of interpretation that emerges when the question of the origin becomes at once unavoidable

and unanswerable, when the origin must be remembered but memory fails utterly, when all the evidence points toward an origin that nevertheless remains unverifiable. The primal scene is the figure of an interpretive dilemma.[195]

From this angle, the fact that Leopardi's *Urszene* takes place within a complex network of intertextual relationships — classical sources, folkloric traces, stylistic echoes of fourteenth-century religious writers — confirms Lukacher's assumption that the primal scene 'defines a kind of historical "event" that cannot be thought outside the question of intertextuality'. Lukacher acknowledges:

> the recognition implicit in a wide range of modern texts that errancy is, and has always been, the only ground of memory. The locks of memory, it appears, have always already been severed. In the place of the transcendental ground of subjective memory, *Primal Scenes* substitutes a textual memory; in lieu of a human subject, a series of intertextual constructions.[...] To paraphrase Althusser, *there is no subject to the primal scene; it is the primal scene itself which is a subject insofar as it does not have a subject*. The notion of the primal scene enables us to grasp historical experience at the interface of language and world, at the interface of consciousness and the unconscious.[196]

In particular, it is relevant to point out how, for Freud, the notion of *Urszene* also possesses, as Ginzburg maintains, 'obvious phylogenetic implications'.[197] Although referring to childhood experiences, Freud's 1897 understanding of *Urszene* does not exclude cultural echoes: in Freud's letters to Fliess, hypotheses are raised that scenes of seduction could actually be memories of ancient, collective traumas, and this possibility remains implicitly present in his re-use of the term in 1918. 'In both cases', Ginzburg concludes, 'the original valence suggested by Freud with the prefix *Ur* is ascribable both to the ontogenetic and the phylogenetic spheres'.[198]

We should not fail to notice that the ambiguity of the prefix 'Ur-' is the same as that of Leopardi's adjective 'antico', and that *Urszenen* could be a perfect German translation for the 'immagini antiche' mentioned by Leopardi in the letter to Giordani of 1820. In Leopardi's text, as well as in Freud's, the spheres of ontogenesis and phylogenesis collide, generating a superimposition of individual and cultural memory from which actuality is excluded.[199] The howling dog evokes Avianus's wolf by association, and implicitly calls to mind the original images of terror recounted by ancient writers: at the same time, primitive beliefs survive in the superstitions of peasants, and are reborn in the fantasies of children via their nurses' frightening stories. Since they are repressed by individual or collective maturity, these relics of the distant past become something 'that ought to have remained secret and hidden but has come to light'. Continuing to analyze these processes with the help of Freudian logic, we cannot help but remark how, in *The Interpretation of Dreams*, Freud asserts that 'the alternative "either-or" cannot be expressed in dreams in any way whatsoever. Both of the alternatives are usually inserted in the text of the dream as though they were equally valid'.[200] Dreams are not concerned with 'the category of contraries and contradictories', and show instead 'a particular preference for combining contraries into a unity'.[201] The conflict between supernatural and rational explanations is therefore condensed into a bipolar textual object, characterized by the undecidability between a set of binary oppositions: dog/wolf, moon/Hecate, actual countryside/mythical space, familiarity and otherness. In the familiar and *heimlich* setting of 'palazzo Bello', an auditory stimulus conjures up the *Unheimlichkeit*: as Freud would have put it, 'an uncanny experience occurs either when infantile complexes which have been repressed are once more revived by some impressions, or when primitive beliefs which have been surmounted seem once more to be confirmed'.[202]

In relating the case of the Wolf Man, Freud highlights how the *Urszene* was brought back not by memory, but by just such a reactivation:

> The activation [*die Aktivierung*] of this scene (I purposely avoid the word 'recollection' [*Erinnerung*]) had the same effect as though it were a recent experience. The effects of the scene were deferred [*nachträglich*], but meanwhile [...] it had lost none of its freshness.[203]

Freud's lexical choice, Jean Laplanche writes, defines 'a kind of memory [...] cut off from its origins and from its access routes, isolated and fixed, reduced to a trace. It is a trace', he continues, 'which is not [...] necessarily more *false*, but which contains a "kernel of truth" that is more essential than the trivial conscious memory'.[204] The process is close to the one described by Leopardi in the letter to Giordani: a set of otherwise irrelevant elements work as a catalyst, activating an *Urszene* that has scarcely anything to do with the usual mechanics of memory. 'Mi si svegliarono alcune immagini antiche', writes Leopardi: the activation is not a recollection, but the awakening of a 'secret and hidden' reminiscence that 'has come to light'. As Gioanola remarks, Leopardi — exactly like Freud — deliberately chooses not to use the word 'ricordo'.[205] He employs instead the nouns 'ricordanza' and 'rimembranza' and the verbs 'rimembrare' or 'sovvenire', using this last, in the *Canti*, only in the first-person form with the pronominal particle 'mi' (e.g. 'mi sovvien l'eterno' in 'L'infinito' [the eternal comes to mind]).[206] This strategy ('mi sovvien', 'mi si svegliarono') de-subjectivizes the process of memory, making it occur outside the subject's control. The subject is a mere witness of an *Urszene* that literally 'enters from below' ('sovviene', Latin *subvenit*) as an unexpected (although obliquely familiar) apparition.

The same process, I argue, structures the first page of the *Zibaldone*, in which — as in Pankeiev's dream — temporal sequence is subverted through the reactivation of the indefinite sphere of origin. As Walter Benjamin would synthesize in the sixth of his theses 'On the Concept of History', the unexpected and fleeting return of the past threatens the historicist illusions of continuity and tradition, establishing in their place the uncanny presence of anachronism:

> Articulating the past historically [...] means appropriating a memory as it flashes up [*aufblitzt*] in a moment of danger [*im Augenblick einer Gefahr*]. Historical materialism wishes to hold fast [*festhalten*] that image of the past which unexpectedly [*unversehens*] appears to the historical subject [*dem historischen Subjekt*] in the moment of danger.[207]

As Lukacher points out, 'The dialectical image is Benjamin's version of the primal scene':

> These images are 'constellations' because they are formed from the interrelations within an aggregate of images and because the historian places them high above the horizon of the past, high enough perhaps to shed some light over

a darkened present and future. [...] Benjamin's dialectical images are situated in the unverifiable preontological zone between memory and imagination. Their authenticity can never be established because the dreaming collective that produced them no longer exists and could not confirm them if it did exist. They are the tentative responses to a politico-interpretive where knowledge of the origin is at once necessary and necessarily flawed.[208]

Equally, Benjamin's dialectical image is poised between 'the remembrance or interiorization (*Erinnerung*) of the individual's primal scene' and 'the deeper reaches of the remembrance (*Gedächtnis*) of a collective primal scene', thus blurring 'the differences between individual and collective experience and between voluntary and involuntary memory'; 'Benjamin's romantic historiography', Lukacher concludes, 'leads us to the deep structures linking literature, philosophy, and psychoanalysis',[209] in the same way — we may add — as Leopardi's hybrid and liminal experience questions the borders between poetry and philosophy, rigour and reverie, rational and mythical thinking. Tellingly, the nebula of the *Urszene*, namely of an abstract and pre-logical ancientness that λόγος inexorably fails to grasp, is given solid form by the opening of the *Zibaldone*, a desperately modern work that — like Benjamin's and Warburg's oeuvres — chooses fragmentariness as an answer to the impossibility of conceptualizing any 'origin' (*Ursprung*) or tradition.[210] At the same time, the beginning of the *Zibaldone* obliquely evokes the image of Hecate, thus recalling her to her ancient role as the 'goddess who guarded entrances and liminal points'.[211] Hecate announces the liminal nature of Leopardi's operation, a Faustian experience, as it has been defined,[212] of confrontation with a sulphurous modernity (it is perhaps not a coincidence that in Goethe's *Faust* the presence of Hell also appears in the guise of a dog); in being literally located 'entre chien et loup' [between dog and wolf] — the French expression for denoting twilight — Leopardi's intellectual endeavour tries to move within a twilight zone between rationality and 'savage mind', μῦθος and λόγος, truth and illusion, whose first allegorical epitome is perhaps the ambiguity between the dog and the big bad wolf of fairy tales portrayed in the first page of the *Zibaldone*.

Notes to Chapter 3

1. Blasucci, 'I tempi dei "Canti"', p. 202.
2. Leopardi, 'Le ricordanze', ll. 1–5.
3. Folin, *Leopardi e il canto dell'addio*, p. 96.
4. Carrera, *La distanza del cielo*, p. 61.
5. Ibid., p. 74.
6. The reference is to Claude Lévi-Strauss, *La Pensée sauvage* (Paris: Plon, 1962).
7. *Zib.* 19.
8. Staël, 'Sulla maniera e l'utilità delle traduzioni', p. 8, '[Gli italiani] per lo più stanno contenti all'antica mitologia, né pensano che quelle favole sono da un pezzo anticate, anzi il resto d'Europa le ha già abbandonate e dimentiche' [Italians are still mainly satisfied with ancient mythology, and do not think that those fables have looked antiquated for quite a while; moreover, that the rest of Europe has now abandoned and forgotten them].
9. *Zib.* 63–64.
10. TPP, pp. 972–73.
11. White, *Metahistory*, pp. 15–16.

12. On the frontispiece, see Hartog, 'Il confronto con gli antichi', pp. 22–23; Michel de Certeau, 'Histoire et anthropologie chez Lafitau', in *Naissance de l'ethnologie? Anthropologie et missions en Amérique, XVIe-XVIIIe siècle*, ed. by Claude Blankaert (Paris: Cerf, 1985), pp. 63–89; and Pierre Vidal-Naquet, *The Black Hunter: Forms of Thought and Forms of Society in the Greek World*, transl. by Andrew Szegedy-Maszak (Baltimore and London: Johns Hopkins University Press, 1986), pp. 129–33. For the expression 'obsolete objects' see Francesco Orlando, *Obsolete Objects in the Literary Imagination: Ruins, Relics, Rarities, Rubbish, Uninhabited Places, and Hidden Treasures*, transl. by Gabriel Pihas and Daniel Seidel, with Alessandra Grego (New Haven and London: Yale University Press, 2006).

13. Leopardi, 'Inno ai Patriarchi', l. 105.

14. Ibid., l. 104. On Leopardi and native Americans see Marco Balzano, *I confini del sole: Leopardi e il nuovo mondo* (Venice: Marsilio, 2008).

15. Aby Warburg, 'A Lecture on Serpent Ritual', transl. by W.F. Mainland, *Journal of the Warburg Institute*, 2, 4 (April 1939), 277–92 (p. 277). The translation of the epigraph is Allan Cameron's, from *The Future of the 'Classical'*, by Salvatore Settis, transl. by Allan Cameron (Cambridge: Polity Press, 2006), p. 88. See also Sabine Mainberger, 'Hamburg-Oraibi via Florence: Aby Warburg's Cultural Geography', *Acta Historiae Artium* 49 (2008), 138–43.

16. The activity of Usener and Lamprecht is to be inscribed within the wider frame of the so-called *Bonner Kreis*, namely the presence, at the University of Bonn, of several scholars such as Friedrich Nietzsche, Ulrich Wilamowitz-Möllendorff, Franz Cumont, and Ernst Cassirer.

17. Warburg, 'A Lecture on Serpent Ritual', pp. 291–92.

18. Ibid., p. 291.

19. Ibid., p. 282.

20. Ibid., p. 291.

21. 'The *Atlas* was a visual instrument of invocation, and its plates, with their meticulously arranged objects, had much in common with the ceremonial altar superstructures of the Hopi', Kurt W. Forster, introduction to Warburg, *The Renewal of Pagan Antiquity*, p. 52.

22. Ibid.

23. SE, XVII, 217–56.

24. SE, XVII, 224.

25. See Anneleen Masschelein, *The Unconcept: The Freudian Uncanny in Late-Twentieth-Century Theory* (Albany: State University of New York Press, 2011), pp. 27–35 for a detailed analysis of the 'surmounted phylogenetic origin' of Freud's conceptualization of the uncanny.

26. SE, XVII, 247–48, my emphases; GW, XII, 262.

27. Ernst Jentsch, 'On the Psychology of the Uncanny', transl. by Roy Sellars, *Angelaki* 2, 1 (1995), 7–16 (p. 11).

28. SE, XVII, 226. For the curious case of a 'kunstvolle Puppe' connected to Leopardi see Mario Andrea Rigoni, 'Un Elzeviro: Opere d'arte per amori mancati', in *Giacomo Leopardi : Viaggio nella memoria*, ed. by Fabiana Cacciapuoti (Milan: Electa, 1999), pp. 147–48.

29. As Giorgio Agamben notes, the doll is a 'signifie[r] of diachrony', afterimage of the small idols found in ancient sepulchres, which belong instead to 'that immutable world of synchrony, the domain of the tomb': Agamben, 'In Playland', in *Infancy and History*, by Giorgio Agamben, pp. 65–87 (p. 81).

30. SE, XVII, 240–41.

31. Gilberto Lonardi has shown how Leopardi's re-elaboration of the theme of return is constructed through an intertextual memory of Achilles's dialogue with his mother Thetis in the *Iliad*, mediated by Vincenzo Monti's translation, *L'oro di Omero*, pp. 13–14.

32. Leopardi, 'Le ricordanze', l. 3.

33. Ibid., ll. 4–5.

34. Ibid., l. 18.

35. Ibid., ll. 20–21.

36. Ibid., l. 53.

37. Ibid., ll. 50–51.

38. Ibid., l. 61.

39. Ibid., ll. 62–64.

40. Ibid., l. 67.

41. Ibid., ll. 68–69.

42. Ibid., l. 107.

43. Ibid., l. 151.

44. Ibid., ll. 166–67.

45. Ibid., l. 144.

46. Jacques Lacan, *Le Séminaire livre X: L'angoisse (1962–1963)*, ed. by Jacques-Alain Miller (Paris: Seuil, 2004), p. 60.

47. Lonardi, *L'oro di Omero*, p. 13.

48. Anthony Vidler, *The Architectural Uncanny: Essays in Modern Unhomely* (Cambridge, MA: MIT Press, 1992), p. 24.

49. Leopardi, 'Le ricordanze', ll. 55–57.

50. *Zib.* 15.

51. *Zib.* 15–16.

52. See Gaetano, *Giacomo Leopardi e il sublime*, p. 319.

53. Leopardi, 'Il pensiero dominante', ll. 18–19, my emphases.

54. Leopardi, 'Il passero solitario', ll. 1–2, my emphases.

55. See for example: *Zib.* 171 (12–23 July 1820), 'Perciò [la curiosità] potrà esser la cagione immediata di questo effetto, (vale a dire che se l'anima non provasse piacere nella vista della *campagna* ec. non desidererebbe l'estensione di questa vista), ma non la primaria [...]. L'anima s'immagina quello che non vede, che quell'albero, quella siepe, quella *torre* gli nasconde, e va errando in uno spazio immaginario' [So curiosity could be the immediate cause of this effect (which is to say that if the soul did not find pleasure in a view of the *countryside*, etc., it would not desire the extension of this view), but it is not the main one [...]. The soul imagines what it cannot see, whatever is hidden by that tree, that hedge, that *tower*, and wanders in an imaginary space]; *Zib.* 1429–30 (1 August 1821), 'è notabile che l'anima in una delle dette estasi, vedendo p.e. una *torre* moderna, ma che non sappia quando fabbricata, e un'altra antica della quale sappia l'epoca precisa, tuttavia è molto più commossa da questa che da quella. [...] Come allorchè vediamo una vasta *campagna*, di cui pur da tutte le parti si scuopra l'orizzonte' [it is noteworthy that the soul in one of these ecstasies, seeing, e.g., a modern *tower*, but not knowing when it was built, and another ancient one whose precise era it knows, is nonetheless far more deeply moved by the latter than by the former. [...] As when we see a vast *expanse of countryside*, whose horizon is yet apparent on every side]; *Zib.* 1430–31 (1 August 1821), 'richiamar l'idea di una *campagna* arditamente declive in guisa che la vista in certa lontananza non arrivi alla valle [...] Una fabbrica una *torre* ec. veduta in modo che ella paia innalzarsi sola sopra l'orizzonte, e questo non si veda, produce un contrasto efficacissimo e sublimissimo tra il finito e l'indefinito [recall the idea of steeply sloping *countryside* where a view at a certain distance does not reach as far as the valley [...] A building, a *tower*, etc., seen in a way that it seems to rise up alone above the horizon, and where the horizon can be seen, produces a most sublime and effective contrast between the finite and the infinite]; *Zib.* 4418 (30 November 1828), 'All'uomo sensibile e immaginoso, che viva, come io sono vissuto gran tempo, sentendo di continuo ed immaginando, il mondo e gli oggetti sono in certo modo doppi. Egli vedrà cogli occhi una *torre*, una *campagna*; udrà cogli orecchi un suono d'una campana; e nel tempo stesso coll'immaginazione vedrà un'altra *torre*, un'altra *campagna*, udrà un altro suono' [To a sensitive and imaginative man, who lives, as I have done for so long, continually feeling and imagining, the world and its objects are in a certain respect double. With his eyes he will see a *tower*, a *country landscape*; with his ears he will hear the sound of a bell; and at the same time with his imagination he will see another *tower*, another *country landscape*, he will hear another sound]. My emphases throughout.

56. Folin, *Leopardi e il canto dell'addio*, p. 96.

57. SE, XVII, 241.

58. *Zib.* 36.

59. Leopardi, 'L'infinito', ll. 7–8.

60. E, II, 1459.

61. SE, XVII, 225.

62. SE, XVII, 245.

63. See Michel de Certeau: *L'Écriture de l'histoire* (Paris: Gallimard, 1975), pp. 337–419; and *Histoire et psychanalyse entre science et fiction* (Paris: Gallimard, 1987).

64. SE, XVII, 244.

65. On Freud's Enlightenment see Oudai Celso, *Freud e la filosofia antica*, pp. 37–39.

66. TPP, p. 873, my emphases. On the model of critique, see Lorenzo Bianchi, 'Critica e libero pensiero', in *Illuminismo: Un vademecum*, ed. by Gianni Paganini and Edoardo Tortarolo (Turin: Bollati Boringhieri, 2008), pp. 88–102. On Leopardi's *Saggio* and the culture of European Enlightenment, see especially Damiani, 'Le "credenze stolte', and Mazzarella, *I dolci inganni*.

67. Francesco Orlando, *Illuminismo, barocco e retorica freudiana* (Turin: Einaudi, 1997), pp. 16–17.

68. Didi-Huberman, *Devant le temps*, pp. 94–95 and 103–04.

69. *Zib.* 143, 1 July 1820.

70. Carlo Ginzburg, 'Mito', in *I Greci. Storia Cultura Arte Società*, I, 197–237.

71. Felici, *L'Olimpo abbandonato*, pp. 69–71.

72. *Zib.* 497–98, 13 January 1821.

73. Felici, *L'Olimpo abbandonato*, p. 17.

74. Leopardi, 'Alla Primavera', ll. 23–38.

75. Cesare Galimberti, 'Un mot sous les mots nella "Canzone alla sua Donna"?', in *Cose che non son cose: Saggi su Leopardi*, by Cesare Galimberti (Venice: Marsilio, 2001), pp. 87–97.

76. *Zib.* 2.

77. TPP, p. 874.

78. SE, XVII, 143.

79. Agamben, *Stanzas*, p. 76.

80. Leopardi, 'Le ricordanze', ll. 55–67.

81. Sigmund Freud, *Aus den Anfängen der Psychoanalyse. 1887–1902. Briefe an Wilhelm Fließ* (Frankfurt am Main: Fischer, 1962), p. 187.

82. SE, XVIII, 60; GW, XIII, 268.

83. Masschelein, *The Unconcept*, pp. 17–48.

84. SE, XVII, 150.

85. H.C. Erik Midelfort, 'Charcot, Freud, and the Demons', in *Werewolves, Witches, and Wandering Spirits: Traditional Belief & Folklore in Early Modern Europe*, ed. by Kathryn A. Edwards (Kirksville: Truman State University Press, 2002), pp. 199–215.

86. Jean Starobinski, 'Virgilio in Freud', transl. by Stefania Cirri, in *Di fronte ai classici. A colloquio con i greci e i latini*, ed. by Ivano Dionigi (Milan: Rizzoli, 2002), pp. 229–57 (p. 249).

87. Agamben, *Stanzas*, pp. 19–21.

88. Lawrence Johnson, *The Wolf Man's Burden* (Ithaca and London: Cornell University Press, 2001), p. 54.

89. Georges Didi-Huberman, *Fra Angelico: Dissemblance and Figuration*, transl. by Jane Marie Todd (London: University of Chicago Press, 1995), p. 8.

90. On childhood fears in Leopardi see Damiani, *All'apparir del vero*, pp. 20–22; Gioanola: *Leopardi, la malinconia*, pp. 144–48, and *Psicanalisi e interpretazione letteraria* (Milan: Jaca Book, 2005), pp. 49–140; and Franco D'Intino, 'I misteri di Silvia', pp. 219–22.

91. SFA, pp. 50–51.

92. Georges Didi-Huberman, 'The Supposition of the Aura: The Now, the Then, and Modernity', transl. by Jane Marie Todd, in *Walter Benjamin and History*, ed. by Alexander Benjamin (London and New York: Continuum, 2005), pp. 3–18 (p. 8).

93. Johnson, *The Wolf Man's Burden*, p. 55.

94. Leopardi, 'Le ricordanze', ll. 51–55.

95. Cfr. Damiani, *All'apparir del vero*, p. 20.

96. Monaldo Leopardi, 'Memoriale autografo ad Antonio Ranieri', in *Carteggio inedito di varii con Giacomo Leopardi con lettere che lo riguardano*, ed. by Giovanni and Raffaele Bresciano (Turin: Rosenberg & Sellier, 1935), pp. 478–82 (p. 478).

97. See Emilio Peruzzi, 'Odi, Melisso', in Id., *Studi leopardiani*, by Emilio Peruzzi, 2 vols. (Florence: Olschki, 1987), II, 75–138 (pp. 78–79).

98. TPP, p. 894.

99. Mazzarella, *I dolci inganni*, p. 21 note.

100. *Zib.* 531–32, 20 January 1821.

101. TPP, p. 892.

102. *Zib.* 262, 5 October 1820.

103. *Zib.* 2803–04, 21 June 1823.

104. *Zib.* 1103, 28 May 1821. See Colaiacomo, *Camera Obscura*, p. 47.

105. TPP, p. 892.

106. TPP, p. 61.

107. Germaine de Staël, *De l'Allemagne*, ed. by Simone Balayé, 2 vols. (Paris: Flammarion, 1968), I, 237–38.

108. Castle, *The Female Thermometer*, p. 8.

109. Leopardi, 'Le ricordanze', ll. 58–60.

110. See Didi-Huberman, *L'Image survivante*, pp. 13 and 17 and, more generally, pp. 11–26, for a comparison of the frontispices of Vasari's *Lives* and Winckelmann's *History of Ancient Art*.

111. Benjamin, 'On the Concept of History', SW, IV, 392.

112. SE, III, 192.

113. Jacques Derrida, *Spectres of Marx: The State of the Debt, the Work of Mourning, & the New International*, transl. by Peggy Kamuf (London: Routledge, 1994).

114. Friedrich Schlegel, *Geschichte der epischen Dichtkunst der Griechen*, in *Sämmtliche Werke*, by Friedrich Schlegel, 10 vols. (Vienna: Jakob Maner, 1822–25), III, 224.

115. Quoted in Christopher D. Johnson, *Memory, Metaphor, and Aby Warburg's Atlas of Images* (Ithaca: Cornell University Press, 2012), p. 13.

116. Aby Warburg, 'Seminarübungen über Jacob Burckhardt' (1927), ed. by Bernd Roeck, *Idea. Jahrbuch der Hamburger Kunsthalle*, 10 (1991), 86–89 (pp. 86–87).

117. Anthony Vidler, *The Architectural Uncanny*, p. 6.

118. SE, II, 7.

119. Graham Frankland stresses the analogies between Freud's clinical cases and detective novels, a 'genre of literature that does [...] structure itelf around meaningful gaps which, when filled, lead to a "solution" [...]. [Freud's] insistence on interpreting every phenomenon he encounters [...] does indeed seem to correspond with a literary-critical paradigm in which detective fiction has played a formative role. [...] The Wolf Man himself spotted the resemblance between his analyst and Sherlock Holmes, and was surprised to hear that Freud had read and enjoyed several Conan Doyle novels. It is also known that in later life Freud's favoured light reading was the fiction of Agatha Christie and Dorothy L. Sayers', *Freud's Literary Culture* (Cambridge: Cambridge University Press, 2004), pp. 151–52.

120. Forster, introduction to Warburg, *The Renewal of Pagan Antiquity*, p. 19.

121. TPP, p. 629.

122. On the ruins of Pompeii in Leopardi's works, see Fedi, *Mausolei di sabbia*, pp. 32–62.

123. Vidler, *The Architectural Uncanny*, p. 45. On Pompeii, see in general pp. 45–55. See also *Pompeii in the Public Imagination from its Rediscovery to Today*, ed. by Shelley Hales and Joanna Paul (Oxford: Oxford University Press, 2011), where no reference to Leopardi is, quite curiously, to be found.

124. 'Delusions and Dreams in Jensen's *Gradiva*', SE, IX, 1–95 (p. 43).

125. Douglas-Fairhurst, *Victorian Afterlives*, p. 37.

126. Didi-Huberman, *L'Image survivante*, pp. 9 and 271 respectively.

127. Ibid., pp. 296–97. See the whole section on 'L'Image-symptôme' for a strict analysis of the notion of 'symptom' between Freud and Warburg (pp. 271–514).

128. Ibid., p. 338.

129. Jacques Lacan, 'The Instance of the Letter in the Unconscious or Reason since Freud', in *Écrits*, by Jacques Lacan, transl. by Bruce Fink, Héloïse Fink and Russell Grigg (London and New York: W.W. Norton, 2006), pp. 412–41 (p. 439).

130. Slavoj Žižek, *Looking Awry: An Introduction to Jacques Lacan Through Popular Culture* (Cambridge, MA: MIT Press, 1992), p. 23.

131. Douglas-Fairhurst, *Victorian Afterlives*, p. 37.

132. *Zib.* 259–60, 4 October 1820.

133. Cacciapuoti, *Dentro lo Zibaldone*, p. 48.

134. Douglas-Fairhurst, *Victorian Afterlives*, p. 148.
135. Blasucci, 'Quattro modi di approccio allo *Zibaldone*', p. 240.
136. See the corresponding note by Pacella in *Zibaldone di pensieri*, by Leopardi, III, 464, and Cacciapuoti, *Dentro lo Zibaldone*, p. 49.
137. Carlo Ossola, 'Leopardi: préludes et passions', in *La Conscience de soi de la poésie*, ed. by Yves Bonnefoy (Paris: Seuil, 2008), pp. 235–68 (p. 256).
138. Lucio Felici, *La luna nel cortile: Capitoli leopardiani* (Soveria Mannelli: Rubbettino, 2006), p. 26.
139. Phaedrus and Avianus, *Fabulae, accedunt fabulae graecae latinis respondentes et Homeri Batrachomyomachia*, ed. by David Hoogstratan (Padua, 1721).
140. Felici, *La luna nel cortile*, p.24
141. See Pacella in *Zibaldone di pensieri*, III, 463.
142. Giulio Augusto Levi, 'Note di cronologia leopardiana', *Giornale storico della letteratura italiana*, 53 (1909), 232–70.
143. TPP, pp. 961–64.
144. E, I, 164.
145. The interest in fourteenth-century writers in the summer 1817 seems to play some part in the style of *Zib.* 1, in which we witness several phenomena of archaism, verging on pastiche. Several elements seem to herald the systematic calque of thirteenth-century style put into practice, years later, in the *Martirio de' Santi Padri* [Martyrdom of the Holy Fathers], of 1822: see D'Intino's linguistic note to the *Martirio* in *Volgarizzamenti in prosa*, by Leopardi, pp. 56–58, with Leopardi's choices, in *Zib.*1, in terms of lexicon and morphology ('onde', 'bambolo', 'aggiugne'), syntax ('minacciogli', 'credettele', 'messosi'), and macro-syntax ('Come poi ristesse tutto quel tempo e la donna non se n'accorgesse e non n'avesse paura e non gli facesse motto con sasso o altro, Aviano lo saprà che lo dice'). Moreover, in fourteenth-century hagiography, 'onde' was often used as a connection between different episodes. I am indebted to Roberta Cella for this observation.
146. TPP, p. 1112.
147. Neuro Bonifazi, 'La libera traduzione leopardiana di una favola di Aviano nel proemio dello "Zibaldone"', in *La corrispondenza imperfetta: Leopardi tradotto e traduttore*, ed. by Anna Dolfi and Adriana Mitescu (Rome: Bulzoni, 1990), pp. 31–39. One year later, Bonifazi developed his considerations in the third chapter of his *Leopardi, l'immagine antica*, pp. 62–99. The hypothesis was, however, already present in his *Lingua mortale: Genesi della poesia leopardiana* (Ravenna: Longo, 1984), pp. 101–05.
148. Leopardi, *Zibaldone di pensieri*, ed. by Giuseppe Pacella, III, 463.
149. Felici, *La luna nel cortile*, p. 24.
150. Ibid., p. 25.
151. *Zibaldone di pensieri*, III, 463.
152. See Elio Gioanola, 'Psicanalisi e critica letteraria', in *Freud and Italian Culture*, ed. by Pierluigi Barrotta and Laura Lepschy with Emma Bond (Bern: Peter Lang, 2009), pp. 9–30 (p. 20).
153. Bonifazi, 'La libera traduzione', p. 39.
154. Orlando, *Illuminismo, barocco e retorica freudiana*.
155. TPP, p. 895.
156. TPP, p. 894, my emphases.
157. TPP, p. 758, my emphases.
158. Robert Graves, *The White Goddess*, p. 88.
159. The connection between the dog and Avianus's wolf is asserted by Franco D'Intino in SFA, pp. 54–55 note 28, and in *L'immagine della voce*, p. 204.
160. E, I, 379, my emphases.
161. *Zib.* 1789.
162. Apuleius of Madauros, *The Isis-Book (Metamorphoses, Book XI)*, ed. and transl. by J. Gwyn Griffiths (Leiden: Brill, 1975), pp. 70–73.
163. E, I, 379.
164. Endel Tulving, 'Episodic and Semantic Memory', in *Organization of Memory*, ed. by Endel Tulving and Wayne Donaldson (New York: Academic Press, 1972), pp. 381–403.
165. Abraham and Torok, *The Wolf Man's Magic Word*, p. 22.

166. SE, IV, 270.

167. SE, IV, 304.

168. SE, IV, 314.

169. D'Intino, *L'immagine della voce*, p. 204.

170. SE, IV, 314–15.

171. SE, IV, 316.

172. SE, IV, 320.

173. Bonifazi, 'La libera traduzione leopardiana', pp. 38–39.

174. TPP, p. 895.

175. Pierre Bayard, *Comment parler des livres que l'on n'a pas lus?* (Paris: Minuit, 2007), p. 61; *How to Talk About Books You Haven't Read*, transl. by Jeffrey Mehlman (New York: Bloomsbury USA, 2007), p. 56.

176. SE, VI, 43.

177. SE, VI, 43.

178. SE, XII, 281–87.

179. SE, XII, 281.

180. Freud, 'From the History of an Infantile Neurosis', SE, XVII, 7–122; GW, XII, 27–157.

181. SE, XVII, 29; GW, XII, 54.

182. SE, XVII, 32.

183. See above, n. 55.

184. Richard Buxton, 'Wolves and Werewolves in Greek Thought', in *Interpretations of Greek Mythology*, ed. by Jan Bremmer (London: Routledge, 1988), pp. 60–79 (p. 65).

185. Carlo Ginzburg, 'Freud, the Wolf-Man, and the Werewolves', in Id., *Clues, Myths, and the Historical Method*, transl. by John and Anne C. Tedeschi (Baltimore, MD: Johns Hopkins University Press, 1989), pp. 146–55 (p. 148). Barbara Creed supports Ginzburg's argument, *Phallic Panic: Film, Horror and the Primal Uncanny* (Melbourne: Melbourne University Press, 2005), pp. 96–123 and, more specifically, pp. 102–03.

186. It is interesting to note that in Michele Mari's novel *Io venìa pien d'angoscia a rimirarti* (Venice: Marsilio, 1998) the young Leopardi is depicted as being a werewolf: Leopardi's lycanthropy becomes the emblem of a repressed yearning for active and instinctive life that is later sublimated into poetry, a transition from a 'primitive' to a 'civilized' state that Leopardi, as we have seen, semanticizes in various ways throughout his oeuvre, and which may echo Robert Eisler's seminal, albeit questionable, *Man Into Wolf: An Anthropological Interpretation of Sadism, Masochism, and Lycanthropy* (London: Routledge & Kegan, 1951). On the ancient roots of beliefs in werewolves, see Buxton, 'Wolves and Werewolves in Greek Thought'.

187. Ginzburg, 'Freud, the Wolf-Man, and the Werewolves', p. 148.

188. Cestaro, *Dante and the Grammar of the Nursing Body*, p. 49.

189. TPP, p. 459, my emphasis.

190. Ginzburg, 'Freud, the Wolf-Man, and the Werewolves', p. 148.

191. Hélène Cixous suggests that even Freud's interpretation of Hoffmann's tale *Der Sandmann* in 'The Uncanny' is 'a surreptitious rereading of the Wolf-Man': 'Fiction and Its Phantoms: A Reading of Freud's Das Unheimliche (The "Uncanny")', *New Literary History*, 7, 3 (1976), 525–48 (p. 537). On the connections between the Wolf-Man's case and Freud's essay, see Masschelein, *The Unconcept*, p. 23.

192. Ginzburg, 'Freud, the Wolf-Man, and the Werewolves', p. 152.

193. Didier Anzieu, *L'Auto-analyse: Son rôle dans la découverte de la psychanalyse par Freud — Sa fonction en psychanalyse* (Paris: Presses Universitaires de France, 1959), pp. 61–62.

194. On the problem of the *Urszene* as an actual or imagined experience, see also Elizabeth Wright, *Speaking Desires Can Be Dangerous: The Poetics of the Unconsciousness* (Cambridge: Polity Press, 1999), pp. 25–30.

195. Ned Lukacher, *Primal Scenes: Literature, Philosophy, Psychoanalysis* (Ithaca, NY, and London: Cornell University Press, 1986), p. 24. The 'interpretive strategy' provided by the primal scene, Lukacher warns, is not uniquely 'a twentieth-century product': his own analysis of Dickens actually testifies to 'the possibility that the *nineteenth*-century author may have evolved, although in a very primitive form, a novelistic strategy that has deep affinities with what I call

the primal scene' (p. 276). Leopardi can offer another example, moreover, of a strategy that is definitely anti-novelistic and rather takes place in the domain of poetry.

196. Ibid., pp. 12–14.

197. Ginzburg, 'Freud, the Wolf-Man, and the Werewolves', p. 151.

198. Ibid., pp. 152–53.

199. Bonifazi, who also focuses his analysis on the notion of 'immagine antica', intends it however as merely referring to the sphere of childhood: for him, the phylogenetic aspect is only a metaphor (or a compromise formation) alluding to a repressed 'immagine fanciullesca' (*Leopardi e l'immagine antica*, p. xii).

200. SE, IV, 316.

201. SE, IV, 318.

202. SE, XVII, 249.

203. SE, XVII, 44; GW, XII, 71.

204. Jean Laplanche, 'Interpretation between Determinism and Hermeneutics: a Restatement of the Problem', transl. by Philip Slotkin, in *Essays on Otherness*, by Jean Laplanche (London and New York: Routledge, 1999), pp. 138–65 (p. 152).

205. Elio Gioanola, *Cesare Pavese: La realtà, l'altrove, il silenzio* (Milan: Jaca Book, 2003), p. 120.

206. Leopardi, 'L'infinito', l. 11. See also Francesco Erspamer, *La creazione del passato*, pp. 112–13.

207. SW, IV, 391; GS, I, 695.

208. Lukacher, *Primal Scenes*, pp. 280–81.

209. Ibid., p. 287.

210. See Didi-Huberman, *L'Image survivante*, p. 175.

211. Sarah Iles Johnston, *Restless Dead*, p. 247.

212. D'Intino, 'Il monaco indiavolato'.

CONCLUSION

Fireflies

[...] eine Nymphe, die im Fliehen schon gefallen ist.
[a nymph already fallen in flight]

FRIEDRICH SCHLEGEL, *Lucinde*, translated by P. Firchow

Vocatus atque non vocatus deus aderit.
[Called or uncalled, a god will be present]

THE DELPHIC ORACLE

The laboratory which opened with the first page of the *Zibaldone* closes in 1832, never to reopen again. Still, as we have said, the role of the *Zibaldone* is *de facto* exhausted in September 1829, concurrently with the state of grace from which 'Le ricordanze' arises. Through four more years, Leopardi continues drafting notes, although ever more sporadically, that barely amount to three pages in total. On 4 December 1832, in Florence, he eventually adds the last fragment.

Curiously, as Franco D'Intino points out, in that very same year, 1832, another 'passeggere' makes his appearance in Leopardi's oeuvre, as if he was a sort of afterimage of the one who had opened the *Zibaldone*, scared by a dog-wolf at some timeless crossroads.[1] In the 'Dialogo di un venditore di almanacchi e di un passeggere' [Dialogue of an Almanac-Pedlar and a Passer-by], being one of the two *Operette morali* written in 1832, we are no longer in the Recanati countryside, although transfigured into the original sphere of myth. We are in a modern city, definitely ruled by history and the calendar. In the days immediately preceding New Year's Eve, a travelling seller advertises his 'new almanacs', when he bumps into an unnamed figure of the *flâneur*: a 'passeggere', precisely, someone who *passes*, promenades, strolls. The two begin to talk.

The dialogue is suffused by a sad irony, and by a sort of compassion. The new year will be good, the pedlar replies to the passer-by's urging questions: still, it will not look like any of the past ones, since none of them has, all things considered, been happy. Life is a fine thing, everybody knows that, but if one were obliged to live again all the past years, under the condition of living them in exactly the same way, with the very same joys and griefs, no one, not even a prince, would accept. What sort of life would you like, then? — the passer-by eventually asks. Thus answers the seller:

VENDITORE: Vorrei una vita così, come Dio me la mandasse, senz'altri patti.
PASSEGGERE: Una vita a caso, e non saperne altro avanti, come non si sa dell'anno nuovo?

VENDITORE: Appunto.

PASSEGGERE: Così vorrei ancor io se avessi a rivivere, e così tutti. [...] Quella vita ch'è una cosa bella, non è la vita che si conosce, ma quella che non si conosce; non la vita passata, ma la futura. Coll'anno nuovo, il caso incomincerà a trattar bene voi e me e tutti gli altri, e si principierà la vita felice. Non è vero?

VENDITORE: Speriamo.

PASSEGGERE: Dunque mostratemi l'almanacco più bello che avete.

VENDITORE: Ecco, illustrissimo. Cotesto vale trenta soldi.

PASSEGGERE: Ecco trenta soldi.

VENDITORE: Grazie, illustrissimo: a rivederla. Almanacchi, almanacchi nuovi; lunari nuovi.[2]

[PEDLAR: A life just as it came, as God gave it, with no strings attached. PASSER-BY: A life accepted at random, knowing nothing of it beforehand, just as we know nothing about this new year? PEDLAR: That's it. PASSER-BY: I would want the same thing if I had to live over again, and so would everyone. [...] That life which is a fine thing is not the life one knows, but the life one does not know; not the life of the past, but of the future. With this new year, chance will begin to treat you and me well, and everyone else too; and so the happy life will start. Isn't this the case? PEDLAR: Let's hope so. PASSER-BY: Well then, show me the best almanac you have. PEDLAR: Here, Your Honour. This one costs half a crown. PASSER-BY: And here's your half-crown. PEDLAR: Thank you, Your Honour. Good day to you. Almanacs, new almanacs, new calendars!]

There is much *charity* in this final answer, following which the passer-by interrupts the conversation and purchases an almanac that he knows to be completely useless — charity, I mean, in the fullest sense of the Greek word χάρις. The passer-by's answer is suffused with lightness, grace, ambiguity; and, at the same time, with a sort of disinterested love, which brings him to play with gently ironic rhetorical questions, in order not to destroy the pedlar's poor illusions. Like many other characters of the *Operette*, the passer-by is a Socratic figure: however, unlike Plato's Socrates, he decides to halt, and not to push his maieutic interrogation to the extreme. His purpose is not to reveal the truth, but only to make some vague allusions that the pedlar is unable to grasp, as if momentarily playing in order to dispel boredom. This corresponds to Leopardi's notion of 'mezza filosofia' [half-philosophy], elaborated in the *Zibaldone* since 1821:[3] unlike the strict interdependence of 'enlightenment' and human happiness postulated by eighteenth-century Eudemonism, for Leopardi, as it will prove for Nietzsche, the full and absolute cognition of truth is not only unrelated, but even opposed to the well-being of human creatures.[4] This consideration allows us to highlight an extremely important aspect that characterizes the legacy of Leopardi's thought especially as far as ethics are concerned. As we have seen, the *Operette morali* underlie Nietzsche's reflection at the time of writing the second of the *Untimely Meditations* and the essay *On Truth and Lies in a Nonmoral Sense*: to some extent, the philosophical implications of Leopardi's dialogues in terms of nihilism, relativity of every point of view, and the ultimate awareness of the culturally constructed nature of every 'illusion', can be seen as a secret filigree resurfacing in the 'paradoxical posthumous destiny' of the latter, in the 1970s and between Paris and Yale, when *On Truth and Lies* becomes one of the foundational texts of deconstruction.[5] Still, the difference between Leopardi's position and the twentieth-century legacy of Nietzsche's manifesto of relativism — and most notably of what Ginzburg terms Paul de Man's 'perpetually vacillating pendulum between truth and falsehood: intellectually a more subtle position, but existentially fragile'[6] — resides, I believe, in turning the awareness about the deceiving power of language and the ultimate equivalence between truth and falsehood into the choice for a charitable action in favour of those who are weaker. In writing *Comparazione delle sentenze di Bruto minore e di Teofrasto vicini a morte* [Comparison between the Sentences Pronounced by Brutus and Theophrastus when Close to Death], in 1822, Leopardi declares that he who knows the emptiness of everything operates in every possible way in order to dissipate that awareness in those who have not fully perceived it — a statement in which D'Intino has seen the most intimate core of Leopardi's ethics, later reverberating in the project of translation of Greek moralists.[7] It is in accordance with this precept that the passer-by acts: man, as Leopardi synthesizes in 1820, 'ha bisogno di credenze' [needs beliefs],[8] and Voltaire's ideal of virtue as 'benevolence for your neighbour' (bienfaisance envers le prochain)[9] can sometimes coincide with cheating him. This deeply ethical choice, which recuperates the Christian notion of a disinterested pity for humanity and its miseries, animates the passer-by's respectful, albeit ironic, answer.

Once the dialogue is over, both passer-by and pedlar go their own way. Theirs has been a momentary and fleeting encounter: the only kind of interaction between individuals that a big city (and modernity in general) can allow, as Walter Benjamin's analysis of Baudelaire's 'A une passante' lucidly acknowledges. Every being passes, Leopardi suggests, and the fate of everything — especially in modern life — is nothing but ephemerality. As we have seen, in April 1827, in the *Zibaldone*, Leopardi connects the fate of human beings to that of modern books, both doomed to a fleeting life. By recuperating an ancient image, already present in Homer and Pindar,[10] he states that men and modern books are 'passers-by' and 'pilgrims' on earth, and resemble the 'efimeri, che vivono nello stato di *larve e di ninfe* per ispazio di un anno, alcuni di due anni, altri di tre' [ephemeral creatures that live in the state of *larvae and nymphs* for the space of a year, some for two years, others for three].[11] The problem is therefore to understand what form of survival such ephemeral and frail creatures can expect, or, within the domain of literature, how it is possible to write poems in the age of disenchantment.

As we have seen, in *Silvio Sarno* Leopardi had drafted a sort of micro-narration, in which the constellation of 'A Silvia' and 'Le ricordanze' was already, somehow, present:

> Giardino presso alla casa del guardiano, io era malinconichiss. e mi posi a una finestra che metteva sulla piazzetta ec. due giovanotti sulla gradinata della chiesa abbandonata [...] sedevano scherzando sotto al lanternone [....] comparisce la prima lucciola ch'io vedessi in quell'anno ec. uno dei due s'alza gli va addosso ec. io domandava fra me misericordia alla poverella l'esortava ad alzarsi ec, ma la colpì e gittò a terra e tornò all'altro ec. intanto la figlia del cocchiere ec. alzandosi da cena e affacciatasi alla finestra per lavare un piattello nel tornare dice a quei dentro = stanotte piove da vero. Se vedeste che tempo. Nero come un cappello. = e poco dopo sparisce il lume di quella finestra ec. intanto la

lucciola era risorta ec. avrei voluto ec. ma quegli se n'accorse tornò = porca buzzarona = un'altra botta la fa cadere già debole com'era ed egli col piede ne fa una striscia lucida fra la polvere ec. e poi ec. finchè la cancella. [...] sento una dolce voce di donna che non conoscea né vedea ec..[12]

[Garden next to the surveyor's place, I was most melancholy and I went to a window that overlooked the small square etc. two youths sat joking on the steps of the abandoned church [...] beneath the big lantern [...] there appears the first firefly I saw that year etc. one of the two gets up and sets upon her etc. I begged within myself pity for the poor creature I exhorted her to take off etc., but he struck her and threw her to the ground and went back to the other youth etc. in the meantime the coachman's daughter etc. getting up from the dining table went to the window to wash a dish and on her way back says to those inside: — tonight it will rain for sure. if you could see the weather. Dark as a hat. — and soon the light of that window disappears etc. in the meantime the firefly had revived etc. I would have etc. but that one saw what had happened and came back — you fucking bitch — another hit and he makes her fall, feeble as she was, and with his foot he makes of her a luminous line in the dust etc. etc. until he rubs it out. [...] I hear the sweet voice of a woman whom I didn't know nor see etc..]

This passage is centred on the image of the firefly, which reappears in 'Le ricordanze' as an emblem of the uncontaminated innocence of childhood, 'E la lucciola errava appo le siepi | E in su l'aiuole' [And the firefly floated over the hedges and flower beds].[13] As such, the firefly works as a powerful emblem of ephemerality:[14] the sources that plausibly construct this episode at an intertextual level — Roberti's Aesopian fable *La lucciola*, Gessner's idyll *La serenata*, Erasmus Darwin's *Amori delle piante* — coagulate around the small insect the ideas of fleetingness, of an intermittent and feeble splendour, of an erratic movement, and that of fall.[15] In the same way, Teresa/Silvia and Nerina — as we have seen — are depicted while performing the dancing, floating movement of someone who passes (away); at the same time, however, this movement intersects that of falling, and of lying down on the soil, 'All'apparir del vero | Tu, misera, cadesti' [When the truth dawned you fell away, poor thing];[16] 'caduta forse | Dal mio pensier sei tu?' [Have you possibly fallen from my thoughts?], 'E giacevi' [and you fell].[17]

We should not neglect to note how this double movement seems to characterize peculiarly the nymphs in the course of their peregrinations through Western art. As Didi-Huberman notes, the nymph, by definition, escapes (*nympha fugitiva*); at the same time, however, her run is coupled and intersected by a downward movement, a perturbing decline that does not tend toward disappearance, but rather to an oblique and imperceptible form of survival.[18] This is an aspect that is not immediately recognizable at a first glance, as it was not, in 1819, for Leopardi, who had, motionless, beheld the way the slaughtered firefly had become a 'luminous line', soon to be erased by the young man's foot. This is probably why the 'falling firefly' haunts modernity as a recurrent motif, embodying an ideal of beauty that so-called 'progress' (or the mere biological process of becoming adult) has dissolved. In 'Le ricordanze', the floating movement of the firefly symbolizes the illusions that later disenchantment has dissolved: exactly as it will be, more than a century later, to Pier Paolo Pasolini's eyes, the loss of innocence is, for Leopardi, best epitomized by the disappearance of fireflies.

In his recent volume, *Survivance des lucioles* [Survival of Fireflies], Didi-Huberman argues that, in Pasolini's famous *Articolo delle lucciole* [Article on Fireflies] of 1975, the disappearance of fireflies from the modern countryside hides an 'apocalyptic' and anti-modern move, namely a bitter nostalgia for the past that rests upon the ideal of an archaic and lost innocence.[19] The firefly, as in the *piazzetta di Monte Morello* in *Silvio Sarno*, is the privileged victim of the most ferocious brutality, which, for Pasolini, has become the predominant feature of society. Still, according to Didi-Huberman, the firefly embodies a possibility of resistance and survival that Pasolini's apocalyptic tones seem to underestimate. This resistance is not grounded in continuity and durability, but rather in the very features themselves of the firefly as an ephemeral creature: its irregular and intermittent light, its fleeting life, its imperceptible smallness. Like Warburg's nymph, the firefly epitomizes a fragmentary and unstable form of knowledge, which survives precisely because of its ephemeral nature, and which may give a clue to 'organising pessimism' in a political way.

In this book, I have tried to show how Leopardi turns his bitter statement of the radically ephemeral nature of human life and culture into a productive employment of that very same ephemerality as the only resource left to moderns. The *Zibaldone* as a 'non-book', the recuperation of the Greek genre of ὑπομνήματα as a device for reassessing the splitting of post-Enlightenment subjectivity, the use of philological skills in order to retrace an alchemy of the charming power of poetry, the theoretical dissection of grace as an aesthetic effect, the way a lost sphere of origin can be re-activated, albeit momentarily, through the subversion of established poetic praxes, and, finally, the reconfiguration of historical and individual time, are all steps in an experience of shock that aims to become direct (but unperceivable) action. By fully acknowledging the fracture that has divided the modern subject from a both historical and autobiographical past, the *Zibaldone* is constructed as a laboratory in motion, in which memory, the past, and the library produce a 'firefly-like' — namely, intermittent and rhizomatic — modality of knowledge.

The direct experience of anamnesis that rules the cantos of 1828 to 1829 engenders a deviation in this process, turning into a further writing praxis. This new experience of composition makes the laboratory unnecessary. The apprenticeship is completed, and the originality and skilful naiveté theorized from a philosophical point of view have been reached, outside the subject's control, in the form of a poetic speech that is immediately concretized into the written page. At this stage, the ὑπομνήματον must needs be left behind, while a both individual and cultural μνήμη directly takes its place.

As we have seen, the *Zibaldone* had opened with the conjuration of a timeless sphere of origin, embodied by the 'immagine antica': the ἀρχή, in other words, which, as Jacques Derrida summarizes, is the space 'where things *commence* — physical, historical, or ontological principle'.[20] The ὑπομνήματον-like form of writing had systematically tried to retrace this *original* space through an archaeological paradigm aimed at recuperating an 'antiquity' that was both individual and collective. We should never forget, Derrida points out, the distinction established in the Greek language between the sphere of μνήμη and that of ὑπόμνημα.[21] The *Zibaldone* is a 'hypomnesic' form of writing, and therefore, to speak in Derrida's terms, belongs to the sphere of the archive.[22] This sphere corresponds to an archaeological paradigm, the same in which Sigmund Freud, or his literary double Norbert Hanold, the main character of Jensen's *Gradiva*, used to move: in being 'incessantly tempted to redirect the original interest he had for the psychic archive toward archaeology', Freud systematically has recourse, in metaphorizing the operation of the unconscious, to 'archaeological parables.[23]

Still, Derrida writes, there may come an instant ('A moment and not a process') that 'does not belong to the laborious deciphering of the archive'.[24] This is:

> The nearly ecstatic instant Freud dreams of, when the very success of the dig must sign the effacement of the archivist: *the origin then speaks by itself.* The *arkhē* appears in the nude, without archive. It presents itself and comments on itself by itself. 'Stones talk!' In the present. *Anamnēsis* withouth *hypomnēsis*! The archaeologist has succeeded in making the archive no longer serve any function. *It comes to efface itself,* it becomes transparent or unessential so as to let the *origin* present itself in person. Live, without mediation and without delay. Without even the memory of a translation, once the intense work of translation has succeeded.

Leopardi's poems of 1828–29 can be assimilated to this ecstatic moment that does not belong to the sphere of archaeology nor of the archive, and which consequently dissolves the *Zibaldone* as a laboratory since origin (the 'immagine antica', or *Urszene*) speaks, at that point, by itself. By employing Ned Lukacher's understanding of the primal scene, Gary Cestaro notes how this notion can help us to 'homologize', within Dante's works, 'a number of what we might call "exile events" both universal and individual: Babel, the Flood, the Fall from grace, political exile, and grammar as loss of linguistic innocence'; all these events rely on 'the generalized cultural notion of a scene of exile in the mother's body'.[25] Not dissimilar is the way in which we can homologize, in Leopardi's oeuvre, all those moments that, being situated in the sphere of origin and having later been erased by a process of civilization and corruption, have now become inaccessible for the modern or grown-up subject, giving the uncanny feeling of an irremediable exile from an original state of grace. What happened in the first years of life, when memories could not be fixed? How did the ancients speak or sing, when writing praxes had not yet been fixed and normalized? The *Zibaldone* had been the venue in which philology and philosophical analysis could help to reconstruct these inaccessible moments of origin, thereby attempting to re-access a state of innocence precisely through those disciplines that epitomize loss of innocence in the highest degree. The cantos of 1828–29, on the contrary, make origin speak directly: the 'canzone libera' and the free associations structuring 'Le ricordanze' reproduce mimetically the freedom that precedes fixation and normativity, thus regaining the lost domain from which the subject had been exiled.

The key device of this process is Leopardi's use of survival. Tellingly, in a *Zibaldone* fragment of May 1821, Leopardi had noted that ancient words and expressions, in writing, should not sound like archaizing and revivalistic insertions:

they should be *known* to be ancient, but by no means be *felt* as such ('Parole e modi, dove l'antichità si può conoscere, ma per nessun conto sentire'), like fruits covered with wax that come out as fresh as if they had just been picked from the tree, 'E sebbene dismessi e ciò da lunghissimo tempo, o nello scrivere, o nel parlare, o in ambedue, non paiono dimenticati, ma come riposti in disparte, e custoditi, per poi ripigliarli' [And though unused, and for a very long time, whether in writing or in speech, or both, they do not seem forgotten but as if set to one side, and kept, in order to be used again later].[26] In the same way, in 1828, poems were seen as the venue in which some relic of past feelings was put 'per conservarla e darle durata, quasi in deposito', and reactivated, after many years, through the process of reading. Again, ontogenesis and phyologenesis are superimposed the one on the other, and the text is constructed as the unique venue in which the survival of antiquity can be possible. Through the poetic speech, the ἀρχή-'immagine antica', reactivated in the moment of anamnesis, is made visible without mediation. Exactly as for Freud-Norbert Hanold, this 'ecstatic instant' is embodied and epitomized by the fleeting footstep of the walking nymph, Nerina or Gradiva: the poem has become 'an archive without archive, where, suddenly indiscernible from the impression of its imprint, Gradiva's footstep speaks by itself! [...] this is exactly', Derrida concludes, 'what Hanold dreamed of in his disenchanted archaeologist's desire, in the moment when he awaited the coming of the "mid-day ghost"'.[27]

Again, myth can be helpful in understanding this moment of ecstasy, and the way it becomes crystallized within the subject's poetic speech. While examining Hecate in the appendixes to *Psyche* (1890–94), Erwin Rohde highlights how, in archaic Greek religion, 'nocturnal terrors' were produced by 'the restless souls of the dead wandering in the train of Hekate. [...] The souls which thus wander about with Hekate are in part those of the ἄωροι, i.e. of those who have died before the completion of their "destined" period of life'.[28] A specific kind of these untimely souls is the one named ἄωρη, namely the maiden (παρθένος) who died before reaching her maturity. As the goddess of liminal points, Hecate rules over 'the girl's passage into womanhood', the moment of transition described in 'A Silvia' as 'il limitare | Di gioventù' [the threshold of youth];[29] by combining 'femaleness and prematurity of death', the ἄωρη happens almost naturally to fall within Hecate's circle, often taking the shape of a female demon.[30] Nocturnal terrors appear therefore as inextricably bound with the fear of premature death, shared by the male subject doomed to die young (ἄωρος) and the dying maiden (ἄωρη). This connection, as we have seen, is made explicit in *Silvio Sarno*: 'storia di Teresa da me poco conosciuta e interesse ch'io ne prendeva come di tutti i morti giovani in quello aspettar la morte per me' [story of Teresa whom I did not know well and the interest I used to have for her as for all those who died young while waiting for my own death].[31]

The poetic space opened by 'A Silvia' and 'Le ricordanze' appears therefore as the liminal zone in which the ἄωροι — Silvia or Nerina — can survive, thereby dissolving the nocturnal fears that torment the subject since his childhood. Once embodied in the poem, the 'stones' start 'talking', and the 'immagine antica' finally becomes manifest, thus bypassing the post-Enlightenment paradigms of historicity and their making the understanding of the past a 'lifeless archaeological intuition (*eine leblose archäologische Anschauung*)': as Derrida puts it, 'when the dead awake (*die Toten wachten auf, und Pompeji fing an, wieder zu leben*), Hanold understands everything'.[32]

As we have seen, Leopardi's choice of speaking of *Canti*, in finally publishing his poems in 1831, is particularly meaningful, as if the poems following the mnestic experience of 1828–29 had regained a pre-scriptural, bodily, and pre-symbolic tonality and mode of signification, that I have chosen, following Kristeva's *Revolution in Poetic Language*, to term the semiotic *chora*. From this angle, the turning point is 'A Silvia': here, the rooms of Silvia's house ('le quiete | *Stanze*' [the quiet rooms])[33] are portrayed as echoing with Silvia's 'perpetuo canto' [endless song],[34] mirroring the way the very living memory of that song animates the *stanzas* of the poem. In other words, as Franco D'Intino notes, the written canto finds its referent in the girl's song recuperated by memory, which enlivens with its breath the scriptural sign: the dialectic relationship between orality and writing is thereby narrativized, and, at the same time, re-transfigured in a mythical way, as a Persephonean movement from life to death and backwards.[35]

This oscillation, D'Intino adds, finds its antecedent in the oppositions of life and death and of speech and writing in Hellenistic funeral poetry as reconstructed by the Swedish classical philologist Jesper Svenbro.[36] In a book originally published in 1988, Svenbro employs as an epitome of his 'anthropology of reading in ancient Greece' the sixth-century BC memorial (σῆμα) of a prematurely dead girl named Phrasikleia. Far than being a mere simulacrum carved out of mourning, the statue of Phrasikleia engenders a circular movement of reciprocal re-semantization with the epigram that accompanies it, by which the dead girl is constantly reborn every time her name is uttered — so to say, re-enlivened by human breath:

> Holding a flower in her hand, a flower unceasingly reborn, [...] the young girl [...] enacts her *kléos* [fame] with a silent gesture. [...] The entire *sêma* may be seen as the staging or representation of her name. [...] Phrasikleia [...] attracts the reader, triggers a reading aloud of the epigram and, in doing so, she may well be said to give birth to a son called *Lógos* [...]. In fact, every period when the *sêma* must endure in darkness, without readers and without spectators, is a state of waiting, in which meaning is hardly more than a spark, reduced to a faint gleam — *zurückgeschraubt*, to use Rilke's very precise word — a seed of fire or a flower cup ready to blossom. [...] [The meaning of Phrasikleia's sepulchral *sêma*] blooms or rekindles whenever its inscription is read aloud.[37]

By pushing this suggestion further, both poems 'A Silvia' and 'Le ricordanze' can be seen as σῆματα in which the two prematurely dead girls are temporarily brought back to life whenever speech enlivens the written or printed words in which they are inscribed, and which are the only actual venue of their ghostly modality of existence. This aspect connects Leopardi's poems of 1828–29 to a much earlier tradition, 'the nexus of Eros and poetic language, the *entrebescamen* of desire, phantasm, and poetry in the *topos outopos* of the poem' in the love lyric of the thirteenth century.[38] The theory of phantasm in which this kind of lyric is rooted, precisely made of *breath* (πνεῦμα), grants a desire to be incessantly fulfilled and renovated within the enclosed space of the poetic stanza: the knot between word, pneumatic phantasm, and desire recomposes the fractures between subject and object, reality and illusion, loss and retrieval, and finally between λόγος and μῦθος, symbolic and semiotic.

Thus can the ἄωρη be transfigured in a mythical way, and be eternalized into the form of the nymph — as her *senhal*, Silvia or Nerina, reveals — namely as an ephemeral, liminal and surviving creature which allows a new experience of poetry. Such is the nature of nymphs, namely of intermediary and demonic beings that constitute the point of junction between subject and image. As Giorgio Agamben writes:

> Created not in the image of God but of man, [nymphs] constitute his shadow or *imago*, and as such, they perpetually accompany and desire that of which they are the image — and by which they are at times themselves desired. And it is only in the encounter with man that the inanimate images acquire a soul, becoming truly alive [...]. The history of the ambiguous relation between men and nymphs is the history of the difficult relation between man and his images.[39]

In commenting the Aristotelian notion of φάντασμα, by which the Christian Middle Ages generally explain the encounters (and intercourses) of mortals with fairies and nymphs, Laurence Harf-Lancner notes how, in Walter Map (*De nugis curialium*, 1181–1193), Geoffrey of Clairvaux (commentary on *Revelation*, 1190), and Gervase of Tilbury ('De lamiis et nocturnis larvis', *Otia imperialia*, c.1210–14), the terms *fantasia, fantasma*, and *fantasticus* are connected to the semantic areas of illusion and unreality.[40] Still, following Agamben, it rather seems that such a notion is not employed in order to stress the fantastic (namely unreal) nature of such apparitions, but rather their demonic nature, namely of beings that form their bodies, as Gervase of Tilbury writes, from the aerial element, reflecting the desire of the subjects who look at them.[41] These 'Ladies that do not exist' are therefore imaginary ladies in that they are imagined, following 'the pneumatic link, uniting phantasm, word, and desire'.[42] The poetic stanza is the only space in which to enjoy the possession of the *imago*, 'the poetic sign appears as the sole enclosure offered to the fulfilment of love and erotic desire in their roles as the foundations and meaning of poetry'.[43]

The nymph, like the imaginary breeze that signals her passing, also alters the very matter she comes into touch with. From this angle, Silvia's and Nerina's 'passing' movement displays — to speak in Didi-Huberman's terms — 'a body agitated by the turmoils of time [*les remous du temps*], [...] whence suddenly emerges a repressed image [*image refoulée*]'.[44] Thus, the passing maiden's image is not only the subject of the poem, but the very poem. By blurring the borders between form and content, as in Eleusinian mysteries, the passing girl's body leaves only, as Agamben writes, the 'unsayable young girl' (ἄρρετος κόρη), that the scholiast Hesychius of Alexandria explains to be Persephone: 'Form and content coincide, not because content now appears unveiled, but because, following the literal meaning of the Latin verb *coincidere*, they "fall together", cease and calm down. What we behold is a mere appearance. The unsayable young girl [*la ragazzina indicibile*] shows herself'.[45]

It should be clear, at this point, that the girl is 'unsayable' because her domain is not that of words and critical reflection — namely, that of the paternal and patriarchal λόγος of philosophical speculation — but rather that of the peculiar undecidability of images, the visual dimension of the unconscious that both Freud and Warburg came to acknowledge, each from their respective backgrounds. Far from finding an easy satisfaction in stating the unutterable 'mystery' of poetry, we should not fail to note that poetry, at this point, works as a 'mystery' in its full Greek and Eleusinian meaning as μυστήριον: as Agamben explains, the nature of Eleusinian mysteries is always expressed in terms that imply a visual dimension, which explains the pertinence of the connection between mysteries and painting, brought to light by Warburg's studies.[46] The image is not to be interpreted: form and content coincide, and have therefore become an unstable and undecidable mixture. Hence Freud's unresolved struggle between the need for an aseptic scientific language and the urgent necessity for a *Bildersprache* in order to give account of the unconscious's visual nature; hence Warburg's choice of composing the *Bilderatlas Mnemosyne* by uniquely juxtaposing images without comment, or Benjamin's montage technique in the *Arcades Project*; hence, finally, Leopardi's choice of operating a montage of images of a different kind — figures, formulas of pathos — within his poetic texture, in order to 'brush history against the grain'.

In Leopardi's melancholy discourse, form and content become indistinguishable the one from the other, through the powerful action of the nymph's mythologem that provides poetry with its unprecedented grace. As Roberto Calasso writes:

> The Nymph is the quivering, sparkling, vibrating, *mental matter* of which the simulacrum, the image, the *eídōlon* is made. It is the very stuff of literature. Every time the Nymph shows herself, this divine material that molds itself into epiphanies and enthrones itself in the mind, this power that precedes and upholds the word, begins once again to throb. The moment that power makes itself manifest, form will follow, adjusting and composing itself with the power's flow.[47]

Such, according to Calasso, is the essence of nympholepsy, the form of possession that is peculiar to the nymphs:[48] 'the frenzy caused by Nymphs', writes Calasso, 'is generated by water and by a body emerging from it, in the same way as the mental image resurfaces from the continuum of consciousness',[49] just as the crab emerging from water in the tarot of the Moon symbolizes the resurfacing of the primal scene from the depths of the unconscious. The 'immagine antica' emerges and subjugates the mind, while the subject beholds with fear and wonder the 'versi [...] all'antica' that flow beyond every rational attempt to decipher them.

In the nymph's dancing gait, through her falling that turns into an imperceptible and intermittent survival, the erratic movement of the firefly is therefore crystallized and made active again, becoming a direct choice for the *present* that eschews the archive-ὑπομνήματον. Not by chance, Leopardi's poetry in the following years, and notably in the so-called 'Aspasia cycle', chooses the present as its dimension,[50] as if the fear of death brought by the 'immagine antica' and its echoes of Hecate's procession of restless souls had been overcome by the new form of knowledge acquired while composing the cantos of 1828–29: the fleeting present in which the passer-by and the almanac-pedlar can meet for a moment, and maybe share a dubious (although potentially true, who knows?) confidence in the future. Leopardi's choice of living in the present, by choosing the firefly's intermittent light as a form of resistance, metamorphoses the Christian idea of wandering and transitory human experience into the *flâneur*-like movement of the 'passeggere'. At the same time, the ideal of χάρις turns into an ironic benevolence that is an ultimate act of love for humanity, unburdened from the confessional burden of Leopardi's Catholic education, as well as from the potential apocalyptic drives of his nihilist reflection.

In the *Silvio Sarno* passage quoted above, the firefly, the first of the year, is the only luminescence enlightening the night that the coachman's daughter describes as 'dark as a hat'. Teresa could not know it, of course, but the image of a dark night was to be employed by Leopardi decades later, in order to describe human experience as a whole, and to an equally transitory moment of bliss, fleeting as a firefly, the only resource left to the human race — with nonchalance, levity, and a certain aristocratic disdain:

> [...] Che se d'affetti
> Orba la vita, e di gentili errori,
> È notte senza stelle a mezzo il verno,
> Già del fato mortale a me bastante
> E conforto e vendetta è che su l'erba
> Qui neghittoso immobile giacendo,
> Il mar la terra e il ciel miro e sorrido.[51]

[For if life, once empty of attachments and sweet illusions, is a starless winter night, still it's enough for me of mortal fate and comfort and revenge that lying here lazy, lifeless on the grass, I may watch the sea and earth and sky, and smile.]

Notes to the Conclusion

1. D'Intino, *L'immagine della voce*, p. 204.
2. TPP, pp. 600–01.
3. *Zib.* 520–22, 17 January 1821.
4. D'Intino, *L'immagine della voce*, pp. 101–05.
5. Ginzburg, *History, Rhetoric, and Proof*, pp. 10 and 29 note 34.
6. Ibid., p. 17.
7. Leopardi, *Volgarizzamenti in prosa*, pp. 13–14.
8. *Zib.* 437, 22 December 1820.
9. Voltaire, 'Vertu', in *Dictionnaire philosophique* (1764), by Voltaire, ed. by René Pomeau (Paris: Garnier-Flammarion, 1964), pp. 373–74 (p. 373).
10. A detailed analysis of this image in Leopardi is in Lorenzo Polato, 'Leopardi e Pindaro: il sogno di un'ombra', in *Il sogno di un'ombra: Leopardi e la verità delle illusioni*, by Lorenzo Polato (Venice: Marsilio 2007), pp. 65–115.
11. *Zib.* 4270–72, 2 April 1827.
12. SFA, pp. 108–11.
13. Leopardi, 'Le ricordanze', ll. 14–15.
14. See Paola Cori, 'Ephemera: The Feeling of Time in Leopardi's "Canto notturno"', *Italian Studies*, 67, 1 (March 2012), 70–91.
15. See D'Intino's corresponding note in SFA, pp. 110–11, note 203.
16. Leopardi, 'A Silvia', ll. 60–61.
17. Leopardi, 'Le ricordanze', ll. 137–38 and 157.
18. Didi-Huberman, *Ninfa moderna*, pp. 11–12.
19. Georges Didi-Huberman, *Survivance des lucioles* (Paris: Minuit, 2009).

20. Jacques Derrida, 'Archive Fever: A Freudian Impression', *Diacritics* 25, 2 (1995), 9–63 (p. 9).
21. Ibid., p. 14.
22. Ibid.
23. Ibid., p. 58.
24. Ibid.
25. Cestaro, *Dante and the Grammar of the Nursing Body*, p. 52.
26. *Zib.* 1099, 28 May 1821.
27. Derrida, 'Archive Fever', p. 61.
28. Erwin Rohde, *Psyche: The Cult of Souls and Belief in Immortality among the Greeks*, transl. by W.B. Hillis (London: Routledge & Kegan Paul, 1950), pp. 593–94.
29. Leopardi, 'A Silvia', ll. 5–6. See also Johnston, *Restless Dead*, p. 216, and, more generally, pp. 216–19.
30. Ibid., pp. 164–65, and pp. 161–99.
31. SFA, pp. 87–88.
32. Derrida, 'Archive Fever', p. 61.
33. Leopardi, 'A Silvia', ll. 7–8, my emphasis.
34. Ibid., l. 9.
35. D'Intino, *L'immagine della voce*, pp. 172–73, and 'I misteri di Silvia', pp. 243 and 270–71.
36. D'Intino, *L'immagine della voce*, p. 172 note 25.
37. Jesper Svenbro, 'Phrasikleia: From Silence to Sound', in *Phrasikleia. An Anthropology of Reading in Ancient Greece*, by Jesper Svenbro, transl. by Janet Lloyd (Ithaca, NY, and London: Cornell University Press, 1993), pp. 8–25 (pp. 23–25).
38. Agamben, *Stanzas*, p. 129.
39. Agamben, 'Nymphs', p. 75.
40. Laurence Harf-Lancner, *Les Fées au moyen âge*, p. 48.
41. Quoted in ibid., p. 51.
42. Agamben, *Stanzas*, p. 128.
43. Ibid..
44. Didi-Huberman, *L'Image survivante*, p. 309.
45. Agamben and Ferrando, *La ragazza indicibile*, p. 24, and p. 7 for the reference to Hesychius.
46. 'Ciò che gli iniziati facevano nella notte eleusina è sempre espresso col verbo "vedere" (*opopen*: Hymn. Cer., v. 480; *idon*: Pind., fr. 137; *derchthentes*: Soph., fr. 837) e "visione" (*epopteia*) è il termine che designa lo stadio supremo dell'iniziazione. *Epoptes*, "iniziato" significa anche "spettatore" e i misteri che gli iniziati contemplavano erano delle specie di "quadri viventi", che comportavano gesti (*dromena*), parole (*legomena*) ed esibizione di oggetti (*deiknymena*). Di qui la pertinenza del nesso fra misteri e pittura, così presente nell'arte rinascimentale [...]. Se la conoscenza suprema era stata assimilata dalla tradizione filosofica alla visione misterica, se essa non aveva carattere discorsivo ma era contratta in vedere, toccare e nominare, allora la pittura offriva a questa conoscenza l'espressione forse più adeguata. La tradizione [...] degli studi della scuola di Warburg è venuta a confermare opportunamente questa tesi', Agamben and Ferrando, *La ragazza indicibile*, p. 21 [What the initiates did in the night of Eleusis is always expressed by the verb 'to see', and 'vision' is the term denoting the final stage of initiation. *Epoptes*, 'initiate', also meant 'spectator', and the mysteries that the initiates used to behold were a sort of 'living picture' that involved gestures, words, and the exhibition of objects. Hence the relevance of the connection between mysteries and painting that is so central in Renaissance art. [...] If supreme knowledge had been assimilated by philosophical tradition to the vision of mysteries, if it possessed no discursive aspect but was rather focused on seeing, touching and naming, painting offered to such knowledge perhaps the most adequate expression. The tradition of the Warburg school has opportunely confirmed this thesis].
47. Roberto Calasso, *Literature and the Gods*, transl. by Tim Parks (New York: Knopf, 2001), p. 32.
48. Larson, *Greek Nymphs*, pp. 11–20.
49. Calasso, 'La follia che viene dalle Ninfe', p. 32.
50. See Margaret Brose, 'Posthumous Poetics: Leopardi's *A se stesso*', *Lingua e stile*, 24, 1 (1989), 89–114.
51. Leopardi, 'Aspasia', ll. 106–12.

BIBLIOGRAPHY

ABRAHAM, NICOLAS, and MARIA TOROK, *The Wolf Man's Magic Word: A Cryptonymy*, transl. by Nicholas Rand (Minneapolis: University of Minnesota Press, 1986)

ABRAMS, M.H., 'The Correspondent Breeze: A Romantic Metaphor', in *The Romantic Breeze: Essays on English Romanticism*, by M.H. Abrams, (New York and London: Norton, 1984), pp. 25–43

AGAMBEN, GIORGIO, *Infanzia e storia: Distruzione dell'esperienza e origine della storia* (Turin: Einaudi, 2001)

——*Infancy and History: The Destruction of Experience*, transl. by Liz Heron (London and New York: Verso, 1993)

——'Nymphs', transl. by Amanda Minervini, in *Releasing the Image: From Literature to New Media*, ed. by Jacques Khalip and Robert Mitchell (Stanford: Stanford University Press, 2011), pp. 65–80

——'In Playland', in *Infancy and History*, pp. 65–87

——*Potentialities: Collected Essays in Philosophy*, ed. and transl. by Daniel Heller-Roazen (Stanford: Stanford University Press, 1999)

——*The Signature of All Things: On Method*, transl. by Luca D'Isanto and Kevin Attell (New York: Zone Books, 2009)

——*Stanzas: Word and Phantasm in Western Culture*, transl. by Ronald L. Martinez (Minneapolis and London: University of Minnesota Press, 1993)

——'Warburg and the Nameless Science', in *Potentialities: Collected Essays in Philosophy*, pp. 89–103

AGAMBEN, GIORGIO, and MONICA FERRANDO, *La ragazza indicibile: Mito e mistero di Kore* (Milan: Electa, 2010)

ALIGHIERI, DANTE, *Purgatorio*, ed. and transl. by Robert M. Durling (New York and Oxford: Oxford University Press, 2003)

ANZIEU, DIDIER, *L'Auto-analyse: Son rôle dans la découverte de la psychanalyse par Freud — Sa fonction en psychanalyse* (Paris: Presses Universitaires de France, 1959)

APULEIUS OF MADAUROS, *The Isis-Book (Metamorphoses, Book XI)*, ed. and transl. by J. Gwyn Griffiths (Leiden: Brill, 1975)

ARMSTRONG, RICHARD H., *A Compulsion for Antiquity: Freud and the Ancient World* (Ithaca: Cornell University Press, 2005)

AVALLE, D'ARCO SILVIO, 'Da Santa Uliva a Justine', in *La fanciulla perseguitata*, by Aleksandr N.J. Veselovskij and Sade, ed. by D'Arco Silvio Avalle (Milan: Bompiani, 1977), pp. 7–33

BALZANO, MARCO, *I confini del sole: Leopardi e il nuovo mondo* (Venice: Marsilio, 2008)

BARTHES, ROLAND, *Fragments d'un discours amoureux* (Paris: Seuil, 1977)

——*A Lover's Discourse: Fragments*, transl. by Richard Howard (New York: Hill & Wang, 2001)

BAYARD, PIERRE, *Comment parler des livres que l'on n'a pas lus?* (Paris: Minuit, 2007)

——*How to Talk About Books You Haven't Read*, transl. by Jeffrey Mehlman (New York: Bloomsbury USA, 2007)

BELLUCCI, NOVELLA, *Il 'gener frale': Saggi leopardiani* (Venice: Marsilio, 2010)

Benjamin, Walter, *The Arcades Project*, transl. by Howard Eiland and Kevin McLaughlin (Cambridge, MA, and London: Belknap Press of Harvard University Press, 1999)

—— *Gesammelte Schriften*, ed. by Rolf Tiedemann and Hermann Schweppenhäuser, 14 vols. (Frankfurt am Main: Suhrkamp, 1991)

—— 'On Some Motifs in Baudelaire', in *Selected Writings*, IV, 313–55

—— 'On the Concept of History', in *Selected Writings*, IV, 389–400

—— 'The Work of Art in the Age of Its Reproducibility', in *Selected Writings*, III, 101–33

—— *Selected Writings*, ed. by Howard Eiland and Michael W. Jennings, transl. by Marcus Paul Bullock and Michael W. Jennings, 4 vols. (Harvard: Harvard University Press, 2003)

Bianchi, Lorenzo, 'Critica e libero pensiero', in *Illuminismo: Un vademecum*, ed. by Gianni Paganini and Edoardo Tortarolo (Turin: Bollati Boringhieri, 2008), pp. 88–102

Bigi, Emilio, and others, *Le città di Giacomo Leopardi* (Florence: Olschki, 1991)

Binswanger, Ludwig, and Aby Warburg, *La guarigione infinita: Storia clinica di Aby Warburg*, ed. by Davide Stimilli (Vicenza: Neri Pozza, 2005)

Blasucci, Luigi, 'Leopardi e Pisa', in *Le città di Giacomo Leopardi*, by Emilio Bigi and others (Florence: Olschki, 1991), pp. 105–31

—— 'Petrarchismo e platonismo nella canzone "Alla sua Donna"', in *I tempi dei 'Canti'*, pp. 62–80

—— 'Quattro modi di approccio allo *Zibaldone*', in *I tempi dei 'Canti'*, pp. 229–42

—— 'Sul libro dei *Canti*', in *Leopardi e il libro nell'età romantica*, ed. by Michael Caesar and Franco D'Intino, (Rome: Bulzoni, 2000), pp. 213–36

—— 'I tempi dei "Canti"', in *I tempi dei 'Canti'*, pp. 177–218

—— *I tempi dei 'Canti'* (Turin: Einaudi, 1996)

Bohrer, Karl Heinz, *Suddenness: On the Moment of Aesthetic Appearance*, transl. by Ruth Crowley (New York: Columbia University Press, 1994)

Bollati, Giulio, introduction to *Crestomazia italiana. La prosa*, by Giacomo Leopardi, ed. by Giulio Bollati (Turin: Einaudi, 1968), pp. xviii–xxx

Bolzoni, Lina, *The Gallery of Memory: Literary and Iconographic Models in the Age of the Printing Press*, transl. by Jeremy Parzen (Toronto: University of Toronto Press, 2001)

Bonifazi, Neuro, 'La libera traduzione leopardiana di una favola di Aviano nel proemio dello "Zibaldone"', in *La corrispondenza imperfetta: Leopardi tradotto e traduttore*, ed. by Anna Dolfi and Adriana Mitescu (Rome: Bulzoni, 1990), pp. 31–39

—— *Lingua mortale: Genesi della poesia leopardiana* (Ravenna: Longo, 1984)

—— *Leopardi e l'immagine antica* (Turin: Einaudi, 1991)

Brilli, Attilio, *In viaggio con Leopardi* (Bologna: Il Mulino, 2000)

Bronzini, Giovanni Battista, *Leopardi e la poesia popolare dell'Ottocento* (Naples: De Simone, 1975)

Brose, Margaret, 'Posthumous Poetics: Leopardi's *A se stesso*', *Lingua e stile*, 24, 1 (1989), 89–114

Brozzi, Elisabetta, 'I demoni di Leopardi', in *La prospettiva antropologica nel pensiero e nella poesia di Giacomo Leopardi*, ed. by Chiara Gaiardoni (Florence: Olschki, 2010), pp. 443–59

Buxton, Richard, 'Wolves and Werewolves in Greek Thought', in *Interpretations of Greek Mythology*, ed. by Jan Bremmer (London: Routledge, 1988), pp. 60–79

Cacciapuoti, Fabiana, *Dentro lo 'Zibaldone': Il tempo circolare della scrittura di Leopardi* (Rome: Donzelli, 2010)

—— 'La scrittura dello *Zibaldone* tra sistema filosofico ed opera aperta', in *Lo 'Zibaldone' cento anni dopo. Composizione, edizioni, temi*, ed. by Ronaldo Garbuglia, 2 vols. (Florence: Olschki, 2001), I, 249–56

Caesar, Michael, '"Mezz'ora di nobiltà": Leopardi e i suoi lettori', in *Leopardi a Firenze*, ed. by Laura Melosi (Florence: Olschki, 2002), pp. 461–72

CAESAR, MICHAEL, and FRANCO D'Intino (eds.), *Leopardi e il libro nell'età romantica* (Rome: Bulzoni, 2000)

CALASSO, ROBERTO, *La follia che viene dalle Ninfe* (Milan: Adelphi, 2005)

—— *Literature and the Gods*, transl. by Tim Parks (New York: Knopf, 2001)

CAMILLETTI, FABIO, *Classicism and Romanticism in Italian Literature: Leopardi's 'Discourse on Romantic Poetry'* (London: Pickering & Chatto, 2013)

—— '"On pleure les lèvres absentes": "Amor di lontano" tra Leopardi e Baudelaire', *Italian Studies*, 64, 1, (2009), 77–90

CANCELLIERI, FRANCESCO, *Dissertazione intorno agli uomini dotati di gran memoria ed a quelli divenuti smemorati con un'appendice delle biblioteche degli scrittori sopra gli eruditi precoci, la memoria artificiale, l'arte di trascegliere e di notare ed il giuoco degli scacchi* (Rome: Bourlie, 1815)

CARRERA, ALESSANDRO, *La distanza del cielo: Leopardi e lo spazio dell'ispirazione* (Milan: Medusa, 2011)

—— (ed.), *Giacomo Leopardi: Poeta e Filosofo* (Fiesole: Cadmo, 1999)

CARRUTHERS, MARY, *The Book of Memory: A Study of Memory in Medieval Culture* (Cambridge: Cambridge University Press, 1990)

CASTLE, TERRY, *The Female Thermometer: Eighteenth-Century Culture and the Invention of the Uncanny* (Oxford: Oxford University Press, 1995)

CATALUCCIO, FRANCESCO M., 'Farfalle russe', in *Vladimir Nabokov*, ed. by Maria Sebregondi and Elisabetta Porfiri (Milan: Marcos y Marcos, 1999), pp. 244–46

CELLERINO, LIANA, 'L'io antico e l'io nuovo', in *L'io del topo: Pensieri e letture dell'ultimo Leopardi*, by Liana Cellerino (Rome: La Nuova Italia Scientifica, 1997), pp. 87–103

CERAGIOLI, FIORENZA, *Giacomo Leopardi e la stagione di Silvia* (Rome: Sossella, 2001)

—— (ed.), *Leopardi a Pisa: Cangiato il mondo appar* (Milan: Electa, 1998)

CERAGIOLI, FIORENZA, and MARCELLO ANDRIA, *Il percorso della poesia: Giacomo Leopardi a Pisa (1827–1828)* (Pisa: ETS, 2005)

CERONETTI, GUIDO, 'Intatta luna', *Belfagor*, 25 (1970), 97–103

CERTEAU, MICHEL DE, *L'Écriture de l'histoire* (Paris: Gallimard, 1975)

—— 'Histoire et anthropologie chez Lafitau', in *Naissance de l'ethnologie? Anthropologie et missions en Amérique, XVIe-XVIIIe siècle*, ed. by Claude Blankaert (Paris: Cerf, 1985), pp. 63–89

—— *Histoire et psychanalyse entre science et fiction* (Paris: Gallimard, 1987)

—— 'Walking in the City', in *The Practice of Everyday Life*, by Michel de Certeau, transl. by Steven Rendall (Berkeley: University of California Press, 1984), pp. 90–110

CESTARO, GARY P., *Dante and the Grammar of the Nursing Body* (Notre Dame, IN: University of Notre Dame Press, 2003)

CEVOLINI, ALBERTO, *De arte excerpendi: Imparare a dimenticare nella modernità* (Florence: Olschki, 2006)

CHARTIER, ROGER, *The Order of Books: Readers, Authors and Libraries in Europe between the Fourteenth and Eighteenth Centuries*, transl. by Lydia G. Cochrane (Stanford: Stanford University Press, 1994)

CHEETHAM, MARK A., *Kant, Art, and Art History: Moments of Discipline* (Cambridge: Cambridge University Press, 2001)

CIERI VIA, CLAUDIA, *Introduzione a Aby Warburg* (Rome and Bari: Laterza, 2011)

CIXOUS, HÉLÈNE, 'Fiction and Its Phantoms: A Reading of Freud's *Das Unheimliche* (The "Uncanny")', *New Literary History*, 7, 3 (1976), 525–48

CLAUDIAN, 'Rape of Proserpine', in *Claudian*, ed. and transl. by Maurice Platnauer, 2 vols. (London: Heinemann, 1922), II, 292–377

COLAIACOMO, CLAUDIO, *Camera obscura: Studio di due canti leopardiani* (Naples: Liguori, 1992)

CONTARINI, SILVIA, and MAURIZIO GHELARDI, '"Die verkörperte Bewegung": la ninfa', in *Aby Warburg: La dialettica dell'immagine*, ed. by Davide Stimilli (Milan: Il Saggiatore, 2004), pp. 32–45;

COPIOLI, ROSITA, introduction to *Discorso di un italiano intorno alla poesia romantica*, by Giacomo Leopardi, ed. by Rosita Copioli (Milan: Rizzoli, 1997), pp. 5–36

CORI, PAOLA, 'Ephemera: The Feeling of Time in Leopardi's "Canto notturno"', *Italian Studies*, 67, 1 (March 2012), 70–91

CREED, BARBARA, *Phallic Panic: Film, Horror and the Primal Uncanny* (Melbourne: Melbourne University Press, 2005)

CURTIUS, ERNST ROBERT, *European Literature and the Latin Middle Ages*, transl. by Willard R. Trask (Princeton: Princeton University Press, 1990)

D'ANGELO, PAOLO, and STEFANO VELOTTI, *Il 'non so che': Storia di un'idea estetica* (Palermo: Aesthetica, 1997)

D'INTINO, FRANCO, 'Errore, ortografia e autobiografia in Leopardi e Stendhal', in *Memoria e infanzia tra Alfieri e Leopardi*, ed. by Marco Dondero and Laura Melosi (Macerata: Quodlibet, 2004), pp. 167–83

——'Il gusto dell'altro: La traduzione come esperienza straniera in Leopardi', in *Hospes: Il volto dello straniero da Leopardi a Jabès*, ed. by Alberto Folin (Venice: Marsilio, 2003), pp. 147–58

——*L'immagine della voce: Leopardi, Platone e il libro morale* (Venice: Marsilio, 2009)

——'Leopardi, Julien Sorel e il diavolo: Il gioco sottile dell'eroe faustiano nell'epoca della Restaurazione', *Igitur*, 3 (1991), 23–47

——'I misteri di Silvia. Motivo persefoneo e mistica eleusina in Leopardi', *Filologia e critica*, XIX, 2 (1994), 211–71

——'Il monaco indiavolato: Lo *Zibaldone* e la tentazione faustiana di Leopardi', in *Lo 'Zibaldone' cento anni dopo*, ed. by Ronaldo Garbuglia, 2 vols. (Florence: Olschki, 2001), II, 467–523

DAMIANI, ROLANDO, *All'apparir del vero: Vita di Giacomo Leopardi* (Milan: Mondadori, 1998)

——'Le "credenze stolte": Leopardi e gli errori popolari', in *L'impero della ragione: Studi leopardiani*, by Rolando Damiani (Ravenna: Longo, 1994), pp. 7–55

DARNTON, ROBERT, *Édition et sedition: L'Univers de la littérature clandestine au XVIIIe siècle* (Paris: Gallimard, 1991)

DE LAUDE, SILVIA, *Continuità e variazioni fra Curtius e Warburg* (Naples: Inprint, 2005)

DEICHGRÄBER, KARL, *Charis und Chariten, Grazie und Grazien* (Munich: Heimeran, 1971)

DEIDIER, ROBERTO (ed.), *Persefone: Variazioni sul mito* (Venice: Marsilio, 2010)

DELON, MICHEL, *Le Savoir-vivre libertin* (Paris: Hachette, 2000)

DERRIDA, JACQUES, 'Archive Fever: A Freudian Impression', *Diacritics* 25, 2 (1995), 9–63

——'Fors: The Anglish Words of Nicolas Abraham and Maria Torok', transl. by Barbara Johnson, in *The Wolf Man's Magic Word*, by Nicolas Abraham and Maria Torok, transl. by Nicholas Rand (Minneapolis: University of Minnesota Press, 1986), pp. xi–xlviii

——*Spectres of Marx: The State of the Debt, the Work of Mourning, & the New International*, transl. by Peggy Kamuf (London: Routledge, 1994)

——*The Truth in Painting*, transl. by Geoffrey Bennington and Ian McLeod (Chicago and London: University of Chicago Press, 1987)

DI RUZZA, FLORIANA, *Onomastica leopardiana: Studio sui nomi propri nei 'Canti', nelle 'Operette morali' e nei 'Paralipomeni'* (Rome: Nuova Cultura, 2010)

DIDI-HUBERMAN, GEORGES, *Devant le temps: Histoire de l'art et anachronisme des images* (Paris: Minuit, 2000)

——*Fra Angelico: Dissemblance and Figuration*, transl. by Jane Marie Todd (London: University of Chicago Press, 1995)

——*L'Image survivante: Histoire de l'art et temps des fantômes selon Aby Warburg* (Paris: Minuit, 2002)

——'The Imaginary Breeze: Remarks on the Air of the Quattrocento', *Journal of Visual Culture*, 2 (2003), 275–89

——*Ninfa Moderna: Essai sur le drapé tombé* (Paris: Gallimard, 2002)

——*La Peinture incarnée, suivi de Le Chef-d'œuvre inconnu par Honoré de Balzac* (Paris: Minuit, 1985)

——'The Supposition of the Aura: The Now, the Then, and Modernity', transl. by Jane Marie Todd, in *Walter Benjamin and History*, ed. by Alexander Benjamin (London and New York: Continuum, 2005), pp. 3–18

——*Survivance des lucioles* (Paris: Minuit, 2009)

——'The Surviving Image: Aby Warburg and Tylorian Anthropology', *Oxford Art Journal*, 25, 1 (2002), 61–69

DISTILLER, NATASHA, *Desire and Gender in the Sonnet Tradition* (Basingstoke and New York: Palgrave Macmillan, 2008)

DOTTI, UGO, 'La poesia leopardiana', in *Canti*, by Giacomo Leopardi, ed. by Ugo Dotti (Milan: Feltrinelli, 1993), pp. 9–150

DOUGLAS-FAIRHURST, ROBERT, *Victorian Afterlives: The Shaping of Influence in Nineteenth-Century Literature* (Oxford: Oxford University Press, 2002)

DUMÉZIL, GEORGES, *Fêtes romaines d'été et d'automne suivi de Dix questions romaines* (Paris: Gallimard, 1975)

EISLER, ROBERT, *Man Into Wolf: An Anthropological Interpretation of Sadism, Masochism, and Lycanthropy* (London: Routledge & Kegan, 1951)

ELLENBERGER, HENRI F., *The Discovery of the Unconscious: The History and Evolution of Dynamic Psychiatry* (New York: Basic Books, 1981)

ERSPAMER, FRANCESCO, *La creazione del passato* (Palermo: Sellerio, 2009)

FAUCHERY, PIERRE, *La Destinée féminine dans le roman européen du dix-huitième siècle 1713–1807: Essai de gynécomythie romanesque* (Paris: Armand Colin, 1972)

FEDI, FRANCESCA, *Mausolei di sabbia: Sulla cultura figurativa di Leopardi* (Lucca: Pacini Fazzi, 1997)

FELICI, LUCIO, *La luna nel cortile: Capitoli leopardiani* (Soveria Mannelli: Rubbettino, 2006)

——*L'Olimpo abbandonato: Leopardi tra 'favole antiche' e 'disperati affetti'* (Venice: Marsilio, 2005)

FERRUCCI, FRANCO, *Il formidabile deserto: Lettura di Giacomo Leopardi* (Rome: Fazi, 1998)

FOLIN, ALBERTO, *Leopardi e il canto dell'addio* (Venice: Marsilio, 2008)

——*Leopardi e la notte chiara* (Venice: Marsilio, 1993)

FORSTER, KURT W., introduction to *The Renewal of Pagan Antiquity*, by Aby Warburg, ed. by Gertrud Bing with Fritz Rougemont, transl. by David Britt (Los Angeles: Getty Research Institute for the History of Art and the Humanities, 1999), pp. 1–75

FORTUNA, SARA, and MANUELE GRAGNOLATI, 'Between Affection and Discipline: Exploring Linguistic Tensions from Dante to *Aracoeli*', in *The Power of Disturbance: Elsa Morante's 'Aracoeli'*, ed. by Sara Fortuna and Manuele Gragnolati (Oxford: Legenda, 2009), pp. 8–19

FOUCAULT, MICHEL, 'Self Writing', in *Ethics: Subjectivity and Truth*, by Michel Foucault (New York: New Press, 1997), pp. 207–21

FRANKLAND, GRAHAM, *Freud's Literary Culture* (Cambridge: Cambridge University Press, 2004)

FREUD, SIGMUND, 'The Aetiology of Hysteria', in *The Standard Edition*, III, 191–221

——*Aus den Anfängen der Psychoanalyse. 1887–1902. Briefe an Wilhelm Fließ* (Frankfurt am Main: Fischer, 1962)

——*Beyond the Pleasure Principle*, in *The Standard Edition*, XVIII, 1–64

——'Creative Writers and Day-dreaming', in *The Standard Edition*, IX, 143–53

——*Delusion and Dream: An Interpretation in the Light of Psychoanalysis of 'Gradiva', a Novel, by Wilhelm Jensen*, transl. by Helen M. Downey (New York: Moffat, Yard & Co., 1917)

——'A Difficulty in the Path of Psychoanalysis', in *The Standard Edition*, XVII, 135–44

——'Fetishism', in *The Standard Edition*, XXI, 147–57

——'From the History of an Infantile Neurosis', in *The Standard Edition*, XVII, 7–122

——*Gesammelte Werke*, ed. by Anna Freud, 18 vols. (Frankfurt am Main: Fischer, 1999)

——*The Interpretation of Dreams*, in *The Standard Edition*, IV–V

——*Jokes and Their Relation to the Unconscious*, in *The Standard Edition*, VIII, 3–243

——'Mourning and Melancholia', in *The Standard Edition*, XIV, 243–58

——'A Note on the Prehistory of the Technique of Analysis', in *The Standard Edition*, XVIII, 263–65

——'The Occurrence in Dreams of Material from Fairy Tales', in *The Standard Edition*, XII, 281–87

——*Psychopathology of Everyday Life*, in *The Standard Edition*, VI, 1–289

——*The Standard Edition of the Complete Psychological Works*, ed. by James Strachey, 24 vols. (London: The Hogarth Press, 1953–74)

——*Studies on Hysteria*, in *The Standard Edition*, II, 21–181

——'The Uncanny', in *The Standard Edition*, XVII, 217–56

——*Der Wahn und die Träume in W. Jensens 'Gradiva' mit dem Text der Erzählung von Wilhelm Jensen*, ed. by Bernd Urban and Johannes Cremerius (Frankfurt am Main: Fischer, 1986)

FUMAROLI, MARC, 'Les Abeilles et les araignées', in *La Querelle des anciens et des modernes XVIIe-XVIIIe siècles*, ed. by Anne-Marie Lecoq (Paris: Gallimard, 2001), pp. 7–220

GAETANO, RAFFAELE, *Giacomo Leopardi e il sublime* (Soveria Mannelli: Rubbettino, 2002)

GALIMBERTI, CESARE, 'Di un Leopardi "patrocinatore del circolo" ', *Sigma*, 8 (1965), 23–42

——'Modi della negazione nei "Canti" ', in *Linguaggio del vero in Leopardi*, by Cesare Galimberti, (Florence: Olschki, 1959), pp. 68–95

——'Un mot sous les mots nella "Canzone alla sua Donna"?', in *Cose che non son cose: Saggi su Leopardi*, by Cesare Galimberti (Venice: Marsilio, 2001), pp. 87–97

GARBUGLIA, ROLANDO (ed.), *Lo 'Zibaldone' cento anni dopo. Composizione, edizioni, temi*, 2 vols. (Florence: Olschki, 2001)

GARDINI, NICOLA, 'Considerazioni sullo stilnovismo novecentesco: Il modello della *Vita nova*', *Italianistica*, 29, 3 (September-December 2000), 445–50

——'Dante as a Gay Poet', in *Metamorphosing Dante: Appropriations, Manipulations, and Rewritings in the Twentieth and Twenty-First Centuries*, ed. by Manuele Gragnolati, Fabio Camilletti and Fabian Lampart (Vienna and Berlin: Turia + Kant, 2010), pp. 61–74

GIACHERY, EMERICO, 'Convergenze su *Aspasia*', in *Motivo e parola*, by Emerico Giachery (Naples: Guida, 1990), pp. 23–42

GINZBURG, CARLO, *Clues, Myths, and the Historical Method*, transl. by John and Anne C. Tedeschi (Baltimore, MD: Johns Hopkins University Press, 1989)

——*Ecstasies: Deciphering the Witches' Sabbath*, transl. by Raymond Rosenthal (New York: Pantheon Books, 1991)

——'Freud, the Wolf-Man, and the Werewolves', in *Clues, Myths, and the Historical Method*, pp. 146–55

——*History, Rhetoric, and Proof (The Menahem Stern Jerusalem Lectures)* (Hanover, NH: University Press of New England, 1999)

——'Mito', in *I greci: Storia, cultura, arte, società*, ed. by Salvatore Settis, 4 vols. (Turin: Einaudi, 1996), I, 197–237

——'Morelli, Freud and Sherlock Holmes: Clues and Scientific Method', *History Workshop Journal*, 9, 1 (1980), 5–36

GIOANOLA, ELIO, *Cesare Pavese: La realtà, l'altrove, il silenzio* (Milan: Jaca Book, 2003)

——*Leopardi: La malinconia* (Milan: Jaca Book, 1995)

——'Psicanalisi e critica letteraria', in *Freud and Italian Culture*, ed. by Pierluigi Barrotta and Laura Lepschy with Emma Bond (Bern: Peter Lang, 2009), pp. 9–30

——*Psicanalisi e interpretazione letteraria* (Milan: Jaca Book, 2005)

GIROLAMI, PATRIZIA, *L'antiteodicea: Dio, dei, religione nello 'Zibaldone' di Giacomo Leopardi* (Florence: Olschki, 1995)

GOETHE, JOHANN WOLFGANG VON, *Faust: A Tragedy*, ed. and transl. by John S. Blackie (Edinburgh: Blackwood, 1834)

GOMBRICH, ERNST, *Aby Warburg: An Intellectual Biography, with a Memoir of the History of the Library by F. Saxl* (Chicago: University of Chicago Press, 1986)

GOULEMOT, JEAN-MARIE, *Ces livres qu'on ne lit que d'une main: Lecture et lecteurs de livres pornographiques au XVIIIe siècle* (Aix-en-Provence: Alinea, 1991)

GRAVES, ROBERT, *The White Goddess: A Historical Grammar of Poetic Myth* (London: Faber & Faber, 1959)

HALES, SHELLEY, and JOANNA PAUL (eds.), *Pompeii in the Public Imagination from its Rediscovery to Today* (Oxford: Oxford University Press, 2011)

HARF-LANCNER, LAURENCE, *Les Fées au moyen âge: Morgane et Mélusine: La Naissance des fées* (Geneva: Slatkine, 1984)

HARTOG, FRANÇOIS, 'Il confronto con gli antichi', in *I greci: Storia, cultura, arte, società*, ed. by Salvatore Settis, 4 vols. (Turin: Einaudi, 1996), i, 3–37

HAVELOCK, ERIC A., *The Muse Learns to Write: Reflections on Orality and Literacy from Antiquity to the Present* (New Haven: Yale University Press, 1986)

HEIDENREICH, MARIANNE, *Christian Gottlob Heyne und die alte Geschichte* (Munich: Saor, 2006)

HOFFMANN, PAUL, *La Femme dans la pensée des Lumières* (Paris: Ophrys, 1977)

JANKÉLÉVITCH, VLADIMIR, *Le Je-ne-sais-quoi et le Presque-rien I: La Manière et l'Occasion* (Paris: Seuil, 1980)

JENSEN, WILHELM, *Gradiva: A Pompeian Fancy* (1903), in *Delusion and Dream: An Interpretation in the Light of Psychoanalysis of 'Gradiva', a Novel, by Wilhelm Jensen*, by Sigmund Freud, transl. by Helen M. Downey (New York: Moffat, Yard & Co., 1917), pp. 3–125

JENTSCH, ERNST, 'On the Psychology of the Uncanny', transl. by Roy Sellars, *Angelaki* 2, 1 (1995), 7–16

JOHNSON, CHRISTOPHER D., *Memory, Metaphor, and Aby Warburg's Atlas of Images* (Ithaca: Cornell University Press, 2012)

JOHNSON, LAWRENCE, *The Wolf Man's Burden* (Ithaca and London: Cornell University Press, 2001)

JOHNSON, ROBERT, *Robert Johnson: I Got the Blues. Testi commentati*, ed. and transl. by Luigi Monge (Rome: Arcana, 2008)

JOHNSTON, SARAH ILES, *Restless Dead: Encounters between the Living and the Dead in Ancient Greece* (Berkeley, Los Angeles and London: University of California Press, 1999)

JONES, VERINA R., 'Le *Dark Ladies* manzoniane', in *Le Dark Ladies manzoniane e altri saggi sui 'Promessi sposi'*, by Verina R. Jones (Rome: Salerno, 1998), pp. 90–108

JUNG, CARL GUSTAV, and CARL KERÉNYI, *Science of Mythology: Essays on the Myth of the Divine Child and the Mysteries of Eleusis*, transl. by R.F.C. Hull (London and New York: Routledge, 2002)

KLEIST, HEINRICH VON, 'Puppet Theatre', transl. by Beryl de Zoete, in *The Thunder and the Freshness*, by Beryl de Zoete (New York: Theatre Arts Books, 1963), pp. 64–71

KLOSSOWSKI, PIERRE, *Le Bain de Diane* (Paris: Pauvert, 1956)

——*Diana at Her Bath/The Women of Rome*, transl. by Stephen Sartarelli and Sophie Hawkes (Boston: Eridanos Press, 1990)

——*Sade mon prochain* (Paris: Seuil, 1947)

KOSELLECK, REINHART, *Futures Past: On the Semantics of Historical Time*, transl. by Keith Tribe (New York: Columbia University Press, 2004)

——*The Practice of Conceptual History: Timing History, Spacing Concepts*, transl. by Todd Samuel Presner and others (Stanford: Stanford University Press, 2002)

KREYDER, LAURA, *La Passion des petites filles: Histoire de l'enfance féminine de la Terreur à Lolita* (Arras: Artois Presses Université, 2003)

KRISTEVA, JULIA, *Black Sun: Depression and Melancholia*, transl. by Leon S. Roudiez (New York: Columbia University Press, 1989)

——*La Révolution du langage poétique. L'Avant-garde à la fin du XIXe siècle: Lautréamont et Mallarmé* (Paris: Seuil, 1974)

——*Revolution in Poetic Language*, transl. by Margaret Waller (New York: Columbia University Press, 1984)

——*Soleil noir: Dépression et mélancolie* (Paris: Gallimard, 1987)

KURZ, OTTO, 'Huius nympha loci', *Journal of the Warburg and Courtauld Institutes*, 16 (1953), 171–77

LACAN, JACQUES, *Écrits*, transl. by Bruce Fink, Héloïse Fink and Russell Grigg (London and New York: W.W. Norton, 2006)

——*On Feminine Sexuality: The Limits of Love and Knowledge, The Seminar Book XX: Encore 1972–1973*, transl. by Bruce Fink (New York and London: Norton, 1998)

——*The Four Fundamental Concepts of Psychoanalysis. The Seminar Book XI*, ed. by Jacques-Alain Miller, transl. by Alan Sheridan (New York and London: Norton, 1998)

——'The Instance of the Letter in the Unconscious or Reason since Freud', in *Écrits*, pp. 412–41

——*Le Séminaire livre X: L'Angoisse (1962–1963)*, ed. by Jacques-Alain Miller (Paris: Seuil, 2004)

——*Le Séminaire livre XI: Les Quatre Concepts fondamentaux de la psychanalyse*, ed. by Jacques-Alain Miller (Paris: Seuil, 1973)

——*Le Séminaire livre XX: Encore*, ed. by Jacques-Alain Miller (Paris: Seuil, 1975)

LAPLANCHE, JEAN, 'Interpretation between Determinism and Hermeneutics: A Restatement of the Problem', transl. by Philip Slotkin, in *Essays on Otherness*, by Jean Laplanche (London and New York: Routledge, 1999), pp. 138–65

LAPLANCHE, JEAN, and JEAN-BERTRAND PONTALIS, 'Fantasy and the Origins of Sexuality', in *Formations of Fantasy*, ed. by Victor Burgin, James Donald and Cora Kaplan (London and New York: Routledge, 1986), pp. 5–34

LARSON, JENNIFER, *Greek Nymphs: Myth, Cult, Lore* (Oxford: Oxford University Press, 2001)

LE BRUN, ANNIE, *Les Châteaux de la subversion* (Paris: Pauvert & Garnier Frères, 1982)

LEONE DE CASTRIS, ARCANGELO, *Il problema Manzoni* (Palermo: Palumbo, 1990)

LEOPARDI, GIACOMO, *Canti*, ed. by Mario Fubini and Emilio Bigi (Turin: Loescher, 1964)

——*Canti*, ed. by Ugo Dotti (Milan: Feltrinelli, 1993)

——*Canti*, ed. by Emilio Peruzzi, 2 vols. (Milan: Rizzoli, 1998)

——*Canti*, ed. and transl. by Jonathan Galassi (London: Penguin, 2010)

——*Crestomazia italiana. La prosa*, ed. by Giulio Bollati (Turin: Einaudi, 1968)

——*Discorso di un italiano intorno alla poesia romantica*, ed. by Rosita Copioli (Milan: Rizzoli, 1997)

——*Discourse of an Italian on Romantic Poetry*, transl. by Gabrielle Sims and Fabio A. Camilletti, in *Classicism and Romanticism in Italian Literature*, by Fabio A. Camilletti, (London: Pickering & Chatto, 2013), pp. 113–73

——*Epistolario*, ed. by Franco Brioschi and Patrizia Landi, 2 vols. (Turin: Bollati Boringhieri, 1998)

——*The Letters of Giacomo Leopardi, 1817–1837*, ed. and transl. by Prue Shaw (Leeds: Northern University Press, 1998)

——*Moral Tales*, transl. by Patrick Creagh (Manchester: Carcanet New Press, 1983)

——*Scritti e frammenti autobiografici*, ed. by Franco D'Intino (Rome: Salerno, 1995)

——*Tutte le poesie e tutte le prose*, ed. by Lucio Felici and Emanuele Trevi (Rome: Newton, 1997)

——*Volgarizzamenti in prosa 1822–1827*, ed. by Franco D'Intino (Venice: Marsilio, 2012)

——*Zibaldone di pensieri*, ed. by Giuseppe Pacella, 3 vols. (Milan: Garzanti, 1991)

——*Zibaldone di pensieri*, ed. by Emilio Peruzzi, 10 vols. (Pisa: Scuola Normale Superiore, 1989–94)

——*Zibaldone di pensieri*, ed. by Fiorenza Ceragioli and Monica Ballerini (Bologna: Zanichelli, 2009)

——*Zibaldone: The Notebooks of Leopardi*, ed. by Michael Caesar and Franco D'Intino, transl. by Kathleen Baldwin, Richard Dixon, David Gibbons and others (Harmondsworth: Penguin, 2013)

LEOPARDI, MONALDO, 'Memoriale autografo ad Antonio Ranieri', in *Carteggio inedito di varii con Giacomo Leopardi con lettere che lo riguardano*, ed. by Giovanni and Raffaele Bresciano (Turin: Rosenberg & Sellier, 1935), pp. 478–82

LEVI, GIULIO AUGUSTO, 'Note di cronologia leopardiana', *Giornale storico della letteratura italiana*, 53 (1909), 232–70

LÉVI-STRAUSS, CLAUDE, *La Pensée sauvage* (Paris: Plon, 1962)

LIDDELL, HENRY GEORGE, and ROBERT SCOTT, *A Greek-English Lexicon* (Oxford: Clarendon Press, 1996)

LONARDI, GILBERTO, *L'oro di Omero. L''Iliade', Saffo: antichissimi di Leopardi* (Venice: Marsilio, 2005)

LONGINUS, *Dionysii Longini quæ supersunt latine et græce*, ed. by Jean Toup (Oxford: Clarendon Press, 1778)

——'On the Sublime', in *The Poetics, On the Sublime, On Style*, by Aristotle, Longinus and Demetrius, ed. and transl. by W. Hamilton Fyfe (London: Heinemann, 1946), pp. 119–254

LÖWY, MICHAEL, *Fire Alarm: Reading Walter Benjamin's 'On the Concept of History'*, transl. by Chris Turner (London: Verso, 2005)

LUKACHER, NED, *Primal Scenes: Literature, Philosophy, Psychoanalysis* (Ithaca, NY, and London: Cornell University Press, 1986)

LUZZI, JOSEPH, *Romantic Europe and the Ghost of Italy* (New Haven and London: Yale University Press, 2008)

LYOTARD, JEAN-FRANÇOIS, *The Inhuman: Reflections on Time*, transl. by Geoffrey Bennington and Rachel Bowlby (Cambridge: Polity Press, 1991)

MACINANTE, ALESSANDRA PAOLA, *'Erano i capei d'oro a l'aura sparsi': Metamorfosi delle chiome femminili tra Petrarca e Tasso* (Rome: Salerno, 2011)

MACLACHLAN, BONNIE, *The Age of Grace* (Princeton: Princeton University Press, 1993)

MAINBERGER, SABINE, 'Hamburg-Oraibi via Florence: Aby Warburg's Cultural Geography', *Acta Historiae Artium* 49 (2008), 138–43.

MANZONI, ALESSANDRO, *The Betrothed*, transl. by Archibald Colquhoun (London: J.M. Dent, 1951)

——*I Promessi sposi (1840)*, ed. by Salvatore Silvano Nigro (Milan: Mondadori, 2002)

——*I Promessi sposi (1827)*, ed. by Salvatore Silvano Nigro (Milan: Mondadori, 2002)

MARI, MICHELE, *Io venìa pien d'angoscia a rimirarti* (Venice: Marsilio, 1998)

MARINELLI, LUCIA, '*Ars memoriae* e *Ars excerpendi*: le alternative del ricordare', in *I libri di Leopardi*, by Maria Gabriella Mansi and others (Naples: De Rosa, 2000), pp. 131–58

MASSCHELEIN, ANNELEEN, *The Unconcept: The Freudian Uncanny in Late-Twentieth-Century Theory* (Albany: State University of New York Press, 2011)

MAZZARELLA, ARTURO, *I dolci inganni: Leopardi, gli errori e le illusioni* (Naples: Liguori, 1996)

MIDELFORT, H.C. ERIK, 'Charcot, Freud, and the Demons', in *Werewolves, Witches, and Wandering Spirits: Traditional Belief & Folklore in Early Modern Europe*, ed. by Kathryn A. Edwards (Kirksville: Truman State University Press, 2002), pp. 199–215

MONSERRATI, MICHELE, *Le 'cognizioni inutili': Saggio su 'Lo Spettatore fiorentino' di Giacomo Leopardi* (Florence: Firenze University Press, 2005)

MONTESQUIEU, CHARLES SECONDAT DE, *Essai sur le goût*, ed. by Charles-Jacques Beyer (Geneva: Droz, 1976)

——*Œuvres* (Amsterdam, 1781)

MOTTA, UBERTO, 'Nel nome della grazia: Leopardi e Castiglione', in *Leopardi e il '500*, ed. by Paola Italia (Pisa: Pacini, 2010), pp. 185–204

MOUSSY, CLAUDE, *Gratia et sa famille* (Paris: Presses Universitaires de France, 1966)

MUSATTI, CESARE L., 'Consulenza psicologica per un film (Autointervista)' (1970), in *Libertà e servitù dello spirito: Diario culturale di uno psicoanalista (1945–1971)*, by Cesare L. Musatti (Turin: Boringhieri, 1971), pp. 337–50

NABOKOV, VLADIMIR, *The Annotated Lolita*, ed. by Alfred Appel Jr. (London: Penguin, 2000)

NATALE, MASSIMO, *Il canto delle idee: Leopardi fra 'Pensiero dominante' e 'Aspasia'* (Venice: Marsilio, 2009)

NESTLE, WILHELM, *Vom Mythos zum Logos: Die Selbstentfaltung des griechischen Denkens von Homer bis auf die Sophistik und Sokrates* (Stuttgart: Metzler, 1940)

NIETZSCHE, FRIEDRICH, *Intorno a Leopardi*, ed. by Cesare Galimberti (Genoa: Il Melangolo, 1999)

NOFERI, ADELIA, 'Petrarca in Leopardi e la funzione di un commento', in *Il gioco delle tracce: Studi su Dante, Petrarca, Bruno, il neo-classicismo, Leopardi, l'informale*, by Adelia Noferi (Florence: La Nuova Italia, 1979), pp. 299–328

O'NEILL, TOM, *Of Virgin Muses and Of Love: A Study of Foscolo's 'Dei Sepolcri'* (Dublin: Irish Academic Press, 1981)

ORLANDO, FRANCESCO, *Illuminismo, barocco e retorica freudiana* (Turin: Einaudi, 1997)

——*Obsolete Objects in the Literary Imagination: Ruins, Relics, Rarities, Rubbish, Uninhabited Places, and Hidden Treasures*, transl. by Gabriel Pihas and Daniel Seidel with Alessandra Grego (New Haven and London: Yale University Press, 2006)

OSSOLA, CARLO, *Dal 'Cortegiano' all'Uomo di mondo': Storia di un libro e di un modello sociale* (Turin: Einaudi, 1987)

——'Leopardi: Préludes et passions', in *La Conscience de soi de la poésie*, ed. by Yves Bonnefoy (Paris: Seuil, 2008), pp. 235–68

OUDAI CELSO, YAMINA, *Freud e la filosofia antica: Genealogia di un fondatore* (Turin: Bollati Boringhieri, 2006)

PARRY, MILMAN, *The Making of Homeric Verse: The Collected Papers*, ed. by Adam Parry (Oxford: Clarendon Press, 1971)

PAVESE, CESARE, *Dialoghi con Leucò* (Turin: Einaudi, 2006)

——*Dialogues with Leucò*, transl. by William Arrowsmith and D.S. Carne-Ross (Ann Arbor: University of Michigan Press, 1965)

PERUZZI, EMILIO, 'Odi, Melisso', in *Studi leopardiani*, by Emilio Peruzzi, 2 vols. (Florence: Olschki, 1987), II, 75–138

PETIT-SKINNER, SOLANGE, 'L'Homme et la sexualité', in *Histoire des moeurs*, ed. by Jean Poirier, 6 vols. (Paris: Gallimard), II, 929–71

PETRARCH, *The Canzoniere, or Rerum vulgarium fragmenta*, ed. and transl. by Mark Musa (Bloomington and Indianapolis: Indiana University Press, 1999)

PFEIFFER, RUDOLF, *Storia della filologia classica: Dalle origini alla fine dell'età ellenistica*, ed. by Marcello Gigante, transl. by Marcello Gigante and Salvatore Cerasuolo (Naples: Macchiaroli, 1973)

PHAEDRUS and AVIANUS, *Fabulae, accedunt fabulae graecae latinis respondentes et Homeri Batrachomyomachia*, ed. by David Hoogstratan (Padua, 1721)

PICHLER, WOLFRAM, WERNER RAPPL, and GUDRUN SWOBODA, 'Metamorphosen des Fluss-gottes und der Nymphe. Aby Waburgs Denk-Haltungen und die Psychoanalyse', in *Die Couch. Vom Denken im Liegen*, ed. by Lydia Marinelli (Munich: Prestel, 2006), pp. 161–86

PINOTTI, ANDREA, 'Nimpha zwischen Eidos und Formel: phänomenologische Aspekte in Warburgs Ikonologie', in *Phänomelität des Kunstwerks*, ed. by Hans Rainer Sepp and Jürgen Trinks (Vienna: Turia + Kant, 2006), pp. 222–32

PLATO, *Euthyphro, Apology, Crito, Phaedo, Phaedrus*, ed. and transl. by Harold North Fowler (London: Heinemann, 1913)

—— *Theaetetus, Sophist*, ed. and transl. by Harold North Fowler (London: Heinemann, 1961)

POLATO, LORENZO, 'Leopardi e Pindaro: il sogno di un'ombra', in *Il sogno di un'ombra: Leopardi e la verità delle illusioni*, by Lorenzo Polato (Venice: Marsilio 2007), pp. 65–115

PORFIRIO, *Sui simulacri*, ed. by Mino Gabriele, transl. by Franco Maltomini (Milan: Adelphi, 2012)

POTTS, ALEX, *Flesh and the Ideal: Winckelmann and the Origins of Art History* (New Haven and London: Yale University Press, 1994)

POZZI, GIOVANNI, 'Il ritratto della donna nella poesia d'inizio Cinquecento e la pittura di Giorgione', *Lettere italiane*, XXXI, 1 (January March 1979), 3–30

PRAZ, MARIO, *The Romantic Agony*, transl. by Angus Davidson (Oxford: Oxford University Press, 1970)

PRETE, ANTONIO, 'Filologia fantastica', in *Leopardi e il libro nell'età romantica*, ed. by Michael Caesar and D'Intino (Rome: Bulzoni, 2000), pp. 29–38

—— *Il pensiero poetante. Saggio su Leopardi* (Turin: Einaudi, 2006)

—— 'Sulla scrittura dello *Zibaldone*: la forma dell'*essai* e i modi del *preludio*', in *Lo 'Zibaldone' cento anni dopo. Composizione, edizioni, temi*, ed. by Ronaldo Garbuglia, 2 vols. (Florence: Olschki, 2001), I, 387–94

—— 'Un anno di Zibaldoni e altre meraviglie' (2004), <http://www.zibaldoni.it/comunicato_stampa/index_frascati_a.htm> [accessed 28 May 2013]

RAMPLEY, MATTHEW, 'Archives of Memory. Walter Benjamin's Arcades Project and Aby Warburg's Mnemosyne Atlas', in *The Optic of Walter Benjamin*, ed. by Alex Coles (London: Black Dog, 1999), pp. 94–117

—— *The Remembrance of Things Past: On Aby Warburg and Walter Benjamin* (Wiesbaden: Harrassowitz, 2000)

RAULFF, ULRICH, 'Die Nimphe und der Dynamo. Warburg aus der Jugendstil', in *Wilde Energien. Vier Versuche zu Aby Warburg*, by Ulrich Raulff (Göttingen: Wallenstein, 2003), pp. 17–47

RICCINI, MARCO, 'Lo *Zibaldone di pensieri*: progettualità e organizzazione del testo', in *Leopardi e il libro nell'età romantica*, ed. by Michael Ceasar and Franco D'Intino (Rome: Bulzoni, 2000), pp. 81–104

RIGONI, MARIO ANDREA, 'Un Elzeviro: Opere d'arte per amori mancati', in *Giacomo Leopardi: Viaggio nella memoria*, ed. by Fabiana Cacciapuoti (Milan: Electa, 1999), pp. 147–48

—— 'L'estetizzazione dell'antico', in *Il pensiero di Leopardi*, pp. 3–40

—— 'Leopardi, Sade e il dio del male', in *Il pensiero di Leopardi*, pp. 111–20

—— *Il pensiero di Leopardi* (Rome: Aragno, 2010)

—— 'Post Scriptum: Sulla fonte della canzone *Alla sua Donna*', in *Il pensiero di Leopardi*, pp. 57–59

ROHDE, ERWIN, *Psyche: The Cult of Souls and Belief in Immortality among the Greeks*, transl. by W.B. Hillis (London: Routledge & Kegan Paul, 1950)

ROSE, LOUIS, *The Survival of Images: Art Historians, Psychoanalysts, and the Ancients* (Detroit: Wayne State University Press, 2001)

ROSSI MONTI, MARTINO, *Il cielo in terra: La grazia fra teologia ed estetica* (Turin: Utet, 2008)

SADE, DONATIEN ALPHONSE FRANÇOIS DE, *Justine, Philosophy in the Bedroom and Other Writings*, ed. and transl. by Richard Seaver and Austryn Wainhouse (London: Arrow Books, 1991)

——*Œuvres*, ed. by Michel Delon, 3 vols. (Paris: Gallimard, 1990–98)

SAINT-AMAND, PIERRE, *Séduire ou la passion des Lumières* (Paris: Klincksieck, 1987)

SANTAGATA, MARCO, *I frammenti dell'anima: Storia e racconto nel Canzoniere di Petrarca* (Bologna: Il Mulino, 1992)

SBRILLI, ANTONELLA, 'Le mani fiorentine di Lolita: Coincidenze warburghiane in Nabokov (e viceversa)', *Engramma* 43 (September 2005), <http://www.engramma.it/engramma_v4/rivista/saggio/43/043_sbrilli_nabokov.html> [accessed 28 May 2013]

SCHLEGEL, FRIEDRICH, *Geschichte der epischen Dichtkunst der Griechen*, in *Sämmtliche Werke*, by Friedrich Schlegel, 10 vols. (Vienna: Jakob Maner, 1822–25), III, 224

——*Lucinde and the Fragments*, transl. by Peter Firchow (Minneapolis: University of Minnesota Press, 1971)

SCHOLAR, RICHARD, *The Je-Ne-Sais-Quoi in Early Modern Europe: Encounters with a Certain Something* (Oxford and New York: Oxford University Press, 2005)

SCHWARZENBERG, ERKINGER, *Die Grazien* (Bonn: Habelt, 1966)

SCIANATICO, GIOVANNA, *La questione neoclassica* (Venice: Marsilio, 2010)

SETTIS, SALVATORE, *The Future of the 'Classical'*, transl. by Allan Cameron (Cambridge: Polity Press, 2006)

—— (ed.), *I greci: Storia, cultura, arte, società*, 4 vols. (Turin: Einaudi, 1996)

——'Presentazione' to Jean Seznec, *La sopravvivenza degli antichi dei. Saggio sul ruolo della tradizione mitologica nella cultura e nell'arte rinascimentali* (Turin: Bollati Boringhieri, 1990), pp. vii–xxix

SIMS, GABRIELLE, 'Speaking about Infinity without Recourse to Fragments: Leopardi's "L'infinito" as a Challenge to the Sublime Ellipsis' (2010), <http://www.birmingham.ac.uk/Documents/college-artslaw/lcahm/leopardi/fragments/leopardi/paper-sims.pdf> [accessed 28 May 2013]

STAËL, GERMAINE DE, *De l'Allemagne*, ed. by Simone Balayé, 2 vols. (Paris: Flammarion, 1968)

——'Sulla maniera e l'utilità delle traduzioni', in *Discussioni e polemiche sul romanticismo (1816–1826)*, ed. by Egidio Bellorini, 2 vols. (Bari: Laterza, 1943), i, 3–9

STAROBINSKI, JEAN, 'Fable et mythologie aux XVIIe et XVIIIe siècles', in *Le Remède dans le mal: Critique et légitimation de l'artifice à l'âge des Lumières*, by Jean Starobinski (Paris: Gallimard, 1989), pp. 233–62

——'Virgilio in Freud', transl. by Stefania Cirri, in *Di fronte ai classici: A colloquio con i greci e i latini*, ed. by Ivano Dionigi (Milan: Rizzoli, 2002), pp. 229–57

STIEGLER, BERNARD, 'Anamnesis and Hypomnesis', *Ars Industrialis*, <http://arsindustrialis.org/anamnesis-and-hypomnesis> [accessed 28 May 2013]

SVENBRO, JESPER, 'Phrasikleia: From Silence to Sound', in *Phrasikleia. An Anthropology of Reading in Ancient Greece*, by Jesper Svenbro, transl. by Janet Lloyd (Ithaca, NY, and London: Cornell University Press, 1993), pp. 8–25

SZONDI, PETER, 'Walter Benjamin's "City Portraits"', in *On Textual Understanding and Other Essays*, by Peter Szondi, transl. by Harvey Mendelsohn (Manchester: Manchester University Press, 1986), pp. 133–43.

TASSO, TORQUATO, 'Il Messaggiero', in *Dialoghi*, by Torquato Tasso, ed. by Giovanni Baffetti, 2 vols. (Milan: Rizzoli, 1998), i, 305–83

——*Opere*, ed. by Bortolo Tommaso Sozzi, 2 vols. (Turin: Utet, 1964)

THOMPSON, RACHEL LEAH, 'The Automatic Hand: Spiritualism, Psychoanalysis, Surrealism', *Invisible Culture: An Electronic Journal for Visual Culture*, 7 (Spring 2004), <http://www.rochester.edu/in_visible_culture/ivchome.html> [accessed 28 May 2013]

TIMPANARO, SEBASTIANO, '"Gli sguardi innamorati e schivi" (A Silvia, 46)', in *Aspetti e figure della cultura ottocentesca*, by Sebastiano Timpanaro (Pisa: Nistri-Lischi, 1980), pp. 277–85

——*La filologia di Giacomo Leopardi* (Bari: Laterza, 1997)

TORRE, ANDREA, *Petrarcheschi segni di memoria: Spie, postille, metafore* (Pisa: Edizioni della Normale, 2007)

TULVING, ENDEL, 'Episodic and Semantic Semory', in *Organization of Memory*, ed. by Endel Tulving and Wayne Donaldson (New York: Academic Press, 1972), pp. 381–403

VERDENELLI, MARCELLO, 'Cronistoria dell'idea leopardiana di "Zibaldone"', *Il Veltro. Rivista della civiltà italiana*, 5–6 (1987), 591–620

——introduction to *Epistolario*, by Giuseppe Antonio Vogel (Ancona: Transeuropa, 1993), pp. 5–33

VERNANT, JEAN-PIERRE, 'Psuche: Simulacrum of the Body or Image of the Divine?', in *Mortals and Immortals: Collected Essays*, by Jean-Pierre Vernant, ed. by Froma I. Zeitlin (Princeton: Princeton University Press, 1991), pp. 186–92

VERONESE, COSETTA, 'Fleetingness and Flâneurie [sic]: Leopardi, Baudelaire and the Experience of Transience' (2010), <http://www.birmingham.ac.uk/Documents/college-artslaw/lcahm/leopardi/fragments/leopardi/paper-veronese.pdf> [accessed 28 May 2013]

——*The Reception of Giacomo Leopardi in the Nineteenth Century: Italy's Greatest Poet After Dante?* (Lewiston, NY: Edwin Mellen, 2008)

VEYNE, PAUL, *Les Grecs ont-ils cru à leurs mythes?* (Paris: Seuil, 1983)

VIDAL-NAQUET, PIERRE, *The Black Hunter: Forms of Thought and Forms of Society in the Greek World*, transl. by Andrew Szegedy-Maszak (Baltimore and London: Johns Hopkins University Press, 1986)

VIDLER, ANTHONY, *The Architectural Uncanny: Essays in Modern Unhomely* (Cambridge, MA: MIT Press, 1992)

VIGARELLO, GEORGES, *Histoire du viol, XVIe-XXe siècle* (Paris: Seuil, 2000)

VOGEL, GIUSEPPE ANTONIO, *Epistolario* (Ancona: Transeuropa, 1993)

VOLTAIRE, *Dictionnaire philosophique*, ed. by René Pomeau (Paris: Garnier-Flammarion, 1964)

YATES, FRANCES, *The Art of Memory* (Chicago: Chicago University Press, 1966)

WARBURG, ABY, 'A Lecture on Serpent Ritual', transl. by W.F. Mainland, *Journal of the Warburg Institute*, 2, 4 (April 1939), 277–92

——'Sandro Botticelli's *Birth of Venus* and *Spring*: An Examination of Concepts of Antiquity in the Italian Early Renaissance', in *The Renewal of Pagan Antiquity*, by Aby Warburg, ed. by Gertrud Bing with Fritz Rougemont, transl. by David Britt (Los Angeles: Getty Research Institute for the History of Art and the Humanities, 1999), pp. 89–156

——'Seminarübungen über Jacob Burckhardt' (1927), ed. by Bernd Roeck, *Idea. Jahrbuch der Hamburger Kunsthalle*, 10 (1991), 86–89

WEIGEL, SIGRID, 'Aby Warburgs "Göttin im Exil": Das "Nymphenfragment" zwischen Brief und Taxonomie', *Vorträge aus dem Warburg-Haus*, 4 (2000), 65–104

WHITE, HAYDEN, foreword to *The Practice of Conceptual History*, by Reinhart Koselleck (Stanford: Stanford University Press, 2002), pp. ix-xiv

——*The Historical Imagination in Nineteenth-Century Europe* (Baltimore and London: Johns Hopkins University Press, 1973)

WORBS, MICHAEL, *Nervenkunst: Literatur und Psychoanalyse im Wien der Jahrhundertwende* (Frankfurt am Main: Athenäum, 1988)

WRIGHT, ELIZABETH, *Speaking Desires Can Be Dangerous: The Poetics of the Unconsciousness* (Cambridge: Polity Press, 1999)

ŽIŽEK, SLAVOJ, *Looking Awry: An Introduction to Jacques Lacan through Popular Culture* (Cambridge, MA: MIT Press, 1992)

INDEX